Economics and the Environment

A Reconciliation

Economics and the Environment

A Reconciliation

**Edited by
Walter Block**

**_Contributors:_
Terry Anderson
John Baden
Walter Block
Thomas Borcherding
John Chant
Edwin Dolan
Donald McFetridge
Murray Rothbard
Douglas Smith
Jane Shaw
Richard Stroup**

THE FRASER
INSTITUTE

Canadian Cataloguing in Publication Data

Main entry under title:
Economics and the environment

Includes bibliographical references.
ISNB 0-88975-067-X

1. Environmental policy — Economic aspects.
I. Block, Walter, 1941–   II. Fraser Institute
(Vancouver, B.C.)

HC79.ESE22   1989   363.7   C89-091582-2

CONTENTS

Preface   vii
About the Authors   xvii

Chapter 1
The Economics of the Conserver Society
John F. Chant, Donald G. McFetridge, and Douglas A. Smith   1

Chapter 2
Natural Resources and Transgenerational Equity
Thomas E. Borcherding   95

Chapter 3
Natural Resource Scarcity, Entrepreneurship, and
the Political Economy of Hope
John Baden and Richard L. Stroup   117

Chapter 4
The Market Process and Environmental Amenities
Terry Anderson   137

Chapter 5
Global Warming and Ozone Depletion
Jane S. Shaw and Richard L. Stroup   159

Chapter 6
The Economics of Protecting the Ozone Layer
Douglas A. Smith   181

Chapter 7
Chemophobia and Activist Environmental Antidotes:
Is the Cure More Deadly than the Disease?
Richard L. Stroup   193

Chapter 8
Controlling Acid Rain
Edwin G. Dolan   215

Chapter 9
Law, Property Rights, and Air Pollution
Murray N. Rothbard 233

Chapter 10
**Environmental Problems, Private Property Rights
Solutions**
Walter E. Block 281

Preface

The title of this book is *Economics and the Environment: A Reconciliation*. On the face of it, two more irreconcilable perspectives could hardly be found. Economists are presumably concerned with the bottom line, with profit and loss, and with matters commercial and financial; "Let the environment watch out for itself" is the attitude attributed to economists by many people. Environmentalists, in sharp and dramatic contrast, want to promote ecologically sound policies, ones that leave the earth's resources unsullied, that preserve its land, water, and air in pristine form for the generations to come. At least in the popular conception, they are supposed to be blissfully unconcerned about the economic implications of such a stance.

Nevertheless, it shall be the burden of this volume to argue that despite these differences, the two very different concerns can be reconciled. How can this be done?

The essence of the reconciliation is that it is possible to use economic means in order to obtain environmental ends. The various authors in this book argue, each in his own way, that by using such economic building blocks as free market prices, private property rights, and, most important, a legal system that carefully defines, delineates, and protects such rights, the goals of the environmentalists can be achieved. They argue, also, that using these building blocks is a better and more effective way of attaining an ecologically sound environment than is directly and explicitly attempting to promote this end. A strict adherence to private property rights, in other words, will do more to secure air and water purity and sound resource management than will centralized control over the economy, even if done with this purpose in mind.

This motif of using free market means for ecological ends is analogous to the attempt to use capitalist means in order to attain socialist goals.

New Zealand

The Honorable Roger Douglas, former Finance Minister of the Labour government of New Zealand, uses this insight to explain why his social democratic government employs such techniques as large-scale privatization of state-owned assets, banking and market deregulation, tax cutting, reducing the public sector deficit, and eliminating wage, interest, import and export controls. States Douglas, "This government is more interested in ends than it is in means. We are hungry for results and not obsessed with process. There is nothing socialistic about high inflation, nor about high levels of foreign debt, about an economy that does not grow for a decade and a half" (Fraser Forum, July 1988, p. 4).

Of course, this economist-ecologist reconciliation now being attempted will be impossible for those who use environmental concerns merely as a stick with which to beat the free-enterprise system. All that can be said to such people is that much of the environmental despoliation in the western nations stems from the public sector (e.g., municipal authorities dumping raw sewage into the ocean), not the private, and that in any case, no matter how badly the ecosystem has been treated by the capitalist countries, communism has a far worse record in this regard. One need only contrast Three Mile Island, the worst nuclear disaster in the U.S., where not one person died, with Chernobyl, its Soviet counterpart, which caused the deaths of hundreds and laid waste to thousands of square miles of our precious spaceship earth.

Similarly, a reconciliation is also impossible for some fanatical anti-environmentalists—those concerned only with the immediate short-run bottom line, who feel that technology, virtually any technology, is per se beneficial. One sometimes supposes that the ideal vision of such people is an earth where all forests and fields have been plowed under and paved over with cement, forming one single gigantic parking lot, or one with smokestacks run riot, where the air is almost blackened with pollution. One can only reply that such a spectre represents a very narrow perspective. Not only would this scenario be an absolute ecological disaster, but the implications for a growing and prospering economy would also be highly problematic, to say the very least.

Moderation

Fortunately, however, most people concerned with economics and ecology fall into neither of these extreme categories. It is to the vast number of people who are open-minded on this issue—and thus fall into an intermediate or more moderate category on this spectrum—that this book is addressed. But even these people will question our attempted reconciliation. After all, it does sound paradoxical, not to say somewhat quixotic: aren't economic growth and environmental protection supposed to be incompatible? All that can be said at this point is that there is certainly no more contradiction between economics and ecology than between socialism and capitalism, and that if the New Zealanders can harmonize the latter pair, then we are at least justified in attempting to do so with the former.

Some of the paradoxical nature of the enterprise can be banished at the outset, however. Much of the seeming incompatibility stems not from any intrinsic opposition between the free marketplace and a sound environment, but rather from a mis-specification of the former. That is, it is commonly assumed that the system now operating in North America, Western Europe, and parts of Asia is one of capitalism. Most people in these countries suppose that free enterprise is the system now in operation.

Nothing could be further from the truth, however. At present, we have a mixed economy. It is partially free, but also partially controlled by government. In a pure free market, there would be no public sector to control or conduct purely economic activities. Government would instead be limited to providing for defence against external enemies, and for protection against internal criminals. As a last resort, it would provide a "safety net" in order to guard against the effects of dire poverty, if private charity were somehow unequal to the task, given the more highly productive society entailed by such arrangements.

A Legal System

But *laissez-faire* capitalism, if it is to function, needs far more than economic freedom. It also needs a legal system based strictly, and rigidly, on the rights of private property. It is thus government's job, too, to organize a body of law based on these principles. It is only if the economic system is embedded in legislation deriving from such principles that a full free market can be said to exist.

It is the contention of this volume that the seeming contradictions between the market and ecological concerns are not due to the free-enterprise part of the mixed economy. Rather, they are caused by government's failure to live up to the role it and only it can play in a truly capitalist system. It is impossible to overemphasize the importance of this claim; it is absolutely crucial to an understanding of our attempted reconciliation.

A statement of this principle, as it applies to the environment, has been expressed as follows by Martin Anderson:

> Fortunately, there is a simple, effective approach available— long appreciated but underused. An approach based solidly on. . . private property rights.
>
> At its root all pollution is garbage disposal in one form or another. The essence of the problem is that our laws and the administration of justice have not kept up with the refuse produced by the exploding growth of industry, technology and science.
>
> If you took a bag of garbage and dropped it on your neighbor's lawn, we all know what would happen. Your neighbor would call the police and you would soon find out that the disposal of your garbage is your responsibility, and

that it must be done in a way that does not violate anyone else's property rights.

But if you took that same bag of garbage and burned it in a backyard incinerator, letting the sooty ash drift over the neighborhood, the problem gets more complicated. The violation of property rights is clear, but protecting them is more difficult. And when the garbage is invisible to the naked eye, as much air and water pollution is, the problem often seems insurmountable.

We have tried many remedies in the past. We have tried to dissuade polluters with fines, with government programs whereby all pay to clean up the garbage produced by the few, with a myriad of detailed regulations to control the degree of pollution. Now some even seriously propose that we should have economic incentives, to charge polluters a fee for polluting—and the more they pollute the more they pay. But that is just like taxing burglars as an economic incentive to deter people from stealing your property, and just as unconscionable.

The only effective way to eliminate serious pollution is to treat it exactly for what it is—garbage. Just as one does not have the right to drop a bag of garbage on his neighbor's lawn, so does one not have the right to place any garbage in the air or the water or the earth, if it in any way violates the property rights of others.

What we need are tougher clearer environmental laws that are enforced—not with economic incentives but with jail terms.

What the strict application of the idea of private property rights will do is to increase the cost of garbage disposal. That increased cost will be reflected in a higher cost for the products and services that resulted from the process that produced the garbage. And that is how it should be. Much of the cost of disposing of waste material is already incorporated in the price of the goods and services produced. All of it should be. Then only those who benefit from the garbage made will pay for its disposal (*The Christian Science Monitor*, January 4, 1989, p. 19).

Alternative Perspective

It must be acknowledged, however, that within what might be called the broadly based free-enterprise camp, there is an alternative perspective. While adherents of this philosophy, too, would focus on the importance of private property rights as the linchpin of the economic defence of the environment, they do not go quite so far in their reliance on this institution. On the contrary, they maintain that there are some cases where government must step in and, despite critics such as Anderson, explicitly allow a certain amount of pollution to occur.

Fortunately, both sides of this internal debate are represented in this book. What might be called the "pure" private property rights view is depicted particularly in the contributions of Murray N. Rothbard and Walter Block, while what might be called the "modified" version is ably delineated by Edwin Dolan, John Chant, Donald McFetridge, and Douglas Smith. The other chapters occupy intermediate points on this spectrum, and several utilize both perspectives.

What reasons are given by the "modified" school of thought for its rejection of the "pure" private property rights scenario? Dolan gives four: lack of knowledge concerning the precise harmful effects of dumping garbage into the air; uncertainty over who is responsible for this activity; the disputatious nature of the property rights in question; and the prohibitively high transaction costs involved in negotiating a solution between numerous polluters and victims.

In order to solve the problem expeditiously, in this view, the government would organize a market in "pollution rights," where those who are most efficient in reducing their pollution levels would be able to purchase these rights from the least efficient. In this way, explain Dolan and Chant-McFetridge-Smith, society would best be able to economize resources, while ensuring that pollution levels stay below certain politically determined limits.

Economic Means, Environmental Ends

But this book is not dedicated to resolving a dispute between two free-enterprise oriented schools of thought. Rather, its purpose, as stated above, is to bring about a resolution between economists and ecologists, by showing how the teachings of the former can be used as means to solving problems that particularly concern the latter.

In this regard it is worth stressing that both the "pure" and the "modified" perspectives pass muster under this criterion. The "pure" private property rights regimen accomplishes this by outlawing what it considers trespassing: the invasive act of dumping air-borne garbage on another person's property. But the "modified" view also discharges this obligation. It does so by setting up a market (surely an economic institution) in pollution rights, under which such despoliations of the environment can be severely limited.

One last word on the attempt at reconciliation—many of the essays in this book are highly critical of the analysis put forth by those calling themselves environmentalists. This criticism must not be interpreted as opposition to the *goals* of those who speak out in defence of spaceship earth. If it is, no reconciliation is possible. On the contrary, the critiques offered here can more properly be seen as being aimed at the *means* to these ends, not the ends themselves. We now move to a more detailed discussion of the chapters of the book.

The Present Study

This book contains essays written by 11 leading North American economists, resource analysts, and environmentalists. It presents a market-oriented perspective on questions of environmentalism, in stark contrast to the approach adopted by many ecologists and biologists.

The authors of this volume are all highly critical of the public policy proposals—but not the goals—put forth by conservation groups such as The Sierra Club, Greenpeace, Friends of the Earth, National Audubon Society, Resources for the Future, National Wildlife Association, and The Club of Rome.

The major contribution to this book is "The Economics of the Conserver Society," written by John Chant, Donald McFetridge, and Douglas Smith. In this lead-off chapter they take to task the Canadian equivalents of those international bodies, specifically The Science Council and the Montreal-based Gamma Group. Although the programmes of these conserver groups were written in the 1970s, they remain the most articulate and definitive Canadian statements of the view that ecological problems are caused by unbridled capitalism, and may best be addressed through greater government involvement in the economy.

Our authors begin by setting the stage. The conservers, they note, are particularly outraged by what they see as the market's tendency to promote harmful technological change, overpopulation and pollution, to create artificial wants, to ignore the future, and to fail to come to grips with non-market interactions, such as externalities and spill-over effects.

Drawing upon Hayek's critique of Galbraith's notion of the "dependence effect," these three authors demonstrate that just because a want is not innate, does not mean it is not valuable. In a modern industrial society, people demand more than what is biologically (i.e., innately) required for life. They learn about such products through advertising, which, as long as there is competition from the non-advertised sector, can only help to promote consumer sovereignty. The conservers, in objecting to it, are trying to impose their own personal tastes on the nation.

Planned Obsolescence

Although many critics of the market charge that businessmen engage in "planned obsolescence," it is simply untrue. Instead, note Chant, McFetridge, and Smith, "durability is simply another commodity characteristic. Firms which provide products with characteristics desired by consumers will prosper relative to those that do not." Unless the firm has the ability to exclude producers of similar but more durable products, it must, in its own interest, act so as to benefit the consumer. That is, manufacturers must refrain from purposefully building obsolescence into their products—unless by so doing they can save customers so much money that the entire package is deemed more attractive.

Contrary to the allegations of the conservers, entrepreneurs are concerned with the future. Capital values depend not only on present receipts, but upon (appropriately discounted) distant ones as well. The economist, moreover, contends with scarcity of all goods and services, not merely, in a uni-dimensional manner, with non-renewable resources alone. On the contrary, it is the public sector, not the private, that is truly fixated upon the near term. It is the rare politician, for example, who can look much past the next election.

The reason there are environmental failures such as pollution is not because of a failure of private enterprise; instead, it is due to the failure of government to clearly and fully define property rights. As a practical solution, a "quasi-market," where rights to pollute are sold to the highest bidder, is far more effective than are the government interventions, regulations, and taxes favoured by the conservers.

Selflessness?

It is not true that the ecology movement is motivated by no more than a selfless desire to improve the environment for all of society. Often, such advocates become involved in "an unlikely and unholy alliance" with resource-based unions such as coal miners; as a result, pollution control is far less efficient than it would otherwise be.

The Science Council is not an objective research organization. It is, rather, a sophisticated public relations spokesman for a special-interest pressure group. It is more like a typical business lobbying organization, such as the National Association of Railroad Passengers, whose sole concern is with the preservation of this mode of transportation no matter what costs are imposed upon the rest of society.

The second chapter was written by Thomas Borcherding. Addressing himself to the question of equity and natural resources, the Claremont University economist shows that intra-generationally, government interference tends to transfer wealth "perversely" from the poor to the rich. And what are the inter-generational effects? First, the market should be preferred to the state as a protector of the interests of future generations on grounds of efficiency; second, to the (very limited) extent that government succeeds in transferring resources from present to future generations, private decisions (lowered bequests, investment offsets) would tend to nullify it.

In chapter 3, John Baden and Richard Stroup paint a grim picture of the modern ecological movement, based as it is in large part on economic and ecological fallacies that first found currency in the Progressive period of American history. Highly popular are the views that environmental problems can best be solved by "apolitical, unselfish technically competent bureaucrats . . . charged with managing for the public good." But a whole raft of gigantic failures has led to a reappraisal, and to a more recent appreciation of the important role that well-defined property rights can play in maintaining ecological balance.

Privatizing Streams of Water

Many economists are now coming to see the benefits of privatizing bodies of water as a way of overcoming the "tragedy of the commons" difficulties associated with public ownership. A leader in this tradition is Montana State University's Terry Anderson, who in chapter 4 develops the property rights/transaction cost approach with regard to streams, rivers, and lakes. He applies it to private instream flows of water in England, the U.S., and Canada, and shows how this privatization process can reduce or eliminate problems of pollution.

In chapter 5 Jane S. Shaw and Richard L. Stroup confront two of the most serious charges made against the market system: that it leads to global warming—the greenhouse effect—that will bring about radical and harmful climatic changes, and to the depletion of the ozone layer, which causes skin cancer and other dangers. They find that although some respected scientists support these charges, others who are equally renowned dismiss them. For example, a team of researchers from the Oceanic and Atmospheric Administration found no evidence of a greenhouse effect in the U.S. weather records of 1895-1987; from 1896 to 1940 there was a "marginally significant" rise in temperatures, but this was countered by a "marginally significant" drop in the latter period. In a most fascinating section of their paper, Shaw and Stroup note, however, that "Chicken Little only has to be right once." They still counsel against precipitous government regulation, given our present lack of knowledge, on several grounds, including the fact that postponement will enhance future flexibility.

In keeping with our desire to present both sides of an issue when there is a dispute within the broadly based free-enterprise camp, chapter 6 by Douglas Smith offers a different perspective on the ozone layer from that of Shaw and Stroup. Although there is some disagreement within the scientific community on the dangers to the ozone layer, Smith notes that the overwhelming preponderance of thought indicates depletion is a severe problem. In his view, it can best be addressed by setting up a market for the right to produce chemicals that deplete ozone. Smith is particularly enthusiastic about the Montreal

Protocol, an international governmental regulation that he views as a thoughtful embodiment of what we have been calling the "modified" free market approach.

Richard Stroup's chapter 7 takes aim at "chemophobia," the unreasoning fear of toxic substances that leads to a call for greater governmental intervention into environmental affairs. This method of solving the problem is rejected not because the chemicals are not dangerous—they are—but because public-sector involvement is the cause of the problem, not the cure. He offers an analysis of the infamous Love Canal crisis, exhibit "A" in the case for greater regulation; it shows, contrary to popular misconception, that this debacle was actually brought about by unwise public policy, not by reliance on the market system of private property rights.

Acid Rain

Of all the environmental problems, that of acid rain is high up on the list of Canadian concerns. In chapter 8, Edwin Dolan maintains that the free unencumbered market cannot solve this problem, given present scientific uncertainties and ambiguities in property rights assignments, and therefore government regulation is needed. But he rejects command-and-control schemes that mandate specific technology (e.g., scrubbers) and source-specific performance standards (e.g., fuel switching), because they are more costly and reduce "incentives to develop new, less expensive technologies." Dolan estimates that allowing a market in tradeable emission rights for pollutants would reduce costs by 47 percent to 60 percent. For example, using this modified market mechanism instead of central controls for a 10-million-ton cutback in utility sulfur-dioxide emissions would lower expenditures from $447 million per year to $182 million, a saving of 60 percent.

In chapter 9, Murray N. Rothbard applies the law of torts and trespass to the question of pollution, carefully defining the relevant property rights, and shows how a failure to scrupulously protect them has led to many of the environmental problems that beset the modern world. He touches upon the legal aspects of invasion, strict liability, the burdens of risk and proof, crimes and torts, causality, homesteading, and nuisance. To illustrate the principles developed, he analyses air pollution, radiation, radio waves, odors, smoke, noise, low-flying airplanes, auto emissions, and other trespasses. His public policy prescription? The law should be interpreted so as to protect properly defined private property rights, the linchpin of the market system.

Ecological Problems

Chapter 10 addresses itself to a whole host of ecological problems. Included are pollution, recycling, oil spills, the allocation of land to recreational parks, forestry, and even the decision to use cloth or disposable diapers. As well, it analyses several proposals near and dear to the heart of Dr. David Suzuki, one of Canada's leading environmentalists—such as species extinction, economic growth, and the killing of fur-bearing animals—relying in each case on a private property rights perspective. The chapter concludes that since the difficulties are caused by governments, not markets, sound public policy includes more reliance on the institutions of free-enterprise, not less.

The Fraser Institute is pleased to support the research reported in this volume in the interest of promoting informed public debate about the vital issue of the environment. However, owing to the independence of the authors, the views expressed may not conform severally or collectively to those of the members of the Institute.

Walter Block

ABOUT THE AUTHORS

Terry L. Anderson

Terry Anderson is professor of economics at Montana State University and a senior associate with the Political Economy Research Center in Bozeman, Montana. Recently returned from New Zealand where he was a Fulbright Fellow working with the New Zealand government on the reform of water management laws, he has also been a visiting scholar at Stanford University, Oxford University, the University of Basel, and Clemson University. He has authored or co-authored five books including *Water Crisis: Ending the Policy Drought* and *Water Rights* as well as numerous articles including several publications in the *Wall Street Journal*. Dr. Anderson is currently writing on Indian policy and free market environmentalism.

John Baden

John Baden is chairman of the Foundation for Research on Economics and the Environment (FREE) in Bozeman, Montana, and Seattle, Washington. He received his B.A. from Wittenberg University and his Ph.D. from Indiana University. He is widely regarded as a leading architect of the new resource economics, an approach to natural resources and environmental policies that relies upon private property rights and market incentives to achieve ecological goals. He is the author/contributing editor of six books, and a frequent contributor to the *Wall Street Journal* and other papers. He is currently involved in developing a "Business and the Environment" curriculum programme for executives and MBA students.

Walter E. Block

Senior research fellow at the Fraser Institute and director of its Centre for the Study of Religion and Economics, Dr. Block is also senior fellow at the Ludwig von Mises Institute and co-editor of its *Review of Austrian Economics*. He received his B.A. from Brooklyn College and Ph.D. from Columbia University. The author of more than 30 scholarly articles, he is also the editor of 15 books including *Rent Control: Myths and Realities and Discrimination, Affirmative Action and Equal Opportunity*. Dr. Block has written five books including *The U.S. Bishops and Their Critics* and *Focus on Employment Equity*.

Thomas E. Borcherding

Professor of economics at Claremont Graduate School in Claremont, California, Thomas Borcherding also holds an Avery Fellows chair with Pitzer College
and is a senior research associate in the Claremont Center for Economic Policy
Studies. A graduate of the University of Cincinnati, he received his Ph.D. at
Duke University. He is managing editor of *Economic Inquiry*, the journal of
the Western Economic Association/International and is on the board of editors
of *The Cato Journal*. His current research interests are in the economics of
social security and the role of norms in constraining social behaviour.

John Chant

A Simon Fraser University professor who specializes in monetary economics,
John Chant served as research director of the Financial Markets Group at the
Economic Council of Canada, producing the study *Efficiency and Regulation*
which had an important impact on the Bank Act of 1980. He is the author of
several books including *The Allocative Effects of Inflation* and *The Market for
Financial Services*. One of the foremost experts in Canada on the regulation of
financial institutions, Dr. Chant has served as a consultant to the Bank of
Canada, the Commission of Inquiry into Residential Tenancies, and the Royal
Commission on the Economic Union and Development Prospects of Canada.
Most recently he has been advising the Government of Indonesia with respect
to the regulation of its banking system.

Edwin G. Dolan

Edwin G. Dolan teaches economics at Gettysburg College in Pennsylvania and
has also taught at George Mason University, Dartmouth College, and at the
University of Chicago. He received a B.A. and M.A. from Indiana University
and a Ph.D. in economics from Yale University. Professor Dolan is the author
of *TANSTAAFL: The Economic Strategy for Environmental Crisis* and, with
David E. Lindsey, of the textbook *Economics*. He has written extensively on
environmental issues. His current research interests include environmental
problems and economic reform in the Soviet Union.

Donald G. McFetridge

Professor of Economics at Carleton University, Donald McFetridge received a
B.Comm. from the University of Saskatchewan and an M.A. and Ph.D. in
economics from the University of Toronto. Dr. McFetridge has written and
edited numerous books and articles on industrial organization and economic
policy issues. He served as a research co-ordinator on the economics of
industrial policy for the Royal Commission on the Economic Union and
Development Prospects for Canada. His current research interests include the
economics of competition policy and economic aspects of technology dif-
fusion.

Murray N. Rothbard

The S.J. Hall distinguished professor of economics at the University of Nevada in Las Vegas, Murray Rothbard is also vice president for academic affairs at the Ludwig von Mises Institute and editor of its *Review of Austrian Economics*. He received his B.S., M.S., and Ph.D. in economics from Columbia University where he studied under Joseph Dorfman. He also studied under Ludwig von Mises at New York University. He is the author of more than one hundred scholarly articles. His 16 books include *The Panic of 1819; Man Economy, and State; America's Great Depression, The Ethics of Liberty; Power and Market;* and *Conceived in Liberty*.

Jane S. Shaw

A senior associate of the Political Economy Research Center in Bozeman, Montana, Jane Shaw directs an editorial outreach programme that prepares and distributes economics articles for the popular and non-academic press. She has written or edited more than 85 articles appearing in newspapers and magazines throughout the U.S. including the *Wall Street Journal, New York Times, Christian Science Monitor,* and *USA Today*. She has also been associate economics editor for *Business Week* and Washington correspondent for Mc-Graw-Hill Publications covering occupational safety and environmental issues.

Douglas A. Smith

Douglas A. Smith teaches in the department of economics at Carleton University. Professor Smith received a B.Comm. and M.A. at the University of Toronto and a Ph.D. in economics from the Massachusetts Institute of Technology. He joined Carleton University in 1972 and was a visiting associate professor at the University of Virginia in 1978-79. He served as chairman of the economics department at Carleton from 1983 to 1988. Dr. Smith's research interests are in the areas of labour economics, labour relations, and the economics of property rights.

Richard L. Stroup

Professor of economics at Montana State University, Richard Stroup is a senior associate of the Political Economy Research Center in Bozeman, Montana. He received a B.A., M.A., and Ph.D. from the University of Washington and has served as director of the Office of Policy Analysis at the Interior Department. A widely published author on natural resources and environmental issues, Dr. Stroup's work has been a major force in the development of the approach to resource problems known as the New Resource Economics. He is co-author of a leading economics principles textbook, *Economics: Private and Public Choice,* and is a Cato adjunct scholar. Dr. Stroup's recent research has focused on hazardous waste policies and ways of coping with environmental risk.

Chapter 1

The Economics of the Conserver Society

John F. Chant
Donald G. McFetridge
and
Douglas A. Smith

The Conservers and Their Case

It is difficult to be against conservation. It is impossible to be against waste. In this sense everyone is in favour of a society that conserves its resources. It is our view, as economists, that market institutions serve to avoid rather than create waste and that a market society is thus a conserver society. In this respect we differ from many critics of contemporary society who regard its market system as inherently wasteful.

The 1960s and early 1970s saw the emergence of a widespread, supposedly apolitical movement that was critical of many trends in western industrial society. Its adherents have focused on three areas of concern: the undesirable growth of technology, the unsustainability of economic growth, and the harmful environmental side-effects of industrial activity. In sum, their common viewpoint could be characterized as "extreme environmentalist" or "radical ecologist." In this study, we prefer to use the label adopted by Canadian advocates of this point of view who describe themselves as "conservers" or advocates of a conserver society.

Technology

The first area of concern has grown out of the work of Jacques Ellul, Lewis Mumford, and E.J. Mishan. These authors share a common hostility toward technology. They argue that technological change has developed its own momentum and is beyond human control. The autonomous force of technology, in concert with a technological elite, obliges ordinary citizens to do tedious and degrading work, to consume things they do not really desire, and to become confused as to their true desires. The notions of autonomous technological forces, of growth and consumption "for their own sake," and of wants "artificially encouraged" to accommodate these forces are central elements in the conserver critique of mass consumption society.

Overpopulation

The second area of concern arose as a result of assertions by Jay Forrester, Dennis Meadows and other investigators commissioned by the Club of Rome that continued population growth and capital accumulation would ultimately be limited by pollution, famine, and the exhaustion of non-renewable resources. Technological change will, in their view, serve to postpone but not to avert the ultimate collapse of the world economy. Even here, reliance on technology will entail its own set of costs. The problem is again one of autonomous growth, called exponential growth by these authors, proceeding without regard to consequences. That the industrial system does not—and indeed, cannot, without significant alteration—respond to anticipations of future scarcities is a second major theme of this literature.

Harmful Side-effects

The third area of concern arose after the publication of Rachel Carson's *Silent Spring*. This and succeeding works demonstrated that much industrial activity—indeed, much of human activity—had harmful environmental side-effects, some of which took years to appear. That economic activity will, in general, have adverse environmental side-effects, and that society's choice of activities will probably be biased toward those that are especially damaging to the environment, became the third major source of inspiration to conserver advocates.

The international conserver movement has, over the past 20 years, laboured to establish the proposition that economic growth is a relentless exogenous force unresponsive to the wishes of individuals or to evidence of either impending exhaustion of natural resources or present environmental deterioration. In this view, the essential problem is the absence of institutional feedback mechanisms. The true preferences of individuals cannot influence the extent and composition of economic activity. Neither future scarcities nor environmental side-effects influence current economic decisions.

Canadian Conservers

Canadian proponents of a conserver society have received much of their inspiration from this movement. The leading Canadian advocate of this viewpoint is the Science Council of Canada. Much of the conserver critique and policy proposals can be found in its *Canada as a Conserver Society* and the *Conserver Society Notes* published by the Council in the 1970s. The other major Canadian source of conserver analysis and recommendations is the four-volume report by the Gamma group, a group of academics affiliated with McGill University and the University of Montreal.

Each of the three elements of the conserver position has been advanced with equal vigour by the Canadian advocates.

■ Production, sustained by artificially created wants, occurs "for its own sake."

Our present economic system is based on persuading and seducing people with incomes (or access to credit) to buy more and more and more. Ephemeral novelties, rapid fashion changes, obsolescence and limited durability of goods offered for sale are combined with the insistent message of the media urging and inciting the public to stake all their hopes for happiness on a constantly expanding stream of purchases, even at the cost of going deeply and miserably into debt. Only so can profits, production and job opportunities be sustained (Spry, *Conserver Society Notes*, Summer 1977, p. 19).

■ Present economic decisions do not take proper account of future consequences.

We recognize that many critical materials are finite in supply and we seriously question the continuation of unrestricted consumption of them. Further as proponents of the Conserver Society, we appreciate that decisions so frequently made today in pursuit of short-term goals may incur serious, and perhaps unacceptable, long-term social costs which should be analyzed before they are accepted (Shepherd cited in *Conserver Society Notes*, Oct. 1975, p. 1).

■ Present economic decisions do not take proper account of environmental side-effects.

Economic growth as it is conventionally measured must involve a continuing externalization of costs over time. Businessmen are not evil in their actions. It is simply that traditional accounting methods have a private orientation and only measure particular aspects of business behaviour... In most cases pollution is caused by externalization of costs (Cordell, *Conserver Society Notes*, Summer 1977, p. 45).

3

Diagnosis and Remedies

While they have the same concerns as their international brethren, Canadian conservers differ in the tone of their writing. There are no prophecies of doom, as there are in Forrester and Meadows. Neither are there the whimsical injunctions of Mumford and others to "return to the woods." Canadian conservers are, to a much greater extent, searching for the source of the problems they perceive and for solutions. In this they are to be commended. It is our view, however, that both their diagnosis and their remedies contain serious errors. It is to the appropriate concerns raised by the conserver movement that this paper addresses itself.

To the conservers, the market system is defective. Non-price competition, manifested in advertising and spurious product differentiation, emphasizes material consumption over leisure and destructive leisure activity over passive. Market prices do not reflect long-run considerations, nor do they reflect costs imposed on third parties due to environmental pollution. The market is systematically biased toward the material, the present, and the polluting.

In theory, the market system is an ideal mechanism for allocating scarce resources among competing uses. We are coming to realize, however, that in practice it becomes so distorted by social costs, market power, non-price competition, and an inadequate view of the future that it systematically misallocates resources over time. Where possible, market forces should be allowed to work but the increasing call for social indicators, energy accounting, technology assessment and environmental impact statements all mean that a large part of our market system is in trouble (*Conserver Society Notes*, Dec. 1975, p. 14).

The Marketplace

Spokesmen for the Science Council have insisted that the market is not the sole source of our problems and that they wish merely to improve it rather than replace it.

We advance a number of arguments that show that the market mechanism can be made to work better. However, we do not cite the market economy as the cause of current Canadian ills. The malfunctioning of the market system is, we think, both a reflection and a cause of some of our problems, however, and we urge a more realistic appreciation of how our economy really functions. Cordell 1976, p. 36).

It is our contention, however, that this analysis consistently ignores the feedback mechanisms inherent in existing market arrangements. Moreover, these policy prescriptions generally ignore the possibility, first, that markets will emerge when required and, second, that the most efficient form of state intervention may involve the employment of a quasi-market mechanism.

A simple illustration of this tendency to ignore existing feedback mechanisms is provided by the study "Exploring Energy-Efficient Futures for Canada." It was written by physicist Amory Lovins and published in *Conserver Society Notes* to the apparent approval of other conserver commentators. This study forecasts energy supply and demand to the year 2025 under the assumption that energy markets are inoperative, so that energy prices have no impact. The methodology, reminiscent of Meadows and Forrester, is to extrapolate past rates of growth and modify them with a set of "technical fixes." It does not occur to the author or, apparently, to his readers, that changes in relative prices could have an effect on demand, supply, or technology.

Balance

In the following pages, we provide a more balanced assessment of the conserver concerns. We will not argue that the market looks after everything. Markets are imperfect and they do fail. Some markets are very costly to operate and their replacement by alternative resource allocation mechanisms is appropriate. Sometimes markets fail because governments intervene to prevent their operation. Sometimes particular objectives are too costly to achieve either through the market or any other institutional mechanism. The Science Council and conserver writers in general have been unable or unwilling to distinguish market failure from a wider institutional failure. As a result, their policy recommendations urge the replacement of one imperfect institution with another that is even more imperfect. In the next section of this chapter, we examine the proposition that wants are created to accommodate the requirements of the industrial system. We discuss the distinction between legitimate and contrived wants, the role of advertising and packaging in our economy, and the determinants of product durability.

In the following section, we discuss the allegations that the market systematically ignores the long-run.

> [A] deficiency of the price mechanism involves its inability to detect long-term problems. The price system operates on signals generated from a market and the time horizon for a market may be too short to take account of changes in resource availability or of environmental adaptability that will not occur for 10 to 25 years in the future. (Brooks, *Conserver Society Notes*, Winter/Spring 1977, p. 29).

As a result, non-renewable resources are underpriced and are being extracted at excessive rates.

> Underlying much of the dramatic growth was an underpricing of fossil fuels. They were thought to be a gift from earlier

5

eras of world development. We now know that the fossil fuels should have been seen as an inheritance or capital account— to be managed wisely (Cordell, *Conserver Society Notes*, Summer 1977, p. 6).

The conclusion that non-renewable resources are under-priced has led conservers, the Science Council in particular, to advocate relatively stringent measures to reduce their rate of extraction and to increase recycling. But if non-renewable resources are not under-priced, these measures will themselves be wasteful. We investigate the possibility that the market ignores information about the future that is known to the Science Council. Historical evidence on the effectiveness of the market in allocating resources over time is also surveyed.

In this chapter, we also confront the problem of pollution. We examine the extent to which market arrangements currently take environmental side-effects into account. We also discuss alternative forms of state participation in dealing with these side-effects and provide an assessment of the relative merits of emission rights, emission charges, and emission controls.

In our final section we provide a brief summary and our assessment of the conserver literature as social criticism and as economic policy.

Who Chooses?

The Conserver Critique of the Mass Consumption Society

The conserver society has been proposed as an alternative to our present consumer society. Critics of consumerism contend that the market system, due to advertising and other artificial inducements, encourages consumption for its own sake. They have proposed a conserver society first because, in their view, the resource depletion and environmental damage associated with the market-oriented consumer society cannot continue. Second, even if it were feasible to continue the existing system, they regard it as undesirable to do so. In their view, much of our consumption is associated with artificially created wants instead of inherent needs.

> A Conserver Society...is a society which...questions the ever-growing per capita demand for consumer goods, artificially encouraged by modern marketing techniques (Science Council 1977, p. 14).

Contrived Wants

The Science Council argues that we are seduced by advertising into trading valuable non-renewable resources for largely unnecessary consumer gadgets.

6

According to conservers, the essence of a consumer society is that it neglects the future.

> As inhabitants of a "consumer society," most Canadians have lived through a period when materials seemed plentiful, energy cheap, and growth in size or quantity, whether of cities, automobiles, monuments or lawnmowers was the natural order of things. Status, of individuals or societies, was measured by conspicuous consumption and economic prosperity was demonstrated by what you could afford to throw away (Science Council 1977, p. 28).

The Science Council argues that advertising leads to ever-increasing sales of marginally differentiated consumer products, most of which fail to meet the expectations of their purchaser. Large corporations make production decisions to maximize profits rather than to meet genuine needs. They employ advertising to ensure that consumers purchase those commodities they have decided to produce. The conservers argue that the existing system attempts "to shape the consumer to suit the convenience and profit of a large-scale system that may have gotten out of touch." (Science Council 1977, p. 33).

Tail Fins

The Science Council points to the automobile as the "prototype for the mass consumption society" in which advertising, annual model changes, and the power of the firm act to condition consumers to purchase the products that car makers choose to sell. In short, the consumer society has distorted individual tastes, values, and preferences in a way that should not and cannot continue.

> A more-is-better philosophy has too often seduced us into thinking that more is necessary. More is almost always costly—economically and socially. With energy constraints, capital shortages, inflationary pressures and environmental limits coming to predominate, we are forced to consider less costly and, in many cases different ways of satisfying the demands and needs of Canadians (Science Council 1977, p. 69).

The message of the Gamma group is similar to that of the Science Council; both hold that many wants are contrived and can no longer be sustained. The Gamma group further argues that the market system leads to growing output but not growing welfare:

> The unlimited marketing of goods leads to a cumulative reduction in the pleasure of people because of the conspicuous external diseconomies produced, noise, pollution, urban congestion etc... Many would argue that the market, rather than being a "want-satisfying mechanism" has become

7

a "want-creating mechanism" principally through marketing
and advertising (Gamma, v. 1, p. 155).

According to Gamma, the market system locks us into an undesirable and
unsustainable pattern of growth that must be altered by collectively prescribed
limits on consumption:

When no idea of an appropriate level of consumption exists...and when prestige itself becomes defined by material
consumption, it is clear that throughput and the unintended
waste products generated by it must increase infinitely until
the environmental limits to throughput threaten our survival
(Gamma, v. 1, p. 155).

Materialism

The conserver diagnosis of the problems of a mass consumption society can be
summarized as follows. The pursuit of continually increasing quantities of
material goods fails to satisfy real needs. It also contributes to pollution,
resource depletion, and other social problems. We produce sufficient output
already to meet our real physical needs. Attempts to further increase output lead
to alienation and frustration of our efforts to meet higher-order social and
psychological needs. An undirected market form of economic organization
bears much of the responsibility for this state of affairs because it gives power
and influence to producers. Without their persuasion, consumers would be less
materialistic. The conserver remedy is to limit persuasive advertising for
unnecessary products, and to educate consumers to counteract the effect of past
advertising.

The proposals for change that have been advocated by the Science Council
include the following individual and institutional changes:

• changes in individual values;

• changes in consumer choice patterns;

• changes in public regulations and procedures; and,

• changes in the process of want creation.

Canadians are portrayed as over-indulgent. Conservers attach great importance to their ability to persuade people to adopt an alternative ethic.

Legislation can only confirm and formalize ethical rules and
principles that are generally believed in. Individual
citizens...will change their perceptions of our society and its
problems and will do things differently...widespread sharing
of perceptions and attitudes is fundamental (Science Council
1977, p. 72).

The way in which individual values will be changed to render them less
materialistic is not completely spelled out. The Science Council does indicate

8

that the "informational, educational and communication processes of society" will be employed to make individual values less materialistic. Propagandizing may be too strong a word for this process, but it is clearly a departure from the traditional liberal view that tastes are subject to a variety of competing pressures dealt with by different individuals in different ways.

Transition Period

If Canadians could be persuaded to adopt this new ethic, it would presumably lead to an "appropriate" pattern of consumer choice. However, the Science Council either foresees a transition period in which this adjustment is incomplete, or it sees difficulties with implementing such a change. This is reflected in their proposals to limit or regulate the scope of consumer choice. As an example, the Science Council would require government measures "to improve fuel economy of automobiles." However, if there is no persuasive advertising and if tastes change appropriately, this type of restriction would appear to be unnecessary. Consumers in such a world would purchase only vehicles with appropriate fuel use characteristics.

In a similar vein, the Science Council foresees fuel shortages and suggests restrictions on the use of gasoline. This also implies that values either will not change or will not change quickly enough.

> As fuel shortages develop and prices rise, social inequities will be aggravated. Gasoline rationing or a two-price quota system will likely be necessary so as to ensure fair distribution and encourage conservation. Preparations should be made (Science Council 1977, p. 74).

Other Science Council proposals would encourage individuals to purchase more insulation, buy products that are more durable, and "cut wasteful consumption." Co-operative forms of ownership and use would be encouraged, since "total inventory and excess capacity can be reduced if home-owners share equipment such as lawnmowers." (Science Council 1977, p. 86).

Fundamental Restructuring

Although the Science Council's specific examples are only suggestive of the complete set of restrictions that would exist in a full-blown conserver society, the fundamental point is clear. For automobiles, lawnmowers, and presumably a variety of other commodities, the interaction of individuals in the marketplace is insufficient—direct regulations and restrictions are necessary.

The government, in its roles as consumer, producer and rule-maker, will be required to operate differently in this new society. The Science Council recommends a variety of government policy changes that would affect individual consumption decisions. These include upgraded public transit, pricing schemes to reduce peak demands for many transportation services, and revised utility rates to increase private incentives to economize on energy use. The desirability of such changes is not necessarily restricted to the case for a conserver society.

It is interesting to note that although the advocates of this new society tend to see government intervention as a panacea, they are also dissatisfied with the results of past intervention.

The Science Council's diagnosis of the problems of the consumer society suggests proposals to limit the role of advertising. This industry is seen as encouraging "wasteful practices," providing misleading information, and distorting preferences. The "Recommendations" section of the Science Council report suggests that we study advertising to discover how best to regulate it:

> What is the role of advertising in a saturated market, where total demand is virtually constant, innovation has almost ceased, and the market is dominated by a few large firms? ... How many of the products advertised on TV need to be advertised? (Science Council 1977, p. 87).

Rent, Don't Buy

The Gamma group's recommendations are very similar to those of the Science Council. They stress the importance of value changes. Changes in values are required if the institutions they propose are to function. For example, Gamma proposes that an alternative society would be based on widespread sharing through rental arrangements in contrast to private ownership, upon which the consumer society is based. Implementing this proposal would create fewer but more durable products, such as lawnmowers, since in a "rental mode" they would be used more often. According to Gamma, this would reduce the quantity of natural resources required to produce such goods.

To succeed, however, this proposal would require changes in values. First, for many goods, the rental option is currently available but infrequently chosen. Second, there is little incentive to maintain rented equipment properly. Therefore, renters will have to adopt different personalities if such plans are not to collapse in a sea of mutilated appliances:

> When a good is produced to be sold, in a profit economy, the producer has little interest in durability, while the consumer does. What happens is, of course, that fast-obsolescing perishable commodities are produced and sold... The result is massive continuous throughput to meet demand. When, on the contrary, a good is rented the lessor wishes to have the good returned in good condition. If the lessor is the producer he will build in durability. The consumer on the other hand will think otherwise. He will tend to abuse the product... We abuse cars when they are rented...and generally have little respect for other people's property unless we are forced to.

In a Rental Society this of course would have to change and both producers and consumers taught product durability (Gamma, v. 1, p. 227).

The focal point for all conserver society proposals is individual values. Some consumer changes are possible through restrictions and regulations, but the intent of these policies will ultimately be thwarted if existing "wasteful" and "individualistic" attitudes persist. The problem of the conserver society "can be conceptualized as the problem of transforming each individual consumer into a conserver." (Gamma, v. 1, p. 155).

Values and Tastes

The Gamma volumes explicitly recognize the potential dangers in such an emphasis on changing individual values in a specific direction at only one point.

Any social reformer who begins with the premise that a society's ills derive from imperfections in the value-system is faced with the serious ethical question of how much persuasion should be employed to change it. When does persuasion become coercion? (Gamma, v. 1, p. 173).

This issue is less troublesome when attention is focused on values and tastes that are viewed as artificially contrived. Gamma shares the view of the Science Council that existing tastes reflect not inherent preferences but attitudes created by the media and corporate marketing techniques. One study for the Gamma group argues that marketing practitioners have promoted a consumer society as a result of a failure to recognize resource realities.

Some farsighted critics have long recognized that many resources were finite and likely to be exhausted within an uncomfortably short period of time. In contrast, both marketing academics and business practitioners of the discipline have only recently become aware of this possibility (Gamma, v. 3, study no. 7, pp. 1-2).

The Gamma group urges a significant reduction in the marketing of consumption goods and greater government advocacy of their own views, which they term "social marketing."

Broadening the application of marketing concepts...leads quite logically to the application of these skills to the problem of promoting societal causes...[and] the use of marketing to facilitate social change (Gamma, v. 3, study no. 7, p. 65).

In summary, our society is wasteful in the use of resources because of inadequacies in our value systems. An individual with a conserver value system would not make wasteful choices. Solutions to the problem of waste necessarily imply an important role for government. This would include restrictions on advertising that reflects inappropriate values, and promotion of advertising that

11

reflects conserver values. To the extent that waste persists, further exhortation, taxation, regulation, and restriction may be required.

Economics and Individual Choice

Consumer sovereignty refers to the uncoerced choice of consumers among products of competing sellers who also provide information about their output. It defines a relationship between the actual composition of the output of an economy and the preferences of consumers. It implies that production decisions made by firms are dictated by the tastes and preferences of consumers. If consumer sovereignty prevails, the fundamental impetus for production decisions comes from consumers, rather than producers. To the extent that firms are accorded an active role in the process, their actions (through surveys and test-marketing) are designed to uncover the preferences of consumers and to provide information on new or existing products. This concept plays an important role in the frequently expressed preferences of economists for market, as opposed to government, allocation of resources.

The context for our discussion of consumer sovereignty is the model of household choice generally used by economists. In this model, the household faces the problem of allocating its income among a variety of commodities. It is assumed that individuals are capable of rational choice based on their preferences in order to maximize satisfaction for a given income level. The assumption is simple; whatever the level of income, individuals attempt to do as well for themselves as possible. This procedure yields a combination of commodities, according to the consumer sovereignty view, that primarily reflects the preferences of consumers limited by income and costs of production.

Consumer Sovereignty

For this reason, economists generally evaluate the performance of an economic system by the extent to which it provides satisfaction to consumers, a practice which dates back to Adam Smith in 1776. Smith's criticism of systems designed to achieve other (mercantilist) ends is similar to our criticism of many Science Council proposals for the promotion of domestic technological development.

> Consumption is the sole end and purpose of all production; and the interest of the producer ought to be attended to, only so far as it may be necessary for promoting that of the consumer... But in the mercantile system, the interest of the consumer is almost constantly sacrificed to that of the producer; and it seems to consider production, and not consumption as the ultimate end and object of all industry and commerce (Adam Smith, p. 625).

The problems that must be resolved by every economic system can be divided into the categories of what, how, and for whom. That is, what shall be produced, by what method, and to whom will the final outputs be distributed.

> What things will be produced is determined by the dollar votes of consumers...not every 2 or 4 years at the polls but every day in their decisions to purchase this item and not that... Note this: Consumer votes do not by themselves determine what goods are produced. Demand has to meet with a supply of goods; so business cost and supply decisions along with consumer demand, do help to determine what (Samuelson, 10th edition, p. 44).

This textbook explanation is broadly representative of the way in which economists view the composition of output. By rewarding firms whose output conforms to what is desired, consumers generally determine what is produced. Consumer sovereignty is limited, however, in that firms will not produce at prices that fail to cover their costs of production. The composition of output reflects the interaction of the preferences of individuals and the costs of production. Given the existence of consumer sovereignty, conserver criticisms of what we produce reflect a judgement on the tastes and preferences of other individuals. Conserver society literature abounds with criticism of "conspicuous consumption," "the proliferation of marginally different competing products," and "fast-obsolescing perishable commodities." To label goods and services consumed by others as conspicuous consumption or as marginally different from competing products is to question the worthiness of the preferences of others.

Producer Sovereignty

To the Science Council and the Gamma group, our economic system is characterized by producer rather than consumer sovereignty. This view of the world, in which production itself serves to create artificial consumer wants, is referred to by John Kenneth Galbraith as the dependence effect.

> As a society becomes increasingly affluent, wants are increasingly created by the process by which they are satisfied. This may operate passively. Increases in consumption, the counterpart of increases in production, act by suggestion or emulation to create wants. Or producers may proceed to actively create wants through advertising and salesmanship. Wants thus come to depend on output. In technical terms it can no longer be assumed that welfare is greater at an all-round higher level of production than at a lower one. It may be the same. The higher level of production has, merely, a higher level of want creation necessitating a higher level of

want satisfaction. There will be occasion to refer to the way wants depend on the process by which they are satisfied. It will be convenient to call it the Dependence Effect (Galbraith 1958, pp. 128-129).

The work of Galbraith constitutes an important challenge to the concept of consumer sovereignty. It is relevant for the conserver society debate, since an important criticism of the market is that we are squandering valuable resources (many of them non-renewable) on the production of a wide variety of trivial, unnecessary products. The solution is the adoption of new personalities and lifestyles in which many consumer products would be rejected. This case is obviously much easier to make if it is first possible to argue that existing consumption patterns are biased in the direction of outputs that conservers find distasteful, such as large automobiles and fast food. The Galbraith thesis serves this purpose. It can be used to justify various forms of coercion (prohibition, regulation) since in Galbraith's world, these individual choices are based on manipulated rather than innate wants and preferences.

Affluent Society

The case against consumer sovereignty as expressed by Galbraith and others has a certain logical attraction. Our society is obviously wealthy. By historical standards, even those who occupy a relatively low position in the income hierarchy consume a large quantity of material goods. Just as clearly, we all purchase many material goods (and services) that are not necessary, and we are all acquainted with others whose profligacy exceeds our own. However, one cannot make the logical jump from the observation of affluence to the conclusion that we are choosing an inappropriate combination of outputs (too many colour TVs and too few walks in the wilderness).

The core of the argument is that since wants are not innate, they are unimportant, and that unimportant demands should not be allowed to use up resources that conservers feel could be more valuably employed elsewhere. This is clearly an indictment by conservers of the tastes of others. They feel it is justified on the grounds that these resources are being used to satisfy not innate but contrived wants. The Gamma report goes even further. It argues that individual consumers are so confused that they mistakenly choose to embark on a consumption treadmill, not recognizing that attempts to meet needs such as water-skiing will act as a barrier to meeting higher order psychological needs, such as getting in touch with oneself.

The distinction between inherent and contrived wants is of crucial importance here. The contention that existing choices must be altered—if not voluntarily, then through government initiatives—is only valid if these choices are based on contrived wants.

Contrived Doesn't Mean Unimportant

The weak link in the argument that we have little consumer sovereignty is the assertion that since wants are not innate, they must be unimportant.[1] That most wants are not innate, and that they are unnecessary in that they are not requirements for survival, is not open to serious question. In a wealthy society, virtually by definition, a small fraction of total output is used to satisfy purely biological needs.

It has been estimated that an adult Canadian could survive on less than $400 worth of food per year. The resulting diet would be monotonous, but contains all necessary nutrients. The diet would include such things as wheat, sugar, skim milk, dry white beans, some canned fruit and vegetables, and a daily vitamin pill. There is no biological "need" to add anything to such a diet. Is it the case that the preferences of those who choose to eat more or different food, perhaps the odd bacon, lettuce, and tomato sandwich, are illegitimate because they are not based on biological need? Any reasonable interpretation of the position that consumers determine the composition of output must recognize that virtually all of our tastes are socially acquired. These tastes may lead consumers to purchase outputs that are aesthetically offensive to some, but it is hard to see how a free society can be maintained without tolerating or even encouraging differing tastes.

> All economically relevant wants are learned and…all better taste has to be acquired by study and practice (H.G. Johnson 1964, p. 241).

The conserver argument founders when it is realized that the innateness test is of no value. We biologically need very little of what we consume. Statements that Canadians don't need particular items improperly imply that we shouldn't want them.

Advertising

While conservers might concede the legitimacy of some acquired wants, they remain insistent that wants associated with advertising are contrived. As a result, they favour restrictions or taxes on advertising. They argue that our society is too materialistic and since it is material goods that are advertised, advertising must be at fault. The contrary view is that

> ours is a materialistic society… People are interested in acquiring material things; advertising simply reflects this fact (H.G. Johnson 1964, p. 281).

The conserver case against advertising is particularly weak since it rests on Galbraith's view of advertising, a view which, although not without adherents, commands little supporting evidence.

> One of the main themes in *The Affluent Society* was the enormous power which Galbraith assigned to advertising:

that these tastes for tailfins were not natural or native, that they were created by greedy producers seeking to shape the tastes of the public to satisfy their own interests. There resulted a considerable expansion in the economic analysis of advertising which tended to demonstrate, first, that a very large fraction of all advertising was informative rather than persuasive, secondly, that even in persuasive advertising the smart and intelligent thing for an enterprise to do was to find out what the public wants and then make it and advise them of it, not to try to shape its tastes. But, more important from Galbraith's general point of view, there was a great deal of emphasis on the extent to which you had advertising not only by private enterprise but also by government and bureaucrats, and that this has at least as widespread an effect as private advertising (Friedman 1977, pp. 14-15).

Free to Choose

The conserver society view of advertising is simply not compelling in a market economy in which advertised and unadvertised products exist side by side. As long as consumers are free to choose unadvertised brands, and as long as firms wishing to produce unadvertised products are free to enter markets, it is hard to accept the normative view that advertising should be restricted. Neither Galbraith nor his supporters have yet provided evidence for their claims of the pernicious effects of advertising. The evidence compiled by economists points in the opposite direction—namely, that the information function of advertising predominates.

Although most advertising clearly provides useful information, we would agree that there is more to the wide array of corporate marketing practices than just the provision of information. However, in its concentration on the information content of advertising, the conserver critique of marketing ignores the productive functions that are served by both packaging and advertising.

Is packaging excessive? Packaging facilitates the handling of goods, the prevention of theft, and the control of inventory, all of which save resources. Packaging assures the buyer that the product has not been tampered with. It is the package that identifies the producer and lists product contents and characteristics. There is little doubt that reliance on packaging has increased. However, much of this can be attributed to increases in the cost of labour, higher health standards and, most importantly, changes in our shopping patterns. Individuals buy a wide variety of goods in many locations. They can no longer rely on an idealized personal relationship with their local merchant to ensure quality. The increased reliance on both packaging and brand names can be seen as an attempt to deal with a world in which people move around and make complex choices.

Indirect Information

Is advertising excessive? We would not deny that some advertising does not convey information. Indeed, for products whose characteristics can be verified only through experience, it would be wasteful to provide any information. Is it also wasteful to advertise these products? Perhaps not. Advertising does convey indirect information about product quality. It is surely the case that a producer will not devote resources to convince individuals to try a product he knows beforehand they will not find satisfactory and will not choose again.

No economist can argue that marketing expenditures are unambiguously good or bad. Critics should recognize that they are a response to the demands of an imperfect world. Here they have a social function. There is little to indicate that their function can be served more efficiently by other institutions.

A Change in Values

For conservers, a sufficient condition for the creation of a better society would be the widespread adoption by individuals of "conserver personalities." Since the Science Council does not believe that we will change our tastes in this direction, they have proposed a variety of taxes and regulations to prevent us from exercising our present tastes.

We currently have a society that differs from the conserver vision because the vast majority of individuals do not share the values of its proponents. Market outcomes reflect a variety of individually held tastes and values rather than the set of values that conservers regard as desirable. As a result, conservers favour an alteration in the market form of economic organization. Their problem with the market is that it allows too much consumer sovereignty. The conserver society proposals, taken as a package, would either eliminate or restrict those market choices that are inconsistent with its principles.

Conserver proposals can be seen as having a basis not in economic necessity, as they would have us believe, but in politics. Our fundamental objection to the entire conserver scenario is that it is based solely on value judgements. More importantly, it is based on value judgements not shared by the majority of Canadians. Conservers as individuals clearly have the right to urge others to adopt their values. They do not have the right to use the coercive powers of the state to tax, regulate, and restrict to force such a change. Further, we question whether they should have the right to use the taxing power of the state to finance their efforts in persuasion.

Imposing Tastes

In a market economy, individual tastes prevail. A cost of the freedom associated with the market is that not all members of society will approve of the choices of others. The proponents of a conserver society prefer Volvos to Cadillacs, health-food stores to McDonald's and backpacking vacations to trips to Las Vegas. This may be, as well, a correct ranking of the preferences of the authors. But we are more than reluctant to establish our standards of taste for others. Conservers, however, would replace individual choices with collective ones that represent their own preferences. It is obviously legitimate for individuals to argue for a change in values. In a free society, it is not legitimate to attempt to impose those values by force on others. The problem is even more serious when the pressure for change and for mandated values comes from an agency supported by government.

Choosing Among Alternative Uses of Resources

Consumer choices determine the way in which different resources are employed. If scarce, they have competing uses, and individuals or groups who value a particular resource less highly than others will find it bid away from them. It is the virtue of a market economy that those who value a particular item most highly are identified and granted certain rights to its use. The fundamental problem of any economic system is scarcity. The use of a resource in one area generally precludes competing uses. Some people are excluded from using a good by the fact that others are willing to pay still more for it. The conserver society debate is over how resources should be used; it stands as an expression of dissatisfaction with the present system, under which the highest bidder wins.

Consider the conflict between logging and recreational uses of a particular parcel of land. Note that it is not competition between recreational users and "the logging interests," but between recreational users and individuals who use forest products. Which of these competing uses should prevail? Presently, the one that will better maximize consumer wellbeing. To reach a decision, we must calculate the value that recreational users attach to the services of this land, and the value attached to it by buyers of wood products. This is simply the total price that each group would be willing to pay to use the land for their own purposes. If the recreational users are willing to pay more than the loggers, we should preserve this land and prevent logging—even though it is privately profitable and employs many workers. If, however, the loggers acting on behalf of consumers of wood products are willing to pay more, then they should prevail. The criticisms of those persons who have been outbid are essentially those of market outcomes made by conserver society proponents.

Not by Dollars Alone

Conservers have several objections to the manner in which the market determines which user should prevail. The first objection is that social decisions, particularly those dealing with natural and non-renewable resources, should not be made on the basis of dollars alone. However, in the case discussed here, the market has merely used dollars as a yardstick for measuring the strength of the preferences of the alternative demanders of the resource. As long as the price paid by users reflects all benefits derived, including aesthetic and other benefits, then the market decision is best.

The second objection has to do with how those competing with conservers for the wood land determine not only the value they attach to the uses of the wood, but also to the recreational services of the land. Proponents of the conserver society have value systems in which environmental goods rank very highly relative to other goods. This may be because these proponents are drawn primarily from the highest income groups so that they already possess large quantities of material goods. In their opinion, wood is being used by others for purposes such as building houses that are "too large," or even worse, for the construction of pleasure boats or other over-valued consumer society items.

De Gustibus non est Disputandum

The conserver criticism of the decision to allow logging is that the outcome would have been different if only the consumers of wood were sufficiently sensitive to value wood less highly and environmental goods more highly. Their dislike of market outcomes and their desire to regulate market processes stem from the fact that a market economy often allocates resources to the highest bidders, precisely to the people whose preferences they regard as "ecologically unsound." Conserver regulations would attempt to alter market results to achieve the outcome that would have been reached if all individuals had conserver values and preferences. Our rejection of their scenario and our case in favour of market outcomes is made on opposite grounds: Market outcomes prevent any group from imposing its preferences on others.

The Political Economy of the Conserver Society

The distinguishing characteristic of conserver society proposals is their rejection of free choice by those who do not share their values. They do more than urge others to change. They propose using the coercive power of the state to compel this change. In this section, we explore the implications of their proposals to replace market processes and outcomes with government control.

A market form of organization is one possible way of organizing ourselves to deal with scarcity.[2] Command systems in which government decisions allocate resources among competing users are another obvious alternative.

Scarcity necessarily implies competition for resources. Any form of social organization must provide a mechanism for choosing between competing ends. The winner in this competition can be determined in a variety of ways, and the method chosen will have important social implications.

A major advantage of the market as an allocational device is that it provides a non-political solution to the social conflict raised by resource scarcity. Individuals obtain title to scarce resources through voluntary exchange and each such exchange represents a solution to what would otherwise be a political issue.

> The solution is essentially the transformation of the *conflict* from a political *problem* to an economic transaction. An economic *transaction* is a solved political problem. (Lerner 1972, p. 259)

The case being made here is not that we should prevent problems from becoming political issues at any cost. There are problems and activities, particularly associated with the production of collectively consumed goods and the control of external effects, for which political solutions are essential. It is precisely because there are so many important areas for government participation that it should not be overloaded with problems that markets can resolve well. A major criticism of the conserver society documents is that they select a large number of issues that have been resolved by the market and advocate returning these issues to the status of political problems through their proposals for restrictions, regulation, and government initiatives.

Planned Obsolescence

Consider the conserver approach to product durability. It asserts that market outcomes persistently provide us with products of less than desired durability. The Science Council argues that we should "make products more durable" and urges the establishment of "durability and efficiency standards." (Conserver Society, p. 79). The Gamma group asserts that in a profit economy, the producer has little interest "when a good is produced to be sold, in durability, while the consumer does." (Conserver Society, p. 80).

Our view is that durability is simply another commodity characteristic and that firms providing products with characteristics desired by consumers will prosper relative to those that do not. The Gamma statement that producers have no interest in durability is inaccurate. Unless the firm has the ability to exclude producers of similar but more durable products, it must, in its own interest, provide this and other desired characteristics.

It is true that many products are now less durable than is technically possible. This is, however, not evidence that products should be more durable. Many products are technically inefficient but economically efficient. Durability is not costless. It is likely that automobiles with a useful lifespan of 30 years could be produced—say for $100,000. The Rolls Royce company likes to claim that virtually all of the cars it has ever produced are still functioning. These cars are built expensively and substantial resources are devoted to their maintenance. That most consumers choose to pay less and purchase less durability is not surprising. A standard of technical efficiency could minimize, for example, the quantity of steel used per automobile, in that one durable 30-year car might produce the same number of passenger miles as six five-year cars. The savings in steel use, however, would be more than offset by the value of the extra resources consumed in producing and maintaining more durability.

Market is Imperfect

We concede that it is possible that the durability buyers might want will not be supplied. The reason is that claims of durability are difficult to verify prior to purchase. Buyers are likely to discount such claims, whether made by private companies or government producers. In a better world, buyers would have no reason to doubt the claims of sellers. The case for governmental mandates on durability rests on a confusion between technical and economic efficiency and on a failure to see that market competition restricts the ability of firms to produce outputs less durable than desired by their customers. Conservers also fail to recognize that the provision of desired durability is a problem faced by market and non-market regimes alike.

Conserver proposals, of which a durability standard is but one example, are based in part on a misunderstanding of how markets work to allocate resources, and in part on their advocates' desire to substitute their preferences for those of consumers as reflected in current market outcomes. These proposals require, in general, an expansion of non-market decision-making (i.e. more government) and a curtailment of the scope of markets.

Competition for scarce resources would be unaffected by such a change. Only the method of competition would be changed. Instead of the operation of market forces, there would be political decisions. Competing users of resources would be forced to channel their energies into influencing the political process to obtain resources. The competition for scarce resources would shift from the impersonality of the market to the political arena. A major drawback of such a shift in the mechanism for allocating resources is that the politicization of allocation decisions intensifies social divisiveness. A conserver society would be a highly politicized society. Do we really wish to use the government decision-making process for decisions regarding the production of television sets, microwave ovens, pizzas and all other items to which conservers take exception?

Who Looks After the Future?

A persistent theme of the conserver literature is that our society pays too much attention to the present and too little to the future. The Science Council alleges that:

> the time horizons of individuals, businesses, and governments are too short... [T]he planning being done is too often of a kind that is short-term or is aimed at solving yesterday's problems. (Science Council 1977, p. 24).

As an antidote, the Council proposes "a conserver society [that] will conserve to gain manoeuvering room to keep all options open, rather than being driven by one supply crisis after another to desperate solutions that box us in for many decades." (Science Council 1977, p. 25). Concern over our legacy to the future is not new. The Science Council has embraced a tradition that in the early 1800s originated with the writings of Parson Thomas Malthus, ironically an economist and not an ecologist.

Scarcity is nothing new to economists. In fact, economics has been defined as the study of how man uses scarce resources to fulfill competing objectives. Moreover, for the economist, it is not just one or even a few resources that are scarce. Scarcity exists whenever the quantity of some resource is insufficient to satisfy all possible uses for it. As a consequence, the economist's list of scarce resources is very long and in addition to the usual non-renewable resources, it includes renewable and human resources.

One-dimensionality

The economist's view of scarcity contrasts sharply with the approach of the advocates of the conserver society. We believe that conservers deal only with "one-dimensional scarcity." They focus on the decreasing abundance of natural resources and, at times, even on adequacy for the future of particular non-renewable resources. The nearest the Science Council comes to a recognition of general scarcity is its concession that "it is an oversimplification to think in terms of energy efficiency." (Conserver Society, p. 50). Still, the limited extent of this recognition is revealed as they continue: "More fundamentally we should be concerned with the use-efficiency of whichever is the limiting resource—and there may be several." (Conserver Society, p. 50). The shortcoming of this attachment to one-dimensional scarcity is that it overemphasizes the necessity of specific inputs in meeting society's needs. In so doing, it neglects the impressive substitutions in industrial processes that have served to limit the use of resources in short supply.

Substitutes

Much can be learned from historical experience about the potential for substitution. One of the most dramatic examples is provided by the German mobilization efforts during the Second World War. The German economy was expected to be especially vulnerable to shortages of metals. Examples include copper, where output from domestic sources accounted for no more than 10 percent of production, and steel, where the dependency on imported ferro-alloys seemed certain to create shortages. Technical substitution played a substantial role in overcoming these anticipated problems.

> At the beginning of 1942 railway locomotives contained, on the average, 2.3 metric tons of copper, but by the middle of 1943 this had been reduced to 237 kilograms, or about one-tenth of the original amount. Early in the war the building of a submarine required 56 tons of copper; this was later reduced to 26 tons. The use of alloy steel was virtually eliminated from railway car construction, and iron radiators were substituted for copper radiators in all motor vehicles. In the case of ferro-alloys, relatively plentiful vanadium and silicon were substituted for molybdenum in gun tubes under 21 centimeters in length. Nickel was replaced by vanadium in gun tubes under 10.5 centimeters in length. In addition, new processes were devised for working lower grade ore supplies, such as chrome supplies in the Balkans. (Mason 1977, p. 2.)

These measures were so successful that they led to substantial miscalculations by Allied intelligence of German stockpiles of strategic materials. The British Ministry of Economic Warfare, for example, estimated that German copper stocks had declined from 200,000 to 75,000 metric tons over the period from 1940 to 1942; actually, they had risen from 183,000 to 265,000 thousand metric tons at the same time as meeting the demands of the expanded war effort (Klein 1959, p. 114). A similar story occurred with respect to ferro-alloys. The bottleneck for steel production turned out not to be ferro-alloys, but coke. In turn, the shortage of coke resulted not from limited raw materials but, rather, from a lack of skilled labour.

Waste

Once the possibilities for substitution become recognized, one-dimensional scarcity encounters severe difficulties. Should the range of scarcity be extended to include close substitutes for the resource being considered? If so, where does this process end? As the German example and others show, man has been ingenious in devising alternatives. Some require renewable resources, but others, such as the search for scrap metal, involve the use of labour.

A greater danger from a fixation on one—or at the most, several—scarce resources is the possibility of contributing to rather than preventing waste. Consider two farmers, Jones and Green, who both face identical conditions. They have the same weather, land, machinery, and technology. The only difference is that Green hires more labour to work his farm. As a result, we would not expect the two farmers to practise the same methods of cultivation. With more labour, Green will plant parts of his land that are hard to reach. He will have his crops weeded more frequently and more thoroughly. Clearly, Green will have a higher yield per acre than Jones.

From a one-dimensional viewpoint and with land the scarce resource, Jones clearly is more wasteful than Green. But note the arbitrary nature of one-dimensional scarcity. If labour were deemed the scarcer resource, Jones becomes less wasteful than Green! The economist, however, would not necessarily agree. Before making any judgement he would want to know the other productive uses to which the labour could have been put and the value society attaches to their foregone output.

To an economist, not one, not a few, but all resources are scarce and should not be wasted. This point of view has profound implications for the future. Unused natural resources are only one of the ways of providing for posterity. Past generations have looked after our future in many other ways. They have given us tangible assets, such as railroads and factories. They have also left us the intangible assets of knowledge and technical skills, important sources of our well-being. They have also given us poetry, paintings, and music. These diverse man-made resources have one feature in common. Their creation required using up previously available stocks of scarce natural resources. In the case of the factory, the coal and iron ore used to make steel come readily to mind. Less obvious in the case of knowledge is the training and sustenance of the scientist, which required the use of natural resources, many of them non-renewable.

Recycling

The Science Council's attachment to one-dimensional scarcity carries through into its recommendations for policy. The Council, for example, argues "recycling must become part of the fabric of all productive activities" (Science Council 1977, p. 29) and urges a massive programme of support for recycling through such diverse means as subsidy, tax holidays, forgivable loans, freight subsidies, and a host of other means.

The brunt of the Science Council case rests on its commitment to one-dimensional scarcity. According to the Council, recycling ought to be encouraged because it saves non-renewable resources and, in particular, energy resources.

Energy expended in collecting, transporting and reprocessing waste materials is usually far less than the energy required for the extraction, refining and transportation of virgin materials.

As the extraction of minerals continues and lower grade ore is used, the energy expenditure involved in extraction and refining is likely to increase.

Recycling is essential if we wish to extend the life of our non-renewable resources and keep down their cost. (Science Council 1977, p. 79)

While the list continues to include other factors, including environmental benefits and the costs of waste disposal, nowhere does the Council show that recycling costs less in terms of overall resources. Often, the limit to recycling is that it does not cover its costs. Paradoxically, at least to the conservers, extending recycling on the basis of energy-efficiency or even on non-renewable resource efficiency alone could reduce the possible output from our total resources and would be detrimental to future generations.

Objections

The economist's view of the future immediately raises a number of possible objections. Has the conversion of natural resources into man-made resources foreclosed our options? Would we not be better off if these resources had been left in their natural state? The issue of options obscures rather than illuminates. It is true we do not now have certain options we would have had if natural resources had remained unused. Canadians cannot now use the long depleted oil reserves of the Sarnia region. But just as important is the other side. The option of using insulin to provide longer, more meaningful lives for diabetics would not have been available to us unless earlier generations had devoted natural resources, including non-renewables, to scientific endeavour. Use of natural resources in the present need not reduce the options of future generations; instead, it gives them a different set of options. The relevant question is which set of options is preferable.

A further objection to the economist's broad concept of scarcity arises from the inclusion of human time as a scarce resource. Labour, it is argued, can be viewed very differently from natural and man-made resources in terms of its contribution to posterity. If we do not use our existing labour today, the services it would have provided are lost forever. Labour services cannot be preserved for the future. Clearly, acceptance of this view has substantial consequences. Every effort should be made to substitute labour for more durable resources, since only by conserving can we protect the interests of future generations.

Echoes of this variant of one-dimensional scarcity permeate the *Conserver Society*, especially in its attack on the passenger car for urban commuting.

While recognizing both the "trade-offs in time and convenience" for inter-city travel and also the "privacy, mobility and convenience offered by the automobile," the Science Council argues the upgrading of urban public transit "is essential because urban travel is the least fuel-efficient use of the private automobile." (p. 73)

The focus on fuel-efficiency alone fails to recognize the importance of labour in the economy. Labour is just as much a productive resource as man-made capital, renewable resources, and even non-renewable resources. Any movement of labour from its current uses must be assessed in terms of its value in alternative options. Labour, like any resource, can be directed to satisfying current demand or toward meeting the needs of the future. To judge otherwise is to depreciate the contributions of a Darwin or a Wordsworth, a Beethoven or a de Vinci.

Passenger transportation provides an example of an area where well-intentioned policies based on the single dimension of fuel-efficiency can have unintended detrimental effects. Subsidy of urban transport, as urged by the Science Council, could be used either to upgrade service or reduce fares. But there is a very real danger of devoting resources to urban transit and being unable to persuade commuters to switch. In such a case, resources will have been wasted because of duplication of transport facilities. Lower fares are unlikely to be adequate in the face of large differentials in the cost of time. It is even possible that improvements in urban transport merely generate increased traffic, offsetting the effects of any shift among modes. Such a change could, incidentally, lead to greater overall consumption of fuel, despite the improvement of fuel-efficiency in terms of passenger miles per gallon. The use of the one-dimensional guide of fuel-efficiency carries the potential for mischievous unintended outcomes that are wasteful from a social viewpoint.

The Market and the Future

Not surprisingly, the Science Council plunges onward from its diagnosis of social myopia to prescription. It proposes a massive programme of government involvement and intervention. Before accepting this programme, many questions should be asked. Have other generations provided for us? If so, what mechanisms did they use? Can these mechanisms play a role in providing for the future in our society? As a result of answering these questions, we must part company with the advocates of the conserver society.

At an abstract level, the economist can demonstrate the logical beauty of the market for making choices about the future. One necessary ingredient in this demonstration is the existence of a separate market for every commodity during each time period in the future. Not only is a market for coal needed; a market must exist in which coal can be traded now for 1990, 1991, and into the future forever. Clearly, not even the most ardent defender of the market believes these conditions exist. Since existing markets fall far short of meeting these requirements, is the economist's demonstration in vain? The market in abstract works perfectly because decision-makers are faced with prices for resources at all times in the future. Any resource owner is able to sell his resources at the times that are to his greatest benefit. However, actual markets for non-renewable resources work the same way in principle as the theoretical abstractions of markets. Resource owners must decide how much to use today and how much to save for the future. If the resource owner is economically rational, he tries to gain the most he can for his resources by comparing current prices with prices he expects in the future and plans his use of the resource accordingly. The higher the price he expects in the future, the more the owner will conserve his resource so as to increase profits.

Negative Feedback

Many critics of the free-enterprise system fail to recognize that the market works much like the negative feedback mechanisms found in nature. In nature, a negative feedback mechanism exists in a system when a stimulus provokes an offsetting response. A similar feedback mechanism ensures that the market works as a conserving force.

For example, suppose new information suggests that existing estimates of the availability of coal are overly optimistic. Resource owners will react to this by revising upward their expectations of the future price. This higher future price will lead owners to use less of their resources today and preserve more for the future.

The reduced supply of coal at present will have important consequences. Current prices will be forced to rise to bring demand into balance with the reduced supply. On the demand side, the higher prices will lead users of coal and its by products to find substitutes. The incentive to develop techniques that economize on the use of coal will be increased.

Similar adjustments will occur on the supply side. The search for new deposits will intensify and lower-grade sources will become more profitable to use. For many non-renewable resources there will also be a greater incentive for recycling and other measures to stretch their use.

The Conserver Critique of the Market

The price system as a feedback mechanism serves the ends of conservation by invoking many of the responses desired by advocates of the conserver society. Consumers are led to reduce their consumption of scarce materials, manufacturers are encouraged to substitute for scarce commodities as inputs, and businesses have greater incentives for recycling. Yet the Science Council tends to reject the market as a device for achieving their aims. Among their grounds for rejecting the use of the market are the following:

- consumers do not respond to prices;
- producers do not respond to prices—the opportunities for substitution are extremely limited;
- the price system has allowed depletion of resources in the past;
- producers and consumers are not adequately informed;
- resource owners' time horizons do not extend far enough into the future; and
- the working of the price system is unfair.

Consumers Do Not Respond to Prices

Critics of the market argue that economists overestimate the role of prices in determining consumer choices. Economic theory and reality are two different things, they say. How can we be sure that consumers will respond to higher prices in the real world? Are economists not aware that people make many choices by habit and, in any case, are conditioned by the pervasive influences of consumerism? Moreover, it is easy to point to people who persist in driving excessively large cars and live in poorly insulated houses. In the Science Council's words, "prices may have to be raised to quite artificially high levels before the behaviour of individuals is influenced on self-interest alone." (Science Council 1977, p. 40)

The suggestion that consumers do not respond sufficiently to prices in itself reveals a lack of understanding of the workings of the market as a negative feedback mechanism. A given shortfall between demand and supply of a resource will not have exactly the same price impact in all markets. In any particular case, prices will respond to any shortage until their increase has eliminated that shortage. If consumers are very responsive to price, only a small increase is needed. The less responsive consumers are to prices, the larger the increase must be to bring demand and supply together again. But as long as consumers respond at all to price, and the price is free to move, the market mechanism can ration the limited supply. To characterize the resulting prices as "artificial" merely clouds the issue.

Relative versus Absolute Prices

Some observers have underestimated the role of prices in governing energy demands because they have confused movements of energy prices that are part of an overall inflation with relative movements in energy prices. The economist is willing to predict the effect of prices on energy demands when energy prices are changing relative to other prices. Only then will energy users have an incentive to economize on the use of energy in their choice of production techniques and in their final demands. When energy price increases are part of a general rise in prices, the incentive to economize is no greater than if all prices had been stable. Thus any argument on the effect of prices must be based on changes in the price of energy relative to other prices.

Before turning to evidence on how consumers respond to prices, it is useful to examine the nature of this response. Consumers react to higher prices differently according to the good or service under consideration. Some consumer reactions occur immediately. We may switch from planning to buy spinach to actually buying broccoli when we arrive at the supermarket and discover a much lower price for broccoli than anticipated. However, not all adjustments to higher prices will be so prompt.

Car size, house design, type of heating fuel, and similar choices lock consumers into technologies, which will continue for some time after the choice is made. The initial reaction to a price change may then be limited by the existing technology. Car owners may decide to travel less and to drive at more economical speeds when they do travel. Similarly, home owners may decide to maintain their houses at lower temperatures. Only after some time may more substantial reactions be made. When considering the purchase of a new car, a person may then try to find a more fuel-efficient car. Similarly, home buyers may insist on furnaces that use cheaper fuel and on insulation that meets a higher standard. The insulation standards of some houses may be upgraded through renovation. In other cases, it still may not pay to make such adjustments. Nevertheless, with new housing being built and with the renovation of other homes, the share of houses in the housing stock that are less fuel-efficient will fall over time. Thus the response to a price change can be expected in some cases to continue for many years. The initial response to a price change will often be only a fraction of the total response.

Elasticities Increase Over Time

Failure to appreciate the time pattern of the response to changing prices can lead sceptics to unjustifiably condemn the market as an adjustment mechanism. Even after a large shift in prices, people may persist in driving large cars and living in poorly insulated houses judged in terms of the new energy prices. To argue that the failure to shift immediately to small cars and better insulated houses in the name of energy efficiency indicates the inadequacy of market adjustments is to fall into the trap of one-dimensional scarcity again.

Energy is only one among many scarce resources used in producing passenger transportation and housing. Immediate shifts to smaller cars would waste other scarce resources used in their production. It is not even clear such a move would necessarily be useful even in the conservers' reference term of one-dimensional efficiency. Premature scrapping of large gas guzzlers to replace them by small fuel-efficient cars may use more energy resources than might be saved, leaving less energy for future generations.

29

Evidence

Still, to this point, the question of consumer responses to higher prices remains open. What evidence have economists accumulated on this question? A useful source providing tentative answers from a Canadian standpoint is study of energy demands by Ernst Berndt. Berndt explores the evidence on the response of demands for specific forms of energy to changes in their price, and is able to conclude:

> evidence on Canadian final demand for energy is somewhat fragmentary but reasonable. In the short run, prices have only a small effect but in the longer run the price elasticities appear to be in the -.3 to -.6 range (1977, p. 65).

What do these studies tell us about energy demands? In particular, what does the price elasticity of -.3 to -.6 found by Berndt mean? The term "price elasticity" is used by economists as a measure of the responsiveness of demand to price. It indicates the ratio of the percentage change in quantity demanded for some good to the percentage change in its price. Thus, when Berndt finds a price elasticity of -.6 for the residential demand for natural gas, it means that a 10 percent increase in natural gas prices can be expected to lead households to reduce their purchases of natural gas by 6 per cent, given no change in the other influences on demand such as household income and average temperature.

More Recent Evidence

The studies cited by Berndt all covered periods prior to the drastic increases in oil prices in the 1970s. The evidence for more recent periods has led to a strengthening of the view that energy consumption responds effectively to prices. Professor Robert Pindyck of the Massachusetts Institute of Technology has concluded on the basis of more recent studies that:

> we now believe energy is much more price-sensitive than we have previously expected... For example, in the case of industrial energy use we have found that the long-run price elasticity of total energy demand with respect to changes in the aggregate price index of energy is around -0.8 (about twice as large as earlier studies—based on time series data for single countries and therefore picking up shorter run effects—had indicated)... We have found similar results for the residential sector (an own price elasticity for total energy use of about -1.1) and the transportation sector (it appears that the price elasticity of demand for motor gasoline is around -1. (pp. 12-13)

Pindyck relates this evidence to patterns of energy use in industrialized economies.

Countries that have used stiff taxes and other price incentives to reduce energy demand have indeed found these policies to be successful. We now observe *decreases* in energy consumption since 1973 of roughly 5 or even 10 percent for such countries as Britain, France, West Germany and Italy, while the United States, which has continued to maintain domestic energy prices below world levels, has experienced increases in energy use. (p. 13)

Economists recognize that consumer demands are subject to a multitude of influences: habit, advertising, social pressures, and even whim. The failure of prices to influence consumer demand is an important element of the conserver critique of the market. In the absence of any role for prices, arguments for direct controls over consumers are more persuasive. However, the evidence that non-economic factors also shape consumer demands does not preclude an important role for prices. The available evidence on consumer demand for energy in Canada leaves little doubt that prices do play an important role in rationing our scarce resources.

Producers Do Not Respond to Prices

A 1977 study conducted for Resources for the Future shows that Canada has the highest ratio of energy consumption to Gross Domestic Product of the nine major industrialized countries surveyed (see table 1). On the basis of this type of evidence, the Science Council observes:

We begin from a standpoint of a society that is acknowledged to be wasteful in energy, consuming in some cases almost twice as much energy per capita and/or per unit of industrial output as some countries with comparable or higher GNP per capita and similar industrial mix... (Science Council 1977, p. 41)

Canadian industry is, they contend, less energy conscious and more prone to waste than its foreign counterparts. Further, if Canadian industry has ignored opportunities for conservation in the past, how can we be assured they will respond to higher energy prices in the future?

The validity of the argument that North American industry is inherently less sensitive to the need to conserve energy was examined by Darmstadter and his associates, who concluded:

Variations in energy/output ratios should not in themselves be viewed as indicators of economic efficiency or even of energy efficiency. Economic efficiency depends on how energy is used in combination with other resources—particularly capital and labour—and the relative costs of all these. (1977, p. 207).

Table 1
Energy/Output Relationships, 1972

Country	Gross Domestic Product per capita (dollars)	Energy Consumption per capita (tons oil equivalent)	Energy/GDP ratio (tons oil equivalent) per $million	Indexes U.S.=100
United States	5,643	8.35	1,480	100
Canada	4,728	8.38	1,772	120
France	4,168	3.31	795	54
West Germany	3,991	4.12	1,031	70
Italy	2,612	2.39	915	62
Netherlands	3,678	4.68	1,272	86
United Kingdom	3,401	3.81	1,121	76
Sweden	5,000	5.31	1,062	72
Japan	3,423	2.90	849	57

Source: Joel Darmstadter, Joy Dunkerley, and Jack Alterman, *How Industrial Societies Use Energy: A Comparative Analysis*, Baltimore, Johns Hopkins Press, 1977.

They also concluded:

> It is nevertheless our firm judgement that, in the comparative intercountry setting of this report, the assumed presence of an energy-conservation ethic and abhorrence of waste "over time" is simply not supported by the facts and is simplistic in its view of the evidence. (1977, p. 207)

Other Variables

Darmstadter and associates turned to a variety of factors other than differences in energy consciousness to explain the patterns of energy use across countries. Factors include geography, energy resource endowment, import dependence, and fuel mix. They also reserve an important role for price, citing favourably a study by William D. Nordhaus, who found that a 10 percent increase in prices would be associated with a 5 percent decline in energy use by industry. Nordhaus concluded in his study that "relative prices play a crucial role in determining the energy intensiveness across space and time." (Nordhaus 1975, p. 588).

Studies of energy use in Canadian industry serve to buttress the findings of Nordhaus and indicate a price responsiveness similar to those found in consumer demand for energy. Ernst Berndt reports:

> A number of studies have been cited which vary with respect to data base—cross section, time series or combination of both—and in terms of statistical methodology. The principal findings, however, are remarkably similar. Demand for energy in the intermediate demand sector in Canada is price responsive. Our own price elasticities vary from -.3 to -.6... Finally, demand for specific fuels is even more price responsible because of possibilities for inter-fuel competition. (1977, p. 62)

Berndt suggests that neglecting the effect of technical change on factor demands in these studies may even reinforce the conclusions:

> Technological progress may of course be non-neutral in the sense that some inputs are augmented or conserved more than others. A recent study by E. R. Berndt and David O. Wood finds that technological change in post-war U.S. manufacturing has been labour-saving and energy-using. An intriguing aspect of this result is that the pattern of technological change has been to conserve on the input whose price has risen the greatest (labour), and to utilize more extensively the input whose price has risen least (energy). This suggests that even the bias of technological innovations may be price-responsive (1977, p. 63).

The possibility that price changes can affect the direction of technological changes comes as little surprise to economists; it reinforces our confidence in the role of market forces.

Are Canadians less energy-conscious or inherently more wasteful than the Japanese? Has Canadian industry lagged in its adjustment to the new reality of the energy situation? Must direct measures be implemented to enforce conservation actions that industry seems unwilling to carry out? We would say no to each question. Differences in industrial energy use among countries correspond to differences in price.

Depletion of Resources

The best test of the market is its actual performance in rationing scarce resources in the past. Has the market stretched our scarce supplies of resources over time, or has it allowed us to run out? Can we assume that prices will rise as they are supposed to in order to preserve threatened resources?

Before judging the working of the market in a specific case, some insight can be gained from reviewing the way in which prices can be expected to ration scarce resources over time. Economists have long noted that as a resource becomes scarcer relative to its demands, its price rises over time, calling forth new supplies, rationing its use, and conserving more of the resource for the future. But this is not the only possibility. Prices will rise continuously over time only for those resources that have few close substitutes. If, on the other hand, there is a substitute, and if its production can be expanded readily at some constant price, the pattern of price change and resource use over time will differ from the usual case.

The term "back-stop" describes a close substitute resource that can be brought into use at a particular price. The potential switch to the "back-stop technology" places a limit on the price increase of any given scarce resource. If the back-stop is competitive in all uses, the original resource will ultimately disappear from the market. On the other hand, if the back-stop technology is competitive in only some uses, the price of the scarce resource will continue to rise. Its use will be confined to those purposes where the back-stop is a less effective replacement.

Misinterpretation Easy

It would be easy to misinterpret the sequence of events leading to the replacement of a resource with a back-stop technology. Observers would note that the scarce resource supplied a smaller and smaller proportion of needs over time. Some might even be tempted to say that the market has let us down, permitting us to squander the reserve to such a degree that we cannot even meet traditional demands with what is left. An alternative interpretation is that the market adjustment has led us to substitute a cheaper back-stop technology to meet these demands.

The substitution of coal for firewood in England over the period from 1450 to 1700 provides an example of a back-stop technology at work. By 1500 a shortage of firewood had become increasingly apparent. Nef, in his classic *The Rise of the British Coal Industry*, declared:

> All the evidence suggests that between the accession of Elizabeth and the Civil War, England, Wales and Scotland faced an acute shortage of wood, which was common to most parts of the island... (p. 161).

The extent of this shortage can be seen by following the path of firewood prices shown in table 2. The price of firewood increased by two and one-half times as much as the general price level during the period 1450 to 1640.

Table 2
The Relative Price of Firewood, 1451 - 1642

Time Period	Money Price of Firewood	General Prices Index	Real Price of Firewood
1451 - 1500	100	100	100
1531 - 1540	94	105	90
1551 - 1560	163	132	123
1583 - 1592	277	198	140
1603 - 1612	366	251	146
1613 - 1622	457	257	178
1623 - 1632	677	282	240
1633 - 1642	780	291	268

Source:John U. Nef, *The Rise of the British Coal Industry*, p. 158.

Coal as Back-stop

The "back-stop technology" for firewood turned out to be coal. As might be expected, the substitution of coal for wood proceeded at different rates in different industries, spreading from the trades of the "limeburner and smith" to the making of salt, soap, and sugar. Finally, as reported by Nef:

> There were a large number of industrial situations in which coal could not be substituted at all until some technical alteration had been made in the process of manufacture. It was necessary either to free the coal from its damaging properties or to invent a device to protect the raw material from the flames and fumes. (p. 215)

During the 1600s, the technical problems were gradually solved so that coal had replaced firewood in the baking of bricks, the drying of meat, and the making of glass. Nef concluded that "by 1700 the substitution of coal for firewood had relieved the pressure upon timber supplies in England except in those localities where metallic ores were smelted." (p. 221)

How well does the firewood example fit our expectations for a resource with a back-stop technology? Were the British driven to the use of coal only after squandering their forests to the point of exhaustion? To the contrary, the woodlands were far from depleted. Nef writes:

.The danger of exhaustion was far less ominous in the decade from 1690 to 1700 than in the decade from 1600 to 1610. A French visitor, well informed on many questions, could write in 1689 of the abundant forests, and could argue that use of coal by the English would not be ascribed to any lack of wood. (p. 221)

By this time, the remaining forests were no longer threatened by the demands from industry. Ironically, a greater threat arose from a lack of demand. As a contemporary observer noted:

It is not immaterial to observe what an alternative it (the use of coal fires in London taverns) makes in the value of these woods in Kent, and how many more of them, than usual, are yearly grabbed up, and made fit for the plough. (p. 222)

Much the same story can be seen from the movement of prices. From 1642 to 1702 the price of firewood, if anything, declined.

Informed Decision-makers

In government, decisions are typically made by a few individuals on behalf of many. In the market, decision-making is diffused among numerous individual consumers and producers. This difference leads some critics to question the outcome of market processes, arguing that it is unlikely this many decision-makers could be adequately informed.

In examining the validity of this criticism of the market, several issues need to be kept separate. First, does the government necessarily have better information for decision-making than market participants? Second, what would proven superiority of government information imply for reliance on the market? Each of these issues will be treated more fully in the remainder of this section.

Hindsight

One difficulty in judging this line of criticism is that it leads too easily into the "what we know now" fallacy. The chances that the Toronto Argonauts would have won would surely be increased if only the quarterback had kept the ball and not thrown an interception. Similarly, Detroit was silly to keep on producing large gas-guzzlers when the OPEC cartel was just around the corner. We might just as well argue that if Newton was so smart, why did he not discover Einstein's theory of relativity rather than causing us to wait another century? In each of these cases, we must resist the temptation to judge past decisions on the basis of perfect hindsight. We can judge past decisions only on the reasonable interpretation of information available at the time, and even then we must allow for differences of opinion. The intercepted pass, before it was thrown, was the best chance the quarterback had to pull the game out. Detroit had observed constant, if not falling, real prices of gasoline for many years after World War II.

The message of the "what we know now" fallacy is that we cannot reject reliance on the use of prices just because it can be shown that some past market decisions could have been better. Instead, it must be shown that government decision-makers would have consistently possessed and acted on superior information.

Market Imperfect. Government Perfect?

Many critics of the market tend to overestimate the difficulties faced by market participants in obtaining sufficient information. The market provides incentives for participants to seek superior information. It also provides an outlet for those whose judgements differ from the consensus. The nature of government organization means that even though diverse viewpoints may contribute to the final choice, only a single judgement—often the result of weighting arguments brought to bear on the issue—can prevail. In the market, in contrast, those whose information and judgement leads them to differ with the consensus can act on their differences of opinion. For example, those who believe that the market consensus reflects an over-estimate of a resource can act on this belief and buy up the resource to hold for the future.

Anyone whose judgement differs from the market will earn profits if this judgement ultimately proves correct. The incentive of profits, together with the discipline of losses, creates strong pressure for decision-makers to seek out information needed for effective decision-making. Of course, the greater the stakes in any decision, the greater will be the incentive to seek out information.

Assume Government Superiority

Conservers appear to have found the preceding argument unconvincing. But what if they happen to be right? What would the superiority of information available to the government imply for the scope of the market? Surprisingly enough, the answer may be "very little." Consider an example where the government accurately assesses that the recoverable stocks of some non-renewable resources are no more than half the amount judged to be present by the private sector. Conservers would argue that the government must take direct measures to reduce present consumption. Laws must be passed to restrict its current use. Taxes must be increased on both extraction and use.

But direct action by government is hardly the only possibility. On the contrary, the government could share its superior information with market participants. With better information, producers would realize that future prices will be higher than earlier expected. They would then hold more of their resources for sale in the future.

Interestingly enough, the possibility of the government sharing its superior information with the private sector is not without precedent. The belief that government has superior knowledge with respect to agricultural techniques has not led to government intervention to force their adoption. Rather, the government has chosen to share this supposedly superior knowledge by means of agricultural extension services that provide advice to farmers. Thus, unless the costs of conveying information to the public are high, possession of superior information by governments is not a sufficient argument for intervention through regulation and taxation.

Resource Owners' Horizons Are Limited

Many conservers question reliance on the market because they believe the horizons of individual resource owners are too limited to reflect the interests of future generations. Will resource owners hold their resources aside for future generations when they can sell now for current use? How can future generations express their demands for non-renewable resources when they have yet to be born? The arguments implied by these questions might appear to damage the case for the price system. However, they ignore several of its important features. In particular, they fail to consider the range of alternatives available to resource owners. They also neglect the institutional forms through which people are able to hold resources.

Resource owners strive to sell their resources so they gain the maximum benefit from them. When resource prices are expected to rise, owners are encouraged to hold their resources into the future to gain from the higher prices. Thus, if shortages of a particular item are expected in the future, its owners will respond by shifting their planned use of these resources away from the present and toward the future. This way, they can take advantage of higher prices.

Conservers are unlikely to be reassured by this account of the incentives created by the market and would raise many questions. What if the resource owner's horizon is very limited? What if he wants to enjoy consumption now and is unwilling to wait for higher prices to develop? Clearly, one alternative open to him would be extraction and sale today. If resource owners decide to respond in this way, the higher prices expected in the future will have failed to preserve the resource for future generations.

Other Alternatives

It should be clear, however, that selling the resource for current use is not the only available alternative. The owner can sell the resource to someone else who anticipates a future shortage and higher prices. If prices are expected to be higher by at least enough to cover holding costs, the buyer who plans to hold the resource will be willing to pay more than present users. Thus, even though the horizon of a single owner may be very limited, preservation of the resource for future uses would be achieved by its transfer among different investors, each with a short horizon.

So far, our analysis has not taken into account one of the most important features of resource ownership in our economy. In reality, we find very few people hold stocks of non-renewable resources directly; instead, they hold resources indirectly through corporate share ownership. Investors do not buy stocks merely for the profits the corporations will earn during the time the investor holds the stocks. They are well aware that shares can be sold at any time at a value based on market expectations of future profits. For resource firms, these profits depend on expected future sales, as well as on sales for current use. The corporate form of organization serves to insulate resources from owners with limited horizons.

Sophisticated institutions, such as stock exchanges and mutual funds, permit the continual buying and selling of claims to corporate ownership. These institutions are an important part of the way our economy incorporates the future into present decision-making. They permit the transfer of ownership of non-renewable resources at low cost and allow decisions about the use of resources to be separated from the specific time horizons of their owners.

Breaking the Link

While the market can allow the needs of future generations to influence the timing of resource use, it may not work as described. The link between future scarcity and the preservation of resources can be broken in a number of ways. The mechanisms described above cannot be expected to function, for example, when ownership rights to natural resources are limited in duration. The temporary owner of the resources will not gain from higher prices that occur after the end of his tenure. With limited tenure, there is a strong incentive to extract the resource while he still has the claim to ownership, regardless of the prospect of higher prices in the future.

The link also can be broken under supposedly permanent ownership if resource owners feel the existing rules of the game will be altered. For example, the rules of the game would definitely be changed by nationalization of resources presently held by private owners. The threat of nationalization creates the same incentives for shorter horizons in resource use as does limited tenure.

The former owner gains no advantage from higher resource prices that occur only after nationalization.

Market incentives can be rendered impotent in less drastic ways than nationalization. Any action that prevents future prices from rising to reflect resource shortages reduces the inducement to hold resources for the future. Similarly, any policy that prevents resource owners from realizing higher returns from these higher prices also encourages current use.

There Is Always Uncertainty

To see how continual changes in the rules of the game can shorten the horizons of resource owners, we must recognize that their decisions are not made with absolute certainty of future prices. Rather, the resource owner expects a range of possible prices. Within this range the extreme prices, both high and low, are viewed as improbable but still play a role in shaping expectations. If owners are prevented from realizing the gains higher prices would imply, they will revise their expectation of future prices downwards and choose to hold less for the future. Policies to keep current prices low carry the danger of persuading resource owners that they will also be unable to benefit from higher prices expected in the future. Such policies will lead them to divert resources away from future uses.[3]

To summarize, the fact that resource owners' time horizons may be limited does not imply that the interests of future generations are ignored. The possibility of transferred resource ownership from one generation to another, together with the corporate form of organization, extends the horizon for decision-making beyond that of any single owner. Shorter horizons arise when resource ownership is limited in its tenure and when government is expected to change the rules of the game. Similarly, government policies that alter the rules of the game have the same effect. The market, in the absence of this form of intervention, leads participants to take the long view.

The Working of the Market Is Unfair

At any time, a variety of influences operating through the market affect the incomes of the poor or, for that matter, any income group. Some improve the position of the poor, while others are clearly harmful. In recent years, the rapid increase in energy prices has been deemed especially detrimental to the well-being of the low-income groups. Does the market protect the interests of future generations at the expense of less privileged members of the current generation?

The unfairness argument involves first the purely factual question of the impact of higher energy prices on different income groups. Second, and more complex, is the question of whether suppression of the market is the appropriate response to any inequities that arise from its operation.

The available evidence supports the view that expenditures on fuel and power in Canada are a higher proportion of total expenditures for the poor than they are for the rich. Leonard Waverman found that while energy accounted for only 6.2 percent of total expenditure for the average Canadian family in 1969, it accounted for over 8.9 percent of expenditures for the very poorest families with an income under $3,000, (Waverman, p. 85). Clearly, the impact of higher energy prices on the poor is greater than for others.

While on average the poor allocate a larger fraction of their expenditures to fuel than do the rich, the aggregate data mask substantial regional differences. The lowest income group in the Atlantic provinces devotes 11.4 percent of its total expenditures to energy while the same group in Quebec allocates only 6.1 percent to energy. The poor of Quebec directed roughly the same proportion of expenditures to energy as did those with much higher incomes in other regions. A policy of low energy prices does not benefit the poor uniformly across regions and, in addition, will benefit some high-income groups more than some of the low ones.

Granting that the poor are harmed on average disproportionately by higher energy prices, is maintaining lower energy prices the best way of protecting them? Do we wish to help the poor merely because they have been harmed by higher oil prices or because they are poor? If the answer is the latter, then our concern should be direct support to low-income groups through the tax system.

The use of the income tax system has the advantage that it can be directed at all the poor, rather than those who consume disproportionate amounts of energy. In addition, the use of general tax measures permits us to relieve the burden of poverty without encouraging high levels of energy use and subsidizing wealthy consumers of energy.

The view that the workings of the price system are inherently unfair poses the unnecessary dilemma of having to choose between the interests of future generations and those of today's poor. Higher energy prices may harm the poor to a greater degree than other income groups, whereas lower energy prices will not check current consumption. The argument that the interests of today's poor require foregoing the use of the market reflects a failure of the imagination. Problems of equity in income distribution are important, but need not involve interference with market allocation of resources over time.

Alternatives to the Market

Critics of the market can be grouped into optimists and pessimists. The former tend to deplore the apparent cynicism of economists for proclaiming that man acts in his own self-interest. They argue that once individuals recognize the dimensions of the crisis they will act in a socially responsible way to protect the interests of future generations. In the optimist's view, changes in attitude

41

are required. This will involve programmes to inform the public about the crisis and to define social responsibility.

In contrast, the pessimists accept the economist's perception of man and argue that an objectionable motive, pursuit of self-interest, can lead only to an objectionable outcome. For this reason, they advocate coercive intervention by government to protect future generations from the avarice of the present generation. The alternatives to the market proposed by both optimists and pessimists will now be examined.

Changing Attitudes

The conservers see acceptance by the public of new attitudes toward our limited resources as an important alternative to the market in looking after the future. While in theory the workings of the market are predicated on the pursuit of self-interest, a preferable outcome can be expected if people would only adopt a broader, more humane perspective. The Science Council asserts that, "substantial changes could follow from widespread shifts of attitude, a new ethic" (Science Council 1977, p. 54) and cites favourably a former member, who argued:

> A preference for the optimum rather than the maximum, for renewal rather than exploitation, requires some form of self denial or austerity. I have often advocated a *joyous austerity* as the key to a wise utilization of our resources and a just distribution of their products (Science Council 1977, p. 54).

What prospects, then, do shifts in attitude or adoption of new ethics have as alternatives to the market in looking after the future?

The adoption of a conserver ethic would appear to painlessly solve the problem of future resource scarcity. Many contentious political issues would disappear as a consequence. For example, preservation of scarce energy resources could be achieved without price increases through voluntary demand reductions. It would thus be possible to avoid, in part, the debate over the division of revenues from energy resources and the undesirable effects of higher energy prices on the poor.

What are the conditions under which public acceptance of new attitudes could be expected to be effective in looking after the future? A prerequisite for the success of new attitudes toward conservation is that they be held with near unanimity. If only a handful adopt the new ethic, they may have the self-satisfaction of acting in a more "socially responsible" way, but they will not make any substantial contribution to increasing the availability of resources to subsequent generations.

Emergency

The statement that new attitudes must be accepted with near unanimity does little to help us understand the circumstances in which this approach could be successful. Experience suggests, however, that new attitudes would most likely be adopted where the threatened consequences of not conforming are substantial and where the degree of personal sacrifice required is minimal.

Although history records many instances where the public has made immense voluntary sacrifices for the common good, almost all of these cases have involved a national emergency in time of war. There is little to suggest that distant concerns, such as the welfare of future generations, will lead to sacrifices.

The effectiveness of a sense of emergency in encouraging the acceptance of new attitudes has been documented by Sue Anne Blackman in her contribution to *Economics, Environmental Policy and the Quality of Life*. A striking case is that of appeals for blood donations. In September 1970, when New York blood reserves dropped to less than a day's supply, there was a public appeal for voluntary donors. Blackman observed:

> The response to a massive appeal for voluntary donation was described as "fantastic"; donors stood in line up to 90 minutes to give blood. (Baumol et.al., p. 297)

The public response has been less striking in cases where the threat of emergency or crisis was tenuous. Share-the-Ride Day was an attempt by a citizen group in Los Angeles to reduce air pollution by car-pooling. It was supported by extensive television, radio, and handbill advertising. Blackman's assessment was:

> Unfortunately, the day was a dismal failure. There was apparently no difference in traffic density or air quality. Buses carried only a handful of passengers. The organizers concluded that, while most people think car pooling is a good idea, when it comes down to it they will not make the sacrifice. (Baumol et.al., p. 290)

More successful were two other car-pooling experiments described by Blackman. The first, Operation Oxygen, was conducted by the Burroughs Corporation in Pasadena and the other was carried out by the Office of Price Administration during World War II. In both cases, however, direct incentives reinforced an appeal to voluntarism. Burroughs Corporation offered free gas, preferential parking, and raffles with prizes for co-operation. The Office of Price Administration gave supplementary gas rations to drivers in car pools.

No Incentives

Further evidence of unwillingness to incur personal costs to achieve a distant or uncertain public benefit is provided by two cases in which consumers had the opportunity to reduce pollution and improve air quality.

In the first case, a small differential in price prevented the public from switching to less-polluting low-lead or non-leaded gas, despite heavy advertising campaigns. Shell's experiment was so discouraging the company took "Shell of the Future," its unleaded gas, off the market.

The second case involved the introduction of emission control kits by major auto firms. A device introduced by General Motors reduced emissions by 30 to 50 percent and cost only $15-$20 installed. Yet "despite an aggressive marketing campaign, only 528 kits were sold." (Baumol et.al., p. 289) Similarly, Chrysler Corporation found that more than half of the 22,000 used-car emission-control kits it produced remained unsold.

Unreliable

What can we conclude about the role of attitude changes in protecting the interests of future generations? The adoption of a new ethic cannot be expected to reduce the cost of protecting the future. That cost is reduced current consumption; it is inescapable whatever system—markets, government or persuasion—we use. Voluntarism carries the illusion we can avoid this cost. It may only shift it into the future.

An example is provided by the simultaneous advocacy of low energy prices and comprehensive public education about energy conservation. Such a programme eliminates the protection that the market does provide for future generations. It replaces that protection with a set of voluntary standards drawn up without the participation of future generations. Moreover, evidence shows that the voluntary standards are unlikely to work. This leaves no restriction at all on the extent to which the present generation uses the stock of non-renewable resources.

Good will is at best an adjunct to other means of dealing with the future. Persuasion will be most successful when the personal costs of compliance are small and when there is widespread agreement on the desirability of its objectives. Not surprisingly, successful measures include anti-litter campaigns and the imaginative forest-fire prevention programmes in the United States exemplified by Smokey the Bear. Thoughtful use of this type of voluntarism can play a limited role in looking after the future. But widespread reliance runs the risk of jeopardizing rather than protecting the interests of future generations.

Government and the Future

The conservers emphasize the role of government relative to the market in protecting the interests of future generations. A glance at the recommendations of the Science Council reveals that governments would tax and subsidize, support and restrict, and inform and assist in a wide variety of areas ranging from home insulation and modes of transportation to patterns of employment. The basis for this advocacy of government intervention, however, is far from clear.

The current generation may act in the interests of following generations for a variety of motives. Some may wish to make provision for the future out of a concern for humanity in general and a resulting desire to ensure that future living standards are not eroded by short-sighted actions taken at present. For others, the concern may be more specific; they are interested in the well-being of particular individuals, especially their children and grandchildren. In fact, the present generation may be financing their education and accumulating real capital, which is subsequently transferred to them. It is not clear how private decisions in this regard can be augmented by government action. If individuals feel that their current provisions for their own children are inadequate, they can always increase them.

The conserver case for government action is that society as a whole directs too many resources to current consumption and too few to the future. The implication is that we are either ill-informed about future resource scarcity or that we do not value the prosperity of the future to the same degree as the conservers. The Science Council argues that to the extent that misinformation causes the failure to provide for the future, there may be a role for government in supplying the public with better information. In addition, until the public assimilates the new information, government intervention of a more direct variety may be necessary. That is, the public may have to be coerced into adopting practices that they would choose voluntarily if they understood the situation. However, this coercion carries the danger that legitimate differences in preferences will be interpreted as failure to understand.

Ethically Unacceptable

The second interpretation of the conservers' position is that the public's failure to weigh the future highly is ethically unacceptable. Government must coerce the majority to behave in a manner judged socially responsible by the conserver minority. The justification for government action on behalf of the future is, in fact, an argument for adherence to the preferences of the conserver elite.

Unless it is conceded that the views of an elite must prevail, there is no argument that leads uniquely to greater government action. The case for more government involvement must be based on the comparative performance of government and other institutions in providing for future generations. Under what circumstances is government best equipped to protect the interests of future generations?

Asymmetry

In the naive view, the market process and the political process may be judged equally suspect in their ability to consider the future. Future generations do not participate directly in today's markets, nor are they voters in today's elections. There is, however, a fundamental asymmetry between the market and the political process. A resource owner has the opportunity to hold his resources for sale in the future and will do so if the expected returns exceed those of sale for current use. The demands of future generations provide an incentive to hold for future use. It is self-interest, rather than a concern for the well-being of future generations, that leads the resource owner to heed these demands.

No such linkage exists in the political process, however. While future generations are indirectly represented in the marketplace, they lack any franchise in elections and are unrepresented in our legislatures. Future generations can influence the political process only through a concern for their interests on the part of current voters.

Another difference in the way in which the market and government regard the future results from the nature of decision-making in each case. An individual sensing inadequate provision for the future can take steps to direct resources toward the future and away from the present. This step can be taken independently of the actions of others. Any government action involves a collective decision. The need to gain widespread support must lead to politicization of the issue. While many will support the measure on the basis of its merits, others approve for other reasons. Some will trade off their votes for reciprocal support for their own interests, but others may offer support with an eye to modifying the proposal to promote their own objectives. A policy will gain widespread support only by catering to a wide range of interests at the expense of the original objective.

Misplaced Confidence

There are strong theoretical grounds on which to argue that the conservers' confidence in the government's ability to look after future generations is misplaced. Arguments over government intervention cannot stand or fall on theoretical grounds alone. Actual instances of intervention on behalf of the future must be judged on their merits. One government programme that has encouraged excessive use of energy and capital in production is the system of accelerated depreciation and investment tax credits. How has this has occurred?

It is in the interest of firms to combine their inputs of labour, capital, materials, and energy so they minimize their cost of production. The more costly the labour, for example, the greater is the incentive to substitute capital, energy, and materials for this factor in the production process.

Capital and energy are complementary inputs. If the cost of capital relative to other inputs is lower, the incentive to substitute in favour of both capital and energy in the production process will be greater. A reduction in the cost of capital will therefore result in the adoption of a more energy-intensive production process.

Unwise Tax Policy

With the presence of a corporate income tax, firms will combine inputs to minimize their cost of production measured on an after-tax basis. The lower is the after-tax cost of capital relative to the after-tax cost of other inputs, the greater is the extent to which both capital and energy will be substituted for labour and materials in the production process.

The tax system may favour the use of certain factors of production. That is, it may provide an incentive to substitute one input for another, not because it reduces costs, but because it reduces the firm's tax liability. In this case, the firm will be employing an input combination that minimizes its after-tax costs but does not minimize the before-tax or true cost of the goods and services it elects to produce.

The Canadian corporate tax system favours the use of capital. Its accelerated depreciation provisions allow firms to deduct the cost of capital from their taxable income before that capital is used. The cost of other inputs, labour for example, can be deducted from taxable income but only as these inputs are used. Since a dollar spent on capital can be deducted from taxable income earlier than a dollar spent on labour, the tax saving involved is available to be reinvested earlier. This reduces the after-tax cost of capital relative to labour and increases the relative attractiveness of capital and energy as inputs.

Accelerated Depreciation

The government has defended its use of accelerated depreciation on the grounds that it is necessary to create a strong Canadian manufacturing sector, to provide jobs, and to maintain a balanced economy. While there may be some merit in reducing the tax burden borne by Canadian manufacturers, the use of accelerated depreciation to achieve this has biased input decisions in the direction of excessive capital and energy intensity.

The effect of accelerated depreciation on the energy intensity of Canadian production is illustrated by the two-year write-off of machinery and equipment introduced by the federal government in 1972. This reduced the after-tax cost of capital by approximately 10 percent. As a result, there was an estimated increase of 30 percent or more in the energy intensity of production—that is, in the energy:capital ratio (Berndt and Wood 1975, and Benny et. al. 1978).

Another interpretation is that the two-year write-off increased by approximately 2 percent the quantity of energy required to sustain a given level of manufacturing activity (Denny et al. 1979).

If Canadian firms are the energy gluttons the Science Council alleges them to be, this is partly due not to the ignorance and perversity of market participants, but to the incentives provided by government. The cost of this policy, measured in terms of the goods and services that this energy could have provided if used elsewhere, will be borne by both the present and future generations. As seen in this case, increases in the extent of government involvement in allocation decisions are unlikely to promote the objectives of conservers.

Managing the Common

No man is an island, entire of itself; every man is a piece of the continent, a part of the main. If a clod be washed away by the sea, Europe is the less, as well as if a promontory were, as well as if a manor of thy friend's or of thine own were. Any man's death diminishes me because I am involved in mankind, and therefore never send to know for whom the bell tolls; it tolls for thee (John Donne (1572-1631) Meditation XVII).

The Problem of Interdependence: The Conserver View

Differences between private and social cost play an important role in the conserver diagnosis of the ills of our existing economic system. These side-effects are sometimes referred to as externalities. Pollution is an important example of such a problem. If a firm disposes of the by-products of its production process into the air or water, costs are incurred by others (e.g., the reduced recreation value of a lake) that are external to the relevant decision-makers. There is a clear difference between the cost incurred by the firm, the private cost, and the total cost or social cost of using the environment for waste disposal. Concern for this problem by advocates of the conserver society is found in the following excerpt from the definition of a conserver society.

In a Conserver Society, the pricing mechanism should reflect, not just the private cost but as much as possible the total cost to society, including energy and materials used, ecological impact and social considerations. This will permit the market system to allocate resources in a manner that more closely reflects societal needs, both immediate and long term (Science Council 1977, p. 14).

48

In the opinion of the Science Council, adopting a conserver society will focus concerns about divergences between private and social costs.

> Environmental problems will move from concern to action. The widespread externalization of costs (that is, the avoidance of costs by poor housekeeping, pollution of the environment etc.) that has characterized Canadian industrial history needs increasingly to be controlled by legislation and a demand for the reckoning of total costs (Science Council 1977, p. 21).

We later argue that the Science Council misconstrues the economics of externalities. However, parts of their diagnosis, as in the following, are in accord with what we believe to be the majority position of economists:

> When costs are incurred or induced which are not reflected in the price to the consumer, or when the individual firm consciously or unconsciously externalizes costs (into the air, or water, or noise into the surroundings) then prices do not reflect all the costs and the possibility for misallocation of resources arises. To the extent that costs are externalized and become social rather than private, or are deferred into the future, prices are lower than they should be. With lower prices, we tend to produce and consume more than if prices reflected all costs (Science Council 1977, p. 34).

The Science Council raises an obviously legitimate issue in its discussion of potential and actual differences between private and social cost. We will return to their policy proposals in a later section.

Goods and Services

The Gamma group distinguishes between the production of goods and the production of services. As a result, they analyze the limits to throughput rather than the limits to all forms of growth. The throughput process involves the transformation of inputs in industrial processes to produce commodities. The Gamma group's diagnosis of the problems of the existing industrial system is expressed in terms of the side-effects or externalities of the throughput process.

> It would appear that most if not all throughput processes in Nature have a common characteristic: they result in the production both of an intended output and, in addition, *an unintended by-product*. The unintended by-product in biological metabolism is human or animal waste. In economic metabolism the unintended by-product is composed of air, soil and water pollution, garbage, noise, etc... This unintended by-product is one of the major problems associated with throughput (Gamma, v. 1, p. 28).

The Gamma analysis is similar to that of the Science Council. Externalities are defined as arising in the industrial system when important elements of costs are not taken into account by decision makers.

> "Externalities" are produced through effluents which escape the concern of any one individual or firm in the throughput process. Everyone is responsible and no one is. The biosphere cannot function as a garbage dump indefinitely. Ultimately the system will self-destruct or come to a natural balance through Malthusian means (Gamma, v. 1, p. 36).

Inadequate Response

The Gamma group points out that various measures to deal with externalities have been taken, but argues that existing restrictions have been an inadequate response to the distorted incentives facing firms as producers of throughput.

> It would appear then, that *in toto*, there is a strong case against the business-as-usual *laissez-faire* scenario. We are in fact not in a *laissez-faire* situation now, since conservationist measures and pollution-control laws are slowly being drawn up and implemented. The projected Conserver Society would reinforce and extend those measures (Gamma, v. 1, p. 69).

There is little disagreement between most economists and the proponents of the conserver society on problems related to externalities. Any economic system in which there are differences between private and social cost is likely to produce too many smoking factories and too few clean lakes and rivers. Firms and governments in both capitalist and non-capitalist societies have ignored the total costs of polluting activities. Concerns for the environmental consequences of these activities have increased. These concerns have led to many studies of the problem by environmentalists, economists, and representatives of the physical sciences.

Pollution problems have been regarded by many as evidence of "market failure." Conserver society proposals reflect the apparent fact that externality-generating activities in the economic system have increased as a fraction of total activity. Proponents of the conserver society argue that our institutions must be altered to force firms to recognize the total costs of their actions. Governments would use regulations and incentives to achieve this end.

> We often do not know how to measure the costs we may impose on others or on the future by our careless housekeeping. They may be smaller than the costs we avoid, but they may also be much larger. For that reason it is not always enough to depend on prices and the market system. The influence of prices often has to be augmented by the dis-

cipline of regulation, taxation and other penalties (Science Council, p. 35).

A Critique

Our major criticism of the Science Council proposals is that they are not based on a specific framework. If regulation, taxation, and other penalties are to be used, the levels for each must be specified. If this task involves specialized resources going beyond the boundaries of their preliminary report, then criteria are required for application in further work. Nowhere in the Science Council report is there a specific framework for policy. The Council does suggest feasibility studies of the total-costing of products, proposing that:

the importance of having market prices reflect more of the total social costs consequent on manufacturing and using a product suggests that the following types of tax merit study:

- a disposal tax on some forms of packaging and on some"throwaway" products

- a health-care tax on cigarettes, alcohol, caffeine, etc.

- an energy tax on gasoline, fuel oil, large automobile engines, plastics, electric appliances

- an environment tax on paper, coal, fertilizers, aerosols, insecticides, gasoline, etc.

- a resource extraction or severance tax on virgin non-renewable materials (Science Council 1977, p. 87).

All of these policy proposals are quite specific. However, as we argue later, the necessary first step of specifying the precise objectives of taxes and regulations is absent. In the absence of such a framework, we have no way of knowing whether these proposals are likely to make us better or worse off.

The general position of the Science Council on divergences between private and social costs is clear. There are too many such situations. They impose substantial costs and this must be corrected. Methods of correction are not clearly specified but combinations of taxes, regulations, and alterations of property rights are required.

Scenarios

The Gamma group employs the scenario technique in proposing alternatives to the existing consumer society. Their conserver society scenarios range from a "growth with efficiency scenario" to a "Buddhist scenario." Partly because the growth with efficiency scenario is closest to the Science Council proposals and partly because analyses of other variants might be interpreted as attacks on a straw man, we limit our attention to this one.

The Gamma group, in its vision of a conserver society, suggests three basic strategies for reducing waste and externalities.

1) *Full Cost Pricing* (an attempt to reflect within money-cost the total cost of production including environmental damage, health hazards, reduction in quality of life, etc.);

2) *Public Regulation* (government intervention needed to reduce waste);

3) *Technological Improvements* (including reduction of effluents at source, use of renewables instead of non-renewables, recycling, improved durability of products, etc.) (Gamma, v. 1, p. 213).

Full cost pricing as recommended by the Gamma group is very much in the spirit of proposals to deal with externalities suggested by economist A. C. Pigou in 1918. Through the imposition of taxes to reflect "full" costs, currently undesirable side-effects would be discouraged. The Gamma group argues that taxation is an efficient—and presumably the most efficient—form of government intervention.

> An efficient method of intervention by the State in a market economy is taxation. Selective and incentive taxation alters factors costs without destroying the nature of market forces. Instead by changing factor costs, it redirects these forces, hopefully toward more socially desirable goals (Gamma, v. 1, p. 244).

Information and Externalities

As with the Science Council, the precise objective of taxation is not presented in operational form, although selection criteria are discussed (pp. 202-204). The Gamma group does point out an important aspect of the externality problem and one that must be faced under any control programme—namely, that information on divergences between private and social cost is neither completely available nor without cost. It notes that "we not only require selection criteria but empirical indicators to inform us as to the degree of pathology in the environment, economy and society." (Gamma, v. 1, p. 205).

Based on information about the private and social costs of pollution, environmental taxes would be used to induce a variety of behaviours deemed desirable by Gamma. However, Gamma further argues that these taxes are necessary but not sufficient: they must be supplemented by a direct regulatory approach.

> Such public regulation could fall into the following categories: i) Regulation to discourage the production of non-recyclable products; ii) Regulation to ensure the absorption of the unemployed into the recycling industries; iii) Regulation to improve management of the size and structure of cities; iv) Regulation to protect the Sea and the North; v)

Direct government sponsorship of projects with high public
value and low private profitability; vi) Higher efficiency
standards for government agencies; vii) Regulation to ensure
a more equal distribution of income and wealth (Gamma, v.
1, p. 249).

Tax and Regulate

In summary, the conserver solutions are best presented as the answer to a
question: What would be done differently if we followed the Science Council
and Gamma recommendations and instituted a conserver society? To control
the harmful effects of divergences between private and social cost, conserver
society advocates would use a variety of taxes designed to increase producer
costs, thereby reducing the quantity of externality-generating items produced.
Although operational targets are not specified, this approach is regarded by
conservers as insufficient. As a result, a variety of supplementary regulations
would also be required. These regulations would affect not only direct externalities, such as pollution, but would also be applied to the types of products
that could be produced.

The conserver society proposals are derived primarily from analyses of
harmful external effects that have been conducted by a number of environmental groups. The solutions proposed occasionally do employ market
mechanisms. However, their general message is that the market has served us
badly.

Conservers argue that much more direct government regulation of and
intervention in the market is necessary to avoid serious ecological problems in
the future. This intervention, in at least some of the conserver scenarios, would
attempt to stop economic growth and even to reduce existing levels of output.
This is a result of the perceived relationship between rates of economic growth
and environmental problems.

The conserver proposals in this area involve substantial costs and almost
certainly imply a significantly greater role for government in our socioeconomic structure. These sweeping proposals cannot be taken lightly. In the
sections that follow, we examine them in detail. We explore their motivations
and implications in light of possible alternative approaches.

Alternative Approaches to Interdependence

Pollution is a problem of interdependence. Controlling pollution requires some
mechanism for dealing with harmful interactions in the economy. These harmful interactions, such as the impact of smoking factories on local residents, are
what economists call external effects. In particular, it is important to understand
how market situations generating external effects differ from circumstances in
markets where no such effects arise.

Consider as an example of this distinction the production of wheat in a market economy. Between the extremes of producing no wheat at all and using all of society's resources for wheat production, there is a wide range of possible alternatives. The fundamental principle of economics is that resources are scarce. As a result, decisions on the quantity of resources actually devoted to the production of wheat must be made on the basis of the benefits of wheat production at different output levels relative to the costs of producing them. Cost is measured here as opportunity cost—that is, the quantity of other goods that must be sacrificed to produce more wheat. The tools of economics can be used to define a level of wheat production beyond which the benefits provided by further wheat do not justify its production.

The Geometry of Wheat Production

In terms of the usual diagrams employed by economists, we can define a marginal or incremental benefit (MB) schedule that shows in dollar terms the benefits attached to different quantities of wheat. The curve slopes downward to the right, as is shown in figure 1. The diagram shows that the more wheat you produce, the less valuable is an additional bushel.

Similarly, we can show the cost side, where the marginal or incremental cost (MC) of additional bushels of wheat is related to different quantities. If we were now producing wheat, we would begin wheat production by transferring to that market resources now providing the fewest benefits in other industries. As wheat production increases, we are forced to divert increasingly valuable resources out of other markets and into the market for wheat. For this reason, MC slopes upward; further bushels are obtainable only at increasing cost in terms of what is being sacrificed elsewhere. In figure 1, the upward-sloping MC intersects the downward-sloping MB at a dollar price per bushel of P_O at quantity W_O.

The MB curve shows the benefits attached to different quantities in terms of dollars. As a result, this curve is equivalent to the demand curve for wheat. Similarly, MC is the supply curve. In a market system, the forces of competition would lead market participants to produce the quantity indicated by the intersection point at price P_O.

A Counter-example

The desirability of this level of production relative to the available alternatives can be indicated by counter-example. Consider first a choice to produce less than W_O, say W_2. For bushels of wheat between W_2 and W_O, MB lies above MC. Resources used in increasing output to W_O will provide greater benefits than will be foregone by reducing production elsewhere. The additional benefits from moving to W_O are indicated by the triangular area ABC. Similarly, if we begin at W_1, marginal costs exceed marginal benefits for units beyond W_O.

There is a net gain of ADE from reducing output to W_O. From the point of view of suppliers, there is a profit opportunity whenever output diverges from W_O as in the case of W_2, where output increases provide marginal benefits in excess of marginal costs.

The intersection of MB and MC in this case indicates the best allocation of resources to the production of wheat. In a competitive market economy, the undirected actions of individual consumers and producers will, according to the famous "invisible hand" proposition of Adam Smith, lead to this result.

The results of figure 1 indicate in simplified terms the reasons economists are enthusiastic about markets as efficient mechanisms for the allocation of resources. On the other hand, ecologists and the proponents of the conserver society show a distinct lack of enthusiasm for market processes. What are the sources of this disagreement?

Figure 1
The Market for Wheat

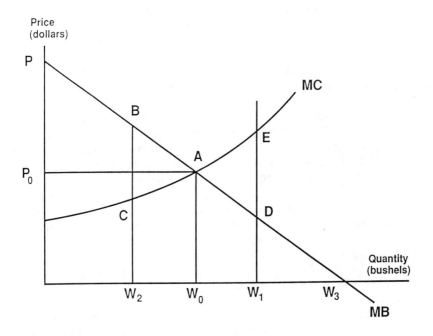

Note: The curve MB indicates the perceived incremental benefits of different quantities of wheat. The curve MC indicates the additional costs associated with alternative output levels measured in terms of benefits elsewhere that are given up. In a market economy, these represent the conditions of demand and supply. The forces of competition will lead to the production of W_O units at the price P_O.

Disagreement

The Science Council and Gamma are concerned with the determinants of tastes, which are taken as given in drawing up MB. This has been discussed in detail. The second area of disagreement, and the one that we are concerned with here, is that the MC curve in figure 1 may not reflect the total costs of production. In the view of the Science Council and the Gamma group, this leads to an inappropriate allocation of resources.

To focus on the differences raised by the conservers between private and total cost consider a different example. This example involves the production of units of travel between two points, a problem initially discussed by economist Frank Knight in 1924.

> Suppose that between two points there are two highways, one of which is broad enough to accommodate without crowding all the traffic which may care to use it but is poorly graded and surfaced, while the other is a much better road but narrow and quite limited in capacity. If a large number of trucks operate between the two termini and are free to choose either of the two routes, they will tend to distribute themselves between the roads in such proportions that the cost per unit of transportation, or effective result per unit of investment, will be the same for every truck on both routes. As more trucks use the narrower and better road, congestion develops, until at a certain point it becomes equally profitable to use the broader but poorer highway (Knight 1924, p. 162).

This example differs from the wheat case only on the cost side, where the costs of congestion have entered the picture. The congestion costs reflect the type of external effect with which we are concerned. For highway congestion, we can think of costs to an individual driver as being the time costs of travel plus vehicle operation costs. For reasons discussed above, these costs will increase for any driver with the number of other drivers making the trip. In other words, the total costs to society of one further trip consist of the costs to the driver himself, plus the congestion costs he imposes on all other drivers. The impact of congestion costs is shown diagrammatically in figure 2.

In this diagram there is a clear difference between the costs to an individual driver (MC_N) and the costs to all drivers (MC_S) of a trip in which he adds to congestion. The pursuit of private self-interest in this example leads to a quantity of T_1, whereas the interest of all drivers would be served if T_2 were actually chosen. The "invisible hand" discussed in connection with the production of wheat does not produce the desired result in this case. The Science Council of Canada criticizes economists for neglecting this type of situation. They say economists traditionally argue for a market solution for all problems, even when these problems are being caused by market processes. They note that "economists used to say that the market would look after everything" (Science Council 1977, p. 24).

Although the phrase "used to" is ambiguous, the statement in its context appears demonstrably false. At least since Pigou in 1918, economists have recognized the possibility of differences between private and total cost. They have realized also that the "invisible hand" result does not necessarily hold in the presence of external effects.

Figure 2
The Production of Inter-urban Trips

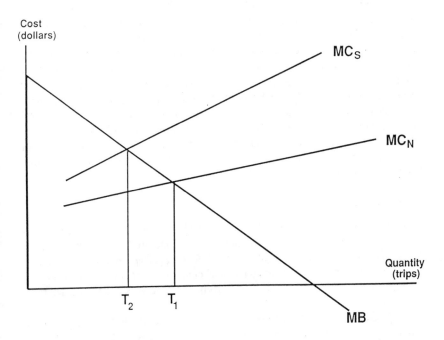

Note: The traditional external-effects case involves the decisions of individual drivers producing T_1 where $MB = MC_N$, with "too many" trips and "too much" congestion. Conserver society full-cost proposals are based on such differences between private cost (MC_N) and social cost (MC_S). The difference between MC_S and MC_N reflects the congestion costs drivers impose on each other.

Externality Literature

Still, the case may be made that economists have accepted externalities as theoretically possible but viewed them as not likely to occur with much frequency. There is some truth to this contention and to the parallel statement that in the years following Pigou, externalities were less important in an empirical sense than is now the case. However, in recent years, the literature on externalities has grown rapidly, particularly with regard to pollution and congestion. This growth has been characterized not only by frequent articles in established economic journals, but also by the creation of new journals devoted specifically to the economic analysis of environmental issues. The advocates of a conserver society seem unaware of the substantial volume of work done on the subject. In our opinion, many of their errors and misinterpretations are attributable to this oversight.

The contention that economists argue that the market will look after everything is particularly misleading when combined with the general conserver disposition against market forms of organization. As Knight argued in the example above, the cause of road congestion externalities was not the pernicious impact of market organization on human behaviour, but rather the *absence* of market or other devices permitting individuals to take account of their interdependence. The policy conclusion in the case of road congestion was that "over-use" resulted from the absence of road ownership and the consequent absence of a market in road usage. As we will show, an important policy option in dealing with differences between private and total cost will be measures to define ownership of scarce resources. Such measures permit the establishment of markets and prices in areas where the absence of a market creates a zero price and excessive use.

A Summary

This section has defined the "best" output of a particular commodity. It has compared a situation in which market forces alone are likely to produce this result with situations where differences between private and total cost imply that intervention may improve on the market result. The central point—and our departure from the conservers—is specifying a framework to define a desirable objective.

The Science Council and Gamma discuss taxes and regulation and indicate that the scale of certain harmful activities should be reduced. However, they fail to show how far the reduction should be carried or what framework should be used to decide this question. The strength of economics is in establishing explicit criteria. These criteria state that a given activity should be extended up to point beyond which the activity provides benefits smaller than the alternatives being sacrificed. There may be objections to this standard, but unlike conserver society proposals it is specific, objective, and openly defined.

Conservers suffer from the problem of "misplaced concreteness." This leads them to attack specific problems without a coherent framework specifying the objective that is being pursued. Such a lapse from scientific method is particularly puzzling and disturbing given its source. Were economists to propose solutions to problems in the physical sciences that are as simplistic as those put forth for economic problems by the Science Council, the result would surely be a well-deserved rebuke.

A Framework for Analysing Interdependence

Interdependence requires mechanisms to control harmful interactions. These mechanisms must be selected on the basis of the costs of different ways of controlling external effects. Taxes would be one such mechanism, while direct regulation would be another. The conservers fail to consider the relative costs of these mechanisms. Their disposition, in the presence of externalities, is to directly regulate the activity in question without considering the costs of alternative approaches.

The growing literature in this area reflects a concern among economists over developing a framework for choosing among alternative arrangements for resource allocation. Property rights can differ across time or social systems, but a defined set of property rights to establish the terms of relations among individuals is an essential element of any rational system of social interaction. As a simple example, if the right of a smoking factory to pollute without paying for the damage is altered, the quantity of smoke emissions will change. The question being raised by environmentalists relates to the possible changes in property rights that would oblige polluters to take into account the damage imposed on others. Canadian economist John Dales suggests the following framework for choosing among alternative property rights systems.

> Different rights systems create different incentives, lead to different behaviour, display different characteristics and produce different social outcomes. I discuss three rights systems: exclusive and transferable rights (price systems); non-exclusive but non-exclusive rights (common property systems); and exclusive but non-transferable rights (command systems)... In nearly all situations human behaviour can be made subject to different constraints, and rights systems should be thought of as having different "comparative advantages" in different situations... (Dales 1975, pp. 486-487).

Dales' central point is that there are alternative institutional devices for producing a system in which the pursuit of individual self-interest leads to socially desirable results. In a market economy, individual behaviour is guided by prices. Demands for virtually all commodities would be different if prices were not attached to their consumption. In a command system, non-transferable property rights are vested in the state, and centralized decisions determine individual behaviour. The third alternative is a system of common property rights. Common property resources are characterized by unrestricted access. Examples include air, water, the fishery and the common pasture.[7]

Dales argues that different rights systems have different comparative advantages. Each limits side-effects in a different way and with different costs. The desirability of one set of property rights can be assessed in terms of the benefits associated with that system relative to the costs.

The Market and Interdependence

In a major departure in the analysis of side-effects, economist Ronald Coase demonstrated in 1960 that a decentralized market economy could produce an efficient allocation of resources even in the presence of significant external effects. Coase argued that participants in a market economy could take account of their interdependence without governmental intervention to tax, subsidize, or regulate the activity in question. The implication of this work is that the question of whether interdependence can be taken into account more effectively by the government or by the market is empirical.

Since the work of Coase, economists have known that if property rights are well-defined, there is nothing unique about external effects that prevents them from being the subject of market transactions. With established property rights, economic agents can enter into contracts to minimize the impact of harmful side-effects, subject to the overall costs of drawing up and enforcing these contracts. Coase stressed that individuals have an incentive to negotiate whenever interdependencies exist. If the costs of negotiating and enforcing agreements are relatively low, and if property rights are defined, then the expectation of mutual gains will lead the affected parties to take proper account of their impact on one another. If they do this, there is nothing more to be gained from taxes, subsidies, or regulations. A corollary is that the more costly it is for individuals to reach such agreements, the greater is the potential role for government intervention.

Collective Judgement

The framework for policy analysis provided by the choice among market, command, and common property systems clearly indicates the course of past decisions and the choices now available to us. For many years, our collective judgement has been that, air and water in particular could be effectively allocated under a common property system. Other property systems were feasible and would have provided benefits but not of sufficient magnitude to cover costs. If this is so, why focus on change now? The answer is that with a growing population and growing output in Canada, the relationship of costs and benefits has altered. The contribution of the environmental movement has been to draw attention to this change in circumstance. Although correctly identifying the possibilities for improvement, the proponents of a conserver society have incorrectly diagnosed the causes by confusing the breakdown of a market with the absence of a market. As a result, they have argued for the replacement of the market where it has not yet been tested.

We have identified the conserver society diagnosis and remedies for problems raised by interdependence. Their diagnosis identified side-effects as an important and growing result of a market form of organizing economic activity. Their remedies involved exhortation, regulation, taxation, and restriction. By contrast, we have identified external effects as arising when it has been too costly to bring these effects within the market. In our view, a framework of analysis must precede *ad hoc* intervention; contrary to the conserver view, economics provides criteria for defining desirable output levels and for choosing among alternative ways of limiting side-effects.

Preferability

Our point is not that markets must deal with everything. Market mechanisms are frequently preferable because of their flexibility: there can, however, be situations in which establishing markets is simply too expensive, making direct regulation preferable. Even under these circumstances, however, it may be possible to design a regulatory system that retains the virtues of the market mechanism.

Many of the issues raised by proponents of the conserver society are worthy of careful scrutiny. The evolution of property rights over air and water appears to have lagged behind population and production. This should not, however, lead us to hastily choose a conserver society that rests on little more than the enthusiasm of its proponents. This philosophy offers an unfocused solution to a number of serious and specific problems. We believe it is possible to do better. We have outlined a framework for structuring responses to these problems that is analytical, rather than emotional. In the following section, we apply this framework to air and water pollution.

How Much Pollution?

Pollution occurs as a by-product of producing goods and services that satisfy certain wants. The satisfaction of this set of wants has a cost that can be expressed in terms of environmental goods that are foregone. Balancing the benefits associated with environmental and other outputs will determine the amount of pollution that is created. Pollution is no more than a standard resource allocation problem that can be analysed with the traditional tools of economics.

The economic approach implies neither a lack of concern for the environment nor a disregard for health and other costs associated with pollution. On the contrary, we regard environmental problems as too important to be left to the environmentalists alone. We have already considered the general question of resource allocation to the production of wheat. It is clear that there is an infinite number of possible outcomes between the extremes of producing no wheat and using our resources to produce only wheat. Just as we must decide how to allocate resources among wheat and other goods and services, so must we choose between environmental and other goods. How many environmental goods should we produce? It is the quantity beyond which the value of other forgone goods exceeds the value of more environmental goods. The pollution problem that the conservers have pointed out is equivalent to the claim that we are now under-producing environmental goods.

Pollution and Property Rights

The "invisible hand" doctrine of Adam Smith argues that many individuals interacting through markets will provide the best allocation of society's resources. Implicit, however, is the assumption that property rights are well-defined and enforced. Where this assumption does not hold, private decision-making may not lead to the best allocation of society's resources. The type of property right that is assigned to the environment—whether private, common, or centrally held—will be the crucial determinant of how much pollution is generated.

Property rights affect the way in which resources are used. Rented cars are treated differently than cars driven by owners. Private lakes, with access legally controlled by owners, are treated differently than lakes that are more widely available for use. Many resources are potentially subject to pollution (e.g. your front lawn being used as a garbage dump) while only some are actually polluted. The difference reflects the assignment of property rights. Until recently, air and water in Canada have been common property resources, allowing access to any and all users essentially without charge. Contrary to the popular view that a market system leads to the abuse of the environment, our property rights framework demonstrates that with such common property rights there are no markets serving to price and allocate valuable environmental assets. It is because markets to allocate air and water to more valuable uses are absent that we produce too few environmental goods. More precisely, the absence of a market in air and water sets an implicit price of zero on the use of these assets. Individuals and firms are then led to use these resources as if the cost to society were actually zero.

Property Rights

To understand why the existing legal definition of property rights leads to excessive pollution, it is important to consider how property rights emerge. The definition and enforcement of property rights are costly activities. New property rights emerge as changes render prior arrangements obsolete. Evolving property rights allow interactions among members of society to make them better off than would have been the case under the old set of property rights.

The Great Lakes are an example of an environmental asset to which we have, until recently, attached common property rights. The Lakes were used for recreational purposes, for fishing, and for dumping the by-products of many production processes. It is the nature of common property rights that all users face a zero price for this resource. For many years, this was perfectly sensible. Relative to the volume of the Lakes and their natural carrying capacity (i.e., ability to recycle wastes), users of the resource were essentially not competing; the Lakes could accommodate them with little conflict. With industrial progress and population growth in the Lakes area, however, demand for their services grew relative to capacity. The efficient price rose from zero. Yet, because the Lakes were common property, no mechanism existed for excluding users or making them pay. The emergence of the environmental movement is evidence that treating the Lakes as common property was increasingly inappropriate.

Rationing

Exclusive property rights, held and exercised either publicly or privately, are the only means of rationing environmental goods among competing users. An illustration of the potential for private holding of exclusive rights can be seen in the context of privately owned lakes and trout streams. In contrast to the common property situation, in which no individual has a financial incentive to protect the asset, privately held lakes and rivers are appropriately used because of the exercise of property rights. Efficient use of the environment requires that environmental assets be privately held or that public bodies exercise such rights on our behalf.

We have now identified the central issue in the use of environmental assets: existing common property rights designed for an earlier time are no longer appropriate. They fail to provide signals of overuse, as would excess demand at the existing price for a privately held asset. They provide no incentive to economize on the use of the resource. In fact, common property rights were established at a time when there was no need to economize. But this is clearly no longer the case. The environment can no longer be used at zero cost and would not be if property rights were defined and enforced. The existing pollution problem thus is due not to the workings of a market economy, but to its very absence.

The Private Sector

Privately held rights have the advantages of greater diversity and freedom of choice than is generally possible via government control. For some environmental assets, this is a feasible and efficient solution. However, for air pollution and many cases of water pollution, publicly held property rights have a strong cost advantage due to the lower enforcement costs associated with the police powers of the state. For this reason, a large portion of our environmental assets will be subject to publicly held property rights. The government must then determine the best use of the environmental assets for which it now exercises ownership rights. There can no longer be an absence of price or quantity restrictions on users of the environment.

Recognizing the importance of publicly held property rights implies three major options for the government agency responsible for exercising these property rights:

- instituting a tax on pollution (i.e. price per unit to produce the desired combination of environmental and other outputs);

- setting admissible quantities of pollution and thereby of environmental goods; and

- selling some fraction of publicly held property rights over the environment to private bidders, whether they be firms wishing to dispose of production by-products or groups of individuals who wish to purchase more environmental goods.

These three options appear in the pollution control literature as taxing, regulating or selling licences in order to achieve a desired degree of pollution reduction. Among these alternatives, direct regulation is the option that will provide the greatest bureaucratic discretion and influence; the other two options are more market-oriented.

Market Approaches to Pollution

Given their incomplete understanding of the sources of pollution, it is hardly surprising that environmentalists have concluded that pollution must be a result of a market form of economic organization, since we have a market economy. Their reaction has been to campaign for a variety of regulations, restrictions, subsidies, and lifestyle changes as a solution to the problem. The environmentalists should recognize, however, that non-market forms of economic organization—namely, the centrally directed Soviet system—face similar problems. Well-known U.S. economist Marshall Goldman argues that the U. S. S. R. "is a chronicle of environmental disruption that is as serious as almost any that exists in the world (Goldman 1970, pp. 37-42)."

The regulatory approach to pollution offers some obvious attractions. It singles out those segments of society deemed to be responsible for our problems and provides direct limits on their offending behaviour. In a property rights framework, regulation can be viewed as a situation in which the regulatory agency assumes exclusive property rights over environmental assets. This situation will, in general, be preferable to a continuation of a common property regime, but in many cases it will fail to produce the maximum pollution reduction for a given expenditure.

An Illustration

Consider, for example, the case illustrated in figure 3 in which total pollution of a lake is Y units, Y_1 from firm 1 and Y_2 from firm 2. If the regulatory agency sets a total allowable amount of X (less than Y), each firm may be required to reduce pollution in equal proportions. This approach would be the cheapest method of reaching the new standard only if the costs of pollution reduction were the same for all producers. We have illustrated a case in figure 3 where firm 2 can achieve a given reduction in pollution at a lower cost than is the case for firm 1. An arrangement that leads firm 2 to accept one further unit of pollution reduction, allowing firm 2 one further unit of pollution would mean a saving of a_1-a_2 dollars. The lack of flexibility inherent in regulated standards explains the general lack of enthusiasm among economists for such solutions.

Figure 3
Regulation-mandated Pollution Reductions

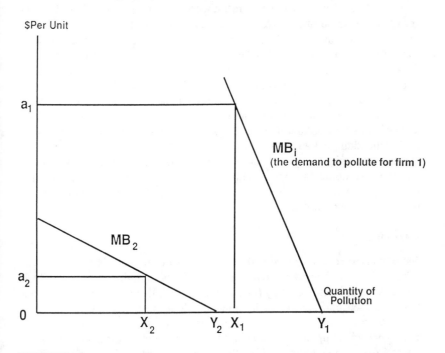

Note: Initially, with common property rights, the effective price is zero, so that total pollution is $Y = Y_1 + Y_2$. The regulatory agency then sets a total pollution standard X $< Y$. That is, $X_1 = X/Y(Y_1)$ and $X_2 = X/Y(Y_2)$. The uniform redution means that for firm 1 the last unit of pollution reduction has a cost equal to a_1, whereas for firm 2 the corresponding cost is a_2.

Regulated standards are the predominant institutional form of pollution control. This is because of the apparent certainty of result under regulation, bureaucratic support for measures creating demand for their own services, and, until relatively recently, the absence of pressure for market-oriented alternatives. As original property rights become inappropriate, regulatory approaches emerged to deal with increasingly visible problems. Initially, regulation was sufficiently limited so that the inefficiencies noted here were not terribly costly. However, with the extension of environmental regulations, these costs have escalated and have created a demand for more efficient institutions.

Effluent Tax

A modification of the regulatory approach involving the use of a market device is the effluent tax. Figure 3 can also be used to illustrate the advantages of such an approach. In this diagram, we show the demand to pollute for two firms. At higher prices per unit of pollution, we observe less pollution. The quantity of pollution Y is the amount that will result when the price per unit of pollution is zero. There is some emission tax per unit of pollution that will reduce pollution by an amount equal to Y - X, the same amount achieved under the regulatory standard. An emission tax will make the marginal cost of pollution control equal for all polluters, distributing the burden of pollution control to minimize its cost. In terms of figure 3, the emission tax would fall somewhere between a_1 and a_2.

Economists have for some time stressed the advantages of a pricing mechanism to control pollution over regulated standards to efficiently achieve a given amount of pollution reduction. The use of the price mechanism has an important additional advantage in that it extends the operation of the market system and limits the growth of bureaucratic forms of government control. Conserver solutions to a large number of problems inevitably imply a greater role for government, which we argue is not required for dealing with environmental and other problems.

Intrusive

Many conserver solutions would extend government controls not only over firms, but also over individual lifestyle and consumption decisions. Such changes are neither necessary (in a technical sense), nor desirable (to us in a normative sense). Sensible environmental policies need not reduce the scope of a market economy. It is possible that proponents of the Conserver Society may have seized upon environmental issues as a pretext for expanding state control over the economy, which they favour on ideological grounds. That issue, on which we obviously have strong views, should be debated on its own merits. Environmental issues are susceptible to solutions that either promote or limit the use of the market. The Science Council and others appear eager to restrict the scope of the market economy, while we argue that much of their argument is without merit.

The case in favour of market approaches to pollution control is reinforced by the point made earlier that environmental problems are caused not by a market form of organization, but by the absence of market forces in allocating environmental assets. One of the most potentially useful arrangements for dealing with pollution treats the problem precisely in this light by creating markets in environmental assets.[5] This approach combines the certainty of outcome from regulated standards with the flexibility of market forces. It involves the sale of licences to pollute.

Selling Pollution Rights

Consider the case of a lake with a single pollutant, where measuring and determining the source is relatively inexpensive. Assume also that the carrying capacity of the lake and the nature of alternative uses can be used to determine an acceptable level of pollution of X units (say 10 tons of pollutant per year). The pollution rights approach would have a government agency (a water quality board) exercise exclusive property rights to this environmental asset by first determining X and then offering for sale "rights" or licences to pollute up to a total of 10 tons. By assumption, monitoring the outputs of individual polluters is inexpensive and the water control board could—through its own powers and/or the courts—deal with discharges beyond the quantity of rights purchased by each firm. The rights would be sold to the highest bidders—that is, to those firms for whom the costs of other methods of waste disposal are the greatest.

The attractiveness of this plan lies in its flexibility. Only the total quantity of pollution would be regulated; market forces would determine the allocation of these rights among competing firms. If stiffer standards were later deemed desirable, the rights could either be time-dated and later issued in smaller quantities, or the water quality board could re-purchase and retire some of the rights. Similarly, if environmental groups regarded a given standard to be too lenient they could also purchase and permanently retire some of these rights. This particular solution is attractive since it retains the certainty of standards but, through market flexibility, provides more pollution control per unit of resource expenditure.

Information

Most pollution control approaches, including the market alternative, require a great deal of information. In the case of a lake, for example, we may have fairly clear evidence of the cost of pollution in terms of other uses no longer possible. However, a scientific determination of the precise contribution of each of a variety of pollutants may be very costly, as may be identifying the emission quantities of a large number of polluters.

In designing a reasonable policy and choosing among alternative routes to a particular goal, the costs of different institutional arrangements become important. In general, we presume market-oriented solutions have lower administrative costs than regulatory options. The metering requirements of market solutions, however, may be high, since both emission taxes or pollution rights require data on individual polluters. Similar information is required to implement a policy of regulated emission reductions. Other regulatory approaches, such as mandated installation of either pollution control equipment or of a non-polluting technology, do not require this information. While it may be possible in some cases to measure pollution indirectly (e.g., on the basis of inputs used) we do not wish to minimize the potential problems in this area.

Neither taxes nor pollution rights appeal to many environmentalists. There is often extreme aversion expressed in moral terms to selling the right to pollute. To us, this indicates either a failure to grasp the concept of choosing between environmental and other goods, or a view that no environmental goods should be foregone. Surely, setting an emission tax producing a level of pollution of X, selling rights to X units of pollution, or otherwise regulating pollution to X units are all presumably equally moral or immoral when each produces the identical level of pollution.

As Baumol and Oates emphasize:

> Society has been giving away free too many of its resources for too long. It is *not* scandalous to decide that everything has its price; the real scandal lies in setting that price at zero or at some token level that invites us all to destroy these resources....Unless we recognize the legitimate role of price incentives for the control of pollution, we may end up with our sense of morality intact but our environment the worse for continued abuse (1979, p. 245).

Survey of Price Incentives

Although their perspective is somewhat different than that adopted in this volume, noted U.S. economists W.J. Baumol and W.E. Oates argue for an extension of market approaches to pollution control. Their reason for doing so is the same as ours: to the extent that taxes and pollution rights offer efficiency gains over a regulated standards approach, society can buy more pollution reduction for a given resource expenditure. As advocates of greater use of price incentives, Baumol and Oates feel (as we do) that it is important to demonstrate how price incentives have worked (i.e., case studies) and how they might work (i.e., simulation studies). In this section, we briefly summarize the Baumol and Oates findings on the effectiveness of price incentives. In the following section we consider simulation models that describe how such incentives might work.

A frequently cited example of the application of economic incentives to pollution control involves the case of the Ruhr River basin in West Germany. This area accounts for approximately 40 percent of industrial production and 70 percent to 90 percent of coal, iron, and steel production in that country. Pollution control is accomplished through regional water authorities that "impose effluent charges, which are dependent *both* on the quality and quantity of emissions, and thus provide incentives to industry to reduce waste discharges" (Baumol and Oates, p. 256). This approach has achieved a standard that makes effluent discharge compatible with fishing and recreation.

Sewage

In the United States, municipal sewage treatment systems provide some evidence on the responsiveness of firms to effluent charges. For many years, treatment authorities paid for such facilities through user charges based on the quantity of water intake. This allows firms with production processes that produce highly concentrated wastes to pollute at a lower price per unit than is faced by other firms. As Baumol and Oates point out, such a system provides an incentive to economize on water, but not necessarily to reduce pollution.

In response to the heavy demands placed on the sewage authority by their pricing system, many jurisdictions have established surcharges based on the quantity of harmful effluent released, not merely on water intake. These surcharges take the form of a price or tax per unit on the excess of biochemical oxygen demand (BOD) over some defined "normal" level. The price is generally in the vicinity of 2 cents per pound of BOD beyond the normal level. A number of different studies have found very significant reductions in BOD discharges in response to this tax. For example, Elliot and Seagraves report that, on the basis of data for 35 cities with such an effluent fee, a relatively small fee increase (from approximately 2 cents to 2.2 cents per pound) led to an 8 percent reduction in BOD discharge. In another study, Ethridge (Baumol *et al.*, p. 259) examines 27 observations on five poultry-producing plants and found that a 10 percent fee increase led to a 5 percent decrease in BOD discharge per unit of output.

In addition to case-study evidence, Lof and Kneese (Baumol *et al.*, p. 260) model the use of water and quantity of BOD effluent discharge in the beet-sugar industry. This industry uses very large quantities of water (estimated as approximately 6 million gallons per day in the United States) and produces relatively large quantities of BOD discharge. The large variation in the production processes shows the potential for efficiency gains over fees relative to regulated standards for pollution reduction. In all processes, water is used as an input, but it ranges from 270 to 5,250 gallons of water per ton of beets. This variation indicates that there is a great range of choice available in methods of beet-sugar production. By the recirculation of water and more effective treatment of wastes (both of which can be accomplished at rather modest costs), levels of water usage and the BOD and suspended-solid content of factory effluents can be cut substantially (Baumol and Oates, p. 260).

Using the results obtained by Lof and Kneese, Ethridge determined the impact of typical sewer surcharge rates on industry emissions. The results are dramatic and underscore the enthusiasm of economists for price incentives. In the beet-sugar industry, Ethridge estimated that a 10 percent increase in the BOD surcharge leads to an average 60 percent reduction in BOD discharge. A regulated standards approach, on the other hand, applied either within this industry or across industrial sources of BOD discharge, would fail to take advantage of the very large cost differences faced by firms in reacting to that standard.

Price System Works

The fundamental message is that the price system is an effective mechanism for pollution control. Although the price system will not always be the most efficient mechanism (for example, in cases where sources of pollution are remote or where there are relatively small cost differences among polluters), it is our contention that the scope of its comparative advantage extends beyond its existing uses. It is unclear how much the disinclination to use the price system is attributable to the novelty of the idea and how much to the antagonism to the market evident in the writings of many conservationists.

A study by Bingham et al. provides a quantitative estimate of the costs of failing to use market approaches to pollution control. This cost can be visualized in two ways. It can be viewed as the value of resources that could be saved from achieving a given degree of pollution control in the least cost way. Alternatively, there is the perspective of the environmentalists. Here, it is seen as the value of resources available to purchase even more pollution abatement once initial targets are achieved efficiently.

Bingham et al. construct a model of sulfur emissions for St. Louis and Cleveland that includes estimates of abatement costs for the different sources. The benchmark for their calculations is the mandated reduction in sulfur emissions of 55 percent in St. Louis and 78 percent in Cleveland. Their model produces estimates of the costs of achieving this reduction via regulated standards and via effluent fees, which would be set at 13 cents per pound of sulfur emissions in St. Louis and 19 cents per pound in Cleveland. Table 3 indicates resource savings of $20.4 million in St. Louis and $11.3 million in Cleveland from achieving the same degree of pollution abatement in the more efficient way. The cost savings reflect the fact that in these cities there are many sources of sulfur emissions and some face very high abatement payments, while others face relatively low ones.

Table 3

Estimated Costs of Reductions in Sulfur Emissions
(millions of dollars)

	Controls	Charges	Use of Emission Charges
St. Louis	$49.5	$29.1	$20.4
Cleveland	45.5	34.2	11.3

Source: Bingham et al. (1973) as cited in Baumol and Oates (1979), p. 267

Pulp and Paper in B.C.

The central advantage of market approaches is their greater flexibility for allocating pollution reductions among sources. In his analysis of the B.C. pulp and paper industry, James Stephenson highlights several important factors in determining and implementing an appropriate pollution standard. First, consider enforcement. It is possible that this process may be more effective in a market that defines rather than negotiates standards. It is also possible that a price system may achieve efficiency gains relative even to flexible standards.

Stephenson constructs a model of the costs of alternative pollution control procedures from the technical relationship between pulp and paper production and the generation of two forms of pollution. These are suspended solids (SS) and biochemical oxygen demand (BOD). The exercise first estimates SS and BOD discharges in the absence of pollution controls of any kind. It then simulates the impact first of effluent standards and second of effluent fees, from which demand curves for pollution rights can be inferred. A profit-maximizing firm (assuming away enforcement problems) will, in the case of the effluent standard, select the least cost treatment procedures. In the case of fees, the firm will attempt to minimize the sum of treatment costs and payments resulting from the effluent fee.

The Results

Although this is only a simulation of the response of a profit-maximizing firm to effluent fees, the results are instructive. First, firms do respond as expected to a charge on polluting activities. Holding the BOD charge constant, for example, we find that an increase in the effluent fee for SS from 0.5 cents to 1 cent per pound reduces the discharge of suspended solids per day from 21,000 pounds to 7,000. A further increase in the SS fee to 10 cents/pound leads to a decline to 2,000 pounds/day. The results also show that the lowest fees lead to a low ratio of abatement costs to fee payments, while at higher fees, the abatement fraction rises quickly. In particular, at the lowest fee schedule simulated, abatement costs were less than 15 percent of fee payments, while for the highest schedule, abatement costs rose to more than three times fee payments. To the extent that the simulation model represents actual firm response, these results contradict the charge often made by conservationists that fees are just a licence to continue to pollute at unchanged levels.

Economic Incentives to Reduce Motor Vehicle Emissions

Canada is quite clearly limited in the extent to which policies independent of those in the U.S. can be implemented to control new vehicle emissions. Any policy that imposed standards beyond that of the U.S. would likely be excessively costly, while less stringent standards may have little impact. What follows below should, therefore, be regarded as an alternative for North American vehicle emission policy and a policy for dealing with pollution from vehicles in use (i.e. maintenance of pollution control equipment).

The history of motor vehicle emission regulation reveals the problems that result from the regulated standards approach to pollution control.[6] Progress under the Clean Air Act (U.S.) and subsequent amendments has been slow and costly. Moreover, the approach since 1970 has been highly adversarial. This may appeal to some environmentalists but it has not been conducive to meeting established goals. The 1970 legislation established standards requiring reduction by 90 percent, of emissions of hydrocarbons (HC), carbon monoxide (CO), and nitrogen oxide (NOX) by 1975 (for HC and CO) and 1976 (NOX). These standards exceeded emission reductions that could be produced with the technology available at that time. The only method for dealing with non-compliance was to prevent the sale of all such vehicles. It was recognized by all parties, however, that the probability of GM being entirely shut down by the Environmental Protection Agency (EPA) for non-compliance, for example, was essentially zero.

Over-penalizing

In this case, the very size of the penalty meant it was virtually certain that it would not be imposed. An advantage of the economic approach is that although non-compliance penalties are lower, they are more certain. This creates a more credible expected cost of non-compliance and a greater incentive to produce vehicles with fewer emissions. Since the standards were so strict that they required substantial and subsequent re-negotiation, a frequently cited advantage of negotiated standards relative to the price mechanism was absent, namely the certainty of the quantity of pollution. A review of U.S. experience since the mid-1960s would almost certainly convince all except those totally committed to regulated standards that almost any alternative policy could have produced better pollution control and more abatement at a lower cost.

Table 4
Automobile Emission Standards
(grams per mile)

	HC	CO	NO[X]
Uncontrolled car	8.7	87.0	4.0
1968	5.9	50.8	-
1970	3.9	33.3	-
1972	3.0	28.0	-
1972-74 federal standards	3.0	28.0	3.1
1975[c] and 1976			
Federal 49-state standards	15.0	3.1	
California standards	0.9	9.0	2.0
1977 federal 50-state standards	1.5	15.0	2.0
1978 statutory standards	0.41	3.4	.4
Administration bill (January 1975)			
197-81 50-state standards	0.9	9.0	3.1
EPA recommendation (March 1975)			
1977-79	1.5	15.0	2.0
1980-81	0.9	9.0	2.0
Post-1981	0.41	3.4	
Revised administration proposal			
(June 1975) Through 1981	1.5	15.0	3.1

Source: Mills and White (1978), p. 353 and Baumol and Oates

Mills and White have suggested a system of motor vehicle pollution control via price incentives. The objective of such a policy can be stated as follows:

> The proximate goal of an automobile pollution control policy should be to motivate competition in the production of clean non-polluting cars. It should reward those who produce clean cars and those who maintain their cars so as to keep them clean; it should penalize those who produce dirty cars or allow them to become dirty (Mills and White, p. 385).

The context for the Mills-White plan is the existing set of emission regulations shown in table 4. These regulations have little flexibility (with the sole exception of the California standard) for dealing with geographical differences in the cost of pollution. They also prevent the use of abatement technologies that offer trade-offs in pollutant reduction (as is the case for many technologies that can substantially reduce HC and CO at the cost of some increase in NOX.)

In the Mills-White plan, manufacturers would have to pay a total pollution fee (F), which would be the sum of charges for the HC, CO, and NOX emissions for that particular automobile as determined by tests of production line vehicles. Ideally, each individual fee should be set to produce what we have described above as the best quantity of pollution. It would, in other words, allow pollution up to the point at which the additional costs were just equal to the additional benefits of abatement. On the basis of admittedly crude estimates of desirable fees per unit of pollution, the proposed fees are:

Hydrocarbons	$ 6.33/gram/mile
Carbon monoxide	$ 1.15/gram/mile
Nitrogen oxide	$25.00/gram/mile

This set of fees would be established as a floor level for places with relatively minor pollution problems; areas with greater problems would specify higher fees. Assuming that fee schedules would be differentiated by states, manufacturers would pay on the basis of the state to which vehicles are shipped. The plan allows further local differentiation, say by county of registration if pollution costs are much higher in particular areas. For illustrative purposes, a set of fees is proposed for high pollution areas that is exactly three times the fee on each pollutant shown above. Table 5 shows what this approach might cost for vehicles meeting different standards. This is shown for both the benchmark fee schedule and the higher fee schedule.

This table shows that manufacturers faced with the low fee schedule would produce vehicles meeting the 1970 standard. This standard minimizes the sum of abatement cost and fee payments. With the higher schedule, the 1975 California standards would be met. This example confirms that pollution taxes are not simply a licence to pollute, as environmentalists often contend. In fact, these taxes are a mechanism for achieving the desired level of pollution on the basis of cost and benefit calculations.

Potential for Market Solutions

A further advantage of this system is that it can be extended to vehicles in use and can thus provide incentives for owners to properly maintain pollution control equipment. Car owners pay a fee at the time of purchase based on properly functioning control devices. Depending on the costs of periodic inspections, it may be worthwhile to test automobiles regularly to determine that they continue to meet their expected standard. Owners would not be forced

Table 5
Effluent Fees (Low Schedule) on Cars that Meet the Various Standards

	Fee Paid				Estimated Discounted Cost of Meeting Standards	Total of Fee and Cost of Meeting Standards
	HC	CO	NO_x	Total		
Uncontrolled car	$100	$100	$100	$300		$300
1968 standards	56	59	125	240	20	260
1970 standards	44	39	125	208	30	238
1972 standards	20	32	125	177	72	249
1973 standards	20	32	78	120	280	400
1975 interim standards	11	17	78	106	280	386
1975 California standards	7	10	50	67	380	447
1975 original standards	4	4	50	58	430	488
1976 original standards	4	4	10	18	630	648

(F_{HC} = $6.33, F_{CO} = $1.15, F_{NOx} = $25.00)

Continued

Table 5 (continued)

Effluent Fees (High Schedule) on Cars that Meet the Various Standards

	Fee Paid				Estimated Discounted Cost of Meeting Standards	Total of Fee and Cost of Meeting Standards
	HC	CO	NO_x	Total		
Uncontrolled car	$300	$300	$300	$900		$900
1968 standards	169	176	375	720	20	740
1970 standards	131	116	375	622	30	652
1972 standards	61	97	375	533	72	605
1973 standards	61	97	232	390	280	670
1975 interim standards	32	52	232	316	280	596
1975 California standards	21	31	150	202	380	582
1975 original standards	11	12	150	173	430	603
1976 original standards	11	12	30	53	630	683

(F_{HC} = $19.00, F_{CO} = $3.45, F_{NO_x} = $75.00)

Source: Adapted from Mills and White, pp. 388-9.

to maintain pollution control equipment but would be required to pay for external costs generated. Clearly, a good deal of research is required for the implementation of such a plan. However, our purpose in this section has been to indicate the potential for economic solutions to various pollution problems. These solutions illustrate the diversity and flexibility that would result from incentives rather than restrictions and regulations.

The Plot Thickens

Robert Crandall, a Senior Fellow of the Brookings Institution, has examined the consequences of seemingly innocuous proposals made to Congress by the Environmental Protection Agency "to require electric utilities to install the best available continuous emission reduction technology in all new plants." As Crandall notes, the effects of such measures were far from innocent.

> In practice, the amendment calls upon [the] E.P.A. to require the scrubbing of stack gases from new plants regardless of the sulphur content of the coal they burn. Obviously this reduces the incentives of the utilities in the Midwest to use the abundant supplies of low-sulphur coal available in the West. Since the new-plant standard does not limit sulphur emissions, but simply requires removal of a large proportion of the sulphur emitted, utilities will burn much higher sulphur coal from nearby regions, which is cheaper. In many cases, the total cost of the full-scrubbing requirement will substantially exceed the cost of burning low-sulphur coal and partially treating the stack gases (Crandall 1979 p. 2).

Why would such a measure be undertaken? Why wouldn't the legislators directly control the source of pollution—sulfur emissions—rather than adopting such an ineffectual, indirect tack? Crandall attributes these measures to an unlikely alliance of environmentalists and midwestern coal workers who found sulfur emission standards would cause the substitution of low-sulfur coal from the west for their product. In this example, the government measure taken to protect the environment for posterity by maintaining clean air standards became subordinated through the political process to the achievement of other goals.

Does It Matter?

Why does it matter if the clean air proposal became aligned with employment protection measures of the midwestern coal workers? Wasn't clean air achieved as an outcome? Crandall provides a clear answer to these questions: clean air was achieved at a far greater expense than it could have been by other means. He suggests:

> If [the] E.P.A. were simply to set a performance standard or tighten existing standards to obtain the same 2.5 million ton

reduction in emissions, it probably could reduce the cost of removal by one-half, from $800 a ton to $400 a ton. The net annual saving would be $1 billion by 1990 (Crandall, p. 3).

Concluding that the major effect of the measures was a $1-billion subsidy to create 13,500 additional jobs in midwestern coal mining, at a cost of $70,000 a year per job, Crandall suggested,

Those 13,500 would be better off to accept, say $30,000 a year to retrain, allowing the rest of the public to save more than $0.5 billion a year (Crandall, p. 3).

The $0.5 billion could be used to purchase even more pollution reduction. Here and elsewhere, we argue that market solutions reduce the probability that the direct objective (here, pollution control) will be submerged in a variety of conflicting purposes.

Bubbles

The economic approach to pollution control is designed to produce the maximum pollution reduction for a given expenditure. We have argued that conventional approaches involving the regulated standards favoured by conservers fail to do this. The inefficiency of the "command-and-control" system has generated interest in more flexible market-oriented approaches.[7]

The inefficiency of regulated standards can be traced to the prohibition of trading among polluters. We pointed out above that efficient pollution control requires that emission reductions should be undertaken by the polluter for whom emission reduction costs are lowest. This is prevented in across-the-board reductions.

In the United States, a series of approaches to allow trading in emission reductions have been developed in recent years. One of the best-known is the "bubble policy." In this approach, a series of polluters are assumed to be enclosed in an imaginary bubble. Standards are developed, not for the individual polluters, but for the entire bubble. In this way, firms for whom emission reduction is not costly can sell their excess reductions to firms for whom such reductions are more costly. In recent years, the U.S. Environmental Protection Agency has taken on the responsibility of monitoring the emissions trading programme.

Society can receive substantial gains from this type of approach. The extent of the gain depends on the deviation between the minimum cost option and the regulated standards alternative. As an example of the gains available, Tietenberg (1985, p. 85) cites a 1983 study of the control of particulates in the Baltimore region. In this case, a restricted form of trading in emissions allowed firms to achieve the overall pollution standard at less than 50 percent of the cost of the command-and-control system.

The gains cited in this example are just further evidence that market-oriented flexibility can substantially contribute to meeting our environmental goals. A recent survey tabulated the results of 11 studies of the ratio of command-and-control costs to the least-cost method of pollution control (Tietenberg 1985, pp. 42-43). This survey indicates that, on average, the costs associated with regulated standards exceed minimum costs (attainable with market-oriented approaches) by a factor of more than six.

The Canadian Case

The same holds true for Canada. Evidence from the operation of sewer surcharge systems in a number of Canadian cities indicates that the use of a market mechanism to control effluent discharge is not just a theoretical abstraction, but is, in fact, a viable strategy.

The use of effluent charges requires data on discharges by type of pollutant. In Canada, the most commonly metered pollutants are the extent of organic material as measured by biochemical oxygen demand (BOD), the quantity of suspended solids (SS), grease, and specific chemical content, such as phenol or chlorine.

In 1958, the city of Winnipeg instituted a sewer surcharge scheme (Bubbis 1983). Polluting firms were required to pay a surcharge based on their emission of specific pollutants, including SS, BOD, grease, and chlorine, in addition to the standard industrial sewage fee. The engineering staff of the city waterworks, waste and disposal division argues that response to the effluent charges has been substantially greater than the response to earlier regulatory approaches. A continuing programme of metering is clearly necessary, but the evidence from Winnipeg is that a market-oriented system is not prohibitively expensive; in 1971, effluent sampling was carried out for less than $15,000. Effluent charges clearly provide a viable method of pollution control.

Further evidence is available from other cities with effluent charges. The city of Toronto permits BOD discharge up to 500 ppm, SS to 600 ppm, grease to 150 ppm, and phenol to 1 ppm as part of the regular sewage charge. Beyond these limits there is a surcharge of one and one-half cents per pound.

An effluent surcharge provides a vehicle for tightening standards if this is justified in terms of the criteria discussed previously. The city of Edmonton, for example, moved to more stringent standards between 1971 and 1977 as shown below.

POLLUTANT	SURCHARGE LEVELS		
(ppm)	1-6-1971	1-1-1975	1-1-1977
BOD	700	500	300
SS	400	350	300
Grease	200	150	100

Emissions beyond these limits are charged at the rate of 1.4 cents per pound of BOD, 0.45 cents per pound for SS, and 0.60 cents per pound for grease. Similar systems operate in London, Calgary, Kitchener, Hamilton, and Charlottetown.

Effluent Fees

The responsiveness of the brewing industry to municipal effluent fees has been examined in detail by Concordia University economist William Sims (February 1979). His conclusions are based on data collected from breweries situated in various Canadian municipalities that charge sewer effluent fees. Contrary to conserver contentions, firms responded significantly to price incentives. A 0.573 percent reduction in BOD emission was estimated to result from a 1 percent increase in the BOD price, while a 0.45 reduction in SS emission was estimated to result from a 1 percent increase in its price. This is further empirical evidence to support our position that a system of economic incentives is, in many cases, preferable to the plethora of regulations apparently favoured by conservers.

What can we expect from a system of effluent fees? Environmentalists are suspicious of this device because it allows some firms to continue polluting. Municipal water quality engineers also have lamented that some firms continue to pay and pollute. These criticisms miss the point. Under an effluent fee system the price per unit of pollutant is set at a level designed to induce the appropriate quantity of emission. Appropriate, as defined earlier, means that further pollution reductions would cost more than society is willing to pay. Neither effluent fees nor any other central mechanism can be judged in relation to a total reduction in emissions. Judged by the standard of attaching an appropriate value to the environment, a system of market-oriented effluent fees has much to recommend it.

Individualism

The conserver critique of the market system raises the fundamental economic problem of choice. All societies must choose what to produce and how and for whom to produce it.

Conservers argue that the bundle of goods and services we produce and the leisure or other non-work activity in which we engage do not reflect the preferences of individual citizens. As a result, the state should protect individuals from those who might convince them they want something that they really do not—or, in the opinion of conservers, should not—want.

The essential question here is the extent to which individuals should be allowed to decide what is in their own best interest. The conserver view is that individuals are to be trusted only with certain kinds of information and certain kinds of products. We find it exceedingly paradoxical that individuals who are expected to make complex political choices are not to be trusted with relatively simple market choices.

Individuals may well decide to delegate their rights to choose in complex situations—but they are unlikely always to delegate them to the government. We believe that conservers err in advocating the delegation of choice in situations that are not particularly complex, but in which existing choices are not to their tastes. They are also mistaken in assuming that all such delegation necessarily should be to the government.

Market Bias

Conservers believe that the market allocation of production is biased in favour of the present at the expense of future generations. In their view, government must ensure that people living today take proper account of those who will come later. Conservers have failed to support this position with a demonstration that future generations can participate in political decisions and thus lobby for their interests. Conservers have also underestimated the extent to which the market mechanism reflects the preferences of future as well as present generations. Many of the remaining shortcomings of the market are attributable to the type of government intervention advocated by conservers.

The political suppression of market outcomes is a common occurrence in a democratic society. Economists have produced mountains of evidence showing that a certain type of intervention is more or less costly than voters might have supposed. They argue that the distribution of its cost is different than voters might have expected. However, as economists, they cannot question the legitimacy of the intervention itself, as long as it is undertaken with a recognition of true costs.

We have argued that political intervention involving future generations is likely to be to their detriment. The marketplace reflects to a considerable extent the preferences of future generations; it is unwise to replace it with political decisions that do not. As citizens, we question the legitimacy of politicizing decisions in which so many of the interested parties are disenfranchised.

Bias Toward Pollution Externalities

Turning to the problem of pollution, conservers argue that market decisions on how to produce are biased in favour of methods that impose costs on others. Firms adopt techniques that are noisy and pollute both the air and the water because they are, in the myopic sense, cheaper.

Since, in their view, pollution is a consequence of the free-enterprise form of organization, conservers see suspension of market incentives as necessary for its control. They advocate emission standards enforced by government as the principal means of controlling pollution. They tend to ignore market

81

approaches that would enable affected individuals to balance the benefits of reduced pollution against the value of the goods and services they must forgo to obtain it.

Our advocacy of market or quasi-market approaches to pollution control is not an advocacy of *laissez-faire*. It is the responsibility of the judicial system and, in some cases, the legislature, to define and assign the right to use the air or a river. Having done this, the state may find it has no further role. The right to use the air or a body of water will be purchased by the highest-valued user, and if recreational and other related benefits are large, pollution will be curtailed.

In many cases, however, the definition and assignment of property rights by the courts or legislature will be insufficient. The affected parties may not be able to reach an agreement that allows the higher-valued use to prevail. In this case, an exchange between competing users of the air or river can be consummated in the courts. The party buying the right pays judicially determined "damages" to the party selling it. The price paid for the right to pollute or to be free of pollution is determined not by the invisible hand of the market, but by the visible hand of the courts.

Theft

When one party continues to pollute despite a ruling that the other has a right to be free of pollution, it is the same as theft. Like other types of theft, this situation is covered by the criminal law.

In some cases, a regulatory tribunal will be better equipped than the courts to decide the values of competing uses of the air and bodies of water. As long as these tribunals have as their objective the allocation of rights to the highest-valued users, there can be no objection to them. Too often, however, the call for regulation is a call for the arbitrary creation and distribution of rights to pollute. We object to this, since it will fail to produce the maximum reduction in pollution for a given expenditure.

In sum, pollution is but one of many manifestations of our interdependence. Much of what each of us does affects others and ought to be taken into account. A well-developed set of market and quasi-market institutions enables us to do this. The same institutions can and do assist us in dealing with pollution problems. We suggest that the operation of these market institutions be first studied by those who see a need to augment or replace them.

Ecology and Economics: Different Approaches?

To many, the environmental debate can be cast as a western movie with good guys (ecologists) and bad guys (economists). Surprisingly, both the terms "ecology" and "economics" are derived from the Greek word *oikos*, meaning home or household. Economics and ecology share a further and far more important feature. Both involve the study of unintended consequences in interdependent systems. Both convey the message that measures taken to achieve one purpose can have substantial, frequently undesirable, and unanticipated effects on attaining other objectives. Moreover, these unintended effects can sometimes swamp the intended in terms of their overall consequences. Garrett Hardin, the eloquent spokesman for many environmentalists, has aptly summed it up: "We can never do one thing." This is called the law of unintended effects.

The relevance of the law of unintended effects to both economics and ecology should come as no surprise once one considers their respective subject matters. Economics studies the working of the market system, a complex, interdependent social system. Ecology studies the functioning of equally complex and interrelated biological systems. Both contain negative feedback loops, in that any change in one part of the system triggers a succession of changes elsewhere. The overall effects of any change cannot be determined solely by examining its immediate effects. Account must be taken of its interactions with all parts of the system.

Unintended Consequences

Examples of the law of unintended effects are numerous in ecology. Hardin notes the contribution of Darwin and his example of the humble bees:

> The great number of humble-bees in any district depends in great measure upon the number of field-mice which destroy their combs and nests; and Colonel Newman who has long attended to the habits of humble-bees, believes that "more than two-thirds of them are thus destroyed all over England." Now the number of mice is largely dependent, as everyone knows, on the number of cats; and Col. Newman says, "near villages and small towns I have found the nests of humble-bees more numerous than elsewhere, which I attribute to the number of cats that destroy the mice." Hence it is quite credible that the presence of a feline animal in large numbers in a district might determine, through the intervention first of mice and then of bees, the frequency of certain flowers in that district! (Hardin, p. 39).

Hardin tells us that others carried Darwin's example several steps further, pointing out:

> that cats are kept (as is well known by old maids) and, on the other, that red clover (which requires humble-bees as pollinators) is used to make hay that nourishes the horses of the cavalry, on which the British Empire depends... Thus "it logically follows" that the perpetuation of the British Empire

is dependent on a bountiful supply of old maids (Hardin, p. 39).

Instances of the law of unintended effects in economics are less familiar, but just as important. Policy measures such as rent controls and minimum wage laws illustrate this principle. Although wage minima have a stated objective of protecting unskilled workers, the evidence accumulated by economists suggests that many low-wage workers are harmed by the unemployment caused by this measure (West/McKee 1980). Similarly, rent controls are designed to provide affordable housing for low-income individuals (Block & Olsen 1981). But the weight of evidence across many countries is that this form of price control has had undesirable and unintended consequences. These include shortages, declines in the standard of maintenance, and in extreme cases, the abandonment of buildings. Noted Swedish economist Assar Lindbeck provides us with a startling conclusion:

> In many cases rent control appears to be the most efficient technique presently known to destroy a city—except for bombing (Lindbeck cited in Rydenfelt 1981, p. 213).

The Road to Hell Is Paved with...

The law of unintended effects has implications at a number of levels for the Conserver Society debate. Most obvious is the proposition that measures involving change, whether in economic or ecological systems, must be examined beyond their superficial and immediate effects to determine as far as possible the impact of their total effects, intended and unintended.

More subtle, but equally important, is the point that policy measures should not be judged by the good intentions of their proponents. Rather, judgement must be based on the overall effects of implementing any change.

We have argued throughout this volume that conservers have not examined the overall consequences of their recommendations, which would lead to many undesirable consequences. This would not have occurred had they employed the methodology of either economics *or* ecology. The failure of conservers to appreciate the subtlety and pervasiveness of the market mechanism does not stem from a general ignorance of feedback loops. What has motivated conservers to use a methodology with which they should feel professionally uncomfortable? The following section attempts to answer this question.

Economic Analysis and Conserver Analysis

The conserver proposals would alter our existing market form of economic organization by substituting greater government control for existing market processes. A fundamental insight of this article, however, is that the conservers fail to appreciate how existing market mechanisms operate. For this reason, their conclusions and recommendations are unlikely to make us better off. Why is it that the conserver case so regularly appears lacking when subjected to analytical scrutiny?

There are two apparent reasons for the poor showing. One is relatively obvious, and the other more subtle. First, many errors result from the apparent fact that no attempt was made to prevent them. Elementary textbooks of economics provide more economic insight into such problems as pollution and resource conservation than do many conserver documents. The authors of *Canada as a Conserver Society*, if one is to judge by their text and references, have simply not consulted the standard works of economists on the various problems with which they are concerned. If for no other reason than to anticipate such criticism as this, it would have been prudent for the Science Council to have attempted to come to grips with the position of economists.

Never Intended to Be Analytical

The second reason for the low quality of *Canada as a Conserver Society* partly explains the failure to deal with the work of economists. Many conserver society proponents have backgrounds in the physical sciences and clearly possess substantial analytical skills. They are accustomed to the analytical treatment of problems. In spite of this, we believe the case can be made that *Canada as a Conserver Society* is not an analytical document—because it was never intended to be one.[8]

If this contention is in fact true, it stands as an indictment both of the authors of the document and of its sponsor, the Science Council of Canada. The Science Council was established for the purpose of providing analysis for the benefit of the people of Canada, not for propagandizing a viewpoint that promises benefit for only a limited segment of the community. Below, we attempt to establish the proposition that rather than being an analysis of alternative social policies, *Canada as a Conserver Society* is, in fact, the pleading of a special-interest group. The intention of this interest group is to benefit from a governmental commitment to "high technology" and increased state control over economic activities and the actions of individuals.

Maximizing Welfare

In economic activity and economic policy, the objective is to provide the greatest net benefit to the individuals who make up a particular society. The goal of public policy is, in other words, to design social institutions to mediate the inevitable conflict among individuals over the allocation of scarce resources. They must do so in such a way that the outcome reflects the preferences of the members of this society. There are significant technical problems in achieving such an end, but what we wish to emphasize here is the objective—to serve the often conflicting interests of individual members of society. Social goals exist only through an aggregation of individual preferences. The role of the state is to provide the means for achieving social goals rather than to set them. Economists do not start out with a specific set of social goals. Rather, they take the approach that our institutions should be structured to achieve in the most efficient manner whatever goals the individuals in a society wish to pursue.

The methodology of economics stands in stark contrast to that of the Science Council. Its report outlines a specific set of goals that we believe are not widely held by individual Canadians. The Science Council then recommends policies to reach those goals without considering alternative objectives. More importantly, they simply assume without analysis that their goals are appropriate and should not only be adopted as government policy, but through taxes, regulations, and restrictions, should be forced on others as well.

Trains, More Trains

George W. Hilton, in commenting on the Ford Foundation Energy Project Report of 1974, has made a similar point about this form of "analysis."

> [It] reads like the publications of organizations formed with a single purpose. For example, the National Association of Railroad Passengers was formed to preserve railroad passenger trains. Its publications do not concern themselves with the benefits versus costs of the survival of passenger trains, or the costs of trains versus buses, or other matters which an economist might consider. Rather, the organization's journals have been concerned at various times with asking whether passenger trains are best preserved by forcing railroads to operate them, having a public monopoly run them, or letting specialized private firms operate them on track owned by various railroads. Such one-sided argument, after all, is what the members pay their dues to secure (Hilton 1975, p. 107).

Our approach explicitly recognizes the multiplicity of desired ends and the inevitable conflict among these ends (e.g., between environmental and non-environmental goods). Devoting all our attention to one or a limited number of the items that are important to social well-being necessarily means accepting less of other important items. Intuitively, it is clear that overall social welfare cannot be maximized by selecting a limited number of desirable ends and enhancing those without regard to all of the other aspects of well-being. Yet this is precisely the methodology of *Canada as a Conserver Society*.

Some disagreement on many aspects of desirable social policy is inevitable. Those supporting the concept of a conserver society are those for whom the limited form of maximization described above creates net benefits (i.e., for whom the gains from maximizing a limited number of variables exceed the costs of neglecting others). A policy that creates a net social loss (costs exceed benefits) can still be attractive to many people. A major purpose of this article is to dispute the claims of potential gainers and to indicate in general terms the nature of the losses that are implicit in the "myopic maximization" advocated by the Science Council.

Myopic Maximization

What, then, are the goals of the proponents of the conserver society? To give them a general identification, they are what Hilton (1975) has referred to as "the goals of the conservationist or popular ecology movement." Given the adoption of these limited goals, it is not surprising that the recommendations of *Canada as a Conserver Society* appear lacking when evaluated in an overall framework. The conserver critique of consumer sovereignty and market processes, as we have discussed earlier, can thus be seen as dissatisfaction with the results of market allocation. Those results are directed to a broader range of ends than the ones drawn by conservationists. Distaste for the market in this context represents distaste for a social device that allows for expression of a multiplicity of goals, some of which conflict with conservationist ends.

We have now identified the issue that is central to the debate between the conservationist and economic point of view. The difference emerges because the conservers have advocated a series of policies designed to achieve their narrowly defined objectives. We have provided various examples that demonstrate rather conclusively that their policy proposals would not necessarily lead to improvements in social well-being. We have pointed out that conservationists do not clearly define the best quantity of environmental goods (hence, of pollution) beyond which the costs of pollution reduction exceed the benefits. We have indicated why extreme conservationist measures do not necessarily make either ourselves or any future generation better off.

Bias in the Name of Science

Since conservationist policies do not translate into generalized benefits, their recommendations necessarily involve replacing markets (which provide individuals with what they want) with allocation by state control to tax, restrict, regulate, and otherwise alter the system to provide the outputs that conservationists have determined people should want. Markets are regarded by conservationists as inefficient devices for maximizing social well-being precisely because markets allow choices that conservationists would restrict.

The apparent lack of logic in *Canada as a Conserver Society* cannot easily be rationalized in any other manner. As an example, consider the goal of conservation of oil, to which conserver documents attach great weight. Their recommendations would force conservation beyond that which would be achieved by the market and would attempt, in some vaguely defined sense, to "minimize" use of the resource. What is not recognized is that such minimization to prevent "waste" will in fact lead to wasteful use of other inputs in the production process. To an economist, this cost must be weighed against the benefits from conserving fuel or other resources. Many conserver proposals involve an excess of cost over benefit when calculated in this way. Economic efficiency involves minimizing the cost of *all* inputs for a given level of output, while conservationist methodology involves minimizing only one input and wastefully using the rest. Only in the myopic maximization world of *Canada as a Conserver Society* can this be regarded as an improvement.

Political Success?

In political terms, conservationists have had a substantial impact. This is evident, at least, in the impressive stream of publications they have successfully convinced the government of Canada to fund. Yet we feel this group will inevitably decline in political influence. As indicated, many conservationist policies reduce economic welfare and require government coercion to implement. Many conservationist policies that are ill-conceived and uneconomic may remain popular, and some may be implemented. Ultimately, however, the costs associated with these misguided policies will galvanize those who must bear the burden of them. The political marketplace does not respond to individual preferences as quickly as traditional markets, but at some point the response will be felt and politicians who continue to support transfers from consumers and tax-payers to conservationists will be defeated

This is not to say that environmental concerns will not continue to be a priority. With increasing real incomes, we expect more concern with the environment. Rather, our point is that the specific anti-market approaches that we have analysed will become less attractive.

Our criticism here is not of conservers or their tastes and values. Although the movement is frequently characterized by anti-market extremes, the conserver influence on pollution has probably been, on balance, positive. Their preference for environmental over non-environmental goods and for future over present consumption is as legitimate as strongly held opposing views. We do, however, criticize their willingness to replace the market with state allocation to achieve their goals by coercion.

Notes

1. This section draws heavily on Hayek (1961).
2. The Science Council blurs the distinction between scarcity and shortage. All resources that are not freely available are scarce. The more scarce a resource is relative to the demand for it, the higher is its price. Gems or unique works of art are extremely scarce, yet we observe no shortage since the high price limits demand to equal available supply. Shortages, on the other hand, can exist for items of relatively low value (e.g., a gallon of gasoline) if price is prevented from balancing demand and supply.
3. The argument in this paragraph has been developed more fully in Grubel and Sydney Smith (1975), pp. 13-29.
4. The problems of the common pasture were made famous by Hardin (1968).
5. This innovative approach, now widely known, is due to Canadian economist John H. Dales. See Dales (1968).
6. For a detailed survey, on which this section draws heavily, see Mills and White (1978).
7. For an extensive survey, see Tietenberg (1985).
8. The following section is based in large part on Hilton (1975).

References

Anderson, F.J., "Ontario Reforestation Policy," *Canadian Public Policy*, Summer 1979.

Baumol, W.J., and W.E. Oates, *Economics, Environmental Policy and the Quality of Life* (1979).

Berndt, E., and D. Wood, "Technology, Prices and the Derived Demand for Energy," *Review of Economics and Statistics*, May 1975, pp. 259-268.

Berndt, Ernst R., "Canadian Energy Demand and Economic Growth" in *Oil in the Seventies: Essays on Energy Policy*, Campbell Watkins and Michael Walker, Vancouver: The Fraser Institute, 1977.

Bingham, T.H., and A.K. Miedema, Final Report, *Allocative and Distributional Effects of Alternative Air Quality Attainment Policies*, Research Triangle, N.C.: Research Triangle Institute, 1974.

Block, Walter, Geoffrey Brennan, Kenneth Elzinga, "Religion, Culture and Technology," in *Morality of the Market: Religious and Economic Perspectives*, eds., Vancouver: The Fraser Institute, 1985. Also see *"Replies"* by David Friedman, Kenneth Elzinga.

Block, Walter, Edgar O. Olsen, *Rent Control: Myths and Realities*, contributors include Milton Friedman and F.A. Hayek, Vancouver: The Fraser Institute, 1981.

Bubbis, N.S., "Industrial Waste Control in Greater Winnipeg," *Journal of the Water Pollution Control Federation*, Vol. 35, No. 11, 1983, p. 1413.

Carson, Rachel, *Silent Spring*, Boston: Houghton, Mifflin, 1962.

Coase, Ronald H., "The Problem of Social Cost," *Journal of Law and Economics*, 3, October 1960, pp. 1-44.

Cordell, Arthur, "Bye-Bye to Buy! Buy!", *Science Forum*, October 1976, pp. 5-18.

Crandall, Robert W., "Curbing the Costs of Social Regulation," *Brookings Bulletin*, 15, Winter 1979, pp. 1-5.

Dales, John H., "Beyond the Marketplace," *Canadian Journal of Economics*, 8, November 1975, pp. 483-503.

_____, *Pollution Property and Prices*, Toronto: University of Toronto Press, 1968.

Darmstadter, Joel, Joy Dunkerley, and Jack Alterman, *How Industrial Societies Use Energy: A Comparative Analysis*, Baltimore: Johns Hopkins Press, 1977.

Denny, M., M. Fuss, and L. Waverman, "The Substitution Possibilities for Energy: Evidence from U.S. and Canadian Manufacturing Industries" in *Modeling and Measuring Natural Resource Substitution*, E. Berndt and R. Fields, Cambridge: MIT Press, 1981.

_____, *Cost Structure of Manufacturing Industries*, Department of Communications, Ottawa, 1979.

Denny, M., J.D. May, and C. Pinto, "The Demand for Energy in Canadian Manufacturing: Prologue to an Energy Policy," *Canadian Journal of Economics*, May 1978, pp. 300-313.

Economic Council of Canada, *One in Three*, Ottawa, 1979.

Ellul, Jacques, *The Technological Society*, New York: Knopf, 1965.

Friedman, Milton, *Friedman on Galbraith and on Curing the British Disease*, Vancouver: Fraser Institute, 1977.

Forrester, Jay W., *World Dynamics*, Cambridge: Wright Allen Press, 1971.

Galbraith, John Kenneth, *The Affluent Society*, Boston: Houghton Mifflin, 1958.

Gamma, Université de Montréal-McGill University, *The Selective Conserver Society*, Montréal, 1977.

_____, *The Physical and Technological Constraints*, Montréal, 1976.

_____, *The Institutional Dimension*, Montréal, 1976.

_____, *Values and the Conserver Society*, Montréal, 1976.

Goldman, Marshall I., "The Convergence of Environmental Disruption," *Science*, vol. 170, October 1970, pp. 37-42.

Grubel, H., and S. Sydney Smith, "The Taxation of Windfall Gains on Stocks of Natural Resources," *Canadian Public Policy*, Winter 1975, pp. 13-29.

Hardin, Garrett, *Exploring New Ethics for Survival: The Voyage of the Spaceship Beagle*, New York: Viking Press, 1972.

_____, "The Tradegy of the Commons," *Science*, December 1968.

Hayek, F.A., "The Non Sequitur of the Dependence Effect," *Southern Economic Journal*, 4, April 1961, pp. 346-348.

_____, "The Use of Knowledge in Society," *American Economic Review*, September 1945, vol. XXXV, pp. 519-30.

Hilton, George W., "A Time to Choose as Economic Thought" in *No Time to Confuse*, M.A. Adelman et al., San Francisco: Institute of Contemporary Studies, 1975.

Johnson, H.G., *The Canadian Quandry; Economic Problems and Policies*, Toronto: McGraw-Hill, 1963.

Klein, Burton H., *Germany's Economic Preparations for the War*, Harvard University Press, Cambridge, Mass.: 1959.

Knight, Frank H., "Some Fallacies in the Interpretation of Social Cost," *Quarterly Journal of Economics*, 38, 1924, pp. 528-606.

Lerner, Abba P., "The Economics and Politics of Consumer Sovereignty," *American Economic Review*, 62, May 1972, pp. 258-266.

Lindbeck, Assar, *The Political Economy of the New Left*, New York: Harper and Row, 1971.

Mason, E.S., "Resources in the Past and for the Future" in *Resources for an Uncertain Future*, Charles Hitch, ed., Washington: Resources for the Future, 1977.

Meadows, Donella H., Dennis L. Meadows, Jorgen Randers, and William W. Behrens III, *The Limits to Growth*, New York: Universe Books, 1972.

Mills, E.S. and L.J. White, "Government Policies Toward Automotive Emissions Control," in *Approaches to Controlling Air Pollution*, Ann F. Friedlaender (ed.), Cambridge: MIT Press, 1978.

Mishan, E.J., *Growth: The Price We Pay*, London: Staples, 1969.

Mumford, Lewis, *The Myth of the Machine*, New York: Harcourt, 1967-70.

Nef, John U., *The Rise of the British Coal Industry*, London: Routledge, 1932.

Nordhaus, W.D., *The Efficient Use of Energy Resources*, New Haven: Yale University Press, 1979.

_____, "The Demand for Energy: An International Perspective," International Institute for Applied Systems Analysis *Proceedings of a Workshop on Energy Demand*. Laxenburg, Austria, May 1975, p. 588. Cited in Darmstadter *et al.* p. 197.

Pigou, A.C., *The Economics of Welfare*, London: Macmillan, 1918.

Pindyck, R., "Interfuel Substitution and the Industrial Demand for Energy: An International Comparison," *Review of Economics and Statistics*, May 1979.

Rydenfelt, Sven, "The Rise, Fall and Revival of Swedish Rent Control," in *Rent Control: Myths and Realities*, Walter Block, ed., Vancouver: The Fraser Institute, 1981.

Samuelson, Paul A., *Economics* (10th edition), New York: McGraw-Hill, 1976.

Science Council of Canada, *Conserver Society Notes*, Ottawa, October 1975-Summer 1977.

_____, *Canada as a Conserver Society: Resource Uncertainties and the Need for New Technologies*, Ottawa, 1977.

Sims, William H., "The Response of Firms to Pollution Charges," *Canadian Journal of Economics*, February 1979, Vol. 12, No. 1, pp. 57-75.

Smith, Adam, *An Introduction to the Nature and Causes of the Wealth of Nations* (1776), New York: Modern Library, 1937.

Spry, Irene, "Consumer Interest and the Future of the Economy," *Science Forum*, October 1976, pp. 19-22.

Stephenson, James B., *Practical Application of Economic Incentives to the Control of Pollution*, Vancouver: University of British Columbia Press, 1977.

Tietenberg, T.H., *Emissions Trading*, Washington: Resources for the Future, 1985.

Waverman, Leonard, "The Two Price System in Energy: Subsidies Forgotten," *Canadian Public Policy* (1975), vol. I, pp. 76-88.

West, E.G., Michael McKee, *Minimum Wages: The New Issue in Theory, Evidence, Policy and Politics*, Ottawa: Economic Council of Canada-Institute for Research and Public Policy, 1980.

Chapter 2

Natural Resources and Transgenerational Equity

Thomas E. Borcherding

Should [parks] be a playground for today or a paradise (i.e. wilderness) to be set aside for all time?
> —*PBS , "National Geographic Special: Playground or Paradise" (1983)*

We will move systematically to reduce the vast [federal] holding of surplus land and property.
> —*Ronald Reagan, 1983 Budget Message*

They paved paradise / And put up a parking lot.
> —*Joni Mitchell song, "Big Yellow Taxi"*

Honourable Intentions Not Sufficient

Like it or not, we are living, as Irving Kristol (1978) notes, in an "entitlement society." Here, attendant social costs are either ignored or deemed worthwhile in pursuit of that hackneyed good, "equity." Equity, ancient and contemporary philosophers tell us, has to do with individuals receiving what they "ought," rather than what they "will" obtain. Kristol has noted, however, that honourable intentions in these matters of redressing moral desserts are not sufficient. Baser egoistic motivations may direct policy and unintended and unpleasant consequences may spill over as well. In short, politics may "pollute" the social order, to use Professor Dwight Lee's apt analogy (1982).

The narrower theme of this paper concerns the possibilities and consequences of redistribution between the generations via ownership and control of natural resources. This will emphasize the question of excessive cost of self-interested redistribution (feigned altruism). But it will more sharply consider the several frustrations to collectivized charity that have, to my mind, not been noted in the social scientific literature on this subject, though they have in other contexts.

Government Ownership and Regulation

To illustrate my thinking, I will draw largely upon examples from two important attempts to alter the time path of resource use by public policy. One is the issue of public ownership of U.S. federal lands. This includes the U.S. national forests, parks, recreation and wilderness areas, and federal monument lands, as well as untold federally owned acres of grazing lands, watershed areas, mineral and wildlife reserves, and so forth. A second policy instrument example, government regulation, is the encompassing California Coastal Act of 1976.

I chose these because of my previous work on the latter subject (Borcherding, 1976) and a long and wide interest in the former (directed, unintentionally, by the director, co-director, and associates of the Center for Political Economy and Natural Resources in Bozeman, Montana). As well, I shall draw occasionally on evidence based on Canadian policy with respect to oil, both at the level of the provincial government (the Alberta Heritage Savings Trust Fund) and inferentially, the federal government (Petro-Canada Ltd. and the Canadian National Energy Program). (See Borcherding, 1983).

This paper is organized into four remaining sections. In the next, I consider the question of allocating natural resources and the employing institutional means to realize efficiency ends. In the third section, some issues of intratemporal equity are developed (i.e., distributional considerations confined to the current generation). In the fourth section, the intergenerational problem is considered at some length. Finally, in the last section V a few comments, speculations, and suggestions are made on the whole question of natural resource policy.

Allocative Efficiency and the Property Right Structure of Natural Resources

The love of Nature among Californians is desperately moderate.
—*John Muir, My First Summer in the Sierra (1869).*

Contemplation of the world's disappearing supplies of minerals, forests and other exhaustible assets has led to demands for regulation of their exploitation. The feeling that these products are now too cheap for the good of future generations, that they are being selfishly exploited at too rapid a rate, and that in their excessive cheapness they are

being produced and consumed wastefully has given rise to
the conservation movement.
—*Harold Hotelling, "The Economics of Exhaustible
Resources," Journal of Political Economy (1931).*

We know in general that even well-functioning complete
markets may fail to allocate resources properly over time.
The reason, I have suggested, is because, in the nature of the
case, the future brings no endowment of its own to whatever
market actually exists.
—*Robert M. Solow, "The Economics of Resources or the
Resources of Economics," American
Economic Review (1974).*

Though the above quotation by Hotelling could have been taken from a recent publication of Friends of the Earth or the Sierra Club, it was taken from a 1931 journal edited then, as now, at the University of Chicago. It represented, as Solow's 1973 American Economic Association's Ely Lecture (Solow 1974) does today, the intellectual mainstream view on natural resources that takes as given that private ownership forms fail to allocate resources optimally over time. Furthermore, both statements imply there are better methods of making temporal resource decisions. Those methods are, of course, ones that employ various methods of government intervention—fiscal and regulatory. That this view is not universally shared is obvious to the student of today's literature in the areas called the economics of property rights and public choice economics. I hope to discuss the main currents of this heterodoxy.

The arguments developed in this section do not relate directly to the question of equity. But the tight interdependence of allocational and distributional considerations makes it necessary to consider the former, for no one suggests that equity ought to be pursued without regard to costs and benefits.

Three Sources of Market Failure?

Generally, public intervention in the resource area is urged to correct various private market impedimenta. These cause the future use of a resource to be undervalued and, perforce, its current exploitation to be excessively encouraged. We shall consider three supposed sources of natural resource market failure.

Time Preference and Rationality

The first problem derives from the supposed upward bias in the private discount rate. Armchair economists, especially the Victorian English doctors of my science (Jevons, Sidgwick, Marshall, and Pigou), took it as given that man was "myopic," or irrational, in his preference for goods and services at present, instead of in the future. This unwillingness to pay a dollar today for a dollar received tomorrow or even more distantly was thought of as a moral imperfection. It meant that people did not treat each moment of their lives as equally important. Today, few take this criticism seriously. Not even the professed liberal and Nobel-anointed economist Kenneth Arrow (1976) holds that people are irrational because they exhibit such a preference for present over future.

Two reasons are often given for this. First, if human nature is generally myopic, there is little that the enlightened can or even should do. After all, *degustibus non est dispuntandum*. This has another implication, as well, that I call "liberal resignation;" namely, this psychic bias, if there really is one, must carry over to decisions in all institutional forms, collective as well as private ones. Second, even if this "myopic" time preference did not affect savings decisions, there still would be the positive productivity of capital to consider. Thus, even if the quantity of savings were totally unrelated to the interest rate, a positive rate of discount would still emerge because of the positive productivity of investment at the margin.

In fact, new studies by Johnson and Libecap (1980) establish that timber markets are "efficient," since they exhibit characteristics consistent with rational decision-making. Berck (1979) offers evidence suggesting that the implicit before-tax rate of discount is only 5 percent. Since Arrow (1976) suggests that 10 percent is the upper-bound of the socially efficient rate, this can be taken as evidence that the future values of resources are being properly weighed vis-à-vis its current use.

Perversities of the Tax System

Tax systems certainly can affect the timing of resource exploitation. The value of a resource in the future is its gross value in that market less all expenses incurred in its capture and delivery. This net sum is discounted from each future period by the ratio $(1/1+r)^t$, where r is the discount rate and t the number of years from the present into the future. Thus, if a resource had a net future value of $10,000, but r is 0.05 (there is a 5 percent discount rate) and t is 10, its present value would be only $6,139.

Tax considerations will, of course, decrease this value, but since they lower the present value of exploitation today, there need be no distortion here, at least none unique to natural resources (Harberger 1974a; 1974b). Suppose, for instance, there is an x percent tax on net returns. If it applies in the current period, t = 0, as well as the future period mentioned, where t = 10, then the optimal time for exploitation will not change. Both values will be depressed by the same percentage. If, however, "depletion allowances" encourage present over future realizations, what is one to say? If the fiscal arm of the government is subsidizing too early usage of a non-renewable natural asset, is one to suggest creating another public agency or regulatory enterprise to correct this bias? In fact, this sleight-of-the-visible-hand is suggested by many policy-oriented analysts, e.g., the Club of Rome (Borcherding 1976). But, of course, a more sensible solution is amending the source of the misallocation, the tax law itself.

Problem of the "Commons"

The third putative source of misallocation is the problem of the "commons." Here incomplete, even absent, private ownership of a resource makes a claim on all or part of its income flow difficult, if not impossible, to enforce. Garrett Hardin's "Tragedy of the Commons" analysis (1968) is widely known. Let me offer a short example. Suppose that there are n private users of a forested area. Each carefully considers the cost of cutting today or tomorrow and the attendant returns on his share of the resource. Since there is no reason owners should be systematically biased in their individual judgements, the outcome is one that maximizes the overall timber resource.

Now assume, however, there is a watershed system, very large compared to the individual ownership packages, that will be degraded as a result of the timber harvesting. Each owner will not consider erosion and flood risk from his clear-cutting, because these effects spill mostly into the commons, i.e., onto the lands of the other $n-1$ owners. Of course, if each of the other owners could enforce his right to maintain soil quality on his own parcel, this would not be the case. In the commons example, however, such precise definition and enforcement of private property rights is not possible because of expensive private legal costs.

The typical solution offered to this "commons tragedy" is either to regulate property or collectivize it. The thought of privatizing the resource by creating larger scale units and thus taking them out of the commons, or more clearly specifying individual property rights, has not been considered by the public at large. (Sell-offs of U.S. federal public lands in smaller chunks in a Reagan programme now known as "Asset Management" is receiving widespread discussion, but hardly much public acceptance (Hales, 1982)).

The problem with regulation or socialization is that these solutions involve putting property into the "political commons." As has been documented, the costs of public ownership of property (Borcherding 1982, 1983) and public regulation of private land are quite high. These "solutions" encourage new sorts of misallocation as individuals strive to appropriate and employ publicly-owned resources for their own narrow ends. Usage in the political commons dissipates wealth as surely, and perhaps even more completely, as in the anarcho-private commons. This is now well understood (Buchanan *et al.*, 1980). Such "rent-seeking" proclivity, the quest for publicly-provided transfers, is encouraged by the instrument of public lands and government regulation of private natural resources. This occurs to such an extent that those who have studied the question in depth, (Baden and Stroup, 1981; Beckwith, 1981; Smith, 1981; Smith, 1982) have suggested a European-type solution. There, rights to private land are both more encompassing over area and more detailed than in North America. The state could persuade owners, by use of easements, to take into account certain remaining commons values, such as amenity and fugitive wildlife considerations. Efficient contracts to preserve scenic and recreational values could be arranged through user charges in ordinary markets. This follows because many of these values are private in nature, so they involve little spillover to non-users.

This private contracting assumption is quite controversial, however, for "users" are hard to identify and even define. If a person never uses recreational or wildlife areas, but still places an "option" value in knowing that they are there, how could a private entrepreneur capture these ephemeral, but perhaps sizeable, benefits?

For this reason, Stroup and Baden (1982) have suggested that title to certain key wilderness endowments and other federal monuments be transferred to private non-profit organizations such as Friends of the Earth, the National Wildlife Association, the Sierra Club, and the like. These societies would have the right to partition the property rights of these resources still further into sub-uses. They could sell or lease some of the more atomistic rights to private users. Since these latter benefits would redound to the association in question, there would be more attention paid to the marketable aspects of the resources than is currently shown by the U.S. Department of the Interior and the U.S. Forest Service. As well, preservationist values would still be taken into account.

Many have noted the cost of "political pollution" of the current regimen. Studies have been done by Resources For the Future and middle-of-the-ideological-road author Marion Clawson (1982), as well as by those of more libertarian persuasions, such as Gordon Tullock (1982) and Barney Dowdle (1981). These scholars find that the land ownership of the U.S. federal government, 20 percent of all land and 25 percent of all forests, has a 1983 market value of between 0.5 to 1.5 trillion dollars. This amounts to $3,500 to $10,000 per U.S. family. Incredibly, the absolute returns today on the marketable rights of the land and natural resources are not even zero, but negative, by about one billion dollars (Dowdle 1981).

Government Land Ownership Excessively Wasteful

What accounts for this massive waste? Several reasons have been given by Tullock, Dowdle, V. Smith, Baden (and others at the Center for Political Economy and Resources), Clawson, and myself to explain this scandal. First, the lack of close political oversight by voters, the general interest group, is obvious for well-known reasons. It does not pay any unorganized individual to become informed when he has little influence over political outcomes. Thus, ignorance by the general group of their individual and collective interests is a hard cost to overcome.

Second, and following from the first, special-interest groups concerned with environmental concerns are over-represented because of the organizational economies they enjoy. The diffuse and general group is too impotent to gain political attention, although President Reagan is certainly trying (Hanke, 1982), with no great success. However, small interest groups facing big per capita gains can impose huge aggregate losses on groups larger in numbers, but smaller in per capita terms.

Third, public managers are sensitive to politically derived criteria of success, not to changes in market-equivalent social wealth. The cost of public enterprise is almost always 20 to 100 percent higher than its private equivalent (Borcherding, 1982, 1983). No public manager thinks this is wasteful, however, for those cost differences represent transfers to politically advantaged interests that monitor him as closely as capital markets mind the managers of private firms.

Finally, public officials and public managers are much more shortsighted than private owners and their agents. The insecurity of public office gives the elected official only a temporary usufruct over state property. It is personally prudent, i.e. rational, for him to concentrate mostly upon the here-and-now. The public manager, because of obedience to his elected masters, reflects this temporal myopia as well. That "holding off" use today implies smaller agency budgets than current exploitations certainly reinforces this obedience. Were public officials and managers able to capitalize future usage values, this would not be such a problem. But if this ever came to pass, the system would be more akin to private ownership (with different owners) than it would be to regulation or public enterprise.

Let us briefly consider regulation over privately owned property—an obvious alternative to public ownership. California's Coastal Act of 1976 and its regulatory commissions have been studied closely and provide some evidence as to efficacy. Hazlett (1980) found that this gargantuan zoning act has led to huge social losses, since the transfer of coastal property from lower to higher valued uses has been considerably impaired by CCA enforcement. Particular users have been protected, but at excessive costs, for Coastal Act commissioners, like public enterprise managers, are sensitive to political, not market, considerations (Frieden, 1979).

The Intragenerational Equity Issue

For it is easier for a camel to go through a needle's eye, than for a rich man to enter the kingdom of God.

—*Gospel of St. Luke, 19:25*

> The more one considers that matter, the clearer it becomes...
> Redistribution is...less a redistribution of free income from
> richer to the poorer, as we imagined, than a redistribution of
> power from the individual to the State.
> —*Bertrand de Jouvenal, The Ethics of*
> *Redistribution (1951)*

> If somebody can afford to drive from New York City to
> Yellowstone, they can afford to pay more than $3 per carload.
> —*"Interior's James Watt—Hero or Villain?" U.S. News*
> *and World Report (June 6, 1983)*

Public Ownership and Social Goals

One cannot come away from perusing studies of the allocative effects of the socialization of natural resources, by public enterprise or by regulatory fiat, and feel confident that the sum of social incomes are enhanced by employment of these instruments. As Professor Armen Alchian (1977) of U.C.L.A. has noted on a number of occasions, this substitution of public for private property rights considerably attenuates the incentive to count costs fully of those charged with managing the resources. As well, special interests are disproportionally rewarded when political assets dominate market consideration. This is not in and of itself a bad thing, e.g., if social goals were enhanced that could not otherwise be attained privately. For instance, military tactical/strategical decisions and their attendant operations could, in principle, be contracted out to private firms. The difficulty for legislatures in writing and enforcing efficient contracts with private suppliers, however, makes a political solution employing a public defence department more palatable. This is true even though "everyone knows" how inefficient military bureaucracies are. The loss associated with high supply cost is thought to be more than made up by benefits of political control on the policy side of the equation. (How vertically integrated defence departments should be below the policy formulation level is, however, a matter of some contention (Borcherding, 1982, 1983).)

An Outstanding Price

There is, as one can imagine, much dispute over the optimal way natural resources should be directed. It is clear, however, that many of the public goods involved—clean air, watershed and wildlife management, parks, etc.—could be, and have been, privately managed by individuals either as owners or as managerial agents contracted by public authorities. The price paid for U.S. public management of public lands is simply astounding. It is at least equivalent to the foregone income that could be earned on dividends, a present value of between $0.5 to $1.5 trillion U.S. Still, if there are some desirable offsetting income distribution effects, perhaps this socialization of ownership could be accepted. This would mean, of course, that (a) there is some general agreement about what is an equitable distribution of income and (b) the economic altera-tions accomplished by the public means actually redistributes according to the ethical criteria developed in (a).

I will not attempt to do even a thumbnail sketch of modern theory of income distributional ethics except to say that variants of the "justice as fairness" methodology developed by philosopher John Rawls (1971) seem to have gained the greatest scholarly acceptance. Essentially, this approach asks people to choose rules for redistribution based on their enlightened self-interest. To affect such a motivation individuals are asked to choose these rules behind a "veil of ignorance" in a pre-social contract setting. Thus, redistribution becomes a type of social insurance to avoid the consequences to individuals from dreadful and unforeseen alterations in social states. The detailed operation of this fairness principle, a willingness of men "to share one another's fate" (Rawls, 1971), is a matter of much debate. A huge body of literature has developed around its interpretations. Nevertheless, one restrictive ethical consensus does emerge from these writings: the state should not be used to transfer income from the less advantaged to the more privileged.

Conservationist Policies Favour the Wealthy

On this last criterion, public natural resource policy looks rather piratical when only the current generation is considered. As conservation historian Samuel Hayes (1959) notes for the past, and Hazlett's aforementioned review of the California Coastal Commission indicates for the present, the effects of conser-vationist policies decidedly favour the wealthy to the detriment of the poorer classes. As illustration, Frieden (1979) points out two interesting things about the Sierra Club, one of the oldest of all environmental pressure groups (founded 1890). First, it is decidedly urban and upper-middle class in its composition. Second, and more to his point, its membership has clearly indicated in surveys (60 percent in agreement) a complete disinterest in the environmental problems of the urban poor or disadvantaged ethnic majorities in non-urban settings. Deacon and Shapiro (1975) and Shapiro and Barkume (1974) give ample evidence for this with respect to the operation of California's Coastal Act and Santa Barbara's environmental zoning regulation. The rich gain, the poor pay in a sort of inverted social democracy.

Why is this? Public choice scholars point out that in an orderly society the state is the only legitimate means of redistributing income and individuals in cohesive groups will employ it for their own selfish purposes. The "suppliers" of these redistributions, the victims in the general group, are, perforce, less cohesive. In the present case, the poor—i.e., the social group with much lower than median family incomes—are at an added disadvantage when dealing with the more patrician group. The latter enjoy superior access to information channels and better social and political "connections" in general. It is reinforced by the political indifference of the lower income group, manifested by their lower rates of political participation. Lewis Lamphan puts it unequivocally: "The environmentalist movement is a rich man's cause... The Club of Rome discovered the limits of growth while gathered on the terrace of a villa overlooking the hillside belonging to its founder" (Hazlett, 1980). Frieden is even more blunt when he refers to the Sierra Club as the "alter ego" of the California Coastal Commission staff.

Intergenerational Equity

For they all seek their own...
—*St. Paul, Epistle to the Philipians, 2:21.*

Now the contract doctrine looks at the problem from...the original position. The parties do not know to which generation they belong... The veil of ignorance is complete in these respects. Thus the persons in the original position are to ask themselves how much they would be willing to save at each stage of advance on the assumption that all other generations are to save at the same rates. That is, they are to consider their willingness to save at any given phase of civilization with the understanding that the rates they propose are to regulate the whole span of accumulation.
—*John Rawls, Theory of Justice (1971).*

One problem with this new political alliance (environmentalists and wealthy homeowners) is that it lends the legitimacy of an environmental crusade in the public interest to what is otherwise a selfish and provincial concern.
—*Bernard Frieden, The Environmental Hustle (1979).*

Resource Policies Hinder Future Generations

A typical statement of aim to help future generations by current environmental and natural policy can be found in the preamble to any agricultural land conservation act. Keeping land in agriculture via restrictions on its transfer to other uses is said to ensure against later "shortages" and the attendant price increases in agriculture products that a free market would otherwise permit. Consider a clear statement found in a 1979 study by the National Agricultural Lands Study group and cited by Pasour (1982):

How can we direct urban development to less productive acres, and thereby protect our irreplaceable prime farm land acres from further encroachment? (p. 739)

The Advantages of Private Markets

Most economists would suggest that private markets be employed in this regard, for the greed of private owners will lead them to consider the value of land assets both in their agricultural use and in alternative occupations. Bureaucrats and politicians, on the other hand, will consider the political returns in each alternative use, now and later. As I have stated earlier, however, congruence between political payoffs and underlying social values is tenuous, though there are those (e.g., Solow (1974) and Bjork (1980)) who hold that land and resources markets are even poorer co-ordination proxies.

We shall not for the moment press those who claim that we need more "planning" (public planning, that is) and greater government ownership and regulation of natural resources. Let us grant them the premise of their argument and ask instead if their preferred policies will really transfer income from the current to the future generations. Suppose one assumes that these various strains of natural resource policy do, in fact, create net wealth for the next generation. All would then agree, I believe, that these current collective acts represent increments of social savings in the form of public bequests. But these changes are closely interrelated to private bequests and, following Becker (1974), will affect the decisions of individuals in the current generation to pass on their private wealth. I would predict, however, that members of the current generation finding themselves forced to make putatively efficient savings through public means will choose to consume more of their private assets today to offset the additional public bequest.

Let us give an example of this substitution. Suppose individual A planned to bequeath an asset worth $1,000 to his heirs, B, in a future generation. The state intervenes and creates a political instrument that transfers $100 to B. In such a case, A will tend to amend his will and leave B a bequest of only $900 (perhaps a bit more, as he feels wealthier by this efficient state intervention).

Of course, if we drop back into the real world of the fallible and venal polity, these offsets may not be dollar for dollar. Actually, they could be the very opposite. If the state offers B $100 but in the process takes $200 from A in an inefficient intergenerational transfer scheme, A will reduce his bequest by more than $100 as he is now a poorer man and poorer men tend to leave smaller estates. Since the likelihood of inefficient intergenerational transfers is at least as high as efficient ones, a dollar-for-dollar substitution is a very conservative expectation.

But this covers only the "supply side" of the public/private savings/invest-ment decision. If one considers the substitution effects among the private demanders of investment, another sort of problem ensues.

The Offset Problem

There are a great number of "hard" and "soft" magazines—running the gamut from the *Journal of Land Economics* to *National Geographic*—that deal with this question. They tend to assume that a public decision that increases agricul-tural land and wilderness areas, or perhaps stretches out the timber-harvesting cycle over a longer period, is the equivalent to an increase (or a reduction in its depletion) in that type of resource for society as a whole. As in Genesis (41:1-57), where Joseph's dream led to net accumulation of grains and storable foods during the seven years of plenty, these writers believe that their visions—or more to the point, those of some government bureaucrats and officials—are neither shared nor considered by non-governmental decision-makers.

That may have been the way the world worked in the Egyptian proprietary state of Pharoanic times, but it certainly is not the way it works now. Suppose private investors put away a silo full of corn with the expectation that it will be worth something more than the various holding costs (including forgone interest). If so, a public decision to supply another silo of grain for future sale will tend to lead private investors to reduce their accumulation by one silo's worth. Thus, the market will offset many resource investment decisions under-taken by the state.

There are two exceptions to this investment substitution effect: one is when the public accumulation of resources (or its equivalent, the postponement of resource consumption) is socially worthless, i.e., it is viewed by the market as having a zero supply effect. The second is when the accumulation involves a resource that is valuable, but would not be provided in the absence of govern-ment intervention by private suppliers. Clearly, fishing and hunting areas, grazing lands, parks and recreation areas, and mineral developments are *not* in this second category (perhaps wilderness areas, too, though I would not press this without more study). It follows, in general, I believe, that except where there are real public goods involved, not those provided by private suppliers, private resource investment offsets will occur. To what degree this charac-terizes the bulk of U.S. federal lands I cannot venture with great certainty, other than to harken back to Clawson, Dowdle, Stroup, Baden, and Tullock, who argue that federal lands are largely an inefficient instrument of redistribution involving very private goods.

The Curmudgeon

Thus, it seems difficult to pass on net assets to the future generations beyond those that individuals as family members desire. What, however, of individuals who do not care one way or another about future generations and plan no bequests? Will they not have their "share" of public assets transferred to the future generations by the aforementioned public natural resource policies? I am not sure they will, since these politically created transfers have current asset complements whose prices ought to rise.

Consider, for example, a public park. Its creation raises the value of private inputs used in conjunction with the park, e.g., motels, restaurants, and stores. People must have places to eat, sleep, and, because of their propensities "to truck, barter and exchange," to shop as well. Thus, things that enhance the future value of a public park raise the future value of those complementary activities consumed along with park services. It follows, therefore, that some of those future transfers will be recouped by the current generation in the form of higher current asset values. Some of this group, indifferent to future generations, will reduce their savings for their old age, hence public transfers are again, at least partially, self-limiting.

The Alberta Heritage Savings Trust Fund

One particular form of social savings is worth looking at with this simple economics in mind—Alberta's Heritage Savings Trust Fund (Alaska's smaller, but still significant, Permanent Fund could be similarly analysed). Alberta has received considerable revenues from its publicly-owned oil leases and royalty receipts. Rather than distributing all of this resource income to its current citizenry, the AHSTF was created (a) to spread these benefits temporally between current and future citizens and (b) to reduce risk over time by investing the undistributed earnings in private activities outside the resources area.

About the success of the second aim, I shall not comment, except to say that a host of political constraints have made the realized rate of return to the AHSTF considerably less than prudent individual investors would generally earn (Mc-Millan and Norrie, 1980; Scarf and Powrie, 1980).

As for (a), it is becoming obvious that distribution to future generations is virtually a hopeless task. To obtain the current and future benefits of the fund, one must only become a citizen of the jurisdiction. Since citizenry in a province is available to any immigrant who is a citizen of the larger Canadian federation, the limiting in-migration factor is the rising price of housing and other amenities that are complementary with state/provincial citizenship. As well, there is the reduction of wages which cheapens Alberta exports.

Owners of specific capital complementary to in-migration labour have clearly gained a great deal. Thus land, capital, and labour market price changes capture and often capitalize much of the future transfers. This offsets the efforts of this petroleum wealth jurisdiction to transfer benefits to future generations. Because real resources are used in the migration process, however, much of the value of the AHSTF is dissipated by migratory rent-seekers. Thus, there is little in the way of net future transfer, but a great deal of inefficiency in its pursuit.

McMillan and Norrie (1980) ask, sensibly, why is it that a collective decision has been made to transfer ownership of Alberta's petroleum resources so inefficiently from present to future generations, since this is a futile and probably wasteful endeavour? Their answer is that public allocation allows greater control over the resources by bureaucrats and special interests. Consequently, this enhances their respective wealth positions more than would an outright privatization.

As an interesting aside, Alaska opted in referendum for a complicated distribution of its Permanent Trust Fund to its existing citizenry. This, however, was seen as violating U.S. and state constitutional guarantees of non-discrimination between citizens. Thus, U.S. courts have acted to maintain the resource in the political commons, instead of a partial privatization.

The present discussion does not preclude the possibility of a collective (public good) motive for state resource redistributions to the future (Marglin, 1963). However, following Tullock (1964), I doubt this motive is very strong. Individuals as members of families already bequeath a great deal of property to their own progeny. Thus, for whatever reasons—cultural altruism and/or genetic selfishness—individuals act as if they subscribe to the Rawlsian intergenerational contract.

But why would such motivation to engage in intergenerational charity extend beyond the family unit ? After all, in a society where the Bs of my previous example are on average much richer than the As, the impetus for A-type individuals of one family group to give to B-type persons in another family unit is probably rather small. The poor do not, voluntarily at least, feel it incumbent upon them to contribute to the rich. Thus, my second question, "Should the current generation publicly provide for the future generation?", would seem to be answered in the negative.

The Morality and Economics of Redistribution

In much of the literature on other aspects of government intervention, the moral as well as economic difficulty of affecting public redistributions of wealth is now a major theme. These concerns link rather well, if not seamlessly, predictive economics with the modern theory of ethics. This holds whether one assumes a Rawlsian pro-redistributional setting or one based on Nozick's radically restrained concept of the "limited state" (Nozick, 1974). They all remind me of a much earlier prediction by one of the founding members of the Mont Pelerin Society, Friedrich A. Hayek (1960). This nicely combines the liberal-individualistic ethics, which are part of the new moral philosophy, with the hard-nosed economics of contemporary public choice/property rights analysis:

> The principle of distributive justice, once introduced, would not be fulfilled until the whole of society was organized in accordance with it. This would produce the kind of society which in all essential respects would be the opposite of a free society—a society in which authority decided what the individual was to do and how he was to do it. (p. 100)

Social theorist Irving Kristol subscribes to this Hayekian hypothesis. His theme in "Two Cheers for Capitalism" (1978) could be summarized as follows: social democracy that intends to collectivize the market sector in the name of redistributional equity, while maintaining a vigorous and competitive polity, is bound to disappoint its advocates. The coercive power necessary to realize the former distributional end is bound to spill over and reduce the vigour of democratic politics.

This "Road to Serfdom" (Hayek 1944) is mercifully reached slowly, but it follows from the economic principles of general equilibrium that if goals of redistribution are not rather modest, their consequences will be realized sooner or later. Those who advocate a further transfer of ownership and control of land and other natural resources to the state should consider the side-effects of their ethical distributive policy preferences more carefully. These transfers are, on the whole, not only allocationally inefficient, but distributionally perverse.

Poetry and Reality

> In wilderness is the preservation of the world.
> —*Henry David Thoreau, Walden (1854).*

> Today, unfortunately, we have two extreme and needlessly hostile groups: Those who speak scornfully of the "wilderness cult" and consider wilderness value a witless return to primitivism, and those who talk about "escaping to the wilderness" as if all man-made landscapes were false and ugly.
> —*Paul Brooks, Speaking for Nature (1971).*

> If men agree on rights, the problem of social order is largely resolved.
> —*James M. Buchanan, "Utopia, the Minimal State and Entitlement," Public Choice (1975).*

Leftist Theory—and Reality

When I was a young man in graduate school (and still a happy pro-interventionist), I asked a question of one of my wisest and most distinguished professors: Why do all the good folk songs not connected with love and death have leftist themes? I do not recall his answer as being very satisfactory, possibly because this scholar was not much addicted to coffee house or beer parlour music. But the answer is clearer to me today. Poetry need not be constrained by reality. Individuals dealing with "free" resources or the equivalent, resources that are not their own, are like poets treating a fanciful subject—sentiment counts, cadence counts, texture and form counts, but substance becomes a boring, extraneous detail.

Rational expectations, on the other hand, naturally dominate where participants are regularly subjected to reality testing. Where links between action and payoffs become more tenuous, the social play between perceptions and reality becomes much greater and theories become more romantic.

Special interests use such slack in understanding to their advantage. In contrast, "honest" political entrepreneurs representing the general interest have a hard time gaining credence for their arguments in a world where almost everyone is dissembling. Not only is it difficult to distinguish their messages as authentic, they have a great deal less incentive to produce them, since truly general interests payoffs are so hard to capture by the politician who seeks them.

Nonetheless, society does pay for thinking on policy subjects, or "preaching," as George Stigler (1982) calls it. Suggestions for superior institutions sometimes do emerge from the subsidized pens of academics or the responsible and highly charitable gentleman-scholar. Unfortunately, most such musings are useless, silly, or even fraudulent. None offers any warranty, nor are they actionable when they prove positively destructive.

Suggestions for Reform

Thus, it is with some trepidation and even less expectation that I offer even modest suggestions for reform in the natural resource policy area. I take several things as given, over which my audience will be forgiven if they quibble. First, like it or not, resources now in the political commons are really "owned" by special interest groups who will not willingly give them up without compensation. Second, compensation to these "owners" in order to accomplish real reform is quite difficult. When a compensation plan is announced, many "non-owners" will feel the call to collect. Third, the average citizen never clearly sees the gain that accrues to him from politically altering the rules of conduct. This is a perception based on a host of past disappointments. The general citizenry's expectations are particularly low. This is understandable in light of the deception practised by special-interest advocates parading their proposals as furthering the common weal.

Thus, I believe that acceptable reforms will hardly ever be radical in such a world. My suggestions are very limited indeed when compared with those of experts in the field, such as Richard Stroup and John Baden (1982), Gordon Tullock (1982), and Vernon Smith (1982). Mine are closer, I am sorry to say, to those of the more pragmatic Resources For the Future and Marian Clawson (1981).

Proposals for the Future

I propose a hodgepodge of alterations. These include a small initial sell-off, just as President Reagan originally suggested. This is especially targeted toward local users (ranchers, farmers, fishermen, miners, foresters, etc.) who have had virtual squatter's rights for some time (Smith 1982). As these modest sales are perceived by the public to "work," resistance to further disposals will be reduced. In addition to these sales, I would endorse transferring ownership of a great deal of the U.S. federal domain to the states, as the Sagebrush Revolutionaries demand. I have no illusion that state bureaucrats and legislatures will be careful and prudent agents of management; I have lived too long in Canada, where Crown lands are largely under provincial domain to believe that. It will, however, encourage state-wide experimentation in development of resources, which should make eventual privatization easier.

Finally, I think it is realistic (politic) to recognize the power of the grand coalition of environmental groups in setting policy over wilderness and wildlife areas. We should follow Stroup and Baden's suggestion and transfer management ownership to such organizations (Stroup and Baden, 1982). As they point out, the Rainey Wildlife Sanctuary of the National Audubon Society is generally deemed superior to its state and federal government counterparts. Other lucrative activities compatible with the Audubon's mandate are carried out on this property, since these revenues enhance the Society's wildlife preservation mission. One can even visualize a type of competitive bidding and operation of many of the U.S. wilderness and wildlife areas by various conservation pressure groups that approximates Demsetz's scheme for public utilities (Demsetz, 1968).

The "Trickle-up" Effect

None of these three proposals is liable to transfer a great deal more to future generations. By enriching the current generation through the reduction of inefficient intragenerational transfer, however, it is more likely to be more generous with future generations. Like it or not, with intergenerational decisions all society really has is this "trickle-up" effect.

Sir Henry Maine notes that the march of civilization is slow and marked by a progression from societies based on status to those based on contract. In point of fact, societies are for a number of historic, cultural, and political reasons mixtures of status and contract, depending on the activity in question. Passage of time can be associated with all sorts of changes, depending on alterations in the factors that determine the cost of social contracting. Property in North America, John Hughes (1977) suggests, was for a number of legal and populist-oriented constraints put into the political commons, but nonetheless most has been privatized.

That one-quarter to one-third of that property is still "publicly owned" is understandable, given the costs to those special interests that realize implicit and uncompensated capital losses from privatization. Thus, just as with Zeno's paradox, society may be able to realize only a portion of the potential larger product by alternating the employment of publicly owned or regulated assets. As long as pathways to realization of efficiency gains are constitutionally protected by competitive political institutions, and as long as individuals are reasonably trustful of each other, privatization will continue.

If I read the Bozeman writers correctly, however, they fear that political competition has been stifled or severely attenuated by a sort of environmental oligopoly. Thus, it is depressing to consider the limited scope of improvement possible in any society, but only because of rational individual impatience (time preference). The pay-offs to the present generations are never very high from any real long-term improvement. Instead, they come in distant times and in unexpected ways. It is these future improvements that are the true public goods that can be collectively transferred to following generations. As individuals representing the current cohort, the best we can do is to propose improvements cheerfully and "conservatively"—and not be offended when our suggestions are ignored.

References

Alchian, Armen A., *Economic Forces at Work* (Indianapolis: Liberty Press, 1977).

Arrow, K. A., "Risk Perception in Psychology and Economics", *Economic Inquiry* (January 1982).

_____, "The Rate of Discount for Long-Term Public Investment." In *Energy and the Environment*, H. Ashley *et al.* (eds.),(New York: Pergamon, 1976).

Baden, J., and R. L. Stroup (eds.), *Bureaucracy vs. Environment: The Environmental Costs of Bureaucratic Governance* (Ann Arbor: University of Michigan Press, 1981).

Becker, G. S., "A Theory of Social Interactions", *Journal of Political Economy* (December 1974).

Beckwith, J. P. Jr., "Parks, Property Rights and the Possibility of the Private Law," *The Cato Journal*, (Fall 1981).

Berck, P., "The Economics of Timber; A Renewable Resource in the Long Run," *Bell Journal of Economics* (Autumn 1979).

Bjork, G., *Life, Liberty and Property: The Economics and Politics of Land-Use Planning and Environmental Controls* (Boston: Lexington Press, 1980).

Borcherding, T. E., "The California Coastal Plan as a Statewide Zoning Ordinance." In *The California Coastal Plan: A Critique*, E. Bardach *et al.* (San Francisco: Institute for Contemporary Studies, 1976).

_____, "Toward a Positive Theory of Public Sector Supply Arrangements." In *Crown Corporations in Canada: The Calculus of Instrument Choice*, J. R. S. Prichard (ed.) (Toronto: Butterworth, 1983).

_____, *et al.*, "Comparing the Efficiency of Private and Public Production: A Survey of the Evidence from Five Federal States," *Journal of Economic Theory*: Public Production (Supplement, 1982).

Buchanan, J. M., *et al.* (eds.) *Toward a Theory of the Rent-Seeking Society* (College Station: Texas A & M University Press, 1980).

Clawson, M., "Public Lands Revisited." Unpublished ms. (Washington, D.C.: Resources For the Future, 1981).

Deacon, R., and P. Shapiro, "Private Preference for Collective Goals Revealed Through Voting on Referenda," *American Economic Review* (December 1975).

Demsetz, H., "Why Regulate Utilities?," *Journal of Law and Economics* (April 1968).

Dowdle, B., "An Institutional Dinosaur with an Ace: Or, How to Piddle Away Public Timber Wealth and Foul the Environment in the Process." In Baden and Stroup (1981).

Hales, Linda, "Who is the Best Steward of America's Public Lands?" *National Wildlife* (April 1983)

Frieden, B., *The Environmental Protection Hustle* (Cambridge: M.I.T. Press, 1979).

Hanke, S. H., "The Privatization Debate: An Insider's View", *The Cato Journal*, (Winter 1982).

Harberger, A. C., "The Taxation of Mineral Industries." In Harberger, *Taxation and Welfare* (Chicago: University of Chicago Press, 1974a).

_____, "The Tax Treatment of Oil Exploration." In Harberger, *Taxation and Welfare*, (1974b).

Hardin, G., "The Tragedy of the Commons", *Science* (December 13, 1968).

Hayek, F. A., *The Constitution of Liberty* (London: Routledge and Kegan, Paul, 1960).

_____, *The Road to Serfdom* (London: Routledge and Kegan Paul, 1944).

Hayes S. P., *Conservation and the Gospel of Efficiency: The Progressive Conservation Movement*, 1890-1920 (Cambridge: Harvard University Press, 1959).

Hazlett, T. W., *The California Coastal Commission and the Economics of Environmentalism* (Los Angeles: International Institute for Economic Research, May 1980).

Hotelling, H., "The Economics of Exhaustible Resource," *Journal of Political Economy* (April 1931).

Hughes, J. R. T., *The Governmental Habit* (New York: Basic Books, 1977).

Johnson, R. N., and G. D. Libecap, "Efficient Markets and Great Lakes Timber: A Conservation Issue Reexamined," *Explorations in Economic History* (No. 2, 1980).

Kristol, I., *Two Cheers for Capitalism* (New York: Basic Books, 1978).

McMilan, M. L., and K. H. Norrie, "Province-Building vs. A Renter Society", *Canadian Public Policy* (February 1980).

Marglin, S. A., "The Social Rate of Discount and the Optimal Rate of Investment", *Quarterly Journal of Economics* (February 1963).

Nozick, R., *Anarchy, State and Utopia* (New York: Basic Books, 1974).

Pasour, E. C., "Agricultural Land Protection: Is Government Intervention Warranted?" *The Cato Journal* (Winter 1982).

Rawls, J. A., *Theory of Justice* (Cambridge: Belknap Press, 1971).

Scarf, B. L., and T. L. Powrie, "The Optimal Savings Question: An Alberta Perspective", *Canadian Public Policy* (February 1980).

Shapiro, P., and A. Barkume, "Political Choice and Environmental Quality", in *Economic Analysis of Pressing Social Problems*, L. Phillips and H. L. Votey Jr. (eds.) (Chicago: Rand McNally, 1974).

Smith, R. J., "Resolving the Tragedy of the Commons by Creating Private Property Rights in Wildlife", *The Cato Journal* (Fall 1981).

Smith, V. L., "On Divestiture and the Creation of Property Rights in Public Lands", *The Cato Journal* (Winter 1982).

Solow, R. M., "The Economics of Resources or the Resources of Economics," *American Economic Review* (May 1974).

Stigler, G. J., "The Economist as Preacher". In Stigler, *The Economist as Preacher and Other Essays* (Chicago: University of Chicago Press, 1982).

Stroup, R. L., and J. Baden, "Endowment Areas: A Clearing in the Policy Wilderness?", *The Cato Journal* (Winter 1982).

Tullock, G., "Comment: The Social Rate of Discount and the Optimal Rate of Investment", *Quarterly Journal of Economics* (May 1964).

_____, "The National Domain and the National Debt." Unpublished ms., 1982.

Chapter 3

Natural Resource Scarcity, Entrepreneurship, and the Political Economy of Hope

John Baden
and
Richard Stroup

> If present trends continue, the world in 2000 will be more crowded, more polluted, less stable ecologically, and more vulnerable to disruption than the world we now live in. Serious stresses involving population, resources, and environment are clearly visible ahead.
>
> —*The Global 2000 Report*[1]
>
> Fortunately for this planet, these gloomy assertions about resources and environment are baseless. The facts point in quite the opposite direction.
>
> —*Julian Simon*[2]

For the last two centuries, the pace of economic and technical advancement has been staggering, especially in North America; and the decisions we make are becoming ever more critical. The potential rate at which wealth can increase is mushrooming, but so is our ability to cause unintended and unwanted secondary effects, such as toxic wastes. Will the finite supply of resources constrain our growth, leading to the grim, polluted future predicted by the doomsayers? Or will the hope and optimism of which Simon spoke be captured by ingenious decision-makers so that we can continue to enhance our wealth and well-being?

It is our thesis that those with entrepreneurial energies and abilities largely determine the fate of a society. When these "movers and shakers" are free to operate, and when they have personal responsibility for their actions, they can be a powerful force for progress. When these same individuals confront a command-and-control environment, however, they are likely to use their talents to seek the same personal goals, but rarely in a socially constructive, truly entrepreneurial manner. When resources are owned or controlled by the state, it is inevitable that the system's formal goals will be subverted as these individuals seek and gain discretionary command over resources without having to obtain voluntary consent from those who pay.[3] Further, when property rights can be transferred coercively by imposing taxes or regulations, rent-seeking competition becomes far more destructive than market-bidding competition, in which the loser tears up his rejected check or seeks another buyer.

A Contrast

Nowhere is the contrast between political and private regimes greater than in the natural resource arena, and nowhere can better illustrations be found to show that individual freedom and full decision-maker responsibility are required to succeed in a changing world. The management of natural resources, which is so important to our material and aesthetic well-being, provides case after case to support this thesis.

In this chapter, we first discuss the Progressive Era and the continued influence of its ideas on those who manage our natural resources and those who profess to care about the environment. We then suggest that a system of marketable, privately held property rights, even though it may increase the number of "wrong" decisions made, is likely to keep the cost of errors low while providing a very high rate of innovation and a rapid spread of successful innovative practices. We will also show that there is reason to believe that while entrepreneurs in the private sector have much to gain by acting in a predictable, principled manner, such behaviour is extremely expensive in a political setting.

Next, we examine how allowing failure to occur in the market can lead to environmentally and economically sound resource management. We then discuss examples of resource management relevant to our argument. As well, we illustrate the prevalent "doomsday" view and explain its utility to those who favour governmental management of resources. The "counsel of doom" programmes and the "zero sum society" myth are, we argue, the most dangerous ideas extant. They legitimize envy, negative-sum coercive institutions, and the destruction of the entrepreneurial environment that is critical to solving the problems they decry. Finally, we discuss how a political economy of hope can be used to protect and foster the institutions that are necessary for the existence of individual freedom and responsibility.

Ideology and Collective Resource Control:
The Progressive Doctrine

Much of the rhetoric associated with scarcity has its roots in the Progressive Era, when conservation first became a truly "social" movement.[4] When

Theodore Roosevelt entered the White House, Progressive conservationism found its first bureaucratic niche. Gifford Pinchot, director of the Bureau of Forestry, led the movement to graft the conservation ethic, which was steadily building a bureaucratic constituency, onto Progressive ideology. This, in turn, stressed the finite nature of natural resources that had become apparent to some when the American frontier was officially declared closed in 1890. Technological and social changes led many to believe that a major problem for society was how to divide the pie equitably, rather than how to increase it. The Progressives anticipated Lester Thurow's "zero-sum society," and like Thurow, they failed to acknowledge that labelling a society "zero sum" converts it to negative sum due to the rent dissipation associated with dividing the spoils.[5] Here, rent dissipation has three elements: rent-seeking activities, such as lobbying; static inefficiencies (so-called welfare triangles); and dynamic losses brought on by the inability of entrepreneurs to gain access to resources in a straightforward manner.

Historians have explained the environmentalism associated with the Progressive Era in two ways: as a democratic movement and as a scientific movement.[6] The latter is more important for this paper, since it had the most effect on how resources were to be managed. The primary spokesmen for the Progressive conservation movement were scientists and technicians who developed and implemented the conservation policy that became known as scientific management.

The supporters of the scientific approach to managing natural resources claimed that most of the problems associated with allocation and use could be solved by political, unselfish, technically competent bureaucrats insulated from profits and politicians, armed with the latest scientific knowledge, and charged with managing for the public good.[7] The policy that emerged from these beliefs represented a major shift away from the ongoing privatization of the public lands and toward its preservation by relying on governmental management of America's natural resources.

Science Run Amok

The reforms advocated by those in the movement supposedly would eliminate the "pillage and rape" attitudes held by those citizens who, some believed, were exploiting the country's resources for private gain, replacing them with governmental, scientific stewardship. The Progressives did not consider an alternative explanation for the exploitation; that is, that resource problems were generated by poorly defined and enforced property rights and, hence, were the result of governmental failure. Roy M. Robbins has summarized the Progressive view:

> No nation in world history had so wasted its natural resources
> or opened up its natural treasure to unbridled exploitation as

had the United States of America, but a halt had been called.
The grizzled hardheaded pioneer of the American West and
the evergrasping corporations stood face to face with the
challenge of a new American order which demanded an end
to the reckless and wasteful methods of the era of *laissez-
faire*. The task which remains was not only to recover lost
ground, and to preserve the fragments of what was left, but
also to educate the public in the intelligent use of the remaining resources...but governmental authorities insisted there
was still much good land left and that immediate steps should
be taken for its protection.[8]

Bernhard Fernow, a colleague of Roosevelt's and author of the first American
text on forest economics, gave the Progressives an economic rationale for
supporting public management:

The natural resources of the earth have in all ages and in all
countries for a time at least been squandered by man with
wanton disregard of the future and are still being squandered
wherever absolute necessity has not yet forced a more careful
utilization.

For private enterprise knows only the immediate future
and has only one aim in the use of these resources. Namely
to obtain from them the greatest possible personal and
present gain.[9]

A Critique

It was not until the late 1950s that systematic critiques of Progressive conservation were forthcoming. In 1958, Scott Gordon separated economics and
ideology and provided an analysis of the conservation problem.[10] He noted that
conservation policy had been a product of "passionate romanticism," which
rarely leads to "rational policies." He attacked the optimists, who "failed to see
that when a resource has the character of a fixed stock...it follows necessarily
that every use diminishes the remaining fund," and the pessimists, who "are
left unimpressed by the history of man's success in discovering new resources
to take the place of the old."[11]

The key to Gordon's analysis lies in demonstrating that in most cases the
application of elemental capital theory answers the "conservation question."
As Thomas Borcherding explains, the issue of the proper allocation of resources
over time is imbedded in the conservation question.[12] It has taken decades to
develop a basic understanding that "the optimum is achieved when the marginal
productivities of the different factors are equal."[13] Traditional resource
managers must make a great leap to understand that, for example, the socially

efficient harvest rule maximizes net present value, not biomass or some other biological measure.

When dealing with timber and rangelands, the Progressive conservationists believed that markets could not account for future demands and that, as a result, resources would be exhausted prematurely. When dealing with water and energy conservation, however, the conservationists feared that private markets could not generate enough capital to adequately develop the resource. Further, they saw the free-enterprise system as chaotic and inequitable and believed that only by turning resources over to governmental agencies could the abuses of the free-enterprise system be curtailed.

Market Not Lawless

Terry Anderson and P.J. Hill have demonstrated, however, that the frontier was hardly as wild and lawless as many Progressives believed.[14] Further, Gary Libecap and Ronald Johnson found that even though conservationists reasoned that a forest reserve system was necessary because of timber fraud and theft in the Pacific Northwest, "costly federal land policy encourage[d] fraud and theft" in American forests.[15] Governmental policy ignored the economics of scale associated with logging by legally restricting timber land claims to under 160 acres. As rational businessmen, timber operators invested in skirting the law to establish legal claims to tracts that were large enough to be economically viable. In essence, federal restrictions increased the transaction costs of establishing property rights to timber and, thus, resulted in rent dissipation activities.[16] Given a vacant economic niche and an opportunity to increase economic co-ordination, entry men became middlemen who established legal rights to land, and then deeded those rights to their employers. These policies postponed the development of secure property rights and prolonged the period of common property, contributing to the timber theft that was used by conservationists to justify the creation of the national forests.[17]

In examining the allegation that markets were unable to halt increased scarcity and that profit-seeking timbermen would deplete the resource, Johnson and Libecap found that the timber market operated in ways that were consistent with the efficient market hypothesis and that future demand and supply conditions were accurately estimated.[18] The timbermen did harvest with future relative scarcity in mind: "Wealth maximization does not, in general, imply that growth should equal cut except at some steady state solution."[19] Given the huge inventory of mature, stagnant, and overmature timber in North America during the 19th century, downward inventory adjustment was a rational management technique. Johnson and Libecap demonstrated that when entrepreneurs can make property rights secure, markets "develop early and effectively to allocate resources over space and time."[20]

Rational Timber Harvest

In a companion study, Peter Berck found that timber harvest rates by private operators in the Douglas Fir region were also conducted at a rational level.[21] Timber harvesters discounted future value at a real rate of 5 percent, a lower rate than was available for most other private investments. We must conclude, therefore, that owners did not cut their forests prematurely and that the repeated predictions of a timber famine have been, and still are, ill-founded.

The same kind of analysis has been applied to range conservation. Libecap's *Locking Up the Range*, an analysis of federal rangeland controls, identified insecure property rights as the cause of many range management problems, such as overstocking and under-investment in productivity-enhancing activities.[22] Again, rent dissipation is linked to the 160-acre limitation on private claims to arid western rangeland. Federal range policy increased the cost of establishing property rights and prolonged the overgrazing problems that are inevitable on property held in common. Under-investment in the form of insufficient cross-fencing, water development, seeding, and so forth can be explained by the tenuous nature of the property rights, which were subject to vacillating policies of bureaucratic management. The insecurity of property rights prevented markets from moving resources to their highest valued uses.

Water

The analysis can be extended to the area of water use and allocation. In *Water Crisis: Ending the Policy Drought*, Anderson demonstrated that the private sector was competent to develop those water resources that merited development.[23] The Progressives' concern that the market was unable to adequately develop water resources in the west is simply unfounded, and their insistence that government intervention was the only rational solution has only exacerbated the growing crisis in water supplies. Entrepreneurs are too often dissuaded by obstacles erected by federal, state, and local institutions that keep water from being allocated to its highest valued uses.

The ideas and ideology of the Progressive Era provided an ideological foundation for adventurous political operators, who embrace any plausible excuse to expand governmental power on behalf of their client groups in response to perceived or projected scarcities. Opportunism provides at least a partial explanation for using natural resource policy issues to expand the coercive sector of the polity.

Entrepreneurship and the Ordeal of Change

If we think of entrepreneurship in a generic sense—that is, as imagination and alertness coupled with the willingness to risk, the requisite energy, and the ability to assemble resources—then potential entrepreneurs are always with us.

Even in a mixed economy, individuals seek to express their will and improve their lot. What entrepreneurs do, we submit, determines the fate of society. It is they who select and offer for our selection branches of the social decision tree. If they, their clients, and their employees act as free and responsible individuals, logic and history indicate that good choices will seldom be passed by and bad ones will seldom persist. If individuals are not free to choose, or if they are not held personally responsible for their wins and losses, however, then only pessimism is justified.

Entrepreneurs see opportunities to solve problems or to create progress and follow up with action. To be successful, an entrepreneur must have much more than the imagination to envision new alternatives and the alertness to match resource allocation alternatives to opportunities. Adding the willingness to risk an investment of time, energy, and effort is not sufficient either. A successful entrepreneur must also be able to marshall resources. This often requires not only a good idea, but the ability to convince others (e.g. bankers, investment firms, or buyers of penny stocks) that the idea deserves their capital investment. This combination of talents is rare, but to varying degrees it exists in every economy. What is missing in most economic systems is a way to allow entrepreneurs access to capital while holding them and their backers accountable for the resources they place at risk.

Problem-solving

In capitalist economies, we accomplish these goals through private property rights and market transactions. Any entrepreneur can attempt to convince any financier, investor, or resource owner of the soundness and profitability of his proposal. If the proposal does increase the value of resources by solving a problem or expanding opportunities, investors should profit. Only when all resource uses are perfectly co-ordinated to provide maximum value from our resource base do profitable opportunities vanish. F.A. Hayek and others have explained why this will never happen, in our society or in any other.[24]

The entrepreneur is a specialist who is able to perceive and act on previously unnoticed opportunities.[25] Entrepreneurship is a creative activity whose net result is to create value, and in the process, produce free lunches for others. This by no means implies that entrepreneurs act out of charity or good will, although these motives may exist. The entrepreneur takes an existing batch of resources—natural and otherwise—combines them in innovative ways, increases their value, and receives a profit for doing so. While the entrepreneur is often concerned with production processes, he or she must also be sensitive to current or prospective consumer demands, institutional opportunities and constraints in the private and public sectors, information, and transaction costs.

Entrepreneurs appear to represent a disequilibrating force in traditional economies and an equilibriating force in modern societies. In both cases, however, the entrepreneur is a disturbing creature—an agent of change whether moving from an old equilibrium or to a new one. For those interested in increased general welfare, entrepreneurs are our most valuable citizens.

General Electricity

Suppose that an individual sees a problem and a potential solution. However, the necessary resources to solve the problem are in the hands of government. In this case, resource allocation decisions will probably differ from those made in a similar, privately controlled situation. Consider the case of electric power generation capacity in the Pacific Northwest.[26] Many industry analysts in the 1970s believed that demand would outstrip the fixed supply of inexpensive hydroelectric power, most of which was marketed by the Bonneville Power Administration (BPA), a federal agency. This would be a problem because the power was priced far below the cost of adding new power. Several solutions were suggested, including a market-clearing price increase and capacity investments based on returns implied by the higher rates. A combination of conservation and capital expansion would then have solved the problem, but that option was politically infeasible. Those with access to the cheap power were politically well-organized and simply would not allow it.

Alternative methods could have been used to approximate the efficient market outcome. Instead of raising rates to market levels, allowing users to trade their rights to the power could have raised the value of that power (its opportunity cost) to existing users, even though the cash flow to BPA would remain constant. Users would be able to sell their access rights and each transacting party would gain. Buyers would purchase power from BPA only at prices at or below the cost of alternative new generation, and sellers would sell only when conservation was cheaper. Substantially more efficient processing techniques are available in the aluminum industry, for example, which is the largest consumer in the region. Utilities could have adopted rate structures to keep average bills at the same level for those with constant use rates, while charging more for marginal power used or saved. This would have encouraged conservation and allowed utilities to market their access rights at a profit, resulting in lower user bills. But this arrangement would expose the implicit subsidies in the low BPA rate structure and, thus, was also politically unacceptable. Since the utility companies currently cannot gain by selling conserved power to others at a profit, they do not do so.

Preventing Entrepreneurship: The WPPSS Case

In this environment, entrepreneurs could find little reason to find and sell ways to conserve electricity. Instead, political operatives had incentives to find ways to help their clients get or retain access to the cheap power. Another political institution was spawned; public utilities in the region joined with BPA to form the Washington Public Power Supply System (WPPSS), or "Whoops." Backed by the seemingly endless potential of BPA to raise its rates "if needed," the combine contracted for and (mis-)managed a series of five financially disastrous nuclear plant projections. Early plans called for a total cost of $4.1 billion. By 1981, the cost estimate was $23.8 billion. None of the directors or managers had their own resources directly on the line, and the results reflected this fact.

As costs ballooned, the utilities refused to come up with further funds. Finally, they decided to back out of the arrangement and refused to pay back bondholders. They simply reneged. Court battles are now being fought over these decisions and will probably continue for years. The utilities argued that they really did not have the authority to sign the agreements they signed; in effect, they had acted illegally. The desperation of the utility managers, presumably necessary for such drastic action, is partially explained in the following:

> The bonds began falling due in 1977, when the first reactor was scheduled for completion. And even though the reactor wasn't finished—which meant it wasn't generating any electricity to sell—bond payments still had to be made. Those payments didn't come out of the salaries of WPPSS executives or administrators; instead, they came out of the pockets of BPA ratepayers. BPA simply jacked up the prices it charged for electricity; after only three minor price hikes in forty years, BPA announced successive 88 percent and 53 percent increases in one disastrous six-month period. Electric bills are projected to rise fivefold within the coming decade. A family of four in a utility district committed to all five reactors is now responsible for a median indebtedness of between $27,000 and $30,000 for WPPSS construction costs alone.[27]

Misallocated Resources

Clearly, the way in which a resource is handled can lead to a bonanza, as it did for some years even in federal hands, as long as plenty was available at a cost that was at least less than its replacement cost. When political operatives controlled the resource, however, disaster was only a few years in coming. Due to its low price, and the inability of decision-makers (e.g., users) to gain by transferring rights to higher valued users, electricity was squandered in relatively low-valued uses. Even worse, the potential revenues were used to "guarantee" the cost of some irresponsibly planned and executed projects. In the end, it bought tens of billions of dollars worth of trouble. The cause, most simply, was the lack of marketable rights.

Entrepreneurs could not control the resource and move it to higher valued uses. Private owners of such rights would not pledge their value to expensive projects without carefully examining the options. In this case, had conservation been properly encouraged by a rate structure or opportunity costs that reflected the true value of the electricity, the nuclear plants probably would not have been planned for this century. A private owner would not have allowed such underpricing, or if he found himself in a long-term contract at very low prices, he would have simply offered to renegotiate, buying back some of the power and selling it to a customer who valued the energy more. The original buyer then would have captured a share of the profit.

Had BPA power been privately controlled, offers to buy hydropower would have impressed upon its owners the fact that co-ordinated resource usage had not yet been achieved. Potential users placed higher value on the power than was obtained by its price to the chosen users. Privately determined electricity prices would have reflected its opportunity cost at the margin. Mismanagement and mistaken forecasts would have been detected sooner and acted upon quickly to protect the decision-makers' wealth. Offers made to buy and sell—that is, market prices—would have provided both information and incentives, motivating and co-ordinating producers and consumers of electricity in the region to act in full consideration of one another with the aid of profit-seeking entrepreneurs. Instead of entrepreneurship, the political environment for electric power in the Pacific Northwest has produced recriminations, excuses, and litigation.

The Importance of Failure

When entrepreneurship flourishes, failure is common. Information is scarce and costly, and predictions are uncertain at best. Successful entrepreneurs need to be innovators, operating on the edge of knowledge. Thus, frequent miscalculation and failure are expected consequences of an open economy. To become averse to risk is to eschew the greatest potential profits.

How failure is handled and the extent to which it is tolerated are critical matters. Progress would be slow without failure, but it would also be slowed if too many resources were devoted to failing projects. Thus, early warnings and the incentive to kill failing projects are required if resources are to be allocated efficiently. Since those who successfully launch projects are likely to be "true believers" and enthusiasts, their decision to abort an enterprise is especially painful. When the investors' own wealth is at stake, however, the grip of reality is relatively secure. A strong, personal financial interest focuses the decision-maker's attention on relevant financial issues. As Kenneth Arrow has suggested, only those whose reputation and financial assets are on the line can be trusted to make good investment decisions.[28]

How quickly will appropriate, successful innovation be spread through the economy? When early adoption is the only chance for profit, as in the marketplace where competition is open, decision-makers gain from being alert and copying the innovation of others. Once again, a personal, financial stake spurs alert, sound action.

"Crackpots"

A key element in a successful market system with privately held property rights is the access to resources it provides even to "crackpots". A mere handful of investors—who may be bankers, institutional investors, professional financiers, corporations, or buyers of penny stock—are sufficient to finance the implementation of a new idea. Since each decision-maker invests his own capital, and since society as a whole is not investing, there is no need for a majority of voters, their representatives, or "the experts" to be convinced of a proposal's promise. Direct, personal responsibility begets and legitimizes individual freedom to act, even if the majority believes the proposal to be insane or irrelevant.

The planet is dotted with expensive "dry holes" drilled in search of oil. But those who were able to spot good prospects, whether by skill or "good luck" (which is not randomly distributed), have become wealthy in money and reputation, giving them increased discretionary command over investment resources.

Synthetic Fuel Fiasco

From society's point of view, access to venture capital is distorted when coercively raised tax dollars are available to politically potent sectors and firms. The developers of synthetic fuel plants provide prime examples. Ventures that not only raise havoc with the environment, produce carcinogens, and voraciously consume scarce water, but that also are also privately shunned by just about every firm and sizeable investor group in the nation, were nevertheless given billions of dollars through the U.S. Synthetic Fuels Corporation (SFC).[29] A taxpayer-funded bureaucracy from its creation in 1980 until its demise in 1984, the SFC waltzed into areas where no privately accountable financial angel dared to tread. Financing decades-old, grossly inefficient technology with money raised in part by "windfall profit" and other taxes on successful energy producers, the SFC vividly illustrated how big engineering and energy firms can take investment capital from highly valued users to finance uneconomical projects.

Protecting a failing industry tends to be politically expedient in the short run, but it is painful and expensive over the long haul. Some of the best examples are the U.S. Forest Service's efforts to maintain "community stability" in declining logging and mill towns. While tariffs, quotas, and subsidies can protect a specific industry or location from the reality checks imposed by the market process, if it fails to make the adjustments required for success, it becomes less competitive with alternative suppliers and the deadweight social loss continues to grow.

Constraints on Resource Owners: The Love Canal Case

Along with the opportunity for profit in the market is the liability for losses. A special case is legal liability for pollution. When the size of damages, the pollutant, and the source can be identified, damages from pollution are typically actionable in court. The Love Canal situation provides a fine example of how private ownership leads to responsible action and how public ownership separates responsibility from authority, with potentially dangerous results.

When Hooker Chemical Company began using the old Love Canal as a waste dump, it was well-aware of its legal liability for potential future damages. For that reason, if no other, its managers took great care in lining the canal and sealing it against leakage of the chemicals to be stored there. The care exercised by Hooker was later nullified, however, when the local school board decided that the landfill Hooker had created over the canal was part of a tract of land they wanted for another school. Hooker, concerned by the potential problems with toxicity (and their legal liability), objected. Under threat of condemnation, however, they sold their landfill. Carefully noting in the transfer paperwork the dangerous potential of the landfill, Hooker bowed to governmental pressure and signed the papers.[30]

Years later, local government decided that the land not being used for schools could be sold to a developer, and housing was eventually constructed. The local government, meanwhile, had constructed sewers, which required digging through the sealed walls of the canal, seriously breaching them and producing leaks and contamination. When the story broke nationally, Hooker Chemical was made the villain. The local government's role, the intermediate ownership, and the blame for breaching the canal vessel was not reported, despite the many newspaper stories that appeared at the time of transfer when Hooker was under threat of eminent domain. Local officials could not be sued. They had no personal wealth or business reputation at risk. Only when *Reason Magazine* broke the story and ABC's "Nightline" picked it up did even a significant fraction of the U.S. population find out what had really happened.[31] Few environmentalists have yet recognized the true history of the case or its significance for the future.

Doomsday Literature as a Growth Industry

The "doomsday" literature, of which *The Global 2000 Report* is a federally sponsored example, has a long, though not very honourable, history. The "ain't it awful" view sells newspapers, books, and movies, and enables people to vent their anger and righteous indignation. The radical environmentalist draws attention to policy issues that, aside from a derivative entertainment value, would not normally command such attention. People naturally devote most of their serious reading time to issues that have more personal impact, such as the weather report or a *Consumer Reports* article. The individual does not have the remotest control over whether mankind will survive the next decade, and only if a report is sensational enough to be discussed over cocktails will it be scanned along with the ball scores.

From a politician's or ambitious bureaucrat's point of view, forecasting a timber famine (made recurrently for decades by the Forest Service), an energy crisis (by those who want to expand the energy bureaucracy), or a disastrous pollution problem (by those who want more power and budget for the EPA) is a way to win more attention, tax money, and coercive powers for the coercive governmental agencies.

Doomsday forecasts sell, despite a rather consistent record of failure:

> Take the Club of Rome's complex calculations of resource depletion, based on existing world reserves and rates of world consumption. It concluded, in 1972, that the world would run out of gold in nine years; silver, mercury, and tin within fifteen years; and oil in twenty. Now, let's see. Gold is still with us; no silver, mercury, or tin shortage is in sight; and if we were to repeat today the same calculations for oil, we'd have to conclude that the world has another thirty years' supply left. When the first calculations were made for oil, the world seemed to have only a nine-year supply left. That was in 1936. The problem with these exercises is that neither numerator nor denominator is fixed. Our horizon keeps receding as we approach it because both demand and supply—which in turn derive from taste, knowledge, technology, and substitution—are responsive to price change, a property not found in the world view of most computers or their catastrophist masters.[32]

On Environmental Forecasts

As recently as 1970, recalls John Silber in *Bostonia* magazine, *Life* reported that there was a probability that by 1980 urban dwellers would have to wear gas masks to breathe, by the early 1980s a smog inversion would kill thousands of people in some major city, and by 1985 the amount of sunlight reaching the earth would be reduced in half and new diseases that man could not resist would reach plague proportions. The Club of Rome's highly influential report, *The Limits to Growth*, based on a sophisticated computer study, predicted in 1972 that the combined effects of pollution, population growth, resource depletion, and industrialization would drive the world system to "the limits of the earth and ultimate collapse." A later version, Willy Brandt's "North-South Report," warned that the immiserization of the third world (the theory that supplants Marx's now defunct prophecy of the immiserization of the industrial working classes) would lead to catastrophic global war. And so on. The bibliography on the subject is so vast as to make one fear, at least, for our forests.[33]

When large gains are possible for the writers, publishers, and governmental promoters of such alarmist views, and when the intended audience—casual readers and voters—has no large personal decisions to make on such matters, we should not be surprised that each new set of alarms is received with serious consideration, each sinking only gradually from relatively informed conversation. Yet, while each new report remains "current," it is useful to those who seek to justify or retain agencies and authorities that limit voluntary responses. Wartime is the most time-honoured emergency. Just as President Carter asked Americans to consider the energy "crisis" as the "moral equivalent of war" so that he could preserve and expand politically attractive programmes, so do other interests use upcoming "emergencies" to legitimize otherwise unsalable programmes. These pose obvious dangers to freedom and responsibility.

The "Zero-sum Society" Myth

Related to the doomsday syndrome and even more hardy is the myth that each society plays a zero-sum game; that is, each winner must deprive losers of all the "winnings." Since there is no free lunch, what one person gains must be taken from others. This fallacy totally ignores improvements in efficiency, the "free lunch" that successful entrepreneurs provide. It ignores how any redistributionist policy imposes deadweight losses, not only operationally, but also in the rent-seeking that inevitably accompanies high-stakes political control over valuable resources. The erroneous view that production is a given, like manna from heaven, rather than created by human ingenuity and efforts, also legitimizes envy of the rich and successful—perhaps the most potent force behind the "levelling" forces thought to accompany governmental direction of the economy. In reality, of course, we know of no society in which wealth and political power are not correlated. Indeed, they most often reinforce one another.

Even Lester Thurow, author of *The Zero-Sum Society*, has argued that while government is good at handing out favours and the added product it has captured, it is not good at apportioning losses.[34] When a new market arrangement causes someone (perhaps a supplier in an old market) to lose, the government faces strong pressures to prohibit the change. The new beneficiaries, especially on the customer side, are seldom aware of the upcoming opportunity. Existing businesses and labour unions, however, usually keep close tabs on upcoming events. Once again, political operators frequently impose a "conservative" (anti-change) bias into markets that otherwise would be more dynamic.

Toward a Political Economy of Hope

The central theme of Earth Day was that there are significant trade-offs necessarily associated with America's traditional pattern of resource use. A substantial proportion of America's youth and many others concerned with preserving and protecting the environment claim that the environmental costs of free-enterprise significantly swamp the benefits it provides. The social cost of congestion, pollution, clearcutting, and population growth is increasingly recognized, while the market system is alleged to ignore future resource scarcities. Public opinion polls indicate that environmental concerns have displaced other policy issues in importance, and the political environment is changing as a reflection of deeply felt environmental concerns. In sum, environmentalism has become a genuine social and, for some, quasi-religious movement.

Along with the legitimate concerns people have for the future allocation and use of natural resources, many environmentalists who are trying to influence the political decision-making process are making claims that have no firm basis in fact. The first claim is that Americans are excessively and irrationally materialistic and self-interested. This is best demonstrated, they say, by their overwhelming acceptance of the automobile, which consumes valuable resources and degrades environmental quality. Unless American consumers are constrained by governmental edict backed by coercion, they will continue to consume too much of the wrong things at the wrong time in the wrong places. Prices are not viewed as even potentially legitimate mechanisms to reconcile private and social costs.

The second claim is that American business is mesmerized by current profits and is quite willing to sacrifice environmental health for corporate wealth. This is held to be evident in the continued production of dangerous chemicals, noxious smoke, and negative externalities in general. That there is a better explanation for the existence of such externalities—that is, that they are caused by government's failure to define and enforce property rights—is either not understood or deliberately ignored.

The third claim is that Americans stress property rights in ways that diminish social welfare. Private property is held to be the problem, not the solution. The argument is that if more management, ownership, and control of natural resources were given to public sector bureaucrats—those purported protectors of the public interest who do not profit from their decisions—then environmental quality and the public interest would be encouraged. By giving control to bureaucrats who lack the profit motive, public welfare would not be sacrificed for personal gain. The themes of the Progressives are being repeated.

A New Approach

In the mid-1970s, small groups of political economists centred in Montana, Chicago, UCLA, and the Public Choice Center began to devote attention to property rights as the key to environmental management. They rediscovered that the absence of clear, enforceable, and transferable property rights uniformly led to environmental problems with varying degrees of severity. The over-harvesting of such fugitive resources as buffalo in the 19th century and whales in the 20th and the over-exploitation of such common pool resources as air, groundwater, and oil pools were recognized as the result of governmental—not market—failure.

Using this perspective, property rights are simply a set of usage and exchange rights held exclusively by specified owners. Clearly defined and enforceable property rights are essential if any economy is to operate efficiently. Property rights determine how resources will be used and who will be allowed to use them. When property rights are privately held, owners are given the exclusive right to control and benefit from the resources they own as long as their actions do not impinge upon others.

It is important to understand that ownership does not entail the right to use that property in a way that is costly to others. The owner of a rifle and ammunition does not have the right to fire it at will; his rights are constrained by those held by others. Property rights, then, are viewed as a way for owners to be protected from the consequences of the actions of others, and offer the best assurance of responsible resource stewardship and environmentally sensitive development. In the area of natural resources, the absence of private property rights leads to politically and bureaucratically opportunistic management that may be articulately defended, but is commonly the antithesis of responsible behaviour using either environmental or economic criteria.

Bureaucracy

To recognize that bureaucracies are often the cause of environmental problems, one must begin with the assumption that bureaucrats are real people.[35] They are not selfless repositories of virtue and wisdom whose only mission is to advance the public interest. Bureaucrats appear to be approximately as self-interested as others, but they operate in an environment in which they are buffered and insulated from the negative consequences of their actions. Typically, bureaucrats are professionally motivated. Bureau of Reclamation professionals, for example, are said to have a "beaver complex," so strongly do they believe in the importance of building dams. They are not incompetent, wicked, or insensitive; they merely respond to the information and incentives they face, in light of the beliefs of their professional calling.

Bureaucratic entrepreneurs, elected politicians, and special-interest groups representing industrial or environmental concerns use the federal treasury as a common pool resource to advance their personal and professional goals.[36] Whether we are talking about the Forest Service terracing the Bitterroot Mountains in Montana and attempting to grow saw logs in Utah while old-growth federal timber rots in the Northwest, or the Bureau of Land Management chaining millions of acres of pinion-juniper forests in the Southwest to produce more grass, or the 18 separate agencies contributing to the destructive modification of the coastal barrier islands, the logic remains intact. None of these activities could be justified on either economic or ecological grounds, yet each was provided with millions of federal tax dollars.

In each case, subsidies drove the projects, and economic inefficiencies were compounded by environmental damage. In essence, money was taken from taxpayers to subsidize the destruction of environmental quality, which amplified the negative consequences of existing natural resource scarcities. Yet, there are grounds for optimism.

Optimism

In the western hemisphere, nations have been consciously created, and there are systematic variations in the degree to which they rely on property rights, the rule of willing consent, and the market process to allocate and manage resources. The correlations across nations and across national sectors provide powerful arguments that suggest the superiority of markets over governments, whether measured in terms of environmental quality, equity, or economic efficiency. Hope is predicated on the assumption that people learn; but the data are coming in. With a model to organize the data, we can draw some conclusions, some of which are truly optimistic.

When each public policy is viewed as an experiment, when we recognize that there are thousands of examples of governmental management of resources as individual experiments, and when we find continued, recurrent, and protracted failure, we must examine the alternatives. Even committed environmentalists who are the intellectual heirs of Progressive ideology and policy have begun to consider alternatives to the governmental model of resource management. The rule of willing-consent market-process alternatives has become increasingly attractive. While those active in the policy arena are seldom in the forefront of intellectual developments, they too are coming to recognize the potential of markets to manage natural resources in ways that are superior to that demonstrated by the government.

For many years, the ideal of governmental management has been contrasted with a distorted interpretation of actual private sector management. We are becoming more successful, however, in demonstrating how observed governmental failures are predictable consequences of institutional arrangements and how successful reform must depend on the information and incentives generated by alternative systems. Further, it is also being demonstrated that a private-sector, operating in an environment where the government defends property rights and provides mechanisms for adjudicating conflicts, provides the best recipe for progress. It is this evolutionary change that permits a rational being, who carefully segregates his hope from his expectations, to harbour a political economy of hope.

Notes

1. CEQ and Department of State, *The Global 2000 Report to the President*, Vol. 1 (Washington, D.C.: Government Printing Office, n.d.) p. 1.
2. Quoted in the *Washington Post*, May 30, 1983, p. A2.
3. *Forbes*, August 1983, pp. 64-67.
4. Research for this section was conducted by Dean Lueck while he was an Earhart Fellow at the Political Economy Research Center.
5. Lester Thurow, *The Zero-Sum Society*, (New York: Basic Books, 1980).
6. Samuel F. Hayes, *Conservation and the Gospel of Efficiency: The Progressive Conservation Movement, 1890-1920* (Cambridge, Mass.: Harvard University Press, 1959).
7. F.A. Hayek, "The Use of Knowledge in Society," *The American Economic Review*, 35 (September 1945): pp. 519-530; and Thomas Sowell, *Knowledge and Decisions* (New York: Basic Books, 1980).
8. Roy M. Robbins, *Our Landed Heritage: The Public Domain 1776-1936* (Princeton, N.J.: Princeton University Press, 1942), pp. 335-336.
9. B.E. Fernow, *Economics of Forestry* (New York: Thomas Y. Crowell, 1902).
10. Scott H. Gordon, "Economics and the Conservation Question," *Journal of Law and Economics* 1 (October 1958): pp. 110-121.1
11. Ibid.
12. Thomas E. Borcherding, "*Natural Resources and Transgenerational Equity*," op. cit., in this volume.
13. Ibid.
14. Terry Anderson and Peter J. Hill, *The Birth of a Transfer Society* (Stanford, Calif.: Hoover Institution, 1980).
15. Gary D. Libecap and Ronald N. Johnson, "Property Rights, Nineteenth-Century Federal Timber Policy and the Conservation Movement," *Journal of Economic History* 39 (March 1979): pp. 129-142.
16. Ibid.
17. For example, under the Timber and Stone Act the California Redwood Company spent $1,120 for a 160-acre plot, $400 of which was payment to the government and $670 of which was evasion costs. See ibid., p. 136.
18. Ibid.
19. Ibid.
10. Ibid.
21. Peter Berck, "The Economics of Timber: A Renewable Resource in the Long Run," *The Bell Journal of Economics* 10 (Autumn 1979): pp. 447-463.
22. Gary D. Libecap, *Locking Up the Range: Federal Land Controls and Grazing* (Cambridge, Mass.: Ballinger Publishing Company, 1981).

23. Terry L. Anderson, *The Water Crisis: Ending the Policy Drought* (Baltimore: John Hopkins University Press, 1983).
24. See Hayek, "The Use of Knowledge," and Sowell, *Knowledge and Decisions.*
25. Israel Kirzner, *Competition and Entrepreneurship* (Chicago: University of Chicago Press, 1973) p. 32.
26. Paul Lobe, "Going Broke on Atoms," *Inquiry*, Mar. 29, 1982, pp. 12-15.
27. Ibid., p. 13. See also David Shapiro, *Generating Failure: Public Power Policy in the Northwest*, (Washington: Cato Institute, forthcoming 1989).
28. *U.S. News and World Report.* Jan. 13, 1983, pp. 66-71.
29. Jonathan Lash and Laura King, eds., *The Synfuels Manual* (New York: National Resources Defense Council, 1983).
30. See chapter 6 for further elucidation of this point.
31. Eric Zuesse, "The Truth Seeps Out," *Reason* 12 (February 1981): p. 16.
32. Charles Krauthammer, "The End of the World," *The New Republic*, Mar. 28, 1983, pp. 12-13.
33. Ibid., pp. 14-15.
34. Thurow, *Zero-Sum Society.*
35. See John Baden and Richard Stroup, eds., *Bureaucracy vs. Environment* (Ann Arbor: University of Michigan Press, 1981); and John Baden, ed., *Earth Day Reconsidered* (Washington, D.C.: The Heritage Foundation, 1980).
36. Rodney D. Fort and John Baden, "The Federal Treasury as a Common Pool Resource and the Development of a Predatory Bureaucracy," in *Bureaucracy vs. Environment*, pp. 9-21.

Chapter 4

The Market Process and Environmental Amenities

Terry L. Anderson

Introduction

No other field of economic inquiry, with the possible exception of industrial organization, has focused more on market failure and its implications than has natural resource economics. In a leading textbook on the subject, Alan Randall states that:

> resource economics...raises questions about the effectiveness of existing market and institutional structure in allocating resources, in adjudicating among the claims of individuals in the present generation and adjudicating among the claims of present and future generations (Randall 1981, p. 42).

In general, resource economists have focused on problems of externalities and public goods. Solutions requiring governmental intervention are then proposed and analysed to determine what taxes, subsidies, and regulations will improve efficiency.

Starting from a perspective of Pareto optimality, most textbooks focus on why such an optimum will not or cannot be achieved through the market process. Charles Howe, for example uncovers what he believes to be a "number of reasons why even well informed competitive markets may fail to allocate resources in the socially, most desirable way over time." His list includes:

- Private markets are likely to overlook the values of environmental services related to stocks of *in situ* resources.

- Private interest rates are likely to be higher than appropriate social rates of discount.

- Common access to *in situ* resources may preclude the establishment of markets for these resources.

- Future production cost savings related to carrying stocks of *in situ* resources may be spread among many producers in common pool resources, causing producers to ignore or undervalue such savings (Howe 1979, p. 103).

- Monopoly will generally result in quite a different time pattern of resource use than a competitive market, but this pattern may be closer to the optimum pattern than the competitive one.

In general, most of the arguments on market failure centre on the divergence of private and social discount rates or private and social costs. Following a Pigovian tradition, economists have tended to see externalities as pervasive cases of market failure calling for governmental intervention. In the textbook that dominated college courses during the 1960s and 1970s, Paul Samuelson states that:

> Wherever there are externalities, a strong case can be made for supplanting complete individualism by some kind of group action... The reader can think of countless...externalities where economics would suggest some limitations on individual freedom in the interest of all (Samuelson 1980, p. 450).

From this perspective, it has been easy to justify governmental intervention in the allocation of almost all natural resources, including land, air, energy, timber, water, and agriculture. Unfortunately, "the Pigovian analysis contains an implicit bias toward 'intervention solutions' for externalities in the form of taxes, subsidies, regulations and prohibitions" because it suggests "that externalities necessitate 'corrective' government action" (Burton 1978, p. 90).

This approach has recently been criticized and challenged. Stimulated by Ronald Coase's article, "The Problem of Social Cost," economists have begun to incorporate property rights and transaction costs into their analysis of market processes. Particularly in the fields of industrial organization, public choice, and economic history, this new brand of institutional economics is generating a body of literature that is changing the way we think about government and its role in the market system.

This paper will attempt to help expand the list of such fields to include natural resource economics. A few economists are beginning to recognize the importance of the new institutional economics to the study of natural resources, and the result is an emerging new resource economics paradigm (see Anderson 1982). The next section of this paper briefly states the elements of the new paradigm. The third section provides examples of how the new institutional economics can be applied to resource problems. It suggests alternatives to the interventionist solutions derived from the Pigovian analysis, and presents evidence that market processes can provide environmental amenities.

The New Resource Economics

In examining the "myth of social cost," Steven Cheung concludes that:

> The question is...why public policies exist in the way they do and why they vary in different economic systems. The answer to this question of the economic interpretation of political behaviour requires an understanding of the real-world constraints relative to government decision-making. A recent shift of interest in that direction and a growing recognition of the importance of the analysis of politics, presage a new momentum in the development of economics, particulary in industrial organization, public choice and economic history (Cheung 1978, pp. 67-68).

These fields place emphasis on the relationships between principals and agents and the effect that transaction costs have on these relationships. As a result, economists are rethinking the concept of monopoly, reconsidering the behaviour of bureaucracies, and asking how and why institutions change over time.

Even more recently, natural resource economists have begun to apply the transaction cost/property rights tool to their analyses. Antony Fisher captures the essence of the change:

> We have already abandoned the assumption of a complete set of competitive markets...but if we now similarly abandon the notion of a perfect planner, it is not clear, in my judgement, that the government will do any better. Apart from the question of the planner's motivation to behave in the way assumed in our models, to allocate resources efficiently, there is the question of the ability to do so (Fisher 1981, p. 54).

The new institutional economics approach is giving the kind of rigorous, theoretical, and empirical attention to governmental failure in natural resource allocation that previous efforts following the Pigovian tradition have given to market failure. Using this approach, it is clear that

> it is not sufficient to compare the performance of either the market or a non-market mechanism against an "ideal," "optimum," or "theoretical" standard and conclude that it is inappropriate for policy purposes. Market "failure" in some abstract sense does not mean that a non-market alternative will not also fail in the same or in some other abstract sense (Castle 1965, p. 552).

Methodological Individualism

The new resource economics begins with the individual, especially the entrepreneur. Following marginal analysis, entrepreneurs search for situations where marginal benefits exceed marginal costs. As they respond to opportunities, the system moves closer to equilibrium. The question is whether the opportunities they discover and the actions they take will increase wealth for society or simply redistribute it.

The answer to this question depends entirely on transaction costs and the resulting contracts. For entrepreneurs to face the full opportunity costs and reap the full benefits of their actions, there must be explicit or implicit contractual terms for all relevant margins. It is the structure of property rights and the cost of specifying, measuring, and enforcing contractual terms that determine resource allocation.

It is also important to recognize that as the values of resources change and as new technologies are developed, different margins will be specified in contracts. Higher resource rents will induce entrepreneurs to accept the contracting costs that were too high given previous values. Similarly, new technologies can reduce the costs of specifying, measuring, and enforcing contractual terms. Both phenomena were at work in the evolution of property rights in the American west (see Anderson and Hill 1975), and both are influencing the provision of environmental amenities through the market process.

When property rights are not well-defined, enforced, and transferable, or when transaction costs are high, the entrepreneur has at least two opportunities for increasing his wealth. First, consider the economics of a common pool. Cheung (1970) has shown how entrepreneurs faced with a common pool resource dissipate rents. Because of high transaction costs, certain marginal impacts will not be the basis of contract. Exploiting a resource under these conditions benefits the individual, but is a negative-sum game for society.

Entrepreneurs also play negative-sum games when they engage in rent-seeking that uses the coercive power of government to increase personal wealth at the expense of others (Anderson and Hill 1980). In the context of new institutional economics, rent-seeking means that entrepreneurs will engage in efforts to raise transaction costs for their competitors or to redefine property rights in their favour. Both of these actions require governmental action. With so many decisions on natural resource use placed in the hands of state and federal bureaucrats, the rent-seeking game is important for coal company executives as well as environmental leaders. Both types of entrepreneurs recognize that their wealth and that of their principals will be affected by bureaucratic decisions. Hence, interest groups spend large amounts of money and other resources trying to influence these decisions.

Rent-seeking

While such entrepreneurial efforts explain the demand for rent-seeking, the activities of politicians and bureaucrats explain the supply. Just as entrepreneurs in the marketplace recognize and fill demands for goods and services, politicians and bureaucrats discover opportunities to meet the demands of their constituencies. The constraints on each, however, are very different. With well-specified contracts, private entrepreneurs provide new goods and services only when they expect the benefits from those items to exceed the opportunity cost of resources used in their production. Politicians and bureaucrats who provide goods and services to interest groups, however, do not have to pay the full opportunity cost of expended resources. They can increase their own utility by increasing budgetary discretion, power, and wealth.

There is a principal/agent relationship between politicians and bureaucrats on the one hand and voters on the other. But this is weakened by such things as voter ignorance, imperfect information, and special-interest effects, which raise the transaction costs of fully specifying contracts between governmental agents and citizen principals. By explicitly incorporating these costs into our models, we can better understand which situations are likely to result in governmental failure.

Natural resource economists who follow this approach question whether allocation problems can be solved simply by asking governmental decision-makers to equate benefits and costs at the margin. As Friedrich Hayek states:

> The problem is thus in no way solved if we can show that all
> the facts, if they were known to a single mind...would
> uniquely determine the solution; instead we must show how
> a solution is produced by the interaction of people each of
> whom possesses only partial knowledge (Hayek 1972, p. 91).

From this perspective, the real question is: What are the relevant contractual margins and what values will be placed on them?

The new paradigm is certainly having an impact on natural resource economics and policy, but developing a new theory is not enough. If "Pigou's contribution to the economic theory of government policy was based on armchair theorizing, rather than empirical investigation" (Burton 1978, p. 72), it is important that the new resource economics do not fall into the same trap. The property rights and transaction costs constraints that are assumed must be carefully examined to see if they are valid. Empirical investigations must be conducted to ensure that the findings are true. Guidelines for conducting these investigations are provided by Coase's evidence (1974) that lighthouses are not public goods and Cheung's examination (1973) of contracts between beekeepers and orchard owners.

Free Market Environmentalism

Those who follow the Pigovian tradition are willing to acknowledge a property rights solution to some problems. But they generally argue that such a solution could not possibly work for water, amenity, and wildlife allocation.

> With respect to bodies of land and water, extension of property rights may effectively internalize what would otherwise remain externalities. But the possibilities of protecting the citizen against at such common environmental blights as filth, fume, stench, noise, visual distractions, etc. by a market and property rights are too remote to be taken seriously (Mishan 1972, p. 62).

But voluntary, contractual solutions to many environmental problems can and do evolve. When they do not, transaction costs can be blamed for the failure. These costs may not simply be those associated with standard market transactions, however; they can be the result of governmental action designed to correct the alleged market failure. Consider the following examples of how the market provides environmental amenities.

Privatizing Instream Flows

There was little need to consider who had the rights to instream flows during the years when water rights were forming in the American west (see Anderson 1983). Since then, however, the demand for instream uses has grown to include waste disposal, recreation, and scenery. Industrialization led to the discharge of effluent into rivers and lakes, and rising incomes and more leisure time led to an increase in aesthetic values.

As instream uses began to compete directly with diversion uses, the institutional structure had to be adjusted to account for the new values. Judicial and administrative agencies responded by instituting new rules governing instream uses. The rationale is that these uses are a public good; that is, it is difficult (some say impossible) to exclude nonpaying uses, and additional units of the good can be provided at zero marginal costs. To compound the problem, it is argued that an existence value can be associated with instream amenities; that is, some people derive satisfaction from simply knowing the amenity is there. A New Yorker may be happy knowing that a free-flowing stream exists in Montana even if he has no intention of ever seeing it. Using these arguments, policy-makers have justified governmental intervention in water allocation. Is the collective action that has been used to provide for instream uses necessary, or could markets be allowed to resolve the conflicts between uses?

If we are to be convinced that markets can provide an alternative for allocating instream flows, it is reasonable to ask why markets are not more active in this area. James Huffman suggests

that existing inefficiencies in water allocation result from
deficiencies in the private right system rather than alleged
market failures. The existing water laws seriously limit
private acquisition of instream flow rights, so we cannot be
sure from experience that the initial public-good assumption
is accurate (Huffman 1983, p. 268).

In many Western states, the institutional structure precludes the private ownership of instream flows. In some cases, the concept of beneficial use—initially
developed for agricultural, mining, and domestic uses—does not include instream flows. In the early mining camps, beneficial use was determined by any
user who was willing to divert the water. Over time, however, beneficial use
has been increasingly determined by judicial and administrative agencies,
which have ruled that reserving instream flows for amenity purposes does not
constitute a beneficial use.

Beneficial Use

The requirement that beneficial use necessitates the diversion of water has
produced perverse results. For example, when the Colorado legislature
authorised the Colorado River Conservation District to reserve water for
instream purposes in any natural streams large enough to support a fish
population, the Colorado Supreme Court ruled that there was

no support in the law of that state for the proposition that a
minimum flow of water may be "appropriate" in a natural
stream for piscatorial purposes without diversion of any
portion of the water "appropriate" from the natural course of
the stream (Huffman 1983, p. 70).

Much earlier, in 1917, a Utah court had ruled on the disputed ownership of
instream flows for the purpose of supporting a duck population. The court found
that it was:

utterly inconceivable that a valid appropriation of water can
be made under the laws of this state, when the beneficial use
of which, after the appropriation is made, will belong equally
to every human being who seeks to enjoy it... [W]e are
decidedly of the opinion that the beneficial use contemplated
in making the appropriation must be one that inures to the
exclusive benefit of the appropriator and subject to his
domain and control (*Lake Shore Duck Club* v. *Lake View
Duck Club*, 50 Utah 76, 309, 1917).

The state was unwilling to allow individuals or groups to appropriate rights
over the "public goods." As long as the maintenance of instream flows does not
constitute a beneficial use of water, private appropriators will not be able to

define and enforce rights to the flows. Thus, a market cannot develop. Again, this is not a case of market failure, but of governmental or institutional failure.

Also hindering the market allocation is the practice in most states of forcing rights holders to forfeit rights if the water is not used. That is, if water is left in a stream to provide a nice view or fish habitat, the law considers it abandoned and the right is lost. The rationale for this law was that speculation in water caused valuable resources to remain idle and unproductive, inhibiting economic growth.

Since water held for speculative purposes cannot be distinguished from water held for instream uses, the latter has fallen under the law of abandonment. The law stifles the establishment of instream water rights and discourages what may be a highly valued use. Removing the beneficial use restrictions and the laws of abandonment would eliminate an institutional barrier to the establishment of instream flow rights and the production of amenity values.

Private Property Instreams

The evidence suggests that if legal obstacles to the establishment of instream rights were removed, contracted arrangements for the private provision of instream uses would develop. On small streams, for example, where some legal restrictions do not apply, private owners are gainfully providing fishing. In the Yellowstone River Valley south of Livingston, Mont., several spring creeks begin and end on private property and are wholly appropriated by the landowners. Since access to the stream can be inexpensively monitored, landowners can collect a fee from fishermen. The fee gives owners the incentive to develop spawning beds, prevent siltation, and keep cattle away from streams to protect the bank vegetation and cover. Owners limit the number of fishermen per day so that the value of the experience is not diminished.

A rather different case, but one that produced similar results, occurred in the Gallatin Valley near Bozeman, Mont. A few years ago, a recreational fisherman purchased some land and a stream from a cattle rancher who had allowed his livestock to graze on the stream banks, eliminating vegetation, causing erosion, and reducing the size and number of trout in the stream. The new owner got rid of the cattle and in three years had reclaimed the stream and revived its fishing potential. The owner bears the cost of not using the land for cattle production, but he reaps the benefits of better fishing.

The results of private ownership of fishing rights are being noted in other parts of the world. On the Southwest Miramichi River in Quebec, the owner of a fishing camp described how he turned his leased section into the perfect place for salmon fishing:

> I made it perfect by rafting a bulldozer in here... We cleared
> away the gravel bar that kept fish from going up the
> tributary...dug the hundred-yard long pool...and shoved a

big-as-a-house boulder in place at the head of it... With all
due respect to Mother Nature, the pool was built by men and
machines, and it seems to be as good now as it was the first
year (Zern 1982, p. 87).

British Experience

The rights to fishing streams in England and Scotland have long encouraged
instream uses. The tradition of trout fishing in Great Britain has led some
owners to maintain their fisheries even though they have not marketed the
fishing rights. As the value of fishing rights has risen with the demand, however,
"there are few landowners...who can afford to ignore the commercial aspect
of the sporting rights which they own" (Southerland 1968, p. 110). It has
become worthwhile to incur the costs of specifying and enforcing contractual
arrangements that govern fishing. As a result, many private voluntary associa-
tions have been formed to purchase rights to instream flows and to charge fees
for fishing.

In the 1960s and 1970s, smaller, privately managed fisheries
that offered exclusivity in exchange for higher rod fees began
to break out like an aquatic rash around [England]. Now
every city and major town...has first-rate trout fishing within
easy reach and at an affordable price (Clarke 1979, p. 219).

In Scotland,

virtually every inch of every major river and most minor ones
is privately owned or leased, and while trespassing isn't quite
as serious a crime as first-degree murder or high treason, it
isn't taken lightly... Many of the stretches, which may be
100 yards of one bank of a river or several miles of both
banks, are reserved years in advance, with a long waiting list
(Zern 1981, pp. 120-136).

In Grantown-on-Spey, the angler can

join the local angling association by paying a weekly fee
about $25 and be free to fish any of seven miles of association
water. Sometimes, too, hotels and inns own or lease a stretch
of river for their guests or make arrangements with the local
owner of fishing rights (Zern 1981, pp. 120-136).

When water for instream uses can be privately owned, there is an incentive to
manage and improve the fishing habitat. In order to capture a return on the
investment, owners must invest in enforcing their property rights, so the British
hire private fish and game managers and invest in capital improvement on their
streams.

To maintain their houses as homes, they retained
housekeepers. To keep a proper garden and park, they had

groundskeepers. Game keepers for stag and grouse. Then, as keepers of the kept, even gatekeepers to further secure things. And eventually, it was for the British to devise the ultimate in the art of maintenance—the riverkeeper.

Now, the name itself could easily be misinterpreted—as it has from time to time by our American "riverkeepers" whom we call "the Corps of Engineers." To keep a river from doing what it is supposed to do would be noxious to the British, as it is to many anglers (Zahner 1988, p. 16).

The British system illustrates how any country might restructure its institutional arrangements to encourage the private ownership of instream flows. With private ownership, instream flow rights acquire a value that cannot be ignored. Southerland points out there is no doubt

that sporting rights are a desirable amenity...but it must be remembered that without careful preservation much of the amenity would not exist. The good-natured farmer who allows anyone to shoot over his land, and does nothing to preserve his stocks, will soon find out there is little left to shoot... [I]f he invests in improving his sporting amenities, he is surely entitled to make what profit he can from his enterprise. That this should result in the rationing of the commodity by prices is no more deplorable than the fact that Dover sole costs more than herring (Southerland 1968, pp. 113-114).

Reduced Pollution

Even pollution can be reduced if individuals are allowed to own water within the confines of a stream's banks. Under these conditions, liability rules can and will evolve. Owners of instream fishing rights, for example, could bring suit against an upstream polluter whose effluent adversely affects their fishing resource. In England, the Angler's Cooperative Association (ACA) has assumed the job of monitoring pollution.

It has investigated nearly 700 pollution cases since it started and very rarely does it fail to get abatement or damages, as the case requires. The anglers have behind them a simple fact. Every fishery in Britain, except for those in public reservoirs, belongs to some private owner (Dales 1968, p. 68).

These efforts have even preserved trout fishing on the Derwent River, which flows through the industrial city of Derby. The ACA prevented the city from dumping sewage into the river and got an injunction against British Electric to stop it from running warm water directly into the river. "A.C.A. also deals with...mud running into a stream from a new road grade, or a ditch... This is actually a good example of a common form of pollution which we [in North America] accept but which is quite unnecessary and not hard to avoid" (Dales 1968, p. 69).

State laws that prohibit the ownership of water for instream uses inhibit market solutions to use conflicts. If these prohibitions were removed, it is likely that we would move a long way toward reaching private, contracted arrangements for instream uses. The existence of British water institutions, which promote high-quality fishing and give owners an incentive to guard against stream pollution, suggest that markets can play a greater role.

Migratory Fish and Wildlife

Even those who concur with a property rights solution to many natural resource problems often argue that such a solution in some cases would be prohibitively expensive. John Burton concludes that

> fish-farming, for instance, is both technically feasible and commercially viable in some types such as oyster-fishing (and probably also shore-based rearing of expensive fish such as turbot and sole). But the establishment of private rights of fishery in migratory fish seems so far technically infeasible (Burton 1978, p. 88).

The fate of whales, sea turtles, buffalo, grizzly bears, and passenger pigeons provide ample ammunition for environmentalists seeking governmental control of wildlife allocation.

As with instream flows, one reason for market failure is the legal restriction on wildlife ownership. An 1896 Supreme Court ruling established the states' proprietary interest in wildlife through the state ownership doctrine. In light of th near extinction of several furbearing species, state control of wildlife seemed like the only alternative. There are cases, however, where these laws have hindered the establishment of private property rights, and, hence, the investment in wildlife preservation. Nonetheless, there are a growing number of examples of markets responding to scarcity conditions in the allocation of this natural resource.

It appears that establishing private rights, even for migratory fish, is technically feasible. In Oregon, companies are investing large amounts of money in breeding salmon in hatcheries and releasing them into the ocean. When the salmon leave the Oregon Aqua Hatchery, they are "imprinted with a chemical odour which will guide them back to this [release] site when they are ready to spawn" (Nova, p. 8).

Private salmon ranching is not unlike the fishing institutions established by the early coastal Indians. Tribes along the coast and up the Columbia River harvested the fish when they returned to their spawning grounds, limiting the take according to tradition and superstition so there was always a sustainable catch. Resources were not expended in fishing the ocean but were conserved by catching fish as they returned to the rivers.

Common Pool Salmon

When white men came to the Pacific Northwest, the ocean became a common pool resource to be exploited by commercial and sport fishermen. Efforts have been made to limit the catch in open waters and to increase the salmon population by using public hatcheries, but many resources are still being invested in trying to catch the fish that are available. Large amounts are invested in boats, nets, electronic gear, and labour, even though the fish could be harvested by channelling them directly into the cannery at spawning time. Estimates suggest that total expenditures may exceed the value of the salmon (Higgs 1982).

Private salmon ranching is a rational alternative. The only piece of equipment required is a concrete fish ladder, and private salmon ranches catch approximately 70 percent of their released stock. The programme is still in its infancy, but it appears to be profitable and is contributing to a growing wild salmon population.

Timber companies in the south are also recognizing the potential for resource management that enhances wildlife. The Southern timber industry is dominated by private land-holdings. In the past, forests have been managed primarily for pulpwood, with little attention paid to wildlife habitat. It simply was not worth incurring the transaction costs. As amenity values have risen, however, companies such as the International Paper Company have begun to change. White-tailed deer, turkeys, rabbits, bob-white quail, mourning doves, and other species are beginning to reap the benefits of new management techniques, and so are International Paper and hunters. Clear-cuts are limited and are made in irregular, narrow patterns to minimize the edge effect. Stream bottoms and natural drainages are left in hard woods to generate food and cover. By increasing phosphorus through legumes, deer body weight and antler size have increased.

Altruism? No.

All of this comes at some cost to the company, so why do they bother to do it? Part of the reason is improving public relations. But the companies also earn as much as $10 per acre in hunting leases. International Paper's 3,500-acre Cherokee Game Management Area in east Texas earns $6 per acre annually. In other states, leases average from 50 cents to $1 per acre, depending on the quality of the site. *Outdoor Life* editor Richard Starnes concludes that

in the future, timber companies will get involved with leasing lands to hunting clubs, which will then provide timber management of their own. This will give hunters an investment in wildlife helping companies manage their lands (Starnes 1982, p. 11).

The number of hunting clubs interested in contracting for land is rapidly increasing. As *Fishing and Hunting News* reports:

> Today, as the ranks of hunters grow and the available public lands shrink, more and more savvy sportsmen are turning their attention to the hunting club. What's more, folks have discovered that these preserves are an affordable option to hanging up the gun at the end of the general season (April 1982, p. 8).

Clubs that support many different bird species can be found from coast to coast and from border to border. The contracts governing the use of private reserves vary with fees charged based on number of birds bagged, number of birds released in the fields, guide services, and annual membership fees.

> In these days of posted farmland, shrinking public access, and growing hordes of hunters, a hunting preserve membership is an absolute guarantee that you will have a place to hunt and a place to take junior, and you won't have to spend half of the day looking for a landowner whose permission to hunt may not come readily... The bottom line is better hunting, more shooting, and a happier end to each excursion. What more can the outdoor sportsman ask for?" (*Fishing and Hunting News*, April 1982, p. 8).

Clearly, some sportsmen are beginning to recognize that private contractual arrangements offer an alternative to the public provision of wildlife.

Hunter and Landowner as Friends

This alternative is especially evident in Texas, where over 85 percent of the land is privately owned. Deer hunters purchase leases to hunt on private land at fees that range from $100 to $2,000 per gun, depending on the quality of the hunting site, the quality and quantity of game, and the facilities and services provided by the landowner. The type of lease varies: 71 percent are deer season leases, 19 percent are year-round leases, 5 percent are day leases, and 5 percent are short-term leases. On a per-acre basis, lease rates range from 25 cents to $10 annually. Taylor, Beattie and Livengood (1980, p. 2) concluded that "the net returns from deer leases equal or exceed the annual net returns from livestock operations in many areas of the state."

Hunter success on leased lands is extremely high relative to public sites. On leased lands, 1.16 deer were killed per hunter in 1978, while on public lands 0.62 deer were killed per hunter (Livengood 1979, p. 2).

> The rancher-landowner is responsible for the wildlife on his place. When the hunter appears, the hunter is charged a fee

> to hunt on the land... [T]he cowman participates because he makes money. By the same token, if that cowman posts his land "no hunting," it costs him money. You just don't see that many acres posted "no hunting" (Chambers 1982, p. 48).

Co-operation between sportsmen and landowners is improved as a result of market contracts that force individuals to take into account costs and benefits. While it is often "assumed that private property rights cannot be enforced in the case of fisheries, wildlife, and whatever other resources economists have chosen to call 'natural' " (Cheung 1973, p. 33), it would appear that such assumptions only generate more fables.

Private Land Conservation

Arguments abound in favour of government intervention for conservation in general and for land conservation in particular. They are based on excludability and the divergence of private and social discount rates. "It is the clear duty of Government, which is the trustee for unborn generations as well as for its present citizens, to watch over, and if need be, by legislative enactment, to defend the exhaustible natural resources from rash and reckless exploitation" (A.C. Pigou, quoted in Milliman 1962, p. 199).

In the case of land, the call for government action is further buttressed by the claim that market information does not clearly reflect the future value of agricultural production. The National Agricultural Land Survey (NALS) purports to show that more than 3 million acres of agricultural land in the United States is being converted annually to other uses. It has given conservationists the ammunition to press even further their demands for legislation designed to preserve agricultural lands (Baden 1983). Since the late 1800s, the same arguments have been used to justify governmental ownership of one-third of America's land. Everything from national parks to wilderness areas to historic sites supposedly fits into the market failure category. On that basis, vast bureaucratic empires have been built.

Leaving aside the question of whether existing landowners will provide sufficient land preservation and whether the government can do any better (see Baden and Stroup 1981), let us examine private options for land preservation.

> The economics of land conservation are currently undergoing some changes. In the past, much of the activity in land conservation centered on moving land from the private sector into governmental ownership and on classifying public lands into protected status (national parks, wilderness, and primitive areas, monuments, etc.). In the present state of tightening public budges, money for land acquisition is rapidly drying up and resource development of public land is receiving federal encouragement. Leaving the issue of struggle over

public land management aside, the strategies of the land conservation movement are adapting accordingly as they look increasingly to the private sector for support and action (Rusmore 1982, p. 87).

The Nature Conservancy

Leading this adaptation on the national level has been The Nature Conservancy, a national conservation organization committed to preserving natural diversity by finding and protecting areas that contain the best examples of all components of the natural world. Since 1950, the Conservancy and its members have been involved in the preservation of nearly 2 million acres in 50 states, the Virgin Islands, Canada and the Caribbean (The Nature Conservancy News 1983, p. 3).

In 1982, the Conservancy held over $261 million in assets, nearly $190 million of which was in natural land areas. At the end of 1982, the Conservancy's portfolio included 689 preserves, a permanent capital fund of $49,5 million, and 3,098 land conservation projects encompassing over 1.9 million acres.

At the local level, land conservation organizations, using primarily volunteer initiatives and private funds, have grown rapidly during the past three decades. In 1950, only 36 conservation organization existed in the United States. By 1975, there were 173, and by 1982 there were 404 groups representing over 250,000 members. Local conservation organizations in 1982 controlled more than 675,000 acres of valuable resource lands, with over 60 percent of that total in the New England and Middle Atlantic states, where private ownership is dominant.

Land conservation trusts are generally established with tax-exempt status. Their purpose is to preserve land for its amenity values and to keep it in agricultural uses. Funds are raised by soliciting members, with membership fees levied at a small amount per year, and by soliciting grants from foundations and corporations, sometimes amounting to hundreds of thousands of dollars. With these funds, the land trusts can purchase fee simple title to land or simply purchase conservation easements. In addition, trusts find that, "given the moral inclination and encouraged by tax incentives, some...[private] owners are committing their properties to conservation purposes" (Rusmore 1982, p. 187).

Tax Incentives

Tax incentives are very important to the land conservation organizations, since individuals can deduct their contributions as charitable donations. Individuals who give conservation easements to these organizations can also deduct the difference between the value of the land without the easement (the development value) and the value with the easement (the conservation value). These "bargain sales are one of the most effective levels the [Nature] Conservancy has to pry loose land it wants" (Wood 1978, p. 79). It might be argued that conservation contracts between private organizations and existing landowners really are stimulated by government, since such contracts depend heavily on tax incentives. Taking the tax institutions as given, however, the "business-suited saviors of the nation's vanishing wilds" (Wood 1978) clearly represent a private response to the provision of amenity values.

Conservation organizations tend to manage lands differently than public bureaucrats. Even land-swapping is not uncommon. For example, when the Nature Conservancy decided that land it had been given in the Virgin Islands was not of prime environmental importance, it exchanged it for land in Wisconsin that could be managed as an integrated watershed for amenity purposes. While land-conservation organization undoubtedly suffer some of the problems faced by all non-profit organizations, there are some important elements of residual claimancy.

Land trusts are also not opposed to charging user fees of people who obtain benefits from their lands. Since these organizations cannot readily tap public funds, they are continually looking for innovative ways to finance projects. Speaking for the Trustees of Reservations in Massachusetts, Gordon Abbot Jr. states that:

> we're also fortunate that user demand enables us to raise 35 percent of our operating income from admission fees and that these can be adjusted within reason to catch up with inflation. We're great believers in the fairness of users paying their way (Abbott 1982, p. 207).

User Fees

Fees are charged for everything from parking to concessions to entrance, demonstrating that excluding non-payers from consuming amenity values is possible at a cost. As the amenity values rise, organizations are finding it worthwhile to undertake exclusion costs in an effort to raise funds. These organizations also have an incentive to charge fees because the revenues can be reinvested. This is in sharp contrast to the policies of the National Park Service, which has kept entrance fees in real terms below pre-1920 levels.

There is little doubt that "the private sector is proving to be a formidable ally" (Rusmore 1982, p. 187) for the conservation movement. As a leader from the New Jersey Conservation Foundation puts it, "We have entered an area when we now acknowledge that government cannot best solve all our problems and that solutions that draw on the private sector will offer greater economic efficiencies and flexibility" (Moore 1982, p. 213).

With the federal government cutting back on its land acquisition programmes, people are turning more to the private sector to provide land-generated amenities. Even though these organizations face an element of the free-rider problem, they have raised significant amounts of money and found ways to overcome the difficulties, at least partially. The groups are unlikely through outright purchase programmes to accomplish what the government agencies can, but they "can significantly contain the threatened damage to...critical areas" (Rusmore 1982, p. 219). Again it is simply not the case that "protecting the citizen against such common environmental blights as filth, fume, stench, noise, visual distractions, etc. by a market and property rights are too remote to be taken seriously" (Mishan 1972, p. 62).

Conclusions

Professor Cheung has suggested that the concept of externalities be discarded in favour of a contractarian analysis.

> The change in view through the analysis of contracting is not a redundant way of treating the same class of problems, for this change in view leads to different...questions. Why do market contracts not exist for certain effects of actions? Because of the absence of exclusive rights, or because transaction costs are prohibitive? Why do exclusive rights not exist for certain actions? Because of legal institutions, or because policing costs are prohibitive (Cheung 1970, p. 58)?

There is certainly good evidence that the externality approach proposed by Pigou has not taken us very far toward an understanding of natural resource allocation. It has basically provided arguments for governmental intervention. The property rights transaction cost approach suggested by Cheung, on the other hand, is helping us identify the relevant margins for deciding on natural resource allocation. By looking at the actual market process—i.e. the contracting process—we often find that assumed external effects can be negated through contract. Further, when we ask why contracts do not take externalities into account, we are forced to examine all transaction costs, including governmental restrictions. The three natural resource uses examined in this paper reveal that contracting processes are working in some cases. In others, it appears that legal restrictions prevent contracting.

Contractarian Directions

The new institutional economics approach suggests two important directions for the study of natural resources. First, more attention must be paid to the nature of existing contracts. In the case of fee hunting, for example, many questions need to be asked about prices, product specifications, length of contract, and provisions for exclusion. Only such an examination can expose the true transaction costs that determine which margins will be important to decision-makers. Natural resource economists are only beginning to turn in this direction.

Second, natural resource economics must develop clearer ways of thinking about the free-rider problem. Environmental groups in general, and land conservation organizations in particular, seem to be overcoming the free-rider problem in a significant way. Again, I suspect, the nature of the contract is important. What economists assume to be free-rider situations may simply be more fables.

As Douglass North suggests, "strong moral and ethical codes of a society is the cement of social stability which makes an economic system viable" (1981, p. 47). The property rights/transaction costs approach draws our attention to the effect that this "cement" has on the contracting process. By focusing our attention on the nature of contracts and transaction costs, we will be able to develop a better understanding of the relationship between the market process and environmental amenities.

References

Abbot, Gordon Jr., "Long-Term Management: Problems and Opportunities." In *Private Options: Tools and Concepts for Land Conservation*, Barbara Rusmore, Alexandra Swaney, and Allan D. Spader, eds. Covello, Calif.: Island Press, 1982.

Anderson, Terry L., "The New Resource Economics: Old Ideas and New Applications", *American Journal of Agricultural Economics* 64 (December 1982): pp. 928-934.

_____, Water Crisis: Ending the Policy Drought. Baltimore: The John Hopkins University Press, 1983.

_____ and Peter J. Hill, *The Birth of a Transfer Society*. Stanford, Calif.: Hoover Institution Press, 1980.

_____, "The Evolution of Property Rights: A Study of the American West", *Journal of Law and Economics* 18 (April 1975): pp. 163-180.

Baden, John, ed., "Agricultural Land Preservation: Economics or Politics?" Bozeman, Mont.: Center for Political Economy and Natural Resources, 1983.

_____ and Richard Stroup, eds., *Bureaucracy vs. Environment*. Ann Arbor: University of Michigan Press, 1981.

Bremer, Terry "A Review of the 1981 National Survey of Local Land Conservation Organizations," In *Private Options: Tools and Concepts for Land Conservation*, Barbara Rusmore, Alexandra Swaney, and Allan D. Spader, eds. Covello, Calif.: Island Press, 1982.

Burton, John, "Epilog." In *The Myth of Social Costs*, by Steven N.S. Cheung. London: The Institute of Economic Affairs, 1978.

Castle, Emery N., "The Market Mechanism, Externalities, and Land Economics," *Journal of Farm Economics* 47 (August 1965): pp. 542-556.

Chambers, Gale, "Cattle and Wildlife—Managing For Both," *Montana Farmer-Stockmen* January 1982) p. 48.

Cheung, Steven N.S., "The Fable of the Bees," *Journal of Law and Economics* 16 (April 1973): pp. 11-34.

_____, *The Myth of Social Costs*. London: The Institute of Economic Affairs, 1978.

_____, "The Structure of a Contract and the Theory of Non-Exclusive Resource," *Journal of Law and Economics* 13 (April 1970): pp. 49-70.

Clarke, Brian, "The Nymph in Still Water." In *The Masters of Nymph* J.M. Migel and L.M. Wright, eds. New York: Nick Lyons Books, 1979.

Coase, Ronald H., "The Lighthouse in Economics," *Journal of Law and Economics* 17 (October 1974): pp. 357-376.

_____, "The Problem of Social Cost," *Journal of Law and Economics* 3 (October 1960): pp. 1-44.

Dales, J.H., *Pollution, Property and Prices*, Toronto: University of Toronto Press, 1968.

Fisher, Antony C., *Resources and Environmental Economics*, Cambridge: Cambridge University Press, 1981.

"Private Clubs Provide Choice Shooting," *Fishing and Hunting News*, April 1982, p. 8.

Hayek, Friedrich A., "The Use of Knowledge in Society," *Individualism and Economic Order*. Chicago: Henry Regnery, 1972.

Higgs, Robert, "Legally Induced Technical Regress in the Washington Salmon Fishery," *Research in Economic History* 7 (1982): pp. 55-86.

Howe, Charles W., *Natural Resource Economics*. New York: John Wiley and Sons, 1979.

Huffman, James, "Instream Water Use: Public and Private Alternatives." In *Water Rights: Scarce Resource Allocation Bureaucracy and the Environment*, ed. Terry L. Anderson. Cambridge, Mass.: Ballinger Press, 1983.

Livengood, Kerry R., "A Comparison of Market and Extra Market Methods of Estimating the Demand and Benefits of Outdoor Recreation." Ph.D. Diss. College Station: Texas A&M University, 1979.

Milliman, J.W., "Can People Be Trusted With Natural Resources?" *Land Economics* 38 (August 1962): pp. 199-218.

Mishan, E.J., "A Reply to Professor Worcester," *Journal of Economic Literature* 10 (March 1972): pp. 59-62.

Moore, David, "Adapting the British Countryside Commission Ideas." In *Private Options: Tools and Concepts for Land Conservation*, Barbara Rusmore, Alexandra Swaney, and Allan D. Spader, eds. Covello, Calif.: Island Press, 1982.

The Nature Conservancy, "Annual Report, 1983." *The Nature Conservancy News* 33 (March/April 1983).

North, Douglass C., *Structure and Change in Economic History*. New York: W.W. Norton and Company, 1981.

Nova, "Salmon on the Run." WGBH Publications and Films/Video Services, no date.

Randall, Alan *Resource Economics*. Columbus, Ohio: Grid Publishing, 1981.

Rusmore, Barbara, "Economic Perspectives on Land Conservation." In *Private Options: Tools and Concepts for Land Conservation*. Barbara Rusmore, Alexandra Swaney, and Allan D. Spader, eds. Covello California: Island Press, 1982.

_____, Alexandra Swaney, and Allan D. Spader, eds., *Private Options: Tools and Concepts for Land Conservation*. Covello, Calif.: Island Press, 1982.

Samuelson, Paul A., *Economics*. 11th ed. New York: McGraw-Hill, 1980.

Starnes, Richard, "International Paper Has a Grand Plan," *Outdoor Life* (January 1982): pp. 11-12.

Southerland, Douglas, *The Landowner*. London: Anthony Bond, 1968.

Taylor, C. Robert, Bruce Beattie, and Kerry R. Livengood, "Public vs. Private Systems for Big Game Hunting." Paper presented at a conference on Property Rights and Natural Resources: A New Paradigm For the Environmental Movement, Center for Political Economy and Natural Resources, Bozeman, Mont., December 1980.

Wood, Peter, "Business-Suited Saviors of Nation's Vanishing Wilds." *Smithsonian* 9 (December 1978): pp. 76-84.

Zahner, Don, "Anglish Spoken Here," *Fly Fisherman* 12 (January 1980): p. 16.

Zern, Ed, "By Yon Bonny Banks," *Field and Stream* (1981): p. 120, pp. 136-137.

_____, "Rx For Ailing Waters," Field and Stream (November 1982): pp. 87-89.

Chapter 5

Global Warming and Ozone Depletion

Jane S. Shaw
and
Richard L. Stroup

Unless the threats of climate change, ozone depletion, soil erosion, deforestation, and population growth are brought under control soon, economic decline is inevitable. Time is not on our side. We have years, not decades, to turn the situation around.

—*Lester R. Brown*[1]

Modest increases in energy efficiency investments or family planning budgets will not suffice. Getting on such a path depends on a wholesale reordering of priorities, a fundamental restructuring of the global economy, and a quantum leap in international cooperation on the scale that occurred after World War II.

—*Lester R. Brown and Edward C. Wolf*[2]

The Earth's atmosphere is a giant global commons. People use it to dispose of wastes as they breathe, light fires, drive cars, and conduct many other daily activities. The air can assimilate pollutants to some extent and pollutants are cleansed from it by many processes. But virtually every day we see reports that human activity is polluting the atmosphere beyond repair. Leading the list of concerns today are fears of global warming and the depletion of ozone in the stratosphere. Some observers are calling for greater collective control over the use of fossil fuels and refrigerants and over other activities that might affect the global atmosphere.

Lester Brown, President of the Worldwatch Institute, is among those leading the fight to control human activities to save the globe. Many years before he and others began to stress the latest global issues to support their case, they were condemning the size and scope of human activity and calling for increased collectivization of decision-making. Some experts on climate, such as Stephen Schneider of the National Center for Atmospheric Research, have followed their lead. Indeed Schneider, in his 1976 book on global warming,[3] prominently gives thanks to Brown for encouraging the book and to Paul Ehrlich, co-founder of Zero Population Growth, for his editorial comments. Thus, the attention given to problems of global warming and ozone depletion is not simply the result of detached scientific observations; it is part and parcel of an ideological commitment to control human activity. Nevertheless, these issues of the global environment—partly because respected experts treat them so seriously—deserve our careful attention.

Is there a strong scientific case for drastic action? In this chapter we provide an overview of the literature on each of these problems and a discussion of the policy issues they pose. The scientific case for rapidly approaching disaster turns out to be weak, with both the evidence, and scientists' interpretation of it, very much mixed. Furthermore, our ability to bring about effective environmental policy on an international scale is poor, with efforts in this direction likely to threaten individual freedom and prosperity without doing much to help the global environment.

The Global Warming Issue

In the summer of 1988, a severe drought with record temperatures in North America dried up fields and streams. Globally, the year was the warmest on record, according to a British climatologist, and in June, James E. Hansen, a scientist with the National Aeronautics and Space Administration (NASA), told a congressional hearing that the "evidence is pretty strong that the greenhouse effect is here."[4] Fears that the world is becoming warmer and causing catastrophic change became big news.

The greenhouse effect has made headlines before, but this time the scientific press echoed the message with gloomy certitude. "Seldom has there been such a strong consensus among scientists on a major environmental issue," wrote Richard A. Houghton and George M. Woodwell, two scientists at the Woods Hole Research Center in Woods Hole, Massachusetts, in *Scientific American.*[5] "The warming, unless consciously checked by human effort, will be rapid and will be felt differentially over the earth." Stephen Schneider calculated that human caused climate change will proceed 10 to 40 times faster than any previous natural climate change.[6] Christopher Flavin of Lester Brown's Worldwatch Institute summarized the worst of the scientific projections: "During the next few decades average global temperatures will increase at 10 times the rate that they did at the end of the last ice age, or as much as 8 degrees Fahrenheit by the middle of the next century."[7]

David Rind, an atmospheric scientist with NASA, wrote in a special issue of the *EPA Journal* devoted to global warming: "The climate of the next century will very likely be substantially different from that to which we have become accustomed... The consequences of the climate change that is currently being estimated would be enormous."[8] The EPA asked analysts to contemplate the effects of significant climate change. Their scenarios, published in the same issue of the *EPA Journal,* included predictions that forests will shift northward; sea-levels will rise, inundating wetlands, beaches and coastal cities; rainfall patterns will change; air pollution will worsen; and catastrophes such as fires, insect plagues, floods, and droughts will increase.[9]

What to do? Scientists concerned about global warming recommend reducing the emissions of "greenhouse gases." This means cutting back on CO_2, which is considered the chief greenhouse gas, but also methane, nitrous oxides, and CFCs (chlorofluorocarbons), all of which also are believed to trap heat radiating from the earth. Methane is considered particularly dangerous because, even though it is a "trace gas" (existing in very small quantities) it traps twenty times as much heat as CO_2, molecule for molecule. Houghton and Woodwell propose cutting back on fossil fuel use, stopping world-wide deforestation (since trees absorb carbon dioxide), and planting more trees.[10]

The popular press has gone even farther with lists of policy changes. *Time* recommended special taxes on carbon-dioxide emissions, increased funding for alternative energy sources, financial aid to developing nations to build higher-efficiency power plants, a mammoth international tree-planting programme, and development of techniques for recovering methane given off by landfills and cattle feedlots.[11] The Worldwatch Institute proposed stricter automobile fuel-economy standards, home weatherization, higher energy taxes, and electric utility investment in higher efficiency units.[12]

The Ozone Depletion Issue

As the apparent crisis built during 1988 and 1989, fears of another global issue—ozone depletion—received a new burst of media attention. Many scientists believe that the layer of ozone, a variant of oxygen that surrounds the globe in the stratosphere, is thinning, and they have discovered a seasonal "hole" in the stratospheric ozone above Antarctica. Concern about the ozone layer has been growing in recent years, and it took on international importance in 1987 when 17 nations signed the Montreal Protocol, which calls for a halving of CFC production by 1998. A 1989 United Nations Environment Programme (UNEP) conference in Helsinki resulted in a "declaration of intent" to take even more severe measures.

Ozone forms naturally in the stratosphere when oxygen molecules are bombarded with solar ultraviolet rays. Since ozone particles filter out ultraviolet (UV) radiation, the fear is that if ozone is disappearing in the upper atmosphere, more ultraviolet radiation will reach the earth. Ultraviolet light is known to cause skin cancer and has been linked to cataracts and a weakening of the immune system.[13]

Carl Sagan, a Cornell University scientist who is well-known as a popular writer about science, says that large increases in UV radiation could be disastrous for other reasons as well. He points to experiments at Texas A & M University showing that moderate increases in UV light harm one-celled plants in the ocean. If UV radiation increased so much that it caused large numbers of these plants to die off, the animals that rely on them for food would also suffer. "The destruction of the little plants at the base of the food chain causes the entire chain to collapse," says Sagan.[14]

Many scientists believe that ozone depletion is caused by CFCs or chlorofluorocarbons. These are man-made chemicals—nontoxic and inert—that are used in refrigeration, foam manufacturing, air conditioning, and to clean electronic equipment. It appears that when the CFC molecules released on earth reach the stratosphere, ultraviolet light breaks them apart. This releases chlorine atoms, which destroy ozone molecules. According to one scientist, F. Sherwood Rowland, one molecule of chlorine can destroy up to 100,000 molecules of ozone.[15]

The Scientific Issues

Are these genuine issues and ones that policy-makers should be concerned about? If so, what insight can economics offer as proposals for reducing damage are considered? The first step is to examine the scientific issues surrounding these two threats.

Global Warming

The claim that the climate is getting warmer goes back to the 1890s when Svante Arrhenius, a Swedish chemist, contended that the unprecedented amount of CO_2 entering the atmosphere would eventually lead to global warming. Since then, scientists have generally agreed that the amount of CO_2 in the atmosphere is increasing. Based on measurements of gas trapped in glacial ice, scientists estimate that in the 1850s, at the start of the industrial revolution, the atmosphere had nearly 290 parts of CO_2 per million parts of air; that has risen to over 340 ppm, an increase of about 20 percent over some 135 years.[16]

There is also evidence that global temperatures have been going up during the past century. James E. Hansen and his colleagues at NASA believe that the average global temperature has increased by between five- and seven-tenths of a degree Celsius since 1860.[17] Another piece of evidence sometimes cited is that the six warmest years globally during the past century were in the 1980s.[18]

But how much consensus is there on the existence and the causes of global warming? Far less than the statement by Houghton and Woodwell quoted above would indicate. While most scientists agree that temperatures have risen over the past century, there are problems with the evidence. Furthermore, even if temperatures have risen, as most scientists believe, the case that carbon dioxide and other "greenhouse gases" are the chief cause is surprisingly weak.

The Northern Hemisphere experienced a cooling period between the 1940s and the 1970s, so the warming is not a consistent trend. Measurements in recent years may be contaminated by urbanization, which creates "heat island effects."[19] And a number of scientists are sure that the recent warm years can be explained by a periodic weather perturbation known as El Niño.[20]

Andrew R. Solow, a statistician at Woods Hole who is skeptical about the greenhouse effect, points out that global temperatures are less than completely reliable. Monitoring stations tend to be located on land (rather than on oceans) and more are in the Northern Hemisphere than in the Southern Hemisphere. Thus they are not "really global at all," he says. Temperature trends over land may be quite different from trends over the oceans, he notes.[21]

Some regions have not shown any observable warming. A recent study of the contiguous U.S., which took into account "heat island" effects, found no warming during the past century. Proponents of the greenhouse theory such as Houghton and Woodwell dismiss this evidence on the grounds that the U.S. represents only 1.5 percent of the globe's surface.[22]

But even if temperatures are warming, as many scientists believe, the relationship between the increase in carbon dioxide and the warming is quite shaky. Solow notes that the warming began before one could expect to see an effect from CO_2, and if it is occurring, we should have seen a systematic acceleration in the rate of warming, but this hasn't happened. "For example, for the planet to warm by 2 degrees C in the next 100 years, the average rate of warming would have to be four times greater than that in the historic record," he says.[23] Greenhouse warming is expected to be greatest at high latitudes and more rapid in the north than in the south, but this pattern hasn't appeared either, he says.

Finally, Solow notes that the computer models used to predict global warming are only "marginally successful" in reproducing today's climate from current information. Climate models, for example, failed to predict the severe drought of the summer of 1988. (Once the drought occurred, though, and new information was factored in, the drought did appear in the model.) Hugh W. Ellsaesser of Lawrence Livermore National Laboratory, says that his strongest reason for questioning current models' estimates of CO_2 warming is due to "the gross differences I see between how the atmosphere works and how it is modeled to work."[24] In a paper he wrote with others at Livermore, he notes that the historical evidence suggests "either that our climate models are inadequate or that there is a fundamental difference in character between climate changes of the past" and those predicted from changes due to CO_2.[25]

If carbon dioxide and other greenhouse gases didn't cause the warming that apparently occurred, what did? Solow and Ellsaesser both have an explanation for the warming. They think that it simply reflects the aftermath of a period of unusual cooling, the so-called "Little Ice Age" that ended during the 19th century. Writes Solow, "the historic warming is consistent with a mild post-glacial period that would follow the end of such a cool event."[26]

But suppose that a correlation can be made between increased greenhouse gases and warming. Even that doesn't mean that the warming will simply continue. Feedback effects might well change the prediction drastically. A great deal remains unknown about the process by which carbon is taken up by plants and released into the atmosphere. Only about half of the 5.5 billion tons of carbon produced per year by the consumption of fossil fuels turns up in the atmosphere as CO_2, explains Solow, and climatologists assume that the rest is stored in the ocean. But the fact that scientists are unable to account for such large quantities of carbon makes predictions highly uncertain.[27]

Furthermore, if warming occurred, a myriad of biological factors could enter in. Trevor Platt, a biological oceanographer at the Bedford Institute of Oceanography in Nova Scotia, has been studying the role of phytoplankton in removing carbon dioxide from the air. These marine plants, like land plants, consume CO_2 (about ten times the annual global emissions of CO_2 from fossil fuel combustion! says Platt). He believes that the phytoplankton thrive on the extra atmospheric CO_2. This creates a new "steady state" that will interfere with the greenhouse effect. And while some CO_2 returns to the atmosphere when the organisms die, Platt believes as much as 33 percent of the plankton sink to the bottom of the ocean, carrying carbon with them.[28]

Another point about plankton is that as they grow they emit greater amounts of dimethyl-sulphide (DMS) gas into the air, which triggers the formation of small water droplets. If there are far more plankton due to the increased CO_2, there will be more droplets, which reflect more sunlight than normal clouds do and therefore would help cool the earth.[29]

If warming occurs, a large volcanic eruption could counteract it.[30] Volcanic fallout tends to cool the earth because the particles help filter out sunlight. Paul Handler, a physics professor at the University of Illinois, claims that the record heat of the 1920s and 1930s and recent years occurred because few volcanos erupted during these times.

Kenneth E.F. Watt, professor of environmental studies at the University of California at Davis, believes that the excess of carbon dioxide in the atmosphere should in fact lead to a long-term cooling, which may have begun. Carbon dioxide will heat tropical ocean surfaces, he explains, leading to additional evaporation. This evaporation "ultimately appears as denser, more widespread clouds at high altitudes, which decrease the penetration by sunlight." This will lead to surface cooling, except in cities, decreasing the photosynthetic rate of forests, and the trees then draw less carbon out of the air. Watt considers the elevated level of the Great Salt Lake a sign of cooling, not warming.[31] Indeed, the idea that another Ice Age was pending was popular enough for a book, *The Cooling*, to be written on the subject in the mid-1970s.[32]

Reid Bryson, director of the Institute of Environmental Studies at the University of Wisconsin, Madison, has a different view. He believes dust and smoke are the primary culprits in climate change, rather than carbon dioxide. He and a colleague, Gerald Dittberner, developed a model which indicates atmospheric dust is responsible for about 90 percent of the Northern Hemisphere's temperature variation in this century.[33] Bryson has been sceptical about global warming, just as he was sceptical about the global cooling in the 1970s.

The point of these examples is not to disprove the greenhouse theory but to indicate that reputable scientists view the available evidence in different ways. No strong evidence of warming caused by CO_2 or other greenhouse gases has been found so far. Even the evidence of global warming itself is less than conclusive.

Ozone Depletion

Unlike the greenhouse effect, worries about ozone depletion have a relatively short history. In 1974 two University of California scientists, Sherwood Rowland and Mario Molina, released a study indicating that the ozone layer was in danger of being destroyed by chlorofluorocarbons, at the time used primarily as propellants in aerosol sprays. Rowland and Molina's findings led to the eventual banning of CFC use in aerosols in the United States in 1978,[34] and the issue of CFCs faded from the public arena.

But another threat to the ozone was discovered in 1985 when scientists with the British Antarctic Survey observed that concentrations of ozone in the stratosphere were dropping dramatically over Antarctica each austral spring and were replenished a few months later.

In 1985 an American satellite, Nimbus 7, confirmed what the British scientists had discovered—that a seasonal hole did exist. But some scientists view the overall data as suspect. S. Fred Singer, designer of the Nimbus 7's ozone meter, says that the instrument was made for short-term duty and over the last ten years it has lost sensitivity. This could lead it to exaggerate the decline in ozone.[35]

Since then, much of the scientific focus on ozone has consisted of efforts to calculate the existence, size, and duration of ozone "holes" in the Antarctic and Arctic, to estimate overall "thinning" where possible, and to determine what factors are influencing any perceived changes. So far, the results have not been conclusive. In 1986 a ground-based experiment in Antarctica found abnormally high levels of chlorine chemicals in the areas where the ozone was missing. This indicated that chlorine from CFCs may have been active in the destruction, although volcanic sources of ozone-destroying chlorine and fluorine also are important, including those such as Mt. Erebus in the Antarctic area. In addition, the peculiar meteorological conditions over Antarctica significantly affect ozone destruction.

In August and September 1987 two NASA research aircraft flew on 25 missions over Antarctica to gather data on the ozone hole. The abundance of certain chemicals within the hole made them certain that CFCs had a role in the depletion, but chemicals alone could not explain it fully, says Robert T. Watson, head of NASA's upper atmospheric research programme. "The evidence strongly suggests that both chemical and meteorological processes were responsible for perturbing ozone this year. It's not meteorology alone, it's not chemistry alone, it's both."[36]

In January 1987, Kenneth P. Bowman of the University of Illinois in Urbana-Champaign published estimates of global ozone levels from data collected by the Nimbus 7 satellite. He concluded that global ozone fell by 5 percent from 1979 to 1986. James K. Angell, a scientist with NOAA in Silver Spring, Maryland, estimated global ozone based on ground measurements. He found a 2.7 percent decrease in global ozone between 1980 and 1985. But both measurement systems suffer from degradation problems that could make the actual depletion rate greater or less than these estimates.[37]

In 1987, several agencies including NOAA and NASA formed the international Ozone Trends Panel, with more than 100 scientists scrutinizing the data from both systems. The panel has concluded from ground-based measurements that between 1969 and 1986 the level of ozone, averaged over the year and taking into account natural trends, decreased by between 1.7 and 3 percent in the Northern Hemisphere. While this represents a smaller annual decline than the other estimates, the panel notes that the evidence "strongly indicates" that chlorine from CFCs is "primarily responsible" for the hole in Antarctica. It is not clear how much is due to other trace gases, but Watson says "everything we do seems to be suggestive that CFCs are responsible for a loss of ozone."[38]

According to *Science News,* most scientists suspect a decrease in ozone of a few percentage points since 1979 could be explained by a combination of CFCs, volcanic eruptions, and the 11-year solar cycle.[39] Volcanoes, both when they erupt and when they are "passively degassing," put millions of tons of chlorine and fluoride chemicals into the atmosphere each year.[40] Some of these volcanoes are in the Antarctic area. The solar cycle may be another key factor. The year 1979 coincided with a solar maximum, in which the sun's output of ultraviolet radiation peaked. As the solar output fell from that time until 1985-86, ozone probably fell as well. The 1986 satellite data hint at an ozone recovery with the upswing in the solar cycle.

In March 1988 the Ozone Trends Panel announced that the ozone layer over the Arctic Circle was thinning. The thinning was found to be occurring mostly in the winter and at higher altitudes, leading the panel's scientists to believe that another hole might exist over the North Pole. As of January 1989 an international team of scientists had been unable to discover an ozone hole over the Arctic Circle. However, they did encounter large quantities of chlorine monoxide. Derived from CFCs, this chemical was found in high levels in Antarctica and is considered the "smoking gun"—a sign of imminent ozone destruction.[41] As this is being written, scientists such as Watson have indicated that they are sure they will find an ozone hole.

While there is little doubt that CFCs have the ability to destroy ozone, some believe the layer may be self-healing. One of the great difficulties in determining cause and making predictions concerning the depletion of the ozone is that computer models are not very accurate. Computer models failed to predict the existence of the ozone "hole" over Antarctica. Only after it was discovered did a scientist introduce the presence of Antarctic ice clouds into the model; then the ozone hole appeared.[42] Initially, environmentalists argued that supersonic transports would deplete the ozone, but now it appears that they increase it.[43]

Indeed, S. Fred Singer, a veteran of successive ozone theories, is sceptical about the usefulness of the current ozone-depletion theory in determining policy. He has worked with stratospheric ozone since 1970, as a scientist and an administrator at the U.S. Environmental Protection Agency. He has seen theories attract a lot of attention only to be disproven or so modified as to suggest policies directly counter to the ones initially indicated. As he says,

> Few outside my special field know about these wild gyrations in the theoretical predictions. But those of us who lived through them have developed a certain humility and affection toward the ozone layer. It's a matter of some irony that current theory predicts that aircraft exhaust counteracts the ozone-destroying effects of CFCs. But remember: it's only a theory, and it could change.[44]

Robert W. Pease, professor emeritus of physical climatology at the University of California, Riverside, disputes virtually all the claims of the ozone depletion theory. He says that the theory ignores the fact that ozone molecules are constantly being created and destroyed by ultraviolet light from the sun. The amount of ozone at any time depends on an equilibrium between the process of creation and destruction. The equilibrium varies around the globe and during the year, and, in his view, is restored rather quickly. Based on NOAA data, he believes that 60,000 ozone molecules are created for every chlorine atom released from a CFC molecule. This leads him to doubt that the ozone layer is being materially reduced. (He disputes the claim by Sherwood Rowland that each chlorine atom destroys 100,000 molecules of ozone because he doesn't think that most CFCs reach a point in the stratosphere where they are broken up by UV radiation.) Pease also notes that NOAA surface measurements indicate that the total amount of ozone above the U.S. is actually increasing.[45]

Another reason to question the ozone depletion theory is that the presumed effect—more ultraviolet radiation from the sun reaching the Earth's atmosphere—has not shown up. In the February 12, 1988, issue of *Science,* Joseph Scotto of the National Cancer Institute and two other scientists from Temple University in Philadelphia reported that the amount of biologically effective ultraviolet radiation (UVB radiation) had decreased, not increased, by as much as 2 to 7 percent between 1974 and 1985 in eight U.S. locations. The authors concluded that "physical and meteorological factors" in the troposphere (the area below the stratosphere) may "diffuse solar energy and thus reduce the amount of UVB radiation reaching the earth's surface."[46]

Similarly, while scientists estimate that the Antarctic has experienced an overall 6 percent decrease in ozone since 1969[47] and a seasonal loss of as much as half its ozone, the UV radiation reaching the continent there has not doubled. This could be because sunlight passes through the polar atmosphere at a very slanted angle and the effective amount of ozone that screens Antarctica's surface from the sun may be greater than in the temperate zones even when the hole is largest. In any case, so far there have been no observed adverse consequences for animal and plant life.[48]

Is ozone depletion something to be concerned about? Of course. Scientific findings suggest a credible link between the existence of chlorine, which may come from CFCs, and a reduction in ozone in the stratosphere. What isn't clear is what role meteorological factors play in the ozone changes and whether what is occurring is actually harmful. There is no finding so far of the predicted effect, an increase in UV radiation; in fact, just the opposite is true.

Policy Choices on Global Warming and Ozone Depletion

As we have shown, there is widespread concern, bordering in some cases on a crisis mentality, over global warming and the extent to which it is caused by greenhouse gases generated by human activity. Similarly, fears of ozone depletion have led to promises by governments to cut down on CFCs and to substantial improvements in the commercial outlook for CFC substitutes.

As we have seen, proposals are on the table to cut back on fossil fuels, and there is already an international agreement, the Montreal Protocol, that purports to set a limit on use of CFCs by industrialized nations. The difficulties of actually implementing and enforcing these agreements are largely ignored, as are the costly impacts of the vague proposals for coping with global warming.

Implementation would require giving governments additional power, would force people to make large sacrifices, and if technologies are specified politically, as they usually are with political control, would limit innovation. Of course, getting effective international agreement on any of these would have ramifications for foreign policy in a wide number of areas.

It is appropriate to seek better information before substantially restricting the freedom of the people of the world to improve their circumstances by the use of modern technologies such as fossil-fuel energy and refrigeration. As we have seen, the knowledge of scientists on the relevant questions of fact and prediction is seriously incomplete, and their claims are often contradictory. More optimistically, scientific understanding of global warming mechanisms and trends is improving, so our ability to discern and predict large-scale atmospheric changes, and thus to make well-informed policy decisions is increasing.

Proposals Are Costly

Measures designed to put less CO_2, CFCs, and other gases into the atmosphere involve serious restrictions on the ability of people to improve their lives, or even to be safe. One proposal, to increase the fuel efficiency of automobiles, will undoubtedly be lethal. A study of fuel efficiency standards by Robert W. Crandall of the Brookings Institution and John D. Graham of the Harvard School of Public Health indicate that current standards are causing deaths because automakers have had to lighten their autos more than they would otherwise. Lighter-weight cars are less safe because they provide less protection in crashes. Crandall and Graham estimated that the congressionally-established standards for the 1989 model year would lead to between 2,200 and 3,900 more deaths by leading to a decrease in auto weight.[49] Less fuel certainly can be burned, but at substantial cost in human life, among other values.

More generally, policy-makers ought to realize that measures to take more CO_2 and other gases out of the atmosphere require the use of land, labour, and other resources which must be diverted from other productive uses. This is true even of reforestation, which is being touted as a benign step that ought to be taken.[50]

One reason CFCs have been so widely used is that they are nontoxic. Substitutes for today's CFCs are likely to be both less safe and significantly more expensive. A number of chemical companies are making large investments in "soft" CFCS, which break down before they reach the stratosphere. But these are not as effective as their "hard" counterparts. Nor are they easy on the local environment. The processes that allow them to break down are the ones that cause car exhaust fumes to form photochemical smogs.[51] Some firms are trying to find completely new products. One, developed by PetroFerm, a Florida research company collaborating with AT&T,[52] apparently performs well but might ignite if sprayed under pressure.[53]

Since refrigeration and air conditioning account for 35 percent of CFC usage, we can expect that more-expensive alternatives will lead to less usage. One way will be to use other preservatives, which may be less safe than refrigeration; another possibility is that more food will spoil, and more microbial illnesses can be expected. Robert Watson of NASA has noted that if CFCs were banned, "probably more people would die from food poisoning as a consequence of inadequate refrigeration than would die from depleting ozone."[54]

Previous Predictions Consistently Wrong

The world has a long history of predictions of environmental doom that never pan out. Competent, highly-respected people have predicted timber famines, worldwide food shortages, permanent energy crises, and critical mineral depletion. But none of these predictions has materialized.

For example, at the turn of the century such eminent individuals as President Teddy Roosevelt and his first chief of the Forest Service, Gifford Pinchot, thought the country was running out of timber. Indeed, a *New York Times* headline which hammered home the urgency of the matter—"Hickory Disappearing, Supply of Wood Nears End: Much Wasted and There's No Substitute"—was typical.[55]

In 1865, the noted British economist William Jevons argued that industrial growth could not be continued for long because the world was running out of coal. He concluded that it was "inevitable, that our present happy progressive condition is a thing of limited duration."[56]

More to the point, perhaps, forecasters of doom who are treated with obeisance today have a track record that ought to encourage caution. For example, in 1968 Paul Ehrlich wrote: "The battle to feed all of humanity is over. In the 1970s, the world will undergo famines—hundreds of millions of people are going to starve to death."[57] Fortunately, this did not prove correct, and increasing privatization of agriculture in the Third World has significantly increased food production. The famines that have occurred were clearly due to political and civil strife. Nor did this 1980 prediction of the much-admired Lester R. Brown pan out. He said that the buyer of a new car should assume that "gas will cost $2 per gallon within a few years and $3 per gallon during the vehicle's lifetime."[58]

Sadly, however, government policies have often been based on such erroneous predictions and have resulted in severe waste and distorted decision-making. For example, in response to a widely-perceived energy crisis, the U.S. government set up the Synthetic Fuels Corporation in 1980 to artificially spur production of energy from new sources. The corporation wasted capital, labour, and natural resources worth billions of dollars to combat a problem that, with no assistance from the corporation, soon turned into a world-wide glut of oil.

Governments have tended to lurch from one policy to another. Sometimes, as in the case of Synfuels, the policies have merely been superfluous, addressing a problem that is in the process of being corrected by market forces. Other policies, such as the price controls placed on oil during the same "energy crisis," actually retarded the market correction.

Sometimes government policies have shifted along with shifts in political power and have distorted decisions of many kinds. The U.S. government's post-World War II aim of nurturing nuclear power for electricity production led to the adoption of the Price-Anderson Act, which limited nuclear power owners' liability. This, in turn, affected the incentives for them to install (and their insurers to require) effective safety measures, making facilities less safe than they could have been. Once anti-nuclear environmental groups became politically powerful, state and federal governments began regulating nuclear utilities so strenuously and inefficiently that costs became prohibitive and safety regulations became so complex that some analysts contend that safety is actually being compromised.[59]

History suggests that mandatory action by governments while the issues are still so debatable is fraught with danger. It could well move us in the wrong direction and stifle activities that would help solve the problem.

Scientific Understanding Is Improving

While our current lack of knowledge makes wise decisions about major policy changes unlikely now, the accumulation of scientific knowledge offers hope that we will be able to act wisely in the future. Atmospheric scientist Stephen Schneider, for example, writing in *Science,* says: "Another decade or two of observations of trends in Earth's climate, of course, should produce signal-to-noise ratios sufficiently high that we will be able to determine conclusively the validity of present estimates of climatic sensitivity to increasing trace greenhouse gases."[60] Meanwhile, research continues not only on the atmosphere, but also on potential ways to deal with the problem, should it prove to be large and real. Any programme begun now would entrench the methods chosen, creating beneficiaries and political clientele which could be counted on to resist any productive change later.

What If the Doomsayers Are Right?

Even though predictions of doom caused by human activities have always been wrong, it is true that "Chicken Little" only has to be right once. What can be done if scientific evidence accumulates to indicate that the greenhouse effect or ozone depletion is critical and that, in addition, changes in human activity could make an important difference? Even at that hypothetical stage, we currently have little reason to expect much in the way of constructive results from international co-operation among sovereign governments. There are a number of reasons for this rather pessimistic outlook, none of which involve the presence of evil or incompetent national leaders.[61]

Nations Differ in Potential Gains or Losses

To stop or counter a truly global pollution problem would probably require large sacrifices on the part of nearly everyone. Yet in the case of global warming, some regions and some activities would benefit while others were harmed.[62] Northern countries might expand their agricultural belts, for example, while other parts of the world experienced severe droughts. However, scientists cannot at this time even predict which areas those would be. Similarly, the negative impact of additional ultraviolet radiation, should it occur, would depend on factors that vary systematically across nations, such as skin colour and geographic latitude. Simply achieving agreement on "How serious is the problem?"—not to mention "What should be done about it?" and "Who should bear the burden?"—would pose huge, intractable difficulties.

Unlike negotiations between individuals, in which property rights are clear and each party must negotiate successfully to obtain benefits from the other, pollution rights among nations are not clearly defined and not easily defended when they are asserted. There is instead a global commons. Negotiations to establish a Law of the Sea Treaty over the past decade illustrate the problems of reaching agreement about the global commons. Third World nations demanded that an international authority be formed to regulate private development of seabed minerals and collect fees that would be distributed to the governments of Third World countries, even those having nothing to do with development of the seabed resources. The U.S. opposed this demand and refused to sign the treaty.[63]

Even though some view the Montreal Protocol as a historic agreement showing that nations can work together, such optimism is unwarranted. Strong differences are in fact present. These appeared in March 1989 at a 123-nation London "Conference to Save the Ozone Layer" hosted by Britain's Prime Minister Margaret Thatcher. Poorer nations resisted the call to cut back on CFCs. The Associated Press reported that "China, India, and other populous developing nations embarking on mass production of consumer goods containing chlorofluorocarbons reason that since the West invented and produces most of the ozone-destroying chemicals, the West should pay to replace them."[64]

Enforcement Difficult and Costly

Even if a workable agreement could be made and kept intact, enforcement would be difficult. Politicians who plan to continue in office must be prepared to help their most powerful constituents rather than society at large. This is evident in the United States as politicians work to preserve regional interests rather than national interests even when claiming to be concerned about the environment.

For example, the 1977 Clean Air Act amendments required that all electric utilities use scrubbers to eliminate sulfur dioxide emissions—even if they could reduce emissions more effectively by just using low-sulfur coal. The scrubber requirement saved the Appalachian coal mine unions and owners from serious competition from low-sulfur Western coal.[65] Similarly, the stricter air pollution regulations placed on undeveloped regions of the U.S. helped protect jobs in the Midwest and Northeast by making development in the South and West more expensive.[66]

Internationally, the problem of enforcement is even more severe. Most traditional pollution problems are local in nature, so that the same political jurisdiction experiences the costs and benefits of control. If rules are violated, there is at least some incentive for enforcement by the political representatives—even though some cheating undoubtedly occurs. The global situation is far more difficult. Any international solution to a global problem will require that local entities bear the control costs, while the benefits of control are global. Local and even national authorities have incentives to allow "cheating" in their own countries, because their constituents gain while the costs of the added pollution are diffused world-wide. Where industrial processes are affected, as in the case of putting controls on CFC production, it is likely that successful restrictions will raise the price of CFCs and thus further encourage cheating.

In sum, the perceptions of each nation's representatives about the seriousness of a specific global problem and the course of action appropriate to deal with it will be conditioned by the best interests of that nation, and more particularly, the nation's political leaders.

Citizens' Demands Based on Misunderstanding

We have already seen how U. S. environmental policies have, quite understandably, been more responsive to powerful political interests than to the environmental problem at hand. An additional problem is that populist pressures from citizens are frequently misinformed.

In democracies of the West, including the U.S., public perceptions of issues that make the headlines are critical to political outcomes. Such public perceptions frequently differ from those of experts. On issues involving technical risk and capitalism, we can expect a strong ideological component to the popular pressure bearing on policy-makers.

A study of nuclear policy in the U.S. by Stanley Rothman and Robert Lichter[67] provides empirical evidence that demonstrates how ideology affects policy in this area. Rothman and Lichter report that most scientists knowledgeable about nuclear energy who publish extensively in peer-reviewed journals consider nuclear energy safe; furthermore, their beliefs about nuclear safety do not correlate with their personal ideologies. A smaller group of scientists, writing more for the public than in peer-reviewed publications, express more opposition to nuclear power. This group's views about nuclear power are closely correlated to their personal ideologies, which are skewed to the left end of the political spectrum.

Journalists, demonstrated by Rothman and Lichter to have the same ideological bent as the smaller group of anti-nuclear scientists, give them much more coverage, thus distorting the public's perception of nuclear power. The combination of these factors leads to policies that discourage nuclear power on grounds of safety, even though substitute forms of power are demonstrably more dangerous.

Given the press treatment of global environmental issues—*Time* made the Earth its "Planet of the Year" for 1988 and featured global warming and ozone depletion—we can expect that in countries such as the U.S. and Canada public policy on these issues will respond to fears exaggerated by ideological influence.

Postponing Commitment while Enhancing Resilience

We have seen that taking the advice of the doomsayers to mandate or force activities such as rationing or taxing the use of fossil fuel and CFCs will probably be costly. In some cases, this will lead to inflexible policies, since beneficiaries and client groups for any given strategy tend to organize and solidify and resist change. In other cases, policies can shift abruptly as the political winds shift. In either case, early decisions end up being very costly.[68] The cost may be appropriate, of course, when early action is urgently needed. With global atmosphere, however, our information is so poor that a plunge into any political strategy seems unwise.

The situation, however, is not hopeless. As the scientific picture continues to unfold, individuals will adapt their plans as they see fit. This will be more effective than people realize.

Political scientist Aaron Wildavsky argues cogently that when there is uncertainty about a potential risk, a strategy of resilience in the face of potential danger is likely to be superior to one of risk prevention.[69] A multiplicity of individual approaches to problems provides a wealth of information to society on the relative value of alternative strategies. In contrast, if individuals believe that the government (or governments world-wide) is handling the problem, less will be tried and less will be learned—and if the government actually fails, then more serious dangers are likely.

Another fundamental fact of life is that, as Wildavsky points out, "richer is safer." When unexpected risks materialize, a richer individual or a richer society is better prepared to cope with them.[70] The countries that can best deal with a catastrophe such as AIDS, for example, are those that have sophisticated medicine, modern hospital facilities, and a population in generally good health. Political scientist Aaron Wildavsky points out that an earthquake in California in 1971 caused 62 deaths. The next year a slightly less powerful earthquake in

Nicaragua killed tens of thousands. Why the difference? The wealthier country had better-built houses, better transportation and communication, better health facilities.

We should be wary of proposals that would slow down the economic progress or squander our resources to "prevent" a risk that may turn out to be the wrong risk to worry about. Resilience rather than anticipation and risk prevention is often the superior strategy for humans.

Conclusion

As with many policy issues, we find that there is good news and bad news. The bad news is that human beings have not learned to successfully explain or predict the weather and other important atmospheric phenomena, nor to cause governments to co-operate constructively in relation to the global environment. Indeed no government, regardless of its form, has been able to achieve an analytically attractive domestic environmental policy. As *Science* editor Daniel Koshland notes, in today's public climate, the system is "tilted to overreaction."[71] Certainly Lester Brown's call for "a wholesale reordering of priorities," and "a fundamental restructuring of the global economy" is unjustified at this point. In western nations, whose economies he would "fundamentally restructure," human health and lifespans have been improving steadily due to technological advance, despite the risks brought on by those advances. It would be foolish to forgo technological means of improving the human condition, unless and until there is far clearer evidence of a need to do so.

The good news is twofold. For one thing, reports implying that we so dominate the environment of our planet we are about to destroy it seem, like early reports of Mark Twain's death, to be greatly exaggerated. Equally important is the news that allowing economic progress to continue will help provide the resilience we will need if our role as polluters should turn out to be as severe as the doomsday forecasters fear.

Notes

1. Quoted in *Chemical & Engineering News,* March 6, 1989, p. 32.
2. *State of the World 1988* (New York: W.W. Norton & Co.), 1988, p. 170.
3. Stephen H. Schneider, *The Genesis Strategy* (New York: Plenum Press), 1976.
4. Reported in "Feeling the Heat," by Michael D. Lemonick, *Time,* January 2, 1989, p. 36.
5. April 1989, Vol. 260, No. 4, p.39.
6. Robin Johnston, "Plan Now For Climate Change, Scientists Say," *The Christian Science Monitor,* February 7, 1989, p. 8.
7. *World Watch,* Vol. 2, No. 2, March/April 1989, p. 6.
8. *EPA Journal,* Vol. 15, No. 1, January/February 1989, p. 7.
9. Ibid.
10. *Scientific American,* op. cit., pp. 36-44.
11. January 2, 1989, p.37.
12. *World Watch,* op. cit., p. 7.
13. The National Academy of Sciences estimates a 1 percent drop in ozone levels could cause a 2 percent increase in cases of skin cancer in the US alone—more than 10,000 additional cases. See "The Heat is On," *Time,* October 19, 1987, p. 60.
14. "A Piece of the Sky is Missing," *Parade,* September 11, 1988, pp. 19-20.
15. Debora MacKenzie and John Gribbin, "Scientists Set to Track Ozone in the Arctic," *New Scientist,* January 14, 1988, p. 30.
16. *Scientific American,* op. cit., p. 39.
17. Ibid., p. 37.
18. Ibid., p. 38.
19. David Rind, "A Character Sketch of Greenhouse," *EPA Journal,* January/February 1989. A more recent report in *Science* (February 3, 1989, p. 603) indicates that one critic of the warming data has reanalysed a temperature monitoring network to correct for the heat island effect. He concludes that the warming is genuine.
20. See Richard A. Kerr, "The Weather in the Wake of El Niño," *Science,* May 13, 1988.
21. Unpublished paper, March 30, 1989.
22. *Scientific American,* op. cit., p. 38.
23. Unpublished paper, op. cit.
24. "The Climatic Effect of CO_2: A Different View," *Atmospheric Environment,* Vol. 18, No. 2 (1984), p.433.
25. Ellsaesser, et al. "Global Climatic Trends as Revealed by the Recorded Data," *Reviews of Geophysics,* Vol. 24, No. 4 (Nov. 1986), p. 785.
26. Unpublished paper, op. cit., p.11.
27. Ibid., p.5.

28. David R. Francis, " Aircleaners in the Ocean," *The Christian Science Monitor*, February 7, 1989, p. 12.

29. Lowell Ponte, "What's Wrong with Our Weather?" *Reader's Digest*, Nov. 1988, p. 74.

30. "The Heat Is On," *Time*, October 19, 1987, p. 63.

31. "Letters," *Time*, January 30, 1989, p. 11.

32. Lowell Ponte, *The Cooling* (Englewood Cliffs, N.J.: Prentice-Hall, Inc.), 1976.

33. Harold W. Bernard, Jr., *The Greenhouse Effect* (Cambridge: Ballinger Publishing Company), 1980, p. 22.

34. Debora MacKenzie and John Gribbin, "Scientists Set to Track Ozone in the Arctic," *New Scientist*, January 14, 1988, p. 30.

35. Alston Chase, "The Ozone Precedent: We've Got a Policy, But Do We Have a Problem?" *Outside*, March 1988. pp. 37-38.

36. "Antarctic Ozone Hole: Expedition Confirms Chlorine Link," *Chemical & Engineering News*, October 5, 1987, p. 6.

37. Idem.

38. "Ultraviolet Verdict," *Scientific American*, May 5, 1988, p. 26.

39. See S. Weisburg, "Ozone Reports Stir Debate," *Science News*, January 9, 1988, p. 20.

40. R. B. Symonds, et al., "Contribution of Cl- and F-bearing gases to the atmosphere by volcanoes," *Nature*, Vol. 334, (August 4, 1988), pp. 415-418.

41. Fred Pearce and Ian Anderson, "Is There an Ozone Hole Over the North Pole?" *New Scientist*, February 25, 1989, p. 32.

42. David Bjerklie, "Cloudy Crystal Balls," *Time*, October 19, 1987, p. 64.

43. Alston Chase, op. cit., p. 39.

44. S. Fred Singer, "My Adventures in the Ozone Layer," *National Review*, June 30, 1989, pp. 34-38.

45. Robert W. Pease, "Ozone Chicken Littles Are at It Again," *The Wall Street Journal*, March 23, 1989.

46. "Letters," *Science*, November 25, 1988, p. 1111.

47. Fred Pearce, "Ozone Threat Spreads from the Arctic," *New Scientist*, March 24, 1988, pp. 22-23.

48. "Biologists Are Assessing Ozone Hole's Effect on Ecology," *Chemical & Engineering News*, November 2, 1988, p. 23.

49. "The Effect of Fuel Economy Standards on Automobile Safety," *Journal of Law and Economics*, Vol. 32, No. 1 (April 1989), pp. 97-118.

50. See quote from Gustav Speth of the World Resources Institute, *Time*, January 2, 1989, p. 38.

51. *New Scientist Alternative*, March 13, 1988.

52. Peter Tonge, "How Orange Rinds Help Save the Ozone," *The Christian Science Monitor*, February 7, 1989, p. 12.

53. Debora MacKenzie, "Industry Develops Ozone-Friendly Processes," *New Scientist,* November 19, 1988, p. 30.

54. Alston Chase, op. cit., pp. 37-38.

55. Charles Maurice and Charles W. Smithson, *The Doomsday Myth* (Stanford, CA.: Hoover Institution Press), 1984, p.46.

56. Quoted in James D. Gwartney and Richard L. Stroup, *Economics: Private and Public Choice* (San Diego: Harcourt Brace Jovanovich), 1987, p. 655.

57. *The Population Bomb* (Ballantine, New York), 1968, p. xi.

58. Quoted in *Policy Review,* Summer 1986, p. 75.

59. See "Does Adding Safety Devices Increase Safety in Nuclear Power Plants?" by Elizabeth Nichols and Aaron Wildavsky, in Wildavsky, *Searching For Safety* (New Brunswick: Transaction Books), 1988, pp. 125-147.

60. S. Schneider,"The Greenhouse Effect: Science and Policy," *Science,* Vol. 243, (February 10, 1989), p. 776. In the same article, Schneider suggests that our current ignorance should not delay strong policy measures, just in case the potential problem is later verified.

61. Similar difficulties are encountered in issues involving oceans. The reader is referred to Ross D. Eckert, *The Enclosure of Ocean Resources: Economics and the Law of the Sea* (Stanford: Hoover Institution Press), 1979, Ch. 6.

62. See Philip H. Abelson, "The Arctic: A Key to World Climate," *Science,* Vol. 243, No. 4893 (February 17, 1989), p. 873.

63. See Doug Bandow, "The Law of the Sea Treaty: Still Flawed and Increasingly Irrelevant" (Backgrounder Update), (Washington: The Heritage Foundation), Jan. 15, 1988.

64. Associated Press, "Industrial Nations Unwilling to Pay for Cleaner Ozone," *Billings Gazette,* March 8, 1989.

65. See R.W. Crandall, *Controlling Industrial Pollution* (Washington, D.C.: Brookings Institution), 1983.

66. See B. Peter Pashigian, "Environmental Regulation: Whose Self-interests Are Being Protected?" *Economic Inquiry,* Vol 23 (October 1985), pp. 551-584.

67. Stanley Rothman and S. Robert Lichter, "Elite Ideology and Risk Perception in Nuclear Energy Policy," *American Political Science Review,* Vol. 81, No.2, June 1987, pp. 384-404. The analysis of this article stood up well to criticism. See also Charles J. Helm, S. Rothman, and S.R. Lichter, "Is Opposition to Nuclear Energy an Ideological Critique?" *APSR,* Vol. 82, No. 3, 1988, pp. 943-951.

68. An interesting example of an unnecessarily costly strategy is the government's attempts to assure the availability of helium. See Richard

L. Stroup and Jane S. Shaw, "Helium—How Much Is Enough?" *Regulation,* March/April 1985, pp. 17-22.

69. See Aaron Wildavsky, *Searching for Safety* op. cit., especially Ch. 4.
70. See Wildavsky, op. cit. Ch. 3.
71. See Daniel E. Koshland, Jr., "Scare of the Week," (Editorial), *Science,* Vol. 244, No. 4900, April 7, 1989.

Chapter 6

The Economics of Protecting
the Ozone Layer

Douglas A. Smith

Introduction

The ozone layer has been the subject of substantial media attention in recent years. It poses interesting and important scientific and economic problems and in many respects is a potentially difficult area in which to implement successful control policies. In spite of these difficulties, the policies that have been developed to preserve the ozone layer can be characterized as an environmental success story. Part of the reason for deeming these policies a success is that there are so many reasons why they could have failed.

Like acid rain and the greenhouse effect, the destruction of the ozone layer is a global environmental problem. The ozone layer is an international open-access resource that is likely to be over-used relative to a theoretical ideal. Control measures to reduce consumption of ozone-depleting chemicals are costly and the benefits of such reductions are shared by all countries, whether or not they also institute such policies. There is, in other words, a potentially serious free-rider problem.

The other difficulty in protecting the ozone layer from the point of view of environmental policy is that there has not been a scientific consensus on the link between emissions of industrial chemicals and the ozone layer. This consensus has grown in recent years, but when the initial policies in this area were developed, the consensus was less strong than it is now.

The scientific uncertainty about ozone meant that it was always possible to argue that waiting for better information would yield more effective policy. This is a standard problem for economists. Frequently there are benefits associated with waiting, but potentially, there are also costs. Determining the appropriate time to act requires information on the probabilities and magnitudes of the effects in question. The possibility of obtaining better information in the future is not necessarily a good reason for delaying action. The impact of waiting must be included in alternative benefit-cost assessments, along with other factors.

This paper also stresses the mechanics of the policies chosen to control emissions of ozone-depleting substances in Canada and the United States. The traditional approach to environmental policy has been to regulate directly—an approach referred to as command and control. As other papers in this volume argue, this approach is almost certain to be inefficient from the point of view of economics. Economists almost universally favour a system that allows transfer of the right to use polluting substances. In contrast to other pollution-control policies, the private sector was involved at an early stage to assist in developing a solution that maximized the role of market forces. This market-oriented approach can serve as a model for pollution-control policies in a wide variety of other areas.

The Ozone Problem

The stratospheric ozone layer lies between six and 30 miles above the surface of the earth. A depleted ozone layer would allow more ultraviolet radiation to reach the earth. The most directly quantifiable impact of increased ultraviolet radiation is on human health, particularly on the incidence of skin cancer and cataracts. Other potentially important effects include reduced crop yields and damage to aquatic ecosystems and the world fishing industry.

The emerging scientific consensus links the use of chlorofluorocarbons (CFCs) and halons to the destruction of stratospheric ozone.[1] CFCs are used primarily in refrigeration and air-conditioning and in the production of rigid insulation foam and flexible foam for furniture.[2] These applications constitute approximately 80 percent of chlorofluorocarbon consumption in Canada. CFCs are also used as a propellant in some aerosols, as a component of sterilant gas to clean hospital equipment, and as a solvent to clean computer circuit boards and other electronic components.[3] Overall, CFC use is confined to a relatively narrow segment of the economy, and this serves to restrain the costs of restricting its consumption. Halons are used primarily in fire-protection systems for computer rooms and other valuable property, because halons are non-toxic and cause minimal damage to protected equipment.

The harmful effects of CFCs and halons on the stratosphere are somewhat counter-intuitive because they result from their chemical stability. These substances have very attractive properties as industrial chemicals because they are safe to work with and do not cause local environmental problems.

Once released, CFC and halon molecules are slowly transported to the upper atmosphere. This movement can take as long as five years. In the stratosphere, ultraviolet light from the sun decomposes the molecule, releasing the chlorine atom in the case of CFCs or the bromine atom in the case of halons. This decomposition may not take place for 50 or more years after the CFC reaches the stratosphere. For this reason, current ultraviolet radiation levels are a misleading guide to policy formation.

In the upper atmosphere, released chlorine and bromine atoms interact with ozone molecules, breaking them down into chlorine monoxide and oxygen. There is some scientific uncertainty about the magnitude of this effect, with estimates of the number of ozone molecules broken down by one chlorine atom ranging from 10,000 to 100,000.

The ozone layer is capable of regenerating itself, but this process clearly depends on the balance between ongoing ozone creation and destruction from CFCs and halons, as well as natural destruction that has always occurred.[4] Existing policy initiatives are aimed at controlling the consumption of CFCs and halons sufficiently to allow regeneration.

Protecting the Ozone Layer

International policies to reduce the extent of ozone depletion were initiated in 1981. The first concrete step was the 1985 Vienna Convention, which established monitoring and scientific assessment activities but stopped short of specific restrictions. This was followed in 1987 by the Montreal Protocol on Substances that Deplete the Ozone Layer.

From the perspective of economics, the Montreal Protocol is noteworthy because most of the members of the international community were able to reach an agreement that deals effectively with the free-rider problem. They achieved this by including provisions for trade sanctions against countries that do not participate. The Protocol is also interesting because it was based on probable—rather than certain—benefits of reducing the consumption of CFCs and halons.

The Montreal Protocol is an international agreement to reduce consumption of controlled CFCs and halons. It establishes the following schedule for reducing consumption:

- Reduce consumption of CFCs in 1989-90 to actual consumption levels in 1986;

- Reduce 1993-1994 consumption of CFCs to 80 percent of 1986 consumption;

- Reduce 1998-1999 consumption of CFCs to 50 percent of 1986 levels; and

- Freeze halon consumption in 1992 at 1986 consumption levels.[5]

It is important to note that specific CFCs, such as CFC-12, used in most refrigeration applications, are not controlled individually. Different CFCs have different ozone-depleting potentials (ODP) and the Protocol restricts consumption of the total ODP of the group of CFCs in each country.[6] This decision not to regulate each CFC and halon on a uniform basis was the first step in the direction of using market forces to implement the Protocol, because it allows users as a group to concentrate CFC reductions where they are cheapest.

The Montreal Protocol entered into force on January 1, 1989, and its consumption restrictions begin on July 1, 1989. The signatories—which include 32 nations and the members of the European Economic Community—constitute over 85 percent of world consumption of CFCs and halons. The Protocol also contains a framework for including non-participating developing countries if their consumption of these chemicals increases. It also contains trade sanctions to deal with countries that choose not to participate.

Costs and Benefits of Environmental Protection

Other chapters in this volume provide a detailed analysis of the economic framework that should guide environmental policy. In practical terms for economists, the framework is implemented through the use of cost-benefit analysis.

The costs of implementing the Montreal Protocol are, at least conceptually, relatively straightforward. The Montreal Protocol restricts consumption of CFCs and halons thereby increasing the prices of products using these substances as inputs. The social costs of restricting consumption would be measured in terms of lost consumers' surplus on units of output that are no longer produced. The administrative costs of implementing and enforcing the Protocol must also be included here.

The benefits of the Montreal Protocol are more complex to measure. Its impact is part of a chain that begins with the link between Protocol-mandated reductions in CFC consumption and reduced ozone destruction. The next link is between reduced ozone destruction and a decreased amount of ultraviolet radiation that reaches the earth. The final step is establishing the relationship between reduced ultraviolet radiation and reduced health impacts.

The first step in this chain requires scientific impact models, while the last step involves a medical impact model to relate different levels of ultraviolet radiation to the incidences of skin cancer, cataracts, and other effects. Each of these models is subject to some degree of scientific uncertainty. It should be emphasized, however, that the existence of uncertainty is not unique to environmental problems. In the absence of uncertainty, most of our economic policy problems would have obvious solutions.

The economic approach to pollution-control policy is relatively straightforward. If property rights are clearly defined and if transactions costs are low, private market participants should be able to resolve pollution-type problems just as they make other voluntary exchanges. In other cases, there may be net social benefits from public sector-involvement. However, most economists would agree that this intervention should make use of the market mechanism.

The fundamental economic point is that policies to deal with all forms of pollution should be based on an assessment of all social costs and social benefits. Only policies that promise an excess of benefits over costs, including all costs associated with the intervention, should be introduced. As well, policies should be implemented in the most efficient possible manner. These principles seem obvious, but they have not always been used to develop pollution-control policies.

The Montreal Protocol is an international regulatory framework. It is being implemented in signatory nations through regulations introduced in each country to conform to Protocol standards. Government policy in both Canada and the United States now requires a "regulatory impact assessment" of all major regulations that are proposed. Such assessments have been carried out for both countries and, as a result, we do have estimates of the social benefits and costs of participating in the Protocol.

A complete review of the benefit-cost models prepared for Environment Canada and the U.S. Environmental Protection Agency (EPA) is beyond the scope of this paper. These models, initially developed by the EPA[7], include all of the links from CFC reduction to health impacts that are outlined above.[8] The Canadian results are assessed in a model that extends from 1989 to 2075 and measures control costs and health benefits. The ratio of benefits to costs varies from scenario to scenario but is almost always greater than ten. The results of the model are not very sensitive to different social discount rates or different values of life used in estimating the health benefits. They indicate that there are likely to be very significant net benefits from implementing the control measures of the Montreal Protocol.[9]

Control Policies

There are, in principle, substantial social gains to be made from reducing CFC and halon consumption if the cost and benefit estimates described above are correct. The size of these gains, however, is very sensitive to the way in which control policies are implemented. In the case of the ozone layer, control policies have been developed with a view to efficiency through the use of market forces.

The Montreal Protocol contains a series of intermediate steps through which CFC consumption would be reduced by 1998 to 50 percent of consumption in 1986.[10] These targets or objectives could be achieved in a variety of ways. If past policy were an accurate predictor, the government would not only have determined the target but would have participated actively in the mechanics of how the target is to be reached. For example, the government could review all of the areas in which CFCs are used and assess the technologies employed within each sector. Almost certainly, CFC inputs per unit of output vary within sectors. This paper argues that the more direct approach of focusing on targets, rather than on how the private sector achieves these targets, produces better environmental policy.

In the development of other environmental policies in North America, regulations frequently have mandated the use of "best available technologies" to reduce pollution. This means that all firms would be required to use the most "CFC-efficient" technology, regardless of other costs that might be involved. In addition, this command-and-control approach usually adopted specific targets for each polluter. For example, if the target was a 20 percent reduction in emissions of a particular pollutant, every firm would be required to reduce emissions by 20 percent. Again, this reduction would be without regard to the other costs involved.

Economists have long criticized command-and-control policies[11] and have argued that their overly restrictive nature generates inefficiency and may even reduce environmental improvement. Command-and-control policies can be described as central planning applied to environmental assets. Economists have argued that environmental assets are too valuable to use such an inefficient mechanism. The efficiencies of the market mechanism should be used to improve the environment.

Pollution reduction should be regarded as a commodity. It can be produced at different cost by different firms. The clear social objective should be concentrating pollution reduction where it can be achieved most efficiently.[12] Across-the-board reductions of 20 percent in pollution as part of the command-and-control approach described above are the antithesis of efficiency. If the economy consists of two firms, it may be most efficient to concentrate all of the pollution reduction in one of the two firms. The market mechanism will act to do exactly this on the basis of relative control costs that will be equated, at the margin, across all polluters.

In the example provided above, the economically efficient solution could be implemented in a number of ways. If there are only two polluters, direct negotiation between the two firms should generate agreement on how to achieve pollution reductions and how to share the costs. In more complex situations, where numbers are larger, the rights to emit the reduced quantities could be sold. This discussion omits measurement and enforcement issues, the costs of which may be a function of the control method chosen.

The distinction between objectives and control policies is crucial to this discussion. Using the market does not reflect a reduced commitment to the environment. The objectives or targets are determined through the cost-benefit analysis described above. The mechanisms for achieving those targets can and should be structured efficiently. In the case of the Montreal Protocol, the use of the market and of private-sector initiatives has been the cornerstone of control policies.

In Canada and the United States, the right to produce the Protocol-determined quantities of CFCs has been allocated to existing producers. There can be legitimate debate about the merit of this decision relative to other allocations, or, more particularly, relative to an auction of rights to use CFCs. However, the key point is that these rights are transferable. Transferability, rather than the identity of initial recipients of allocated rights, should be the paramount concern for economists.

Market Responses

In both Canada and the United States, producers and major users of ozone-depleting substances have been actively working with government to develop control policies. This has led to accelerated research and development work by producers on substitutes for CFCs. It has also led users to review their alternatives prior to the regulations coming into effect. That is, many input substitutions cannot be made instantaneously, so many users are already switching away from CFCs in anticipation of the price increases that will accompany the Montreal Protocol.

A recurring theme throughout this volume is that market responses to higher prices are likely to be swift and substantial. Many demands for CFCs have already been reduced in anticipation of higher prices. In the cleaning of computer circuit boards, for example, most medium and large users are developing relatively low-cost recycling systems that will significantly reduce CFC emissions. Already, producers of extruded polystyrene sheets for egg cartons and fast-food containers have switched entirely to a non-CFC substitute. The largest producer of extruded polystyrene insulation, Dow Chemical, has announced that it will have switched all of its insulation plants to non-CFC substitutes by the end of 1989.

In addition to demand-side market responses, the supply side is very active in developing substitute products that do not deplete the ozone layer. Ideal substitutes share the chemical properties of CFCs but are more volatile, so that the chlorine is released before it reaches the upper atmosphere.

Substitute chemicals have already been developed and tested for refrigeration and air-conditioning applications, most aerosols, most foam products, and solvents. Under the current development schedule, these substitutes will be commercially available during 1993 and 1994. The delay in supplying these chemicals, already being produced in pilot plants relates to necessary toxicity testing under other environmental and health and safety regulations. However, the initial phases of these tests have been completed and it appears likely that substitutes will be available in the timeframe described. DuPont, the largest CFC producer in North America, has announced it will no longer produce the chemical after the year 2000.In fact, market responses on both the demand and supply side are proceeding so rapidly that the standards of the Montreal Protocol may quickly be exceeded. The anticipation of higher CFC prices appears likely to generate quantity reductions greater than those mandated by the Protocol.

This is particularly likely to be the case after 1994, when all of the refrigeration and insulation substitute chemicals are available.

Forecasts of future consumption patterns are always hazardous, but on the basis of the available evidence, it would not be unreasonable to suggest that CFC consumption in North America could be close to zero by 1998. Under the Montreal Protocol, CFC consumption levels in 1998 would still be 50 percent of the 1986 level. If this optimistic forecast is correct, it shows the effectiveness of the market as a tool of environmental policy, and would also be desirable on environmental grounds.

Under the terms of the Montreal Protocol, the signatories also established a process of continued scientific review of ozone levels. Data from this international group suggest that CFC reductions greater than those mandated by the Montreal Protocol may be necessary to stabilize the ozone layer. Different governments are considering or have already announced CFC reduction targets more ambitious than the Protocol. However, the above argument suggests that these more stringent targets may be redundant due to the effectiveness of market responses to the Montreal Protocol.

Some readers of this volume may question the merits of government intervention to control pollution beyond the general establishment of property rights. The pure property rights approach may be sufficient, as in the standard case of the laundry and the smoking factory. However, it is hard to see how the creation of property rights for the stratospheric ozone layer would be superior to the solution outlined in this paper. A truly free-market property rights approach to protecting the ozone layer will never be a realistic possibility. The aspects of the Montreal Protocol that are reviewed positively in this paper are market-oriented, if not completely free-market, in the sense of being negotiated privately.[13] Many pollution problems are likely to share the characteristics of the ozone problem, which provide a comparative advantage for government as opposed to purely private solutions.

Conclusions

The introduction to this paper describes international measures to protect the ozone layer as an environmental success story. Of course, success is always defined in relative terms. Ideally, we would not have damaged the ozone layer at all. Within the realm of realistic policy alternatives, however, our success has been in reacting to an important policy problem.

A fundamental reason for the relative success of ozone policy is that the costs of inaction, however imprecisely measured, threatened to be very large. The potential threats to human health alone imply large benefits from policies to stabilize the ozone layer in order to keep ultraviolet radiation levels from increasing. A related factor deals with control costs. For some industries, these costs will be very high in absolute terms. Overall, however, the social costs of a strategy that ultimately eliminates the use of CFCs are moderate. This is because CFCs constitute only a relatively small component of total production costs and, for most users, substitution possibilities are substantial. The net result is a very favourable ratio of benefits to costs for most CFC reduction scenarios.

In terms of reconciling environmental and economic priorities, implementation of the Montreal Protocol in North America has also been successful and provides important guidelines for solving many other environmental problems. Control mechanisms have been market-oriented and, most importantly, have made the right to use restricted quantities of CFCs transferable. Market responses to the Montreal Protocol on both the supply and demand side have been swift and are likely to go far beyond mandated standards.[14]

In addition, dubbing Protocol initiatives a success also reflects the large potential that existed for failure. The ozone layer is an open-access resource, and any control policy must deal with severe free-rider problems. The Protocol's trade sanctions and its framework for including developing countries if their use of CFCs crosses defined threshold levels break new ground in international environmental policy.

Scientific uncertainty was a further potential barrier to achieving an international agreement. The scientific consensus on this issue is still not complete. This kind of uncertainty is difficult for non-scientists to assess. The media regularly report on ostensibly reputable statisticians who question the link between cigarette smoking and health effects. This problem of establishing causal links is not unique to science. In which category should an environmental policy-maker place a scientist who questions what seems to be a growing scientific consensus that CFCs are a critical factor in the destruction of the ozone layer?

Uncertainty about scientific evidence is likely to be a characteristic of many important environmental problems.[15] Economists can use sensitivity analysis to demonstrate how different scientific views influence the benefits of control measures. However, in the case of ozone destruction, the growing convergence of scientific views contributed to the successful introduction of control policies.

If recent policy to protect the ozone layer is a success what are its implications for other environmental policy issues? The benefits of policies to reduce CFC consumption were defined and assessed in economic terms. Many environmentalists take environmental damage by itself to be evidence that costly controls are necessary. The ozone experience shows that economists can value the benefits of environmental improvement even when the scientific links are complex. Policy initiatives without such documentation will be less likely to succeed.

On the policy side, the Montreal Protocol has focused almost entirely on objectives, leaving the mechanisms for achieving those results to the market. The public-sector role has been primarily to develop a system for monitoring consumption of regulated substances.

The most important component of using a market orientation to implement the Montreal Protocol in Canada and the United States has been transferability. Individual firms are not required to achieve specific reductions. Instead, quantities are restricted, and higher CFC prices will act to allocate reduced supplies to users for whom control costs are highest. Reactions to date suggest the effectiveness of this approach.

Notes

1. Halons are fluorocarbons containing bromine rather than chlorine as in the case of CFCs. Bromine is, in fact, a more potent destroyer of ozone molecules than chlorine.
2. Freon is the DuPont trademark for CFC-12, a commonly used refrigerant.
3. Earlier regulations substantially reduced the use of CFCs in aerosols before the current round of restrictions. Few aerosols now contain CFCs.
4. There are a variety of references to the scientific aspects of ozone destruction by CFCs and the natural regenerative capacity of the stratosphere. For a recent review and further references, see M.B. McElroy and R.J. Salawitch, "Changing Composition of the Global Stratosphere," *Science*, February 1989, pp. 763-770.
5. This section is based on, *Preserving the Ozone Layer: A First Step*, Environment Canada (Ottawa, 1988).
6. The Montreal Protocol assigns each CFC a weight corresponding to its ODP. CFC-11 and CFC-12 have weights of 1.0, while CFC-115 has a weight of 0.6. Among halons, halon 1211 has a weight of 3.0 and halon 1301 a weight of 10.0. The differential ODP weights mean that one unit of halon 1301 (ODP of 10) consumes 10 times more ozone than one unit of CFC-11 (ODP of 1).
7. U.S. Environmental Protection Agency, *Regulatory Impact Analysis: Protection of Stratospheric Ozone* (Washington, 1988).
8. The Canadian results are described in Douglas A. Smith and Keith Vodden, *Global Environmental Policy: The Case of Ozone Depletion* (mimeo, Carleton University, 1989).
9. Reference is made above to the free-rider problem. The obvious response to the Canadian results is that Canada could have the same benefits without the costs by not participating. This ignores the Protocol trade sanctions against non-signatories and the costs of retaliation that would occur in related areas such as acid rain, as well as in non-related areas.
10. The halon target is different, but the point of this section applies to both the CFC and halon targets.
11. See. W.J. Baumol and W.E. Oates, *Economics, Environmental Policy and the Quality of Life* (Englewood Cliffs, N.J.: Prentice Hall, 1979) and other papers in this volume, particularly Chant, McFetridge, and Smith.
12. This may over-simplify in cases where the location of the pollution is important.
13. Edwin Dolan makes a similar point with regard to control measures for acid rain in his paper in this volume.
14. This may seem counter-intuitive to some economists, but the "overshooting" can be explained in terms of the structure of the cost functions involved. The cheapest input configurations would involve

CFCs but for many processes, the decision to switch may be all-or-nothing. Some overshooting also reflects anticipation of future control measures going beyond the Montreal Protocol.

15. The greenhouse effect and acid rain are obvious examples.

Chapter 7

Chemophobia and Activist Environmental Antidotes: Is the Cure More Deadly than the Disease?

*Richard L. Stroup**

The Non-Crisis Dominating Today's Environmental Policy

There is no question that as we become wealthier and more technologically advanced, the potential for man-caused danger increases. New chemicals are introduced constantly, and there is no question that chemophobia—the fear of chemicals—is increasing also. Environmental activists tell us that if the government does not take immediate control of the situation, results will be catastrophic. As in so much of environmental policy, a crisis atmosphere dominates.[1] The results are anything but constructive. In this chapter, we will look at the source of these fears, see why they are so greatly exaggerated, and examine the counterproductive policies that have resulted. We will see also that the procedures inherent in traditional property rights and the common law have the potential to protect us well, as indeed they did for most of the preceding century and more.

Governmental intervention in environmental affairs poses serious dangers to our safety and material well-being, as well as to our liberties. Take, for example, the case of Times Beach. In February 1983, this small Missouri town became nationally famous as newspaper headlines reported that its streets had been contaminated with the chemical dioxin more than 10 years earlier.

*Richard L. Stroup is a Senior Associate of the Political Economy Research Center in Bozeman, Montana. He acknowledges the substantial assistance of Ayn Cabannis, Donald Leal, and Jane Shaw of the Political Economy Research Center in preparing this chapter.

Environmental Protection Agency administrator Anne Gorsuch (later Burford) announced that the EPA would pay $33 million to buy the town's homes and businesses. This decision was made even though there was no evidence that anyone in Times Beach had ever been harmed by the dioxin. Administrator Gorsuch traveled to Times Beach to announce the buyout personally and to demonstrate to the national media her concern over the risks of hazardous waste. But less than two weeks later, she was forced to resign—accused of, among other things, a callous disregard for such risks. There is still no evidence that human health is endangered, but Times Beach remains a ghost town.

The Times Beach affair paralleled the Love Canal disaster that occurred during the Carter administration. In 1978, the New York State Health Commissioner declared an emergency and urged women and young children to move from neighbourhoods near the Love Canal chemical waste site. The governor of New York, up for reelection, called for federal aid and the Carter administration responded with funds to help the state purchase hundreds of homes. Today, many of the purchased houses are in a state of serious disrepair, or have been torn down. Large parts of the community have been destroyed, and more than $250 million has been spent to date for a cleanup that is still unfinished. Although claims of medical effects have been made, no credible evidence has been found that the chemical waste at Love Canal caused any long-term health problems. We shall see below a series of governmental errors led to the escape of the chemicals. But in the end, it was environmental politics and policy, rather than direct chemical damage, that caused the destruction at Love Canal. Of course, the national media has provided precious little coverage of the origins of the chemical leak or the apparent lack of resulting health damage to human health. Yet most people, even today, believe that Love Canal was some sort of health catastrophe, and it was the Love Canal incident that triggered congressional action to establish Superfund legislation.

There is relatively little partisan flavour to the politicization of environmental issues. It occurs in Republican and Democratic administrations alike. The result has been stricter regulations, more tax and spending programmes, and large mandatory private expenditures. Yet demonstrable benefits from these programmes are minimal. For example, even though long-term health problems from industrial waste sites are almost impossible to substantiate, Congress has mandated that another $8.5 billion will be spent on Superfund, with the goal that each hazardous waste site is to be cleaned up to drinking water standards. A recent EPA study reported that "[o]verall, EPA's priorities appear more closely aligned with public opinion than with our estimated risks."[2] Political imperatives are such that crisis generates a strong demand for action but the mere opportunity to improve public health does not.

Crisis Secures Power and Funding

While public opinion has fueled most of today's federal anti-pollution policies, organized special interests have been quick to take advantage of them. Members of Congress, after all, do not have national constituencies, and helping important constituent groups is the name of the legislative game. It is not surprising that many of the costly policies of the Clean Air Act have been used to fight regional economic battles and to protect the powerful eastern coal industry and its unions.[3]

Those whose careers are bound up in "going after" polluters are not necessarily acting selfishly or in bad faith. Many are undoubtedly drawn to their work precisely because they believe deeply in the "anti-pollution" mission of their agencies. But the fact is that additional public fear and outrage expands their agency budgets and thus their career possibilities. The bureaucratic leadership forms one leg of what political scientists call the "Iron Triangle." Special interests, each seeking a competitive edge—or trying to avoid being put at a severe disadvantage through the political process—are willing and able to use their lobbying power to help the bureau, which in turn sees to it that their clients' interests are not forgotten as bureau strategies and tactics are decided and carried out.

The politicians are the third leg of the iron triangle, operating as brokers between special interests, from whom they draw campaign support, and bureaus, which, with carefully manipulated budgets and regulatory authority, can work with politicians to do much, at public expense, for the politically organized special interests.

The power to tax and transfer society's wealth, which is given to government in order to protect the public, is given much more easily when the public is convinced that a crisis is at hand and that disaster may occur without government action. Therefore, members of the "Iron Triangle" have little incentive to stress or publicize facts that might reduce the fear or the uninformed outrage of the public. For this and other reasons, the general public remains badly uninformed about the risks actually posed by man-made chemicals.

In the case of environmental politics, non-profit environmental groups have become almost an adjunct of the bureaucracy. The major environmental groups receive large sums of money from government agencies, and contributions from their donors partly depend on donors' fear, outrage, or even panic about their favourite environmental issues.[4]

Risk, Fear, and the Role of Environmental Activists

Environmental activism took hold in the U.S. in the 1960s as politically active groups shifted their attention from atmospheric nuclear testing to chemical pollutants. The movement began with the publication of Rachel Carson's *Silent Spring* in 1962. As in much environmental literature since that time, the rhetoric in *Silent Spring* was eloquent and full of strong emotions, but the supporting evidence—against DDT, for example—was considered by many scientists to be one-sided and misleading. The book elicited fear and indignation and moved people to demand political action against those who would pollute and plunder the planet. In fact, the fight against DDT was the origin of the Environmental Defense Fund, which from 1967 to 1969 received a reported 19,000 column inches of press coverage on this, the organization's first major issue.[5] By playing on and feeding public fears of such environmental threats, environmental leaders attract thousands of members and hundreds of millions of dollars each year to fight what they view as "the good fight" against potential harms. These harms certainly include chemicals, but for some, the fight is an ideological battle against economic growth.[6] (As we will see below, slowing economic growth itself has some important negative effects on human health and safety.)

Silent Spring inaugurated the view that a whole new regime of governmental controls was required to protect the earth and its inhabitants from technological disasters. This view is still common, and when an environmental crisis stirs public concern, it is the driving force behind public policy. As a result, we are increasingly operating in a new regulatory climate. Among the important changes is the heavy burden of proof on anything new. New activities are often allowed only if shown to be almost "risk-free"—as exemplified by the Delaney clause of the Food, Drug, and Cosmetic Act, which forbids the use of any food additive that can be carcinogenic for humans or for animals, no matter how weak the carcinogenic effect. Faced with the potential risk of new chemicals, drugs, or genetically altered micro-organisms, politicians and bureaucrats are inclined to ban use until safety can be proven. But as AIDs sufferers and the families of those who have died waiting for federal approval of new drugs can attest, "zero risk" is actually a very dangerous strategy.

Although tragically unsafe, this narrow-minded approach is understandable in the government setting. Regulators may not be blamed for the problems faced by people denied the new substance—most of whom will never know about the benefits the government held back—while they most assuredly would be blamed for any untoward effect of a substance they approved. Thus, a drug that could save thousands of lives might be banned to prevent a single death from a carcinogenic side-effect.

Contrast this one-sided pressure on regulators with the balanced set of incentives facing a private firm, such as a drug maker. The firm wants to protect its reputation and avoid liability for selling dangerous drugs. But it also wants to enhance its reputation and its profits by getting out new "miracle drugs" that can help people. Without formal regulation, the company faces the trade-off squarely: Will the added profit from selling new and possibly dangerous drugs to willing buyers (properly warned by the firm, to avoid extra liability problems) be sufficient to offset the likely losses from lawsuits and reputational harm caused by selling the drug? It is highly ironic that in reality, the search for profit provides the private firm with a more balanced view of "the public interest" than that brought to bear on government regulators. Clearly, political safety regulation can be dangerous to our health.

The unintended side-effects of "uncompromisingly tough" environmental standards can be dangerous, too. When DDT was banned because its misuses harmed some wildlife, more dangerous pesticides replaced it. (Elsewhere, the situation was worse: Sri Lanka withdrew from the World Health Organization's large-scale DDT spraying programme, and the number of cases of malaria rebounded from a low of 110 cases in 1961 to 2.5 million cases in 1968 and 1969.) We cannot know just how many farm workers have died from DDT substitutes, but since the replacement pesticides are more harmful to people and must be more frequently applied, banning DDT to avoid risk actually introduced far more human risk.

In general, attempts to achieve "zero risk" in any single arena are dangerous to society because they stifle technical and economic progress. Most research and development efforts in biotechnology have shown no clear and present dangers and, indeed, offer the promise of more effective waste cleanups and less environmentally threatening means of controlling agricultural pests and weeds. But again, the atmosphere of fear and even of crisis has meant that research, testing, and use of these techniques has been hampered needlessly by a web of regulations created by the EPA and the U.S. Department of Agriculture.[7]

Wealthier is Healthier

A common attitude among environmental activists is that we should ignore the economic costs of formulating health, safety, and environmental regulations because safety is an absolute. As Lori Mott of the Environmental Defense Fund puts it, there is "no room for consideration of the benefits of pesticides."[8] Yet from the point of view of health and safety, it's hard to imagine worse advice. Empirical evidence strongly suggests that higher incomes (both for populations of countries and for individuals within those populations) contribute more to good health and life expectancy than whatever risks are introduced in raising those incomes. In general, the higher our incomes, the more options we have—to change our lifestyles, regulate our diets, and choose more selectively among the risks we do take.[9] In addition, when earthquakes, floods, hurricanes, and other natural disasters occur, richer nations can mobilize the resources necessary to save large numbers of citizens in distress.

People in more developed countries have considerably higher life expectancies than people at lower levels of economic development, despite—and in part, because of—the greater use of chemicals. What is true of whole societies is also true of individuals within societies. In England, death from cancer among males in the highest socioeconomic class is 25 percent below the national average, and death from respiratory disease is 63 percent below the national average.[10] In contrast, deaths from cancer and respiratory disease are 31 percent and 87 percent above the national average respectively among males in the lowest socioeconomic class.

Similar evidence exists for the United States. One study of mortality and income for U.S. counties found that each one percent increase in income reduces mortality by 0.05 percent.[11] Based on this study, it is estimated that, for a 45-year-old man working in manufacturing, a 15-percent increase in income would have about the same risk-reducing value as eliminating every single hazard from his workplace.[12] With higher incomes, individuals drive larger, safer cars, fly instead of drive, live in safer houses, eat better, and in a myriad of other ways live safer lives.

In the light of these findings, it appears that government regulation in general, and health and safety regulation in particular, has done a great deal of harm to counter whatever good it has accomplished, even when measured solely in terms of its effects on health. Between 1959 and 1969, productivity in U.S. manufacturing increased by almost 1 percent annually.[13] Between 1973 and 1978, however, manufacturing productivity fell by more than one half of one percent annually.

There is evidence that a significant portion of this drop in productivity was caused by regulations imposed by the Occupational Safety and Health Administration (OSHA) and the Environmental Protection Agency (EPA). One estimate is that 31 percent of the overall drop in manufacturing productivity was due to regulatory burdens created during the 1970s by OSHA and EPA.[14] Nineteen percent of the drop in productivity growth was attributed to OSHA regulations and 12 percent to regulation by the EPA. Moreover, the productivity drop between 1973 and 1978 did not affect all industries equally. Productivity fell by more than 2 percent per year in highly regulated industries, yet it actually rose in the same period in less regulated ones.

Increases in worker incomes are roughly equal to increases in productivity, so whatever the positive impacts of OSHA and EPA may have been, it appears that the damage to health and safety that they have caused by reducing income growth is substantial.

The Risk of Cancer

Fears of chemicals have focused on one potential outcome—cancer. A popular belief is that an epidemic of cancer is sweeping the modern world as a result of increasing chemical inputs into the human body. This "common knowledge" is false. Although new chemicals can, of course, be deadly, chemical production and increasing human exposure to them has been going on for many decades. In their 1981 comprehensive survey "The Causes of Cancer," sponsored by the congressional Office of Technology Assessment and published in the *Journal of the National Cancer Institute*, Richard Doll and Richard Peto conclude that, except for the increase in lung and skin cancer, "examination of the trends in American mortality from cancer over the last decade provides no reason to suppose that any major new hazards were introduced in the preceding decades."[15] Despite claims of a cancer epidemic from toxic chemicals, there is no such thing. Taking age into account, cancer is not increasing in the U.S. Also, our best estimates place the percentage of cancers caused by all man-made chemical and radiational sources at less than 5 percent.[16]

Still, nothing seems to frighten the voting public more, or bring more hurried action from elected officials, than the potential risk of cancer. In the political arena, expressions of outrage are easy since the people demanding action expect others to pay the costs. Often "big corporations" or other faceless entities are thought to be picking up the tab for politically established regulations.

These same citizens, however, act quite differently in accepting and avoiding risk when they control the degree of risk through their own behaviour, and when they bear the direct costs and reap the direct benefits of their actions. Epidemiologists estimate that at least 70 percent of human cancer is avoidable in principle through changes in human behaviour.

Individuals also remain calm and careful in the face of newly revealed dangers such as the natural cancer risk from radon gas in their homes, despite the fact that this danger can be considerable. As many as one million homes are believed to be generating radon decay exposure levels higher than those received by uranium miners, and as much as 10 percent of lung cancer in the United States has been tentatively attributed to radon pollution in houses.[17] Such revelations have not caused panic, but have instead created a market for detection devices, allowing people who are exposed to take cost-effective actions to reduce their exposure to such dangers.

While the risk of cancer may be greatly exaggerated, it is always present. Carcinogens are everywhere. Without any help from man, carcinogens are naturally present in almost every meal. They are present in mushrooms, parsley, basil, celery, cola, wine, beer, mustard, peanut butter, bread, lima beans, and hundreds of other everyday foods. Human beings also produce carcinogens through everyday activities. Baking bread, browning meat, cooking bacon and eggs—all of these activities cause chemical reactions that produce carcinogens. Allowing a sliced apple to become slightly brown involves an oxidation reaction that produces carcinogenic peroxides. Carcinogens also occur naturally inside the human body.

Activist Policies Lead to Counterproductive Actions

Against this backdrop of fear of chemically-caused cancer, and supported by bureaucracies and activist groups whose leaders and missions (and certainly their budgets) benefit from an atmosphere of crisis, environmental policies relating to chemicals are highly counterproductive.

One of the most expensive and ineffective environmental programmes of the past few decades is Superfund, the $10.1-billion programme that is supposed to clean up abandoned waste dumps.[18] The programme was a direct result of the infamous Love Canal crisis. A short history of the Love Canal episode will illustrate how irrational and perverse policy-making in this area has become.

The crisis, which occurred in 1978, began in the 1950s after the local school board purchased a toxic waste site (an abandoned canal) that had been lined with clay, filled, and capped with clay by the Hooker Chemical Company. At that time, the company demonstrated to school board representatives that the site was potentially dangerous and expressed its opposition to selling the property. Under threat of eminent domain, the company sold the property for $1—but only after writing into the transfer documents the nature of the dangers and including a disclaimer of liability for future damages once ownership of the site was transferred.[19]

Despite the warnings from Hooker, the school board removed part of the clay cap (for use as fill at another school site), built a school on the site, and later sold the remaining land to a developer. Even before the land was developed, the city built water and sewer service lines through the clay walls installed by Hooker to contain the wastes. The gaps in the walls from these procedures provided pathways for chemicals to escape, and partial removal of the clay cap had already provided a pathway for rainwater into the formerly sealed dump. The chemicals thus escaped, and were later found in the soils and even the basements of area residents.

Understandably, fear and anger stirred some of the residents to political action. After all, their property and homes had been wrongfully invaded by noxious chemicals. In an election year they had little trouble generating a good deal of action, though few would be satisfied with the results.

The EPA was called in to investigate. In a hastily released statistical study that was later discredited, the EPA announced that it had found evidence of long-term health problems—an increase in chromosome aberrations in a sample of residents.[20] Federal funds were quickly made available to purchase homes in the area. These homes were boarded up and the affected neighbourhoods destroyed. Later, additional federal money purchased more homes. To date, however, detailed studies have turned up no clear evidence of cancers or other long-term health threats in the neighbourhoods. In September 1988, about two-thirds of the area was declared habitable by the New York State Department of Health.

Clearly, there were unacceptable chemical leaks and the potential for chemical risks around Love Canal. However, the case can be made that politics and policy, as practised by levels of government from the local school board and city government up through the presidential level, have so far caused most of the damage to Love Canal and its residents.

California's Proposition 65

Equally disturbing to those who believe that active environmental policy can be established rationally is the enactment of California's Proposition 65, formally called the Safe Drinking Water and Toxics Enforcement Act of 1986. Criticized by pro-business forces as a drag on the growth of the state's economy and praised by a high-profile anti-toxics movement as an effective way to curb consumer demand for chemicals that allegedly cause cancer, Proposition 65 was passed by a voter initiative, receiving 63 percent of the vote. Drafted by the Environmental Defense Fund and the Sierra Club, backed by Tom Hayden, his wife Jane Fonda, and other Hollywood celebrities, Proposition 65 is the most sweeping chemical regulatory law ever enacted by a state government.

Among other provisions, Proposition 65 bans the discharge into drinking water of chemicals "known" to cause cancer or reproductive harm and requires warnings to individuals exposed to these chemicals.[21] As noted earlier, the list of things that cause cancer (in at least some animals, at sufficiently high laboratory doses) is very large. Almost from day one, the list of chemicals covered by the initiative became a political battleground. Environmental and consumer advocates wanted more chemicals added to the official list and businesses struggled to stay abreast of the growing requirements for fulfilling the public's right to know.[22] Interestingly enough, only private water sources were covered.[23] Municipalities, supplying most of the water Californians drink, were exempted.

As of July 1, 1988, 216 substances were listed as carcinogens and 15 substances were listed as reproductive toxins. That list could grow considerably. California officials are considering chemical substances ranging from cocaine to aspirin, and ultimately Californians may discover that it is impossible to enter a retail store or place of work without seeing warning labels.[24]

Public employees are required to notify the news media when they discover violations, and are subject to criminal penalties if they do not disclose the violations that they discover. The law does not merely open the door to numerous lawsuits, it encourages them through bounty-hunter provisions that allow private citizens to collect 25 percent of the fines imposed if they initiate successful suits against violators of the act.

To be guilty of violating Proposition 65, you do not have to actually harm anyone, or even put anyone at risk. Instead, the standards for violations are entirely hypothetical. In the case of carcinogens, a violation has occurred if you expose someone to a chemical and that person would have been at a significant risk if the exposure level had been maintained over the whole of the person's lifetime. In the case of reproductive toxins, a violation has occurred if the chemical would have produced a detectable risk if the person were exposed over the course of a lifetime at a level 1,000 times the level at which the person was actually exposed. Even if we can determine what would have happened, what constitutes a significant risk? "Significant risk" is not a scientific term. There is nothing in science, for example, that says that a one-in-a-million risk of cancer is not significant, while a two-in-a-million risk of cancer is significant.

Under California law there is no penalty for an unnecessary warning. There is a penalty, however, for mistakenly failing to warn. Moreover, those accused of a failure to warn bear the burden to prove that a chemical exposure did not put anyone at a significant risk, a burden that is scientifically impossible to meet. What Proposition 65 does is produce a line-up of suspects that will forever be just that—suspects. Without a viable means of proving innocence, businesses will tend to compound the problem by posting more warnings than necessary. Indeed, they may label all their products just to be on the safe side.[25] Already, homebuilders are posting warnings on all new houses just to play it safe.[26]

Yet if everything is labelled, especially if all labels contain the same warning, then warning labels lose their value. A warning label will affect behaviour only if consumers can distinguish a few especially dangerous risks out of the thousands of minor risks they take in everyday activities. Putting a warning label on every product robs any meaning from the warning label on a truly dangerous product.[27] California law also has the potential to dangerously misdirect attention from non-carcinogenic risks and dangers that we should be concerned about and toward trivial cancer risks. For example, chlorine used in processing milk leads to the production of chloroform, one of the chemicals listed in California as a carcinogen. Yet chlorine helps prevent a much more serious danger—the risk to children of death by food poisoning from milk made without the use of chlorine. The spirit of the California law would appear to require a warning label on milk made with chlorine, but no warning label for the much more dangerous chlorine-free milk.

Environmental Policies versus Property Rights

Traditionally, individuals and their property have been protected against invasion from pollutants primarily by nuisance and tort actions under common law. This system has not been perfect but it has successfully screened us from the worst possible risks. For people fearful of new technologies and moved by stirring prose of the sort in *Silent Spring*, however, the traditional common law system fails to provide adequate safeguards against environmental risks. In their view, the stringent rules of evidence and of standing in court—which have developed to prevent frivolous actions and to balance the interests of plaintiffs and defendants—are unnecessary. Any plausible threat of damage must be eliminated. Since the public is largely ignorant of the facts about environmental risks, this view has stirred up public outrage and led to the policies described above.

But the assumption that government controls aimed at reducing risk to zero are an effective way to make society safer is simply not true. Aaron Wildavsky, in *Searching for Safety*, explains many of the reasons for this fact. For example, he observes that resilience often is a more effective strategy for safety than anticipation. Unlike the turtle, which anticipates blows to its body by growing a shell to hide under, the human body reacts quickly to danger and repairs injuries to itself. Less protected than the turtle in an anticipatory sense, humans are more agile and resilient.

People who gradually build resilience by facing and overcoming risks are better able to survive future dangers. The person who exercises by running, for instance, initially may be at higher risk of suffering a heart attack from the running itself than a person who does not run. The runner, however, by overcoming the initial risk, continues to run and build resilience to ward off future health threats. Similarly, a resilient society often is safer than an anticipatory one, which attempts to protect itself from specific expected threats.

Under current regulatory policies, we, like Wildavsky's turtle, are retreating under a shell to avoid risk, thereby stifling technological development. Yet because wealth and technological advance are important determinants of future safety for citizens, our best strategy for society, even if safety is our only goal, is to recognize the potential danger of chemicals and develop policies to handle the risks without further harming people by hampering technological and economic advancement.

The Case for Property Rights

A strong case can be made that a system of property rights and liability, enforced in common law, is the best way to control the risks we face from hazardous wastes. A strong property rights regime—backed by effective liability and protected by an efficient legal system—holds people accountable. As we shall see in more detail below, owners of property are rewarded when they are good stewards of their property, and penalized—by the loss in value—when they act as poor stewards. When people damage the person or property of others, the law requires them to compensate for the damage.

To illustrate how property rights can protect the environment, consider fishing rights in England and Scotland. There, unlike the U.S., sports and commercial fishing rights are privately owned and transferable.[28] This has led to suits by the owners of fishing rights against polluters of streams. They have obtained damages and injunctions against polluting activities. Such suits occurred well before Earth Day and before pollution control became part of our politically controlled public policy.

To understand how property rights ensure accountability, it is necessary to look at the fundamental characteristics of private property. When an asset, such as a tract of land or a car, is purchased, a property right is exchanged. The asset's title is a paper representation of the exclusive right to use and benefit from the asset's use. Even though for most assets a paper "title" does not exist, the property right nevertheless is owned by someone. In speaking of markets, economists usually assume implicitly that property rights exist and are efficiently configured in three dimensions: they are "3-D" property rights. Property rights must be defined clearly, so as to reside with a specific person or entity; defended easily against non-owners who might wish to use or "steal" the asset; and divestible, or transferable, by the owner to others on whatever terms are mutually satisfactory to buyer and seller.

When "3-D" property rights exist, and when trades can be transacted easily, the owner of any asset—whether land, house, factory, or some other commodity—has both the incentive and the authority to use that asset in such a way as to maximize its value to society. If the asset is used in a way that reduces services available from it, its value falls and the owner loses commensurate wealth. Using land to store chemical wastes, for example, reduces its value in other uses to which it can be put. But costs also are symmetrical. An owner who refuses to use the asset in a fashion valuable to others (storing chemical wastes, for example) forgoes the revenue others would have paid.

A key feature of private property rights is liability. The owner of land or a chemical plant or a stock of chemicals that is misused in a way that damages others is liable for damages. If irreparable harm is threatened, such as clear and immediate danger to life, courts also will grant injunctive relief. Upon proof that the situation really is this serious, and the danger imminent, the person acting to threaten others can be stopped.

Property Rights and Incentives

Property rights also provide long-term incentives for maximizing the value of property, even for owners whose personal outlook is short-term. If I use my land as a toxic waste dump and impair its future productivity or its groundwater, any gains that I make are reduced by the corresponding reduction in the land's value. That is because land's current worth reflects the value of its future services: it is equal to the net revenue from production or the aesthetic pleasure I receive from the land minus the costs (including liabilities) that may arise from the presence of wastes. Fewer services or greater costs in the future mean lower value now. In fact, on the day an appraiser or potential buyer first can see future problems, my wealth declines by the amount of the reduction in the potential buyer's willingness to pay for the land. Not only does using the land to store hazardous waste reduce future options for the land's productivity, the value also may be reduced by increasing my future liability from lawsuits due to damage to other people or property through leakage. The key fact here is that any reduction in future services and future net value due to potential liability is visited on me now, as it directly affects the present capitalized value of my asset.

In effect, the value of the property right, which gives the asset owner the privilege as well as the responsibility of control, serves also as a hostage to the owner's socially responsive stewardship of the asset. Any decision resulting in less value produced, either now or in the future, reduces the land's value now. The reverse also is true: any new and better way found to produce more value now and into the future is capitalized into the asset's present value. Even a short-sighted owner has the incentive to be alert to new possibilities and dangers and to act as if he cares about the future usefulness of the land.[29]

But what if the owner of the land is owned by a corporation, and the corporate officers, rather than the owner-stockholders, are in control? Corporate officers may be concerned mainly about the short term, not expecting to be present when future problems arise. Contrary to much popular opinion, however, property rights hold these decision-makers accountable, too. If current actions are known to cause future problems, or if current expenditures are seen to promise future benefits, the stock price captures the reduction or increase in future net benefits. Current profits do not look to the future, but buyers and sellers of the corporation's stock do. Even the rumour of future benefits or expenses can strongly influence today's stock price. For this reason, even short-sighted decision-makers are immediately visited by the fruits of their actions, even though the "bottom line" of the profit and loss statement may not reflect the results of bad decisions or good investments for a long time to come.

In addition to their implications for stewardship and conservation, three-dimensional ("3-D") property rights also play an important role in stimulating creative and anticipatory investments. A creative landowner's investment might result in the use of a new technology to clean up hazardous waste—bacteria that eat waste, for example—more efficiently than isolating and capping it with clay. Since the property value would immediately be higher if no wastes remain, the long-term benefits accrue immediately, in financial form, to the landowner. For this reason, the landowner becomes an eager customer for improved techniques.

Government decision-makers have no such incentive to capitalize on future values. They needn't fight to pursue efficiency, since costs are very widely shared, and frequently there is no competition from other agencies for funds targeted to their mission. Whereas the owner of a chemical plant, left to his own devices, would try to be cost-effective in minimizing damages and resulting liabilities from hazardous wastes, EPA staffers have no reason to seek such a goal since they cannot be held accountable. Instead, they are more likely to maximize budgets and paperwork in order to demonstrate to constituencies, and their voices in Congress, that they have done as much as possible to fight the hazardous waste problem.

The fundamental problem with current policy in the political arena is that it does not link payment to damages caused, and it often does not allow much freedom to seek cost-effective ways to minimize damages. Ignoring costs may be a plausible strategy in an emergency, but as we have seen, no emergency exists.

As a matter of fact, risk is inevitable. This is important for policy, because the resilience of a richer society will make it safer, and policies intended to bring risks from hazardous waste to zero are not consistent with a richer, safer future for our society. Yet much of today's policy toward hazardous substances aims at eliminating certain chemical risks. To that extent, the policy is negatively productive.

Should Polluters Pay?

Lip-service is often given to the idea that "the polluter should pay." Most analysts agree that the polluter should indeed pay. But for what? Should the polluter pay for cleaning up the soil in a secure (non-leaking) dumpsite to the point where it meets drinking water standards? The cost is likely to be very large—often many millions of dollars' worth of real resources—and yet the benefits tiny if the wastes are, in fact, secure. Payment for damage is different. Most would agree that a polluter should pay for damages caused. The desire to avoid damage gives companies a strong incentive to do what Hooker did at Love Canal while it had control—look ahead and act responsibly.

But in our political world today, the watchword is "producer pays" rather than "polluter pays." Under Superfund, for example, petroleum and chemical companies pay, not according to how much damage they do or even how much waste they generate, but rather according to the amount they produce (of products that consumers want). A firm is charged for this production, even if no pollution is produced and no damage is done. The money collected is used for enormously expensive public works projects, which add little of demonstrated value to public health.

A Better Approach

In common law, unlike politics, forcing polluters to pay for all the damages they have caused has been the standard. Avoiding damage to others is their responsibility, and how they do it is their business. Since the 1950s, however, legal activists have been working to change this system from one of forcing wrongdoers to compensate their victims for the harms done by the defendant to one of compensating victims from whatever deep pocket can be found.[30] Unfortunately, this approach destroys the accountability of potential polluters, reducing their ability to avoid financial loss by avoiding damage to others.

The original system, holding polluters accountable for whatever damage they do without telling them how to do it, is not just good economics; it is also good for public health in the long term. A number of steps could be taken to strengthen the common-law approach, with its rules of evidence and its even-handed treatment of specific risk versus other human values. It could then be more effective in protecting society's overall wealth and its associated health. Strengthening the common law would also increase its political palatability as our primary defence against the unwanted and illegitimate invasion of person and property by another's pollution. These steps might be taken:

1) Allow more freedom of action, using insurance or bonding to guarantee solvency and responsibility.

Accountability through liability is meaningless if a defendant is found to be insolvent, and thus unable to compensate the victim of his actions. Insurance, or its near-equivalent, the posting of a bond as a "hostage" to the successful control of large potential risks, is an answer to this problem. It can provide the appropriate incentives for cost control, both of internal costs and external liability. Insurance companies, after all, want to avoid damages for which they will have to pay. So they will only insure acceptable risks and will work with firms to develop low-risk management techniques and require use of those techniques. Yet insurers must sell policies competitively, so they must also make their demands on customers cost-effective. An insurer who finds a cheaper way to keep risk low will out-compete one requiring more expensive ways of reaching the same low risk levels. Similarly, the firm operating with a large bond posted to guarantee solvency in case of liability claims will have a strong incentive to be both safe and cost-effective in its handling of hazardous materials.

2) Consider strengthening the common law through statute at the state level.

States could do much to restore the ability of insurers to do their job of helping to control risks from unintended pollution, while simultaneously helping to "regulate" smaller firms in their handling of hazardous substances.[31] In recent years, some courts have in effect voided insurance contract clauses defining coverage in order to find "deep pockets" from which to compensate victims of illness that conceivably could have been affected by hazardous wastes.[32] Similarly, when property has been transferred and hazardous liability with it by contract, the courts have sometimes voided that transfer, making all parties liable.[33] This destruction of contract reduces the incentive and ability to put hazardous properties into the hands of competent specialists. When, under full disclosure, such transfers of risk are made among competent (and solvent) parties, contracts should be honoured. That is part of the essence of insurance.

3) Require branding of chemicals when feasible.

Chemicals that might escape into the water or air could probably be "branded" by radioisotopes, dyes, or other means, to help identify their source if later they escape, appear where they are unwanted, and cause damage.

4) Restore basic responsibility for regulation to the state level.

Most chemical pollution problems are local problems. When policies beyond application of the common law are needed, state and local governments can implement them. Many policy nuances and innovations are tried at the state level without the need for national consensus or a national commitment. Differing policies are being tested. This time-honoured variety of approaches among the states is an important part of American life, and an important part of the genius of the federal system. Experiments are small rather than national in scope, and more of them are attempted. The information they yield is useful nationwide.

Would we have had airline deregulation if California and Texas intrastate airlines had not been able to escape CAB regulation and demonstrate how far out of line CAB-regulated prices were? Experimentation is more likely at the state and local level than nationally, and errors much less costly. The results of California's Proposition 65 will provide a useful lesson for other state governments bent on regulating chemicals.

5) Channel federal efforts into research and criminal investigation.

Political demands for a federal role can be focused on basic research into the effects of toxic chemicals and technical forensic mechanisms to help in tracing, or even finding ways to brand, pollutants as they are emitted. The purpose is to help hold polluters accountable in court, so that responsibility can be enhanced. With such mechanisms, polluters would more often be made to pay when harm is done and innocent parties would be less fearful of paying in error. Much of this research will be done privately, of course. Careful firms storing chemical wastes, for example, will want to be able to show through branding that their stored wastes did not show up where damage occurred. Investigation of criminal activity could be another important federal contribution, since organized crime is reputed to be heavily involved in the disposal of hazardous wastes.

6) Make "orphan" waste sites private.

Orphan waste sites, which Superfund was created to clean up, could be transferred to an owner willing, for a price, to take on the cost of cleanup (or containment) and the potential for liability. Using Superfund money, the government could pay the firm making the lowest bid to accept ownership. The new owner would be free to act as it wished, but would be liable for any damages it caused or any threat of imminent danger. A bond posted by the firm could be required as a guarantee that damage would be avoided. The interest-bearing bond, big enough to match the apparent danger of the site, would remain in the hands of the EPA (the bond's income, over and above that needed to keep the bond "whole" in the face of inflation, would go to the firm) until the danger has been permanently eliminated. This could mean that the bond would stay with the EPA indefinitely if the danger is best avoided simply by containing the waste securely. In such a situation, the waste would remain contained until a cheaper hazard-elimination technology came along or a higher-valued use for the site made hazard elimination economical.

With such a plan, the firm with the least-cost way of minimizing the sum of expected liability costs plus control costs would become the owner. A firm that found (or recognized and purchased) the best technology for handling a given site could make a profit, while underbidding all others. This plan would supplant the Superfund programme, and would provide firms with an incentive to find cheap and effective ways to deal with hazardous waste—something that is largely lacking today. No federal funding would be needed for the research, nor would bureaucratic or political approval of the results be necessary. Firms would adopt a new technology at their own risk, since their bonds would be hostage to their successful avoidance of damage. They also would capture the benefit if the new technology reduced total costs.

In Conclusion: A Historical Parallel

Ecologist William Clark has pointed out that in the 16th and 17th centuries half a million people—ostensibly witches—were burned at the stake.[34] These centuries, like most times, were riddled with grievous social ills, such as plagues, mysterious livestock deaths, and disastrous crop failures. No cause could be found for these ill omens, yet the established authorities of the time, church officials, felt obligated to take some action for the benefit of the public good. The blame was placed on "witches."

It was essentially impossible for accused witches to demonstrate that they did not pose a real threat to the community. They could deny that they were harmful, but they certainly could not prove it. With all the terrible societal risks, how could a political authority (or church official) justify not acting against an accused witch? And so it is today with persons using new chemicals, biotechnology, or other innovations. An elected official often is now, as were the ecclesiastical authorities, strongly pressured by an outraged but not very well-informed public for action against polluters, actual and potential.

There is another similarity between the witch-hunts then and governmental programmes today. When witches were burned, their property was confiscated by the authorities. Today, when businesses are "convicted" politically, without evidence or trials, of endangering the public via chemicals, billions of dollars are taken from them (as in Superfund taxes and cleanup provisions), partly to augment the budgets of the agencies in charge of "prosecuting" them.

In sum, a crisis mentality spurs today's environmental regulations, bolstered by well-meaning government officials whose careers benefit from crisis, just as church officials profited four centuries ago. The frequent result, as we have seen, is bad policy that reduces health and safety. Recognizing the value of a property rights regime backed by common law is a first step to correcting this situation. Second, as I have outlined above, some specific changes can be made to strengthen the common law and make it more politically acceptable as a way of dealing with chemical pollution.

The introduction of some detrimental chemicals or hazardous wastes will inevitably occur as man progresses, but their presence does not imply a crisis. With a properly functioning system, the creation of overall improvements for human life is also inevitable.

Notes

1. See Richard L. Stroup, "Environmental Policy," *Regulation*, 1988, No. 3, for a more complete exposition of this section's topic.
2. See "Unfinished Business," an internal EPA document examining EPA programme priorities. It found relatively little correlation between expenditures and their potential for improving the health of U.S. citizens.
3. See, for example, Robert W. Crandall, "Clean Air and Regional Protectionism," *Brookings Review* (Fall, 1981) pp. 17-20.
4. See James T. Bennett and Thomas J. DiLorenzo, *Destroying Democracy: How Government Funds Partisan Politics* (Washington, Cato Institute, 1985), especially Chapter VII, for some details about how dependent many large environmental groups are on government funding.
5. See Elizabeth Whelan, *Toxic Terror* (Ottawa, Ill. Jameson Books, 1985) pp. 16, 73.
6. See Edith Efron, *The Apocalyptics* (New York, Simon and Schuster, 1984) for an account of how ideology has driven many of the media-reported accounts from scientists warning of disaster from man-made chemicals in the environment and the workplace.
7. On the topic of biotechnology and problems in its regulation, see L. R. Batra and W. Klassen, eds., *Public Perceptions of Biotechnology* (Bethesda, Agricultural Research Institute, 1987).
8. Reported in Tom Hazlett, "Ingredients of a Food Phobia," *The Wall Street Journal*, August 5, 1988.
9. For a fuller treatment of this topic, see Aaron Wildavsky's chapter on "Richer is Safer vs. Richer is Sicker," in his important book *Searching for Safety*, (New Brunswick, Transaction Books, 1988).
10. *Ibid.*, Table 2, p. 63.
11. Jack Hadley and Anthony Osei, "Does Income Affect Mortality? An Analysis of the Effects of Different Types of Income on Age/Sex/Race-Specific Mortality Rates in the United States," *Medical Care*, September 1982, Vol. XX., No. 9.
12. Peter Huber, "The Market for Risk," *Regulation*, March/April 1984, p. 37.
13. Wayne B. Gray, "The Cost of Regulation: OSHA, EPA and the Productivity Slowdown," *American Economic Review*, Vol. 77, No. 5, December 1987, pp. 998-1006.
14. *Ibid.*
15. Richard Doll and Richard Peto, "The Causes of Cancer," *Journal of the National Cancer Institute*, Vol. 66, June 1981, p. 1256.
16. *Ibid.*

17. Bruce M. Ames, Renae Magaw and Lois Swirsky Gold, "Ranking Possible Carcinogenic Hazards," *Science,* Vol. 236, April 17, 1987, pp. 274-275.

18. Superfund, or technically the Comprehensive Environmental Response, Compensation, and Liability Act of 1980 (CERCLA) provided for "liability, compensation, cleanup, and emergency response for hazardous substances released into the environment and the cleanup of inactive hazardous waste disposal sites." It provided $1.6 billion to clean up abandoned sites. The Superfund Amendments and Reauthorization Act (SARA), passed in 1986, authorized an additional $8.5 billion to finance the Superfund site cleanup effort. In addition, SARA enlarged the number of enforcement authorities for the purpose of compelling private cleanups. It intends also to shift waste management practices toward long-term prevention, rather than containment of wastes.

19. The origins of the Love Canal crisis are described in Eric Zuesse, "Love Canal: The Truth Seeps Out," *Reason,* Feb. 1981, pp. 16-33.

20. Dante Picciano, "A Pilot Cytogenetic Study of the Residents Living Near Love Canal, A Hazardous Waste Site," *Mammalian Chromosome Newsletter,* 1980, 21 (3).

21. For a summary of the key provisions of Proposition 65, see Richard J. Denny, Jr., "California's Proposition 65: Coming Soon to Your Neighborhood," *Toxics Law Reporter,* Dec. 17, 1986, pp. 789-794; and Jerome H. Heckman, "California's Proposition 65: A Federal Supremacy and States' Rights Conflict in the Health and Safety Arena," *Food Drug Cosmetic Law Journal,* Vol. 43, 1988, pp. 269-282.

22. Paul Jacobs, "27 Chemicals Added to the List," *Los Angeles Times,* June 19, 1987; and Richard C. Paddock, "56 Chemicals to be Added," *Los Angeles Times,* Feb. 2, 1988.

23. See Robert Gottlieb, *A Life of Its Own* (Orlando, Harcourt, Brace, Javonovich, 1988), Chapter 7.

24. Jerome Heckman, "Proposition 65—A Legal Viewpoint: Reflections on the Political Science of How Not To Do It," paper presented to the American Industrial Hygiene Association's Toxicology Symposium on Aug. 8, 1988, in Williamsburg, VA., p. 4.

25. David Roe of the Environmental Defense Fund, a staunch proponent of Proposition 65 and defender of warning requirements, admits that business may trivialize the law with unnecessary warnings. Yet he believes that withdrawing a few products from the market is more than enough compensation. See Michael deCourcy Hinds, "As Warning Labels Multiply, Messages are Often Ignored," *The New York Times,* March 5, 1988.

26. "Houses with Warning Labels," *The Sacramento Bee,* July 25 1988.

27. The authors and major supporters of Proposition 65 have always viewed warnings as an intermediate step, or compromise, toward a more radical goal: the banning of all carcinogenic and reproductive toxins. See the statement attributed to Tom Hayden in Heckman, "Proposition 65," op. cit., p. 271, n. 24.

28. See Jane S. Shaw and Richard L. Stroup, "Gone Fishin'" (Reason, Aug/Sept 1988, pp. 34-37).

29. For example, had the Kesterson Wildlife Refuge in California, which received irrigation drainage waters that damaged the refuge's waterfowl, been privately owned, it seems likely that the owner (unlike the actual "owner," the U.S. Fish and Wildlife Service) would have investigated the possible consequences and discovered the potential disaster brought on by the drainage waters. In fact, it was a neighbouring landowner who "blew the whistle" on the problem, causing it to become a public concern. Certainly, a private owner has more wealth at stake and a greater personal incentive to be alert and protective than does a bureaucratic manager.

30. See Peter W. Huber, *Liability* (New York, Basic Books, 1988) for a fascinating history and analysis of this legal movement.

31. Critics will note that when legislative bodies tamper with the common law, the politics involved may well make the situation worse. Pointing out a possible improvement, as I have done here, is no guarantee that political action will follow the suggested path.

32. See Peter W. Huber, *op cit.*, pp. 142-149; see also Martin t. Katzman, *Chemical Catastrophes: Regulating Environmental Risk through Pollution Liability Insurance*, Homewood, Il., Richard D. Irwin, 1985, especially Chapter 5.

33. *Ibid.*

34. See William C. Clark, "Witches, Floods, and Wonder Drugs: Historical Perspectives on Risk Management," in *Societal Risk Assessment: How Safe is Safe Enough?*, Richard C. Schwing and Walter Albers, Jr., eds. (New York: Plenum Press, 1980), pp. 287-313.

Chapter 8

Controlling Acid Rain

Edwin G. Dolan

As recently as the early 1980s, a thriving forest covered Mount Mitchell in North Carolina, the highest peak east of the Mississippi. Hardy northern species like Fraser fir and red spruce, which grew at the top of the mountain, changed to mixed hardwoods at lower elevations. Today, much of the upper mountain is a wasteland. Only berry bushes survive among the dead trunks of the firs and spruce, and damage is spreading down into the transition zone to the hardwood forest. A prime suspect: acid rain.

Mount Mitchell is not a unique case. Similar forest damage is found all along the crest of the Appalachians from Georgia to Maine and on up into Canada. And it is not only trees that are suffering. In the Adirondack Mountains of New York, 25 percent of the lakes and ponds are so acidic they cannot support fish. Another 20 percent appear headed in the same direction. In Vermont, summer tourists visiting mountaintop viewpoints must often make do with pictures of neighbouring peaks that are now frequently hidden in a thick haze.

Amid the devastation on Mount Mitchell, plant pathologist Robert Bruck has built a pair of sealed plastic enclosures inside of which young trees have been planted. Untreated local air is fanned into one of the enclosures—air containing a mist that ranges in pH from 2.12 to 2.9, more acidic than vinegar even on the best days. Air blown into the other enclosure is passed through an activated carbon filter. After only six weeks of the experiment, the trees receiving unfiltered air showed a 50-percent shortfall in growth compared with those receiving filtered air.

Years ago, coal miners would lower a caged canary into their mineshaft before going down for the day's shift. If the canary died, the miners stayed out. Bruck and others see Mount Mitchell's firs and spruces as modern-day canaries in the coal mine: sensitive systems that, by their death, signal potential disaster.

Ideal World

Can disaster be avoided? In an ideal world, market mechanisms would save the day. First, the owners of the trees would ascertain the cause of the damage. Second, if the cause turned out to be air pollution (as is suspected in the case of Mount Mitchell), the source of the pollution would be identified. Third, a legal determination would be made concerning the property rights of the owners of the trees and the pollution source. Fourth, the parties would enter into negotiations on the basis of that determination.

Suppose it were determined that ownership of the pollution source did not convey the right to send clouds of noxious gases into the neighbouring forest. In that case, the forester would begin by demanding that emissions cease. In response, the polluter might stop the offending activity or install control equipment that allowed production to continue without further emissions. Instead, the polluter might offer a payment to the forester in exchange for allowing continued emissions. If a payment less than the cost of abatement turned out to exceed the forester's evaluation of the damage, a deal would be struck along these lines. As still another alternative, the polluter might offer to buy the forest outright and decide what to do about future emissions on the basis of internal benefit-cost calculations.

On the other hand, suppose it were determined that ownership of the emission source did include the right to use the neighbouring airshed for disposal of waste gases. In that case, it would be up to the forester to make the first offer. In exchange for a payment not exceeding the estimated value of damage to the trees, the owner of the pollution source would be asked to stop the emissions, or reduce them by an agreed amount. If the cost of abatement were less than the payment offered, the parties would strike a deal. Alternatively, the forester might simply offer to buy the pollution source and make an abatement decision on the basis of internal calculations of costs and benefits.

Is it reasonable to expect the acid rain problem to be resolved according to this market-based model? Unfortunately, it is not. There are four principal problems:

- The causes of Mount Mitchell's dying trees, New York's and Canada's dead lakes, and Vermont's summer haze are not known with certainty.
- Even if air pollution is accepted as the culprit, no one area's pollution can be traced to a particular source.
- The property rights of the owners of pollution sources, the owners of damaged properties, and other parties indirectly affected are matters of dispute, and:
- Even if the first three points were resolved, the transactions costs of private negotiations between numerous source owners and numerous owners of damaged property would appear to be prohibitive.

The next section of this chapter will examine each of these barriers to a market-based resolution of the acid rain problem. Following that, regulatory approaches to the problem will be examined, including some that attempt to incorporate market mechanisms. The final section will briefly discuss political barriers to implementing regulatory solutions.

Impediments to a Market-Based Solution

Scientific Uncertainties

Experiments such as those conducted in Bruck's Mount Mitchell enclosures would appear, on the face of it, to establish conclusively the cause of the observed environmental damage. But even Bruck is not willing to go quite that far. In an interview with *Audubon Magazine*, Bruck says "it's plain that no one has proved, or ever will, that air pollution is killing the trees up here." The most he will say is that "far more quickly than we ever expected, we've ended up with a highly correlated bunch of data—high levels of air pollution correlated to a decline we're watching in progress."[1] Off the cuff, he puts the level of certainty at 90 percent.

Even some observers with a direct interest in the health of eastern forests have their doubts. Robert C. Kaufman, director of the air quality programme of the American Paper Institute and National Forest Products Association says "There is no evidence that acid deposition is affecting the soil of commercial forests. We do not see conclusive evidence air pollution in general is causing reduced productivity in commercial forests."[2] Kaufman supports more research before endorsing a regulatory programme for control of acid rain.

Walter L. Warnick, who represented the Energy Department in the Reagan administration's acid-rain study programme, says that the death of trees on a large scale "is not unprecedented in history," and characterizes the scientific consensus that tree damage is due to pollution from fossil fuels as "shaky."[3]

Although in some cases nothing more than self-interest may lie behind dismissals of the link between acid rain and environment damage, there are also many sources of legitimate scientific uncertainty. Three in particular are worth mentioning.

First, environmental damage may be caused by two or more pollutants in combination. For example, acid rain contains both sulfuric acid and nitric acid, the precursors of which—sulfur dioxide and oxides of nitrogen—are emitted in different proportions by utilities, other industrial sources, and automobiles. To complicate matters further, the trees on Mount Mitchell, in addition to being exposed to acid rain and fog, are exposed to high levels of ozone. In the laboratory, both ozone and acid precipitation can be shown to damage trees. When more than one pollutant is present in the environment, determining which is responsible for observed damage becomes difficult.

Second, the formation of acid rain and the damage it causes involve non-linearities and threshold effects that complicate the task of attributing a given increment of damage to a given increment of emissions. One such non-linearity concerns the formation of acid rain. The rate of formation depends not only on the presence of precursors—the oxides of nitrogen and sulfur emitted by pollution sources—but also on the presence of oxidizing agents, which promote acid formation, and alkaline substances, which retard acid formation. Depending on the presence of oxidizing and alkaline agents, an increment of pollution might add greatly, slightly, or not at all to the acidity of precipitation. Another threshold effect involves the "buffering" properties of soils in areas where acid precipitation falls. Buffering compounds in the soil may for years prevent acid rain from doing environmental damage. At some point, however, cumulative acid deposition exhausts the buffering capacity and damage rapidly escalates.

Third, much research indicates that acid rain does not kill trees directly. The mechanisms involved may be quite complicated. To give one example, Lee Klinger, working with the National Center for Atmospheric Research in Boulder, Colo., sees a link between forest diebacks and certain mosses that are nearly always present in dying forests. The mosses produce organic acids that mobilize aluminum naturally present in the soil, forming compounds toxic to the feeder roots of trees. Although the mosses are naturally present in most forests, their growth appears to be greatly promoted by acid precipitation.[4] Other researchers have suggested, in addition to the role of acid mosses, that acid rain weakens the ability of trees to withstand variations in climate that have occurred in the eastern United States in recent decades and harms their ability to withstand microbial and insect pests.

All in all, the complexities of acid rain make it difficult or impossible to attribute a particular increment of environmental damage to a particular increment in one or another kind of pollution. One is reminded of a firing squad in which some of the members fire blanks. There is no doubt that the firing squad is the cause of death, but no one member can definitely be blamed for firing the fatal shot.

The Transportation Problem

Even if the available evidence linking environmental damage to pollution is accepted, there remains the problem of tracing the acid rain at a given site to a particular source of pollution. To date, research on transportation models for pollution has been able to give only general, probabilistic answers. In general, pollution is known to travel from west to east, which is unfortunate in that the largest concentrations of emission sources are in the midwestern United States, and the most vulnerable environments along the eastern seaboard. Some pollution is thought to cross the U.S.-Canadian border, often from south to north, but in the cases of some emitters in Ontario, it travels from north to south. Pollution from sources in the east is often blown out to sea, where the resulting acid precipitation is thought to be relatively harmless.

Incomplete knowledge of pollution transportation pathways is a significant complication in devising regulatory solutions to the acid rain problem. It is an even more serious barrier to implementing market-based pollution control efforts. Unless it is known where the pollution from a given source travels, there is no way to know who is entitled to enjoin whom, who should negotiate with whom, or who should compensate whom.

It has been suggested that major pollution sources could be required to tag their emissions with distinctive combinations of isotope markers that could be read at downwind sites subject to acid precipitation. If technically feasible, that would certainly clarify some of the transportation issues. However, the problem would remain that shifting atmospheric currents would mix pollutants and deposit them in constantly changing and unpredictable patterns, so that a system of compensation founded on the transportation pathways of a base period would not necessarily remain valid for subsequent periods.

Property Rights

If the scientific controversies regarding acid rain were ever settled, a full resolution of the problem would still require a determination of property rights. Environmentalists often implicitly or explicitly take the view that inhabitants of eastern states have a right to exclude pollutants from their airspace. It is certainly possible to construct arguments to this effect on the basis of common law or "natural law." But counterclaims can be made that are difficult to dismiss out of hand.

For example, midwestern utilities assert that all of their plants, including those that are the most serious polluters, were built in accordance with all federal and state emission standards in force at the time of their construction. They argue that the regulations that restricted emissions to a certain level amounted to a grant of a right to release emissions up to that level. Those concerned about acid rain now suggest that the originally established level of emissions may have been too high. That is all well and good, say the utilities, but none the less, they hold "first in time" rights to use of the airshed. That being the case they should be compensated for pollution abatement costs they now incur, especially the heavy costs of retrofitting control equipment to their older plants.

In advancing this line of argument, the midwestern utilities are joined by producers of Appalachian high-sulfur coal. The coal interests point out that they have made long-lived investments and entered into long-term contracts to supply fuel to utilities. These contracts met all environmental regulations in force at the time they were entered into. To change the rules of the game now would impose job and revenue losses that should not go uncompensated.

Before evidence on the seriousness of the environmental effects of acid rain began to accumulate, there was little incentive to resolve the conflicting claims. Paradoxically, however, that is when they could most easily have been resolved. Not knowing the exact nature of environmental effects and transportation patterns, polluters and downwind property owners could have operated behind a "veil of ignorance" to establish general principles for the resolution of future disputes. Advances in knowledge of how damage at specific sites is linked to specific sources threaten to turn the situation more and more into one of particularized conflicts between contending parties, in which the possibility of agreement on general principles disappears.

The lack of clearly established property rights is yet another barrier to a purely market-based solution to the acid rain problem. It means that the issue, if it is to be resolved at all, is likely to be resolved only in the political arena.

Transaction Cost Considerations

In principle, there are always net benefits in excess of costs to be realized by bringing an externality under control. The initial distribution of property rights affects the distribution of costs and benefits, but not their existence. In practice, however, the net benefits can be realized only if they exceed the transaction costs of negotiating and enforcing a control agreement. Thus transaction costs pose a final potential barrier to market-based control of externalities problems, even if scientific issues of cause and effect and property rights can be resolved.

Consider a simple example. Suppose I am looking for a piece of land on which to build a drag strip. In doing so, I must face the possibility that although some people would consider a neighbourhood drag strip an amenity, others are likely to consider it a nuisance. Fortunately, there are many possible sites for the strip. Some will be large enough that noise from the strip will not carry beyond the property line, although, of course, it will be costly to buy so much acreage. Alternatively, there will be smaller, less expensive sites where I can first negotiate an option to buy, and then negotiate with the neighbours regarding compensation for the noise. Through a process of competitive bargaining in which I simultaneously negotiate with owners of various drag-strip sites and with the neighbours of those sites, I finally settle on the alternative that is least costly to me. Because all externalities have been internalized through the competitive bargaining process, that will also be the most efficient solution from the point of view of the community as a whole.

Regrettably, quite aside from scientific and legal uncertainties, the drag-strip model is not workable in the case of acid rain. Two features of the acid rain case enormously raise the transaction costs of a privately negotiated agreement. One is the fact that the number of parties involved is far greater—

dozens of electric utilities, thousands of smaller industrial pollution sources, and millions of downwind property owners. The other is the fact that the pollution sources that cause the greatest concern are already in place, as are their sources of fuel supply, their customers, and their work forces. Thus, in place of the ex-ante competitive bargaining of the drag-strip model, the acid rain issue involves ex-post bargaining among parties who are already locked into inflexible relationships with one another by virtue of non-redeployable, site-specific investments. These circumstances encourage individual parties to play the free-rider if they are on the paying side or to hold out for a greater share of the potential gains from any agreement if they are on the receiving side. If free-riders, holdouts, and the sheer problem of numbers inflate transaction costs to the point where they exceed the potential gains from an agreement, nothing will be done.

What is meant by "doing nothing" depends, it should be noted, on how property rights issues are resolved. If utilities' claims to free use of the airshed are upheld, then doing nothing means letting pollution continue unabated, even if the marginal gains from pollution abatement exceed the marginal costs of abatement. If the claims of downwind landowners are fully upheld against the polluters, then "doing nothing" means no pollution. Sources must either shut down or install equipment that will reduce pollution to an imperceptible level, even if at that opposite margin, marginal abatement costs exceed the marginal benefits of abatement. Neither extreme is optimal, viewed apart from transaction costs.

The Search for a Regulatory Solution

Well-founded doubts about the ability of purely private negotiations to resolve the acid rain problem have led to the search for a regulatory second best. Many market-oriented economists have participated in this search. In doing so, their primary role has not been to argue that regulation is better than doing nothing, a proposition that some may accept and others may not. Rather, it has been to argue that if there are to be regulations, those that incorporate or mimic market mechanisms will reduce the cost of meeting given environmental goals compared to traditional command-and-control approaches.

Command-and-control regulations come in two forms: specific technology and source-specific performance standards. An example of specific technology would be regulation requiring installation of scrubbers to reduce sulfur-dioxide emissions from coal-fired electric power plants. Such regulations are economically flawed in part because the least-cost abatement technology may vary from plant to plant, and in part because such regulations dampen incentives to develop new, less expensive, technologies.[5] An example of a source-specific performance standard would be a requirement that coal-fired power plants limit emissions to, say, 1 pound of sulfur dioxide per million Btus. Such performance standards are a step in the right direction in that they allow each source to chose the least-cost technology. However, they are still seriously flawed in that they do not allow for differences among sources in the marginal cost of abatement.

For example, suppose that the marginal cost of sulfur-dioxide abatement in the neighbourhood of the 1-pound-per-million Btu standard is $0.25 per pound for plant A and $0.50 per pound for plant B. In that case, allowing B to emit an additional ton of sulfur dioxide would save $1,000 in abatement costs, while requiring A to cut emissions by an additional ton would cost just $500 in abatement costs. The result would be a net decrease of $500 in abatement costs and no net increase in emissions. But so long as the two sources were held to a source-specific performance standard, the saving could not be realized.

Finally, neither regulations based on required technology nor those based on source-specific performance standards provide adequate incentives for reducing emissions through cuts in use of the end product—in this case, electricity. It may well be in some cases that the most cost-effective means of abatement is the installation of energy-efficient equipment by users of electric power, rather than reduction of emissions per unit of power generated by utilities. True, the costs of meeting command-and-control regulations, if passed along to customers in the form of higher rates, do provide some incentive for conservation. Such regulations do not, however, permit full flexibility in substituting conservation for other abatement technologies.

The shortcomings of command-and-control regulation suggest three goals for more efficient regulatory mechanisms. First, complete flexibility should be allowed in choice of abatement technology. Second, the total desired reduction in emissions should be distributed among sources so as to equalize the marginal cost of abatement for all sources. And third, conservation by users and abatement by producers should be treated equivalently. Let's look at a specific proposal designed to accomplish these goals in the case of acid rain.

Tradeable Emission Rights.

Much of the discussion of acid rain control has focused on sulfur-dioxide emissions by electric utilities. These emissions are not the whole story of acid rain, but sulfur-dioxide accounts for about three-quarters of acid rain precursors (oxides of nitrogen accounting for the rest), and utilities account for about three-quarters of sulfur-dioxide emissions. The damaging emissions are concentrated in the midwestern United States. Together, Ohio, Pennsylvania, Illinois, West Virginia, Kentucky, Tennessee, and Missouri account for more than half of all sulfur-dioxide emissions by U.S. utilities. When it is taken into account that much of the emissions from such heavy eastern sources as Florida, Georgia, and Massachusetts blows out over the Atlantic, the midwestern utilities figure even larger. Any approach to acid rain control must include major reductions from these sources. A goal incorporated in several proposed pieces of legislation is to reduce sulfur-dioxide emissions by about half, or about 10 million tons annually. Of the 10 million tons of abatement, about three-quarters would need to come from utilities in the seven states listed.

A 10-million-ton reduction in sulfur-dioxide emissions would roughly represent splitting the difference between the conflicting claims to airshed rights by utilities and by downwind property owners. The remaining rights to emit sulfur-dioxide could be apportioned among utilities and other sources on the basis of actual emissions in a base period. If legislators were to cut the Gordian knot of property rights in this way, the regulatory question becomes one of what restrictions, if any, should be placed on utilities' use of the emission rights allotted to them.

Economists have a simple answer to that question. Once emissions rights are established, they say, no restrictions at all should be placed on utilities' rights to do what they want with them. Each utility should be allowed to use its emissions rights at any of its facilities or sell them to someone else. As a market developed, a going price per ton would be established for emission rights. This would lead to equalization of marginal costs of abatement, as sources with marginal abatement costs higher than the going price would buy rights and those with marginal abatement costs below the going price would sell them. In addition, it is conceivable that the governments of downwind states or even private environmental organizations might bid for pollution rights in order to hold them off the market, thus achieving a total reduction in emission greater than 10 million tons. The presence of such bidders would drive up the market price of emission rights, but would not disturb the market's tendency to equalize the marginal abatement costs of various sources.

Tradeable emission rights would have the additional advantage of treating emission reductions through electric power conservation on a par with reductions achieved by emission controls at the source. If utilities encouraged their customers to reduce energy demand (especially demand met by the dirtiest power plants), they would find themselves with surplus permits to sell. Conservation investments could thus become the object of mutually advantageous bargaining between utilities and their customers.

Estimating the Cost Advantage

Just how much would be saved if tradeable emission rights, rather than performance standards, were used to achieve a 10-million-ton cutback in utility sulfur-dioxide emissions? A study conducted by ICF Incorporated on behalf of the Center for Clean Air studied the issue in detail for two of the nation's largest electric utilities.[6] One was American Electric Power (AEP), a family of utilities operating in Ohio and other midwestern states. AEP is the country's largest private utility, accounting for about 5 percent of all electric power generated and about 10 percent of total national sulfur-dioxide emissions. The other was the Tennessee Valley Authority (TVA), the largest public utility, accounting for about 5 percent of electricity output and about 7 percent of sulfur-dioxide emissions. Unlike some other studies based on control costs averaged over many plants, the ICF study used engineering data supplied by the utilities to develop marginal abatement costs for each individual plant under various technologies.

The study compared two principal regulatory alternatives. One was a plant-specific performance standard of 1.2-pounds of sulfur-dioxide per million Btu. The 1.2 pound standard was estimated to be that which, applied to all utilities, would result in a total national emission reduction of 10 million tons of sulfur-dioxide per year. The other scheme would require each utility to reduce total system-wide emissions by its pro-rated share of the national target of 10 million tons annually, with each utility given the flexibility to allocate its share of the reduction among its plants as it chose. No trading of emission rights with other utility systems or non-utility emission sources was envisioned, but because the systems studied are so large, the flexibility allowed by intra-utility trading is quite substantial.

The difference in cost with and without emission-rights trading turns out to be large. For AEP, the cost of meeting the 1.2-pound performance standard was estimated to be $447 million per year. Achieving a system-wide equivalent reduction in pollution with intra-system emission trading was estimated to lower the cost of compliance by 60 percent, to $182 million per year. For TVA, the cost of meeting performance standards was estimated to be $258 million per year, compared to $139 million (47 percent less) when intra-system emission rights trading was permitted. In a different study prepared for the Environmental Protection Agency in 1988, ICF estimated that the cost savings to be realized nationally by permitting utilities to follow least-cost abatement strategies would be approximately 50 percent.[7]

The dramatic difference in compliance costs with and without emissions-rights trading stems from the mix of abatement techniques used under the differing sets of regulatory constraints. The three abatement techniques considered by the ICF study were as follows:

- *Scrubbing*: Scrubbing, which means removal of sulfur-dioxide from exhaust gasses after combustion, is the most expensive of the three techniques considered. Installation of scrubbing equipment is a major capital expense, especially when scrubbers have to be retrofitted to an existing plant. ICI estimated the capital costs at $230 to $550 per kilowatt, depending on the plant. In addition, scrubbing entails considerable operation and maintenance cost.
- *Fuel switching*: An alternative abatement technique is to switch fuels from high-sulfur to low-sulfur coal. The main cost is a price premium for low-sulfur coal estimated at $0.40 to $0.70 per million Btu. Location and boiler design make fuel-switching unworkable for some

plants, but where it can be used, it tends to be less expensive than scrubbing. For example, at AEP's Gavin plant—the system's heaviest single pollution source—fuel switching was estimated to cost $150 per ton of sulfur-dioxide removed compared to $400 per ton for scrubbing.

■ *Least-emission dispatching*: A third abatement technique, known as "least emission dispatching," means distributing the power output of the system at each moment among the available plants in such a way as to minimize emissions. At periods of relatively low demand, only the cleanest plants are used, with the dirtiest plants brought on line only to meet peak loads.

According to the ICF study, AEP could best meet the 1.2-pound plant-specific performance standard by switching fuels at plants representing 9.3 billion watts (GW) of capacity and installing scrubbers at 2.4 GW of capacity where fuel switching was not feasible because of location or boiler design. The average cost per ton of sulfur-dioxide abatement under this variant would be $390. By contrast, if intra-system trading were permitted, only one unit representing 0.4 GW would be scrubbed, and 12.8 GW of capacity would switch fuels. These steps alone would not meet the system-wide abatement requirement without changes in plant utilization. However, through least-emission dispatching, AEP could increase output at 6.4 GW of its cleanest plants, while making equivalent reductions at its dirtiest plants, thereby meeting the system-wide target. The average abatement cost under this combination of scrubbing, fuel-switching, and least-emission dispatching would be just $168 per ton.

The type of regulation applied would, in ICF's estimate, have a similar impact on TVA's choice of abatement technique. To meet the plant-specific performance standard, TVA would have to scrub 1.9 GW of capacity and switch fuels at 7.9 GW. The average cost of abatement would be $361. With intra-system trading, TVA would not retrofit any of its plants with scrubbers. It would switch fuels at 10.6 GW of capacity, and increase output of 4.4 GW of its cleanest capacity through least-emission dispatching. The average cost of abatement would be reduced to $207 per ton.

Determining the Scope of Emission Rights Trading

Among the issues to be faced in implementing any system of emission rights trading is that of how wide the scope of trading should be. The dimensions within which this decision need to be made include location, types of sources, and types of pollution.

The issue of location is important because pollution from any given source does not affect all downwind areas equally. For example, sulfur-dioxide emitted by a TVA plant in Tennessee presumably affects environmental conditions in North Carolina more than those in Quebec; emissions from a source in Ontario may be more damaging to Vermont's maple trees than Georgia's pines; and emissions from a coal-fired power plant on the Massachusetts coast may blow out over the ocean without much or any harm.

Several schemes have been described for handling the locational aspects of emissions trading.[8] A common feature of these schemes is the establishment of multiple "receptor sites," where pollution concentrations are monitored. In the case of acid rain, one might imagine such stations strung out at 100-mile intervals along the ridge of the Appalachians from Georgia to Canada. Any trading of emission rights would be subject to the constraint that the trade not cause pollution concentrations to increase at any site. The general idea is that if the TVA wanted to build a new plant in Tennessee, it would have to buy many "rights units" relating to receptor sites in North Carolina but not as many relating to sites in New England, whereas an AEP plant in Cleveland would need more New England rights units and fewer North Carolina units.

Such multiple-receptor systems have a certain theoretical appeal. Most obviously, they prevent sources in one area from acquiring enough permits to create dangerous pollution hot-spots. More generally, they can be shown to have desirable efficiency properties. Ultimately, as the number of receptor sites is increased, regulation with multiple receptors more and more closely approaches the pure market-based solution that makes each downwind property owner a separate "receptor site," from which each upwind polluter must purchase permission to emit.

However, the multiple-receptor schemes also have their drawbacks. For one thing, they can function only if emissions from a given source can be traced to a given receptor. Doing so requires either an accurate transportation model or some way of tagging emissions. At present, neither is available for the types of emissions implicated in the formation of acid rain.

In addition, multiple-receptor systems increase both the administrative costs of monitoring compliance and the transaction costs to participants of finding worthwhile trades and carrying them out. At some point, these costs become so great that no trades are carried out, another respect in which multiple-receptor systems coverage with purely market-based systems.

A way to get around the drawbacks of multiple-receptor systems, while still recognizing the locational factor in pollution, is to restrict trading of emission rights to sources near to one another—say, those in the same state. The ICF study of the American Electric Power system suggests that the efficiency penalties of such restrictions may not be prohibitive. In one variant, the utility was allowed to trade emission rights freely among its five subsidiary companies, each covering an area about the size of a state. In another variant, emissions were traded only within subsidiary companies, not between them. Even with the restriction, the tradeable emission-rights system had abatement costs less than half those of a system using source-specific standards. The restriction changed the abatement-cost gap by only about 7 percent.

The question of what types of pollution sources to include within an emission-rights trading scheme raises issues similar to those raised by location. As pointed out earlier, much of the acid rain debate has focused on the electric utility industry, which is the source of three-quarters of all sulfur-dioxide emissions. The remaining quarter of sulfur-dioxide emissions comes from industrial and residential fixed sources and transportation equipment. A few large industrial sources might feasibly be brought into the emission-rights trading system on an equal footing with utilities. But to include small sources, such as individual houses, cars, and trucks, in a trading system might well raise prohibitive administrative and transactions costs. It could be that source-specific performance standards make more sense for such small sources.

Finally, there is the question of whether to permit one kind of pollution to be traded off against another. In the case of acid rain, trades of sulfur-dioxide emissions against oxides of nitrogen would be an example. Unfortunately, too little is known at present of the relative contributions of these two pollutants to observed environmental damage to permit a judgement as to what would constitute appropriate trades. The most that can be said is that any regulatory scheme implemented today should not preclude such trading in the future if better understanding of the issues indicates that it would be cost-effective.

Political Impediments to Acid Rain Control

U.S. environmental policy has not, to date, fully addressed the acid rain problem. The 1977 amendments to the Clean Air Act established a set of source-specific performance standards for facilities built after passage of the act, but these left existing sources largely untouched. Emissions of sulfur-dioxide and other major pollutants, as a result, have levelled off but remain at a high-enough level to cause widespread concern. In the last decade, numerous bills have been introduced in Congress calling for a controls on existing pollution sources, especially coal-fired utilities. As of 1988, however, none has passed, and those that have come closest to passing have been based on the least economically attractive control strategies. This section looks at the general reasons for the failure to adopt a strong acid rain policy, and at the specific reasons for rejection of tradeable emissions rights.

One explanation sometimes given for the failure to adopt a stronger acid rain policy is uncertainty that the benefits of such a policy exceed its costs. In the United States, such uncertainty was regularly cited by the Reagan administration as a reason to defer action in favour of further research.

On the cost side of the acid rain issue, the range of uncertainty is relatively narrow. Estimates of the cost of a 10-million-ton annual reduction in sulfur-dioxide emissions fall, for the most part, in the range of $2 billion to $10 billion annually. However, this range overstates the actual extent of uncertainty about costs, since much of the difference among estimates stems from assumptions made regarding characteristics of the programme under consideration—such factors as regulatory restrictions on abatement technology, time allowed to phase in controls, and so on.[9]

Firm estimates of the benefits of acid rain control are much harder to come by. This is partly because, as noted earlier, of scientific uncertainties regarding the mechanisms through which pollution acts on forests, lakes, air quality, and so on. In addition, there are major economic uncertainties over the attribution of dollar values to benefits such as human health and availability of recreational amenities.

But to say that the benefits of a strong acid rain policy are harder to estimate than the costs is not to say that they are smaller than the costs. They may well be greater, in total, than more easily measured benefits, such as changes in crop yields and pollution damage to buildings. Considering that some 100 million people live downwind from the major midwestern sulfur-dioxide sources, annual benefits as small as $20 to $100 per individual would be enough to justify the costs of a 10-million-ton abatement programme. As research results accumulate, the scientific consensus that acid rain is indeed a serious environmental concern seems to be strengthening, rather than weakening. Increasingly, arguments that there is no real problem look like special pleading by parties wishing to avoid bearing their share of the costs of proposed policies.

Be that as it may, it is an axiom of public choice economics that policy decisions depend less on the overall balance between costs and benefits than on the shares of costs and benefits borne by various politically influential groups. To simplify matters to an extreme, the following groups are of key political importance:

- *Victims of pollution*, including those who live downwind from the major pollution sources—that is, in the eastern parts of the United States and Canada—joined by environmentalists from other regions who favour pollution control as a matter of principle, even when it does not personally affect them.
- *Midwestern utilities and their customers*, whose primary interest is to avoid bearing the costs of abatement through lower profits or higher electric rates.[10]
- *High-sulfur coal interests*, which include the owners of high-sulfur coal deposits, the owners of non-redeployable capital invested in mining those deposits, and workers reluctant or unable to retrain or relocate.
- *Bystanders*—that is, those who do not expect to share either the costs or benefits of abatement. Those living upwind (west) of the major pollution sources often perceive themselves as bystanders.

No one of these groups holds a majority that would enable it to impose its will on the others, so every legislative proposal reflects an effort at coalition-building.[11] The 1977 Clean Air Act amendments are an example. In that case, environmentalists, seeing that they did not have the votes to pass strong pollution controls, sought compromise with two other key groups. First, they compromised with the high-sulfur coal interests by mandating scrubbing as the preferred abatement technology. Although often the most expensive choice, scrubbing removes the incentive to switch from high- to low-sulfur coal. Second, they compromised with midwestern utilities and their customers by focusing on controlling new sources of pollution. Existing sources were left largely untouched. Representatives of midwestern states found new-source control attractive because cheap electricity from existing facilities in their states would discourage industries from moving to the west or south, where they would have to be supplied by facilities built to stringent new-source standards.

Many environmentalists now see the 1977 compromise as inadequate. In fact, some studies have indicated that the 1977 amendments may actually have made the acid rain problem worse, partly because scrubbers have not performed as effectively as hoped, and partly because the new-source requirements have slowed the rate at which old, dirty facilities have been abandoned. However, they have not yet succeeded in forging a coalition for a new acid rain policy.

One might think that emissions rights trading, by dramatically lowering the costs of abatement, would make compromise easier. This would indeed be true if the negotiations involved only eastern acid-rain victims and midwestern utility customers. For example, the ICF study of the American Electric Power system indicated that an acid rain programme that included trading of emission rights would raise rates by just 3 percent, compared to 8 percent for a programme based on source-specific standards. However, because emission trading encourages fuel switching and discourages scrubbing, it offends the high-sulfur coal interests, which hold a pivotal political position.

If scrubbing is mandated to bring in the high-sulfur coal interests, the cost of any programme rises and it becomes more strongly opposed by ratepayers. One way to retain the support of both would be to require scrubbing, but to subsidize installation of the necessary equipment. A legislative package known as the "Mitchell Compromise," which included 10 million tons of sulfur-dioxide abatement, 33 GW of scrubbing, and a federal subsidy of about a billion dollars annually came close to adoption by Congress in 1988. The compromise fell apart at the last minute, however, in part because any subsidy from general tax revenues tends to alienate "bystanders," and in part because environmentalists had second thoughts about some of the concessions they had made to coal and utility interests.

No doubt new attempts at compromise will be made. If the benefits of acid rain control do actually exceed the costs, some majority coalition in favour of control ought, in principle, to exist. However, the complex political machinery of modern democratic government is notoriously capricious in translating dollar costs and benefits into legislative votes.[12] In the real world, something like the fact that the Senate majority leader comes from a state that mines a lot of high-sulfur coal can sometimes be crucial. Whether the shifting political winds will bring effective control of acid rain remains open to question, and whether any new control policy will incorporate efficient abatement strategies is even more so.

Notes

1. As quoted in John R. Luoma, "Acid Murder No Longer a Mystery," *Audubon*, November 1988, p. 128.
2. As quoted in Philip Shabecoff, "Deadly Combination Felling Trees in East," *New York Times*, July 24, 1988, p. 18.
3. Ibid.
4. John R. Luoma, p. 132. "Acid Murder," p. 132.
5. There is also the problem that political considerations may lead legislators to require technologies that are know to be more expensive than available alternatives. Regulations favouring scrubbing over fuel switching for midwestern utilities in order to preserve jobs in high-sulfur coal mining are a case in point. This problem will be discussed in the last section of this chapter.
6. *Acid Rain: Road to a Middleground Solution*. Washington, D.C.: Center for Clean Air Policy, 1987.
7. ICF Incorporated, *Analysis of the Mitchell Compromise Acid Rain Proposal*, prepared for the Environmental Protection Agency, September 1988.
8. A description of several such schemes with references to the literature can be found in Albert McGartland, "A Comparison of Two Marketable Discharge Permits Systems," *Journal of Environmental Economics and Management* 15 (1988), pp. 35-44.
9. For example, ICF's estimates of the cost of sulfur-dioxide controls to the AEP system were $171-$192 million, compared to $900 million estimated by the company itself. Although these estimates differ by nearly a factor of five, a large part of the discrepancy turns out to hinge on differing technical assumptions. For example, the AEP estimate assumed a 10-year phase-in period compared to 20 years for the ICF estimate, and the AEP estimate did not consider least-emission dispatching. Put on a comparable basis, the estimates would probably differ by less than a factor of two. The same is true for a comparison of ICF's and TVA's estimates of abatement costs for the TVA system. For a discussion, see *Acid Rain: Road to a Middleground Solution*, pp. 94-96.
10. In theory, the attitude of utilities depends on whether regulators allow them to recover their capital and operating costs in part, exactly in full, or more than in full. If exactly in full, we would expect the utilities to be neutral. If more than in full, we would expect them to lobby hard for the opportunity to add billions of dollars of pollution control equipment, from which they would reap returns in excess of the opportunity costs of capital. Observing that utilities, in practice, tend to be unenthusiastic about acid rain control suggests that they expect regulators to allow them to recover abatement costs only in part.

11. See Robert W. Crandall, "An Acid Test for Congress," *Regulation*, September/December 1984, pp. 21-28, and *Controlling Industrial Pollution: The Economics and Politics of Clean Air* (Washington, D.C.: Brookings, 1983).

12. The political situation is further complicated by the fact that one important group of victims, those living in eastern Canada, has no votes at all in the U.S. Congress. The Canadian government has expressed itself vigourously on their behalf through diplomatic channels but to little effect, at least as of the end of the Reagan administration.

Chapter 9

Law, Property Rights, and Air Pollution*

Murray N. Rothbard

Law as a Normative Discipline

Law is a set of commands; the principles of tort or criminal law, which we shall be dealing with, are negative commands or prohibitions on the order of "thou shalt not" do actions, X, Y, or Z.[1] In short, certain actions are considered wrong to such a degree that it is considered appropriate to use the sanctions of violence (since law is the social embodiment of violence) to combat, defend against, and punish the transgressors.

There are many actions against which it is not considered appropriate to use violence, individual or organized. Mere lying (i.e., where contracts to transfer property titles are not broken), treachery, base ingratitude, being nasty to one's friends or associates, or not showing up for appointments, are generally considered wrong, but few think of using violence to enjoin or combat them. Other sanctions—such as refusing to see the person or have dealings with him, putting him in Coventry, etcetera—may be used by individuals or groups, but using the violence of the law to prohibit such actions is considered excessive and inappropriate.

If ethics is a normative discipline that identifies and classifies certain sets of actions as good or evil, right or wrong, then tort or criminal law is a subset of ethics identifying certain actions as against which using violence is appropriate. The law says that action X should be illegal, and therefore should be combatted by the violence of the law. The law is a set of "ought" or normative propositions.

Many writers and jurists have claimed that the law is a value-free, "positive" discipline. Of course, it is possible to simply list, classify, and analyse existing law without going further into saying what the law should or should not be.[2] But that sort of jurist is not fulfilling his essential task. Since the law is

---

*Reprinted with permission of *The Cato Journal* (vol. 2, no. 1, Spring 1982).

ultimately a set of normative commands, the true jurist or legal philosopher has not completed his task until he sets forth what the law should be, difficult though that might be. If he does not, then he necessarily abdicates his task in favour of individuals or groups untrained in legal principles, who may lay down their commands by sheer fiat and caprice.

Thus, the Austinian jurists proclaim that the king, or sovereign, is supposed to lay down the law, and the law is purely a set of commands emanating from his will. But then the question arises: On what principles does or should the king operate?[3] It is ever possible to say that the king is issuing a "bad" or "improper" decree? Once the jurist admits that, he is going beyond arbitrary will to begin to frame a set of normative principles that should be guiding the sovereign—and then he is back to normative law.

Modern variants of positive legal theory state that the law should be what the legislators say it is. But what principles are to guide the legislators? And if we say that the legislators should be the spokesmen for their constituents, then we simply push the problem one step back, and ask: What principles are supposed to guide the voters? Or is the law, and therefore everyone's freedom of action, to be ruled by the caprice of millions rather than of one man or a few?[4]

Even the older concept that the law should be determined by tribal or common-law judges who are merely interpreting the custom of the tribe or society cannot escape normative judgements basic to the theory. Why must the rules of custom be obeyed? If tribal custom requires the murder of all people over six feet tall, must this custom be obeyed? Why can't reason dictate a set of principles to challenge and overthrow mere custom and tradition? Similarly, why may it not be used to overthrow mere caprice by king or public?

Tort or criminal law is a set of prohibitions against the invasion of, or aggression against, private property rights; that is, spheres of freedom of action by each individual. But if that is the case, then the implication of the command, "Thou shall not interfere with A's property right," is that A's property right is just and therefore should not be invaded. Legal prohibitions, therefore, far from being in some sense value-free, actually imply a set of theories about justice, in particular the just allocation of property rights and property titles. "Justice" is nothing if not a normative concept.

In recent years, however, jurists and "Chicago School" economists have attempted to develop theories of value-free property rights, rights defined and protected not on the basis of ethical norms, such as justice, but of some form of "social efficiency." In one such variant, Ronald Coase and Harold Demsetz have asserted that "it doesn't make any difference" how property rights are allocated in cases of conflicting interests, provided that some property rights are assigned to someone and then defended. In his famous example, Coase discusses a railroad locomotive's blighting of nearby farms and orchards. To Coase and Demsetz, this damage of a farmer's crops by the railroad is an "externality" that should, according to the tenets of social efficiency, be internalized. But to these economists, it doesn't make any difference which of two possible courses of action one adopts. Either one says that the farmer has a property right in his orchard; therefore, the railroad should have to pay damages for his loss, and the farmer should be able to enjoin the railroad's invasive actions. Or, the railroad has the right to spew forth smoke wherever it wishes, and if the farmer wishes to stop the smoke, he must pay the railroad to install a smoke abatement device. It does not matter, from the point of view of expenditure of productive resources, which route is taken.

For example, suppose the railroad causes $100,000 worth of damage, and in Case 1, this action is held to invade the farmer's property. In that case, the railroad must pay $100,000 to the farmer or else invest in a smoke abatement device, whichever is cheaper. But in Case 2, where the railroad has the property right to emit the smoke, the farmer would have to pay the railroad up to $100,000 to stop damaging his farm. If the smoke device costs less than $100,000, say $80,000, then the device will be installed regardless of who was assigned the property right. In Case 1, the railroad will spend $80,000 on the device rather than have to pay $100,000 to the farmer; in Case 2, the farmer will be willing to pay the railroad $80,000 and up to $100,000 to install the device. If, on the other hand, the smoke device costs more than $100,000, say $120,000, then the device will not be installed anyway, regardless of which route is taken. In Case 1, the railroad will keep pouring out smoke and keep paying the farmer damages of $100,000 rather than spend $120,000 on the device; in Case 2, it will not benefit the farmer to bribe the railroad with $120,000 for the device, since this is more of a loss to him than the $100,000 in damage. Therefore, regardless of how property rights are assigned—according to Coase and Demsetz—the allocation of resources will be the same. The difference between the two is only a matter of "distribution"—that is, of income or wealth.[5]

There are many problems with this theory. First, income and wealth are important to the parties involved, although they might not be to uninvolved economists. It makes a great deal of difference to both parties who has to pay whom. Second, this thesis works only if we deliberately ignore psychological factors. Costs are not only monetary. The farmer might well have an attachment to the orchard far beyond the monetary damage. Therefore, the orchard might be worth far more to him than the $100,000 in damages, so that it might take $1 million to compensate him for the full loss. But then the supposed indifference totally breaks down. In Case 1, the farmer will not be content to accept a mere $100,000 in damages. He will take out an injunction against any further aggression against his property, and even if the law allows bargaining between the parties themselves to remove the injunction, he will insist on over $1 million from the railroad, which the railroad will not be willing to pay.[6] Conversely, in

Case 2, there is not likely to be a way for the farmer to raise the $1 million needed to stop the smoke invasion of the orchard.

The love of the farmer for his orchard is part of a larger difficulty with the Coast-Demsetz doctrine: Costs are purely subjective and not measurable in monetary terms. Coase and Demsetz have a proviso in their indifference thesis that all "transaction costs" be zero. If they are not, then they advocate allocating the property rights to the route that entails minimum social transaction costs. But once we understand that costs are subjective to each individual and therefore unmeasurable, we see that costs cannot be added up. But if all costs, including transaction costs, cannot be added, then there is no such thing as "social transaction costs," and they cannot be compared in Cases 1 or 2, or, indeed, in any other situation.[7]

Another serious problem with the Coast-Demsetz approach is that pretending to be value-free, they import the ethical norm of "efficiency" and assert that property rights should be assigned on the basis of such efficiency. But even if the concept of social efficiency were meaningful, they don't answer the questions of why efficiency should be the overriding consideration in establishing legal principles or why externalities should be internalized above all other considerations. We are now out of *Wertfreiheit* and back to unexamined ethical questions.[8,9]

Another attempt by Chicago School economists to make legal public policy recommendations under the guise of *Wertfreiheit* is the contention that common-law judges over the years will always arrive at the socially efficient allocation of property rights and tort liabilities. Demsetz stresses rights that will minimize social transaction costs; Richard Posner stresses maximization of "social wealth." All this adds an unwarranted historical determinism, functioning as a kind of invisible hand guiding judges to the current Chicago School path, to the other fallacies examined above.[10]

If the law is a set of normative principles, it follows that whatever positive or customary law has emerged cannot simply be recorded and blindly followed. All such law must be subject to a thorough critique grounded in such principles. Then, if there are discrepancies between actual law and just principles, as there almost always are, steps must be taken to make the law conform to correct legal principles.

Physical Invasion

The normative principle I am suggesting for the law is simply this: No action should be considered illicit or illegal unless it invades the person or just property of another. Only invasive actions should be declared illegal and combatted with the full powers of the law. The invasion must be concrete and physical. There are degrees of seriousness of such invasion, and hence, different degrees of restitution or punishment. "Burglary," simple invasion of property for purposes of theft, is less serious than "robbery," where armed force is likely to be used against the victim. In this paper, however, we are not concerned with the questions of degrees of invasion or punishment, but simply with invasion *per se*.

If no man may invade another person's "just" property, what is our criterion of justice to be?[11] There is no space here to elaborate on a theory of justice in property titles. Suffice it to say that the basic axiom of libertarian political theory holds that every man is a self-owner, having absolute jurisdiction over his own body. In effect, this means that no one else may justly invade, or commit aggression against, another's person. It follows then that each person justly owns whatever previously unowned resources he appropriates or mixes his labour with. From these twin axioms—self-ownership and "homesteading"—stem the justification for the entire system of property rights titles in a free-market society. This system establishes the right of every man to his own person, the right of donation, the right of bequest (and concomitantly, the right to receive the bequest or inheritance), and the right of contractual exchange of property titles.[12]

Legal and political theory has committed much mischief by failing to pinpoint physical invasion as the only human action that should be illegal and that justifies the use of physical violence to combat it. The vague concept of "harm" is substituted for the precise one of physical violence.[13] Consider the following two examples. Jim is courting Susan and is just about to win her hand in marriage, when suddenly Bob appears on the scene and wins her away. Surely Bob has done great "harm" to Jim. Once a non-physical sense of harm is adopted, almost any outlaw act might be justified. Should Jim be able to enjoin Bob's very existence?[14]

Similarly, A is a successful seller of razor blades. But then B comes along and sells a better blade, teflon-coated to prevent shaving cuts. The value of A's property is greatly affected. Should he be able to collect damages from B or, better yet, to enjoin B's sale of a better blade? The correct answer is not that consumers would be hurt if they were forced to buy the inferior blade, although that is surely the case. Rather, no one has the right to legally prevent or retaliate against "harms" to his property unless it is an act of physical invasion. Everyone has the right to have the physical integrity of his property inviolate; no one has the right to protect the value of his property, for that value is purely the reflection of what people are willing to pay for it. The willingness depends solely on how they decide to use their money. No one can have a right to someone else's money, unless that other person had previously contracted to transfer it to him.

In the law of torts, "harm" is generally treated as physical invasion of person or property. The outlawing of defamation (libel and slander) has always been a glaring anomaly in tort law. Words and opinions are not physical invasions. Analogous to the loss of property value from a better product or a shift in consumer demand, no one has a property right over his "reputation." Reputation is strictly a function of the subjective opinions of other people, who have the absolute right to their own opinions, whatever they may be. Hence, outlawing defamation is itself a gross invasion of the defamer's right of freedom of speech, which is a subset of his property right over his own person.[15]

An even broader assault on freedom of speech is the modern Warren-Brandeis-inspired tort of invasion of the alleged right of privacy, which outlaws free speech and acts using one's own property that are not even false or malicious.[16]

In the law of torts, "harm" is generally treated as physical invasion of person or property and usually requires payment of damages for "emotional" harm, if and only if that harm is a consequence of physical invasion. Thus, within the standard law of trespass—an invasion of person or property—"battery" is the actual invasion of someone else's body, while "assault" is the creation by one person in another of a fear, or apprehension, of battery.[17]

To be a tortious assault and therefore subject to legal action, the threat under tort law is required to be near and imminent. Mere insults and violent words, vague future threats, or simple possession of a weapon cannot constitute an assault; there must be accompanying overt action to cause apprehension of an imminent physical battery.[18,19] Or, to put it another way, there must be a concrete threat of an imminent battery before the prospective victim may legitimately use force and violence to defend himself.

Physical invasion or molestation needs to be actually "harmful" or to inflict severe damage in order to constitute a tort. The courts properly have held that such acts as spitting in someone's face or ripping off someone's hat are batteries. Chief Justice Holt's words in 1704 still seem to apply: "The least touching of another in anger is a battery." While the actual damage may not be substantial, in a profound sense we may conclude that the victim's person was molested, was interfered with, by the physical aggression against him, and that these seemingly minor actions have become legal wrongs.[20]

Initiation of an Overt Act: Strict Liability

If only a physical invasion of person or property constitutes an illicit act or tort, it becomes important to demarcate when a person may act as if such a physical invasion is about to take place. Libertarian legal theory holds that A may not use force against B expect in self-defence—that is, unless B is initiating force against A. But when is A's force against B legitimate self-defence, and when is it itself illegitimate and tortious aggression against B? To answer this question, we must consider what kind of tort liability theory we are prepared to adopt.

Suppose, for example, that Smith sees Jones frowning in his direction across the street, and that Smith has an abnormal fear of being frowned at. Convinced that Jones is about to shoot him, he pulls a gun and shoots Jones in what he is sure is self-defence. Jones presses a charge of assault and battery against Smith.

Was Smith an aggressor and, therefore, should he be liable? One theory of liability—the orthodox "reasonable man" or "reasonable conduct" or "negligence" theory—says he should, because frowning would not rouse apprehension of imminent attack in a "reasonable man." A competing theory, once held and now being revived—that of "strict liability" or "strict causal liability"—agrees, because it should be clear to a judge or jury that Jones was not an imminent aggressor. This would hold regardless of how sincere Smith was in his fear of attack.

Two serious flaws in the "reasonable man" theory are that the definition of "reasonable" is vague and subjective, and that guilty aggressors go unpunished, while their victims remain uncompensated. In this particular case, the two theories happen to coincide, but in many other cases they do not. Take, for example, the case of *Courvoisier* v. *Raymond* (1896).[21] In this case, the defendant, a storekeeper, was threatened by a rioting mob. When a man who happened to be a plainclothes policeman walked up to the defendant, trying to help him, the defendant, mistaking him for a rioter, shot the policeman. Should the storekeeper have been liable?

The trial court decided the case properly—on the basis of strict liability—and the jury decided for the policeman for it is clear that the defendant committed a battery by shooting the plaintiff. In strict liability theory, the question is causation: Who initiated the tort or crime? An overriding defence for the defendant's action was whether the plaintiff had committed an assault, by threatening an imminent initiation of a battery against him. The question traditionally then becomes a factual one for juries to decide: Did the plainclothesman in fact threaten battery against the storekeeper? The jury decided for the policeman.[22] The appeals court, however, reversed the trial court's decision. To the court, the storekeeper acted as a "reasonable man" when he concluded, though incorrectly, that the plainclothesman was out to attack him.

When is an act held to be an assault? Frowning would scarcely qualify. But if Jones had whipped out a gun and pointed it in Smith's direction without firing, this is clearly a threat of imminent aggression, and would properly be countered by Smith plugging Jones in self-defence. (In this case, our view and the "reasonable man" theory again would coincide.) The proper yardstick for determining whether the point of assault had been reached is this: Did Jones initiate an "overt act" threatening battery? As Randy Barnett has pointed out:

> In a case less than certainty, the only justifiable use of force is that used to repel an overt act that is something more than mere preparation, remote from time and place of the intended crime. It must be more than "risky"; it must be done with the specific intent to commit a crime and directly tend in some substantial degree to accomplish it. (Barnett 1977, p. 377).[23]

Similar principles hold in innocent-bystander cases. Jones assaults and attacks Smith; Smith, in self-defence, shoots. The shot goes wild and accidentally hits Brown, an innocent bystander. Should Smith be liable? Unfortunately, the courts, sticking to the traditional "reasonable man" or "negligence" doctrine, have held that Smith is not liable if indeed he was reasonably intending self-defence against Jones.[24] But, in libertarian and in strict liability theory, Smith has indeed aggressed against Brown, albeit unintentionally, and must pay for this tort. Thus, Brown has a proper legal action against Smith. Since Jones coerced or attacked Smith, Smith also has an independent and proper action for assault or battery against Jones. Presumably, the liability or punishment against Jones would be considerably more severe than against Smith.

One of the great flaws in the orthodox negligence approach has been to focus only on one victim's (Smith's) right of self-defence in repelling at attack, or on his good-faith mistake. But orthodox doctrine unfortunately neglects the other victim—the man frowning across the street, the plainclothesman trying to save someone, the innocent bystander. The plaintiff's right of self-defence is being grievously neglected. The proper focus in all these cases is: Would the plaintiff have had the right to plug the defendant in *his* self-defence? Would the frowning man, the plainclothesman, the innocent bystander, if he could have done so in time, have had the right to shoot the sincere but erring defendants in self-defence? Surely, whatever our theory of liability, the answer must be "yes"; hence, the palm must go to the strict liability theory, which focuses on everyone's right of self-defence and not just that of a particular defendant. It is clear that since these plaintiffs had the right to plug the defendant in self-defence, then the defendant must have been the tortious aggressor, regardless of how sincere or "reasonable" his actions may have been.

From various illuminating discussions of Professor Richard A. Epstein, it seems evident that there are three contrasting theories of tort liability interwoven in our legal structure. The oldest, strict causal liability, apportioned blame and burden on the basis of identifiable cause: Who shot whom? Who assaulted whom? Only defence of person and property was a proper defence against a charge of using force. This doctrine was replaced during the 19th century by negligence or "reasonable man" theory, which let many guilty defendants off the hook if their actions were judged reasonable or did not exhibit undue negligence. In effect, negligence theory swung the balance excessively in favour of the defendant and against the plaintiff. In contrast, modern theory, anxious to help plaintiffs (especially if they are poor), seeks ways to find against defendants even if strict cause of physical invasion cannot be proven. If the oldest theory is termed "strict causal liability," the modern one might be termed "presumptive liability," since the presumption seems to be against the defendant, in flagrant violation of the Anglo-Saxon criminal law presumption of innocence on the part of the defendant.[25]

Extending our discussion from crimes against the person to crimes against property, we may apply the same conclusion: Anyone has the right to defend his property against an overt act initiated against it. He may not move with force against an alleged aggressor—a trespasser against his land or chattels—until the latter initiates force by an overt act.

How much force may a victim use to defend either his person or his property against invasion? Here we must reject as hopelessly inadequate the current legal doctrine that he may use only "reasonable" force, which in most cases has reduced the victim's right to defend himself virtually to a nullity.[26] In current law, a victim is allowed only to use maximal, or "deadly," force, (a) in his own home, and then only if he is under direct personal attack; or (b) if there is no way that he can retreat when he is personally under attack. All this is dangerous nonsense. Any personal attack might turn out to be a murderous one; the victim has no way of knowing whether the aggressor is going to stop short of inflicting a grave injury upon him. The victim should be entitled to proceed on the assumption that any attack is implicitly a deadly one, and therefore to use deadly force in return.

In current law, the victim is in even worse straits when it comes to defending the integrity of his own land or movable property. There, he is not allowed to use deadly force in defending his own home, much less other land or properties. The reasoning seems to be that since a victim would not be allowed to kill a thief who steals his watch, he should not be permitted to shoot the thief in the process of stealing the watch or in pursing him. But punishment and defence of person or property are not the same, and must be treated differently. Punishment is an act of retribution after the crime has been committed and the criminal apprehended, tried, and convicted. Defence, while the crime is being committed, or until property is recovered and the criminal apprehended, is a very different story. The victim should be entitled to use any force, including deadly force, to defend or recover his property so long as the crime is in the process of commission—that is, until the criminal is apprehended and duly tried by legal process. In other words, he should be able to shoot looters.[27]

The Proper Burden of Risk

We conclude, then, that no one may use force to defend himself or his property until an overt act of aggression is initiated against him. But doesn't this doctrine impose an undue risk upon everyone?

The reply is that life is always risky and uncertain and that there is no way of getting around this primordial fact. Any shifting of the burden of risk away from one person simply places it upon someone else. Thus, if our doctrine makes it more risky to wait until someone becomes aggressive against you, it also makes life less risky, because non-aggressors are more assured that no excited alleged victim will pounce upon them in supposed self-defence. There is no way for the law to reduce overall risk; it then becomes important to use some other principle to set the limits of permissible action, and thereby allocate the burdens of risk. The libertarian axiom that all actions are permissable except overt acts of aggression provides such a principled basis for risk allocation.

There are deeper reasons why overall risk cannot be reduced or minimized by overt legal action. Risk is a subjective concept unique to each individual; therefore, it cannot be calculated in quantitative form. Hence, no one person's quantitative degree of risk can be compared to another's, and no overall measure of social risk can be obtained. As a quantitative concept, overall or social risk is fully as meaningless as the economist's concept of "social costs" or social benefits.

In a libertarian world, then, everyone would assume the "proper burden of risk" placed upon him as a free human being responsible for himself.[28] That would be the risk involved in each man's person and property. Of course, individuals could voluntarily pool their risks, as in various forms of insurance, in which risks are shared and benefits paid to losers from the pool. Or, speculators could voluntarily assume risks of future price changes that are sloughed off by others in hedging operations on the market. One man could assume another's risks for payment, as in the case of performance and other forms of bonding. What would not be permissible is one group getting together and deciding that another group should be forced into assuming their risks. If one group, for example, forces a second group to guarantee the former's incomes, risks are greatly increased for the latter, to the detriment of their individual rights. In the long run, of course, the whole system might collapse, since the second group can only provide guarantees under their own production and incomes, which are bound to fall as the burden of social parasitism expands and cripples society.

The Proper Burden of Proof

If every man's proper burden of risk is to refrain from coercion unless an overt act against his person or property has been initiated against him, then what is the proper burden of proof against a defendant?[29]

First, there must be some rational standards of proof in order for libertarian principles to operate. Suppose that the basic axiom of libertarianism—no initiation of force against person or property—is enshrined in all judicial proceedings. But suppose that the only criterion of proof is that all persons under six feet tall are considered guilty, while all persons over six feet tall are held to be innocent. It is clear that these procedural standards of proof would be in direct and flagrant violation of libertarian principles. So would tests of proof in which irrelevant or random occurrences would decide the case, such as the medieval trial by ordeal or trial by tea leaves or astrological charts.

From a libertarian point of view, then, proper procedure calls for rational proof about the guilt or innocence of persons charged with a tort or crime. Evidence must be probative in demonstrating a strict causal chain of acts of invasion of person or property. Evidence must be constructed to demonstrate that aggressor A in fact initiated an overt physical act invading the person or property of victim B.[30]

Who, then, should bear the burden of proof in any particular case? And what criterion or standard of proof should be satisfied?

The basic libertarian principle is that everyone should be allowed to do whatever he is doing unless he is committing an overt act of aggression against someone else. But what about situations where it is unclear whether a person is committing aggression? In those cases, the only procedure consonant with libertarian principle is to do nothing; to lean over backwards to ensure that the judicial agency is not coercing an innocent man.[31] If we are unsure, it is far better to let an aggressive act slip through than to impose coercion and therefore to commit aggression ourselves.[32] A fundamental tenet of the Hippocratic oath, "at least, do not harm," should apply to legal or judicial agencies as well.

The presumption of every case, then, must be that every defendant is innocent until proven guilty, and the burden of proof must be squarely upon the plaintiff.[33]

If we must always insist on *laissez-faire*, then it follows that such a weak standard of proof as "preponderance of evidence" must not be allowed to serve as a demonstration of guilt. If the plaintiff produces evidence adjudged in some sense to weigh a mere 51 percent on the guilt of the defendant, this is scarcely better than random chance as justification for the court's using force against the defendant. Presumption of innocence, then, must demand a far higher standard of proof. At present, "preponderance of evidence" is used to decide civil cases, whereas a far tougher standard is used for criminal cases, since penalties are so much stiffer. But, for libertarians, the test of guilt must not be tied to the degree of punishment; regardless of punishment, guilt involves coercion of some sort levied against the convicted defendant. Defendants deserve as much protection in civil torts as in criminal cases.[34]

A few judges, properly shocked by the dominant view that a mere 51 percent of the evidence may serve to convict, have changed the criteria to make sure whoever is trying the case—judge or jury—is convinced of guilt by the preponderance of evidence. A more satisfactory criterion, however, is that the trier must be convinced of the defendant's guilt by "clear, strong, and convincing proof."[35] Fortunately, this test has been used increasingly in civil cases in recent years. Better yet were stronger but generally rejected formulations of certain judges, such as "clear, positive, and unequivocal" proof, and one judge's contention that the phrase means the plaintiffs "must...satisfy you to a moral certainty."[36]

But the best standard for any proof of guilt is the one commonly used in criminal cases: proof "beyond a reasonable doubt." Obviously, some doubt will almost always persist in gauging people's actions, so that a standard such as "beyond a scintilla of doubt" would be hopelessly unrealistic. But the doubt must remain small enough that any "reasonable man" will be convinced of the defendant's guilt. Establishing guilt "beyond a reasonable doubt" appears to be the standard most consonant with libertarian principle.

Lysander Spooner, the outstanding 19th-century libertarian constitutional lawyer, was an ardent advocate of the "beyond a reasonable doubt" standard for all guilt:

> The lives, liberties, and properties of men are too valuable to
> them, and the natural presumptions are too strong in their
> favour, to justify the destruction of them by their fellowmen
> on a mere balancing of probabilities, *or on any ground
> whatever short of certainty beyond a reasonable doubt.*
> [Italics Spooner's] (C. Shiveley 1971, II, pp. 208-209).[37]

While the reasonable doubt criterion generally has not been used in civil cases, there are a few precedents for this seemingly bold and shocking proposal. Thus, in the claim of an orally offered gift in a probate case, the court ruled that the alleged gift "must be proven by forceful, clear and conclusive testimony which convinces the court beyond reasonable doubt of its truthfulness." And in a suit to revise a written contract, the court ruled that the mistake must be "established by evidence so strong and conclusive as to place it beyond reasonable doubt."[38]

Strict Causality

What the plaintiff must prove, then, beyond a reasonable doubt is a strict causal connection between the defendant and his aggression against the plaintiff. He must prove, in short, that A actually "caused" an invasion of the person or property of B.

In a brilliant analysis of causation in the law, Professor Epstein has demonstrated that his own theory of strict tort liability is intimately connected to a direct, strict, common-sense view of "cause." Causal propositions in a strict liability view of the law take such forms as, "A hit B," "A threatened B," or "A compelled B to hit C." Orthodox tort theory, in contrast, by stressing liability for "negligence" rather than for direct aggressive action, is tangled up with vague and complex theories of "cause," far removed from the common-sense "A hit B" variety. Negligence theory postulates a vague, philosophical notion of "cause in fact" that virtually blames everyone and no one, past, present, and future for every act, and then narrows cause in a vague and unsatisfactory manner to "proximate cause" in the specific case. The result, as Epstein trenchantly points out, is to vitiate the concept of cause altogether and to set the courts free to decide cases arbitrarily and in accordance with their own views of social policy.[39]

To establish guilt and liability, strict causality of aggression leading to harm must meet the rigid test of proof beyond a reasonable doubt. Hunch, conjecture, plausibility, even mere probability, are not enough. In recent years, statistical correlation has been commonly used, but it cannot establish causation, certainly not for a rigorous legal proof of guilt or harm. Thus, if lung cancer rates are higher among cigarette smokers than non-cigarette smokers, this does not in itself establish proof of causation. The very fact that many smokers never get lung cancer and that many lung-cancer sufferers have never smoked indicates that there are other complex variables at work. So that while the correlation is suggestive, it hardly suffices to establish medical or scientific proof; *a fortiori* it still less establishes any sort of legal guilt (if, for example, a wife who develops lung cancer should sue a husband for smoking and therefore injuring her lungs).[40]

Milton Katz points out, in a case where the plaintiff sued for air pollution damage:

> Suppose the plaintiff should claim serious damage: for emphysema, perhaps, or for lung cancer, bronchitis or some other comparably serious injury to his lungs. He would face a problem of proof of causation... Medical diagnoses appear to have established that sulphur dioxide and other air pollutants often play a significant role in the etiology of emphysema and other forms of lung damage. But they are by no means the only possible causative factors. Emphysema and lung cancer are complex illnesses which may originate in a variety of causes, for example, cigarette smoking, to name one familiar example. If and when the plaintiff should succeed in establishing that the defendants' conduct polluted the air of his home, it would not follow that the pollution caused his illness. The plaintiff would still have to meet the separate burden of proving the etiology of his lung damage (Katz 1969, p. 6220).

Thus, a strict causal connection must exist between an aggressor and a victim and this connection must be provable beyond a reasonable doubt. It must be causality in the common-sense concept of strict proof of the "A hit B" variety, not mere probability or statistical correlation.

Liability of the Aggressor Only

Under strict liability theory, it might be assumed that if "A hit B," then A is the aggressor, and that A—and only A—is liable to B. And yet the legal doctrine has arisen and triumphed, approved even by Professor Epstein, in which sometimes C, innocent and not the aggressor, is also held liable. This is the notorious theory of "vicarious liability."

Vicarious liability grew up in medieval law, when a master was responsible for the torts committed by his servants, serfs, slaves, and wife. As individualism and capitalism developed, the common law changed and vicarious liability disappeared in the 16th and 17th centuries, when it was sensibly concluded that "the master should not be liable for his servant's torts unless he had commanded the particular act." (Prosser 1971, p. 458).

Since the 18th and 19th centuries, however, the vicarious liability of masters or employers is back with a vengeance. As long as the tort is committed by the employee in the course of furthering, even if only in part, his employer's business, then the employer is also liable. The only exception is when the servant goes "on a frolic of his own" unconnected with the employer's business. William L. Prosser writes:

> The fact that the servant's act is expressly forbidden by the master, or is done in a manner which he has prohibited, is...usually not conclusive, and does not in itself prevent an act from being within the scope of employment [and therefore making the master liable]. A master cannot escape liability merely by ordering his servant to act carefully... Thus instructions to a sales clerk never to load a gun while exhibiting it will not prevent liability when the clerk does so, in an effort to sell the gun... [T]he master cannot escape responsibility no matter how specific, detailed, and emphatic his orders may have been to the contrary. This has been clear since the leading English case (*Limpus* v. *London General Omnibus Co.*, [1862] 1H. & C. 526, 158 Eng. Rep. 993) in which an omnibus company was held liable notwithstanding definite orders to its driver not to obstruct other vehicles (Prosser 1971, p. 464).

Even more remarkably, the master is now held responsible even for intentional torts committed by the servant without the master's consent:

> In general, the master is held liable for any intentional tort committed by the servant where its purpose, however misguided, is wholly or in part to further the master's business.
>
> Thus he will be held liable where his bus driver crowds a competitor's bus into a ditch, or assaults a trespasser to eject him from the bus, or a salesman makes fraudulent statements about the product he is selling (Prosser 1971, p.464).

Prosser is properly scornful of the tortured reasoning by which the courts have tried to justify a legal concept so at war with libertarianism, individualism, and capitalism, and suited only to a pre-capitalist society:

A multitude of very ingenious reasons have been offered for the vicarious liability of a master: he has a more or less fictitious "control" over the behaviour of a servant; he has "set the whole thing in motion," and is therefore responsible for what has happened; he has selected the servant and trusted him, and so should suffer for his wrongs, rather than an innocent stranger who has had no opportunity to protect himself; it is a great concession that any man should be permitted to employ another at all, and there should be a corresponding responsibility as the price to be paid for it...

Most courts have made little or no effort to explain the result, and have taken refuge in rather empty phrases, such as...the endlessly repeated formula of "respondeat superior," which in itself means nothing more than "look to the man higher up"(Prosser 1971, p. 459).

In fact, as Prosser indicates, the only real justification for vicarious liability is that employers generally have more money than employees, so that it becomes more convenient (if one is not the employer), to stick the wealthier class with the liability. In the cynical words of Thomas Baty: "In hard fact, the reason for the employers' liability is the damages are taken from a deep pocket."(Prosser 1971, p. 459).

In opposition, too, we have Justice Holmes' lucid critique: "I assume that common-sense is opposed to making one man pay for another man's wrong, unless he has actually brought the wrong to pass... I therefore assume that common-sense is opposed to the fundamental theory of agency."[41]

One would expect that in a strict causal liability theory, vicarious liability would be tossed out with little ceremony. It is therefore surprising to see Professor Epstein violate the spirit of his own theory. He seems to have two defences for the doctrine of *respondeat superior* and vicarious liability. One is the curious argument that "just as the employer gets and benefits from the gains for his worker's activities, so too should he be required to bear the losses from these activities" (Epstein 1977, p.707). This statement fails to appreciate the nature of voluntary exchange: Both employer and employee benefit from the wage contract. Moreover, the employer does bear the "losses" in the event his production (and, therefore, his resources) turn out to be misdirected. Or, suppose the employer makes a mistake and hires an incompetent person, who is paid $10,000. The employer may fire this worker, but he and he alone bears the $10,000 loss. Thus, there appears to be no legitimate reason for forcing the employer to bear the additional cost of his employee's tortious behaviour.

Epstein's second argument is contained in the sentence: "X corporation hurt me because its servant did so in the course of his employment." Here Epstein commits the error of conceptual realm, since he supposes that a "corporation" actually exists, and that it committed an act of aggression. In reality, a corporation does not act; only individuals act, and each must be responsible for his own actions and those alone. Epstein may deride Holmes' position as being based on the "nineteenth century premise that individual conduct alone was the basis of individual responsibility," but Holmes was right nevertheless (Epstein 1977, p. 705).

A Theory of Just Property: Homesteading

There are two fundamental principles upon which the libertarian theory of just property rests: Everyone has an absolute property right over his or her own body; and everyone has an absolute property right over previously unowned natural resources (land) that he first occupies and brings into use (in the Lockean phrase, "mixing his labour with the land").

The "first ownership to first use" principle for natural resources is also popularly called the "homesteading principle." If each man owns the land that he mixes his labour with, then he owns the product of that mixture, and he has the right to exchange property titles with other, similar producers. This establishes the right of free contract over the transfer of property titles. It also establishes the right to give away such titles, either as a gift or bequest.

Most of us think of homesteading unused resources in the old-fashioned sense of clearing a piece of unowned land and farming the soil. There are, however, more sophisticated and modern forms of homesteading that should establish a property right. Suppose, for example, that an airport is built with a great deal of empty land around it. The airport exudes a noise level of, say, X decibels, with the sound waves travelling over the empty land. A housing development then buys land near the airport. Some time later, the homeowners sue the airport for excessive noise interfering with the use and quiet enjoyment of their homes.

Excessive noise can be considered a form of aggression, but in this case the airport has already homesteaded X decibels worth of noise. By its prior claim, the airport now "owns the right" to emit X decibels of noise into the surrounding area. In legal terms, we can say that the airport, through homesteading, has earned an easement right to creating X decibels of noise. This homestead easement is an example of the ancient legal concept of "prescription," in which a certain activity earns a prescriptive property right for the person engaging in the action.

On the other hand, if the airport starts to increase noise levels, then the homeowners could sue or enjoin the airport from its noise aggression for the extra decibels, which had not been homesteaded. Of course, if a new airport is built and begins to send out noise of X decibels onto the existing surrounding homes, the airport becomes fully liable for the noise invasion.

It should be clear that the same theory should apply to air pollution. If A is causing pollution of B's air, and this can be proven beyond a reasonable doubt, then this is aggression. It should be enjoined and damages paid in accordance with strict liability unless A had been there first and had already been polluting the air before B's property was developed. For example, if a factory owned by A polluted originally unused property up to a certain amount of pollutant X, then A can be said to have homesteaded a pollution easement of a certain degree and type.

The courts have generally done well in deciding the limits of a prescriptive easement. In *Kerlin* v. *Southern Telephone and Telegraph Co.* (1941), the public utility had maintained an easement by prescription of telephone poles and wires over someone else's land (called the "servient estate" in law). The utility wished to string up two additional wires, and the servient estate challenged its right to do so. The court decided correctly that the utility had the right because there was no proposed change in the "outer limits of space utilized by the owner of the easement..." On the other hand, an early English case decided that an easement for moving carts could not later be used for the purpose of driving cattle.[42]

Unfortunately, the courts have not honoured the concept of homestead in a noise or pollution easement. The classic case is *Sturges* v. *Bridgman* (1879) in England. The plaintiff, a physician, had purchased land in 1865; on the property next to him the defendant, a pharmacist, used a mortar and pestle, which caused vibrations on the physician's property. There was no problem, however, until the physician built a consultation room 10 years later. He then sued to enjoin the pharmacist, claiming that his work constituted a nuisance. The defendant properly argued that the vibrations were going on before the construction of the consultation room, that they did not then constitute a nuisance, and that he had a prescriptive right to keep operating his business. Nevertheless, defendant's claim was denied.

Consequently, we have such injustice as compulsory changes of character in a business and a failure to provide prescription through first use. Thus, Prosser notes that "the character of a district may change with the passage of time, and the industry set up in the open country may become a nuisance, or be required to modify its activities, when residences spring up around it. It will acquire no prescriptive right" (Prosser 1971, pp. 600-601).[43] A just law would tell the residents arriving later that they knew what they were getting into, and that they must adapt to the industrial ambience rather than vice versa.

In some cases, however, the courts have held or at least considered that by the plaintiff's "coming to the nuisance," he has voluntarily entered a pre-existing situation, and therefore the defendant is not guilty. Prosser states that "in the absence of a prescriptive right the defendant cannot condemn the surrounding premises to endure the nuisance," but our whole point here is that the homesteader of a noise or a pollution easement has indeed earned that right in cases of "coming to the nuisance" (Prosser 1971, p. 611).

Dominant court option, as in the case of *Ensign* v. *Walls* (1948), discards or minimizes "coming to the nuisance" and dismisses the idea of a homestead easement. But minority opinion has strongly supported it, as in the New York case of *Bove* v. *Donner-Hanna Coke Co.* (1932). The plaintiff had moved into an industrial region, where the defendant was operating a coke oven on the opposite side of the street. When the plaintiff tried to enjoin the coke oven out of existence, the court rejected the plea with these exemplary words:

> With all the dirt, smoke and gas which necessarily come from factory chimneys, trains and boats, and with full knowledge that this region was especially adapted for industrial rather than residential purposes, and that factories would increase in the future, plaintiff selected this locality as the site of her future home. She voluntarily moved into this district, fully aware of the fact that the atmosphere would constantly be contaminated by dirt, gas and foul odors; and that she could not hope to find in this locality the pure air of a strictly residential zone. She evidently saw certain advantages in living in this congested centre. This is not the case of an industry, with its attendant noise and dirt, invading a quiet, residential district. This is just the opposite. Here a residence is built in an area naturally adapted for industrial purposes and already dedicated to that use. Plaintiff can hardly be heard to complain at this late date that her peace and comfort have been disturbed by a situation which existed, to some extent at least, at the very time she bought her property(Epstein 1977, p. 535).[44]

Nuisance, Visible and Invisible

An invasion of someone else's land can be considered a trespass or a nuisance, and there is considerable confusion about the boundaries of each. For our purposes, the classic distinction between the two is important. Trespass occurs when "there is a physical entry that is a direct interference with the possession of land, which usually must be accomplished by a tangible mass" (Columbia Law Review 1960, p. 879). On the other hand, "contact by minute particles or intangibles, such as industrial dust, noxious fumes, or light rays, has heretofore generally been held insufficient to constitute a trespassory entry, on the ground that there is no interference with possession, or that the entry is not direct, or that the invasion failed to qualify as an entry because of its imponderable or intangible nature" (Columbia Law Review 1960, pp. 879-880).[45]

These more intangible invasions qualify as private nuisances and can be prosecuted as such. A nuisance may be, as Prosser points out:

an interference with the physical condition of the land itself, as by vibration or blasting which damages a house, the destruction of crops, flooding, raising the water table, or the pollution of a stream or of an underground water supply. It may consist of a disturbance of the comfort or convenience of the occupant, as by unpleasant odors, smoke or dust or gas, loud noises, excessive light or high temperatures, or even repeated telephone calls (Prosser 1971, pp. 591-592).

Prosser sums up the difference between trespass and nuisance:

Trespass is an invasion of the plaintiff's interest in the exclusive possession of his land, while nuisance is an interference with his use and enjoyment of it. The difference is that between...felling a tree across his boundary line and keeping him awake at night with the noise of a rolling mill (Prosser 1971, p. 595).[46]

But what precisely does the difference between "exclusive possession" and "interference with use" mean? Furthermore, the practical difference between a tort action for trespass and for nuisance is that a trespass is illegal per se, where a nuisance, to be actionable, has to damage the victim beyond the mere fact of invasion itself. What, if any, is the justification for treating a trespass and nuisance so differently? And is the old distinction between tangible and invisible invasion really now obsolete, as Prosser maintains, "in the light of modern scientific tests" (Prosser 1971, p. 66). As a *Columbia Law Review* note put it:

The federal court...suggested that historically the reluctance of courts to find that invasion by gases and minute particles [was] trespassory resulted from the requirement that to find a trespass a court must be able to see some physical intrusion by tangible matter; it then found that this difficulty no longer exists because courts may today rely on scientific detecting methods, which can make accurate quantitative measurements of gases and minute solids, to determine the existence of a physical entry of tangible matter (Columbia Law Review 1960, pp. 880-881).

The distinction between visible and invisible, however, is not completely swept away by modern scientific detection methods. Let us take two opposite situations. First, a direct trespass: A rolls his car onto B's lawn or places a heavy object on B's grounds. Why is this an invasion and illegal per se? Partly because, in the words of an old English case, "the law infers some damage; if nothing more, the treading down of grass or herbage" (Prosser 1971, p. 66). But it is not just treading down; a tangible invasion of B's property interferes with his exclusive use of the property, if only by taking up tangible square feet (or cubic feet). If A walks on or puts an object on B's land, then B cannot use the space A or his object have taken up. An invasion by a tangible mass is an interference with someone else's property and therefore illegal.

In contrast, consider the case of radio waves, which cross other people's boundaries in a way that is invisible and insensible in every way to the property owner. We are all bombarded by radio waves that cross our properties without our knowledge or consent. Are they invasive and should they therefore be illegal, now that we have scientific devices to detect such waves? Are we then to outlaw all radio transmission? And if not, why not?

The reason why not is that these boundary crossings do not interfere with anyone's exclusive possession, use, or enjoyment of his property. They are invisible, undetected by man's senses, and harmless. They are therefore not really invasions of property, for we must refine our concept of invasion to mean not just boundary crossings, but boundary crossings that in some way interfere with the owner's use or enjoyment of his property. What counts is whether the senses of the property owner are interfered with.

But suppose it is later discovered that radio waves are harmful, that they cause cancer or some other illness? Then they would be interfering with the use one's person and should be illegal and enjoined, provided of course that proof of harm and causal connection between specific invaders and specific victims are established beyond a reasonable doubt.

So we see that the proper distinction between trespass and nuisance, between strict liability per se and strict liability only on proof of harm, is not really based on "exclusive possession" as opposed to "use and enjoyment." The proper distinction is between visible and tangible, or "sensible," invasion— which interferes with possession and use of the property—and invisible, "insensible" boundary crossings that do not, which should be outlawed only on proof of harm.

The same doctrine applies to low-level radiation, which virtually everyone and every object in the world emanates, and therefore everyone receives. Outlawing or enjoining low-level radiation, as some of our environmental fanatics seem to be advocating, would be tantamount to enjoining the entire human race and all the world around us. Low-level radiation, precisely because it is undetectable by man's senses, interferes with no one's use or possession of his property, and therefore may only be acted against upon strict causal proof of harm beyond a reasonable doubt.

The theory of homestead easements discussed earlier would require no restriction on radio transmissions or on people's low-level radiation. In the case of radio transmissions, Smith's ownership of land and all of its appurtenances does not entitle him to own all radio waves passing over and across his land, for Smith has not homesteaded or transmitted radio frequencies there. Hence, Jones, who transmits a wave on, say, 1200 kilohertz, homesteads the ownership of that wave as far as it travels, even if it travels across Smith's property. If

Smith tries to interfere with or otherwise disrupt Jones' transmissions, he is guilty of interfering with Jones' just property.[47]

Only if the radio transmissions are proven to be harmful to Smith's person beyond a reasonable doubt should Jones' activities be subject to injunction. The same type of argument, of course, applies to radiation transmissions.

Between tangible trespass and radio waves or low-level radiation, there is a range of intermediate nuisances. How should they be treated?

Air pollution, consisting of noxious odors, smoke, or other visible matter, definitely constitutes an invasive interference. These particles can be seen, smelled, or touched, and should therefore constitute invasion per se, except in the case of homesteaded air pollution easements (Damages beyond simple invasion would, of course, call for further liability.) Air pollution, however, of gases or particles that are invisible or undetectable by the senses should not constitute aggression per se, because being insensible, they do not interfere with the owner's possession or use. They take on the status of invisible radio waves or radiation unless they are proven to be harmful, and unless this proof and the causal connection from aggressor to victim can be established beyond a reasonable doubt.[48]

Excessive noise is certainly a tort of nuisance, since it interferes with a person's enjoyment of his property, including his health. However, no one would maintain that every man has the right to live as if he is in a soundproof room; only excessive noise, however vague the concept, can be actionable.

In a sense, life itself homesteads noise easements. Every area has certain noises, and people moving into an area must anticipate a reasonable amount of noise. As Terry Yamada ruefully concedes:

> An urban resident must accept the consequences of a noisy environment situation. Courts generally hold that persons who live or work in densely populated communities must necessarily endure the usual annoyances and discomforts of those trades and business located in the neighbourhood where they live or work; such annoyances and discomforts, however, must not be more than those reasonably expected in the community and lawful to the conduct of the trade of business (Yamada 1975, p. 64).[49]

In short, he who wants a soundproof room must pay for its installation.

The current general rule of the civil courts on nuisance suits for noise is cogent:

> A noise source is not a nuisance per se but only becomes a nuisance under certain conditions. These conditions depend on a consideration of the surrounding area, the time of day or night when the noise-producing activities take place and the manner in which the activity is conducted. A private nuisance is compensable only when it is unreasonable or

excessive and when it produces actual physical discomfort or injury to a person of ordinary sensibilities so as to interfere with the use and enjoyment of the property[50] (Yamada 1975, p. 63).

Owning the Technological Unit: Land and Air

In our discussion of homesteading, we did not stress the problem of the size of the area to be homesteaded. If A uses a certain amount of a resource, how much of that resource accrues to his ownership? Our answer is that he owns a technological unit of the resource. The size of that unit depends on the type of good or resource in question, and must be determined by judges, juries, or arbitrators who are expert in the particular resource or industry in question. If resource X is owned by A, then A must own enough of it so as to include necessary appurtenances. For example, in the court's determination of radio frequency ownership in the 1920s, the extent of ownership depended on the technological unit of the radio wave—its width on the electromagnetic spectrum so, that another wave would not interfere with the signal, and its length over space. The ownership of the frequency was then determined by width, length, and location.

American land settlement is a history of grappling, often unsuccessfully, with the size of the homestead unit. Thus, the homesteading provision in the federal land law of 1861 provided a unit of 160 acres, the clearing and use of which over a certain term would convey ownership to the homesteader. Unfortunately, in a few years, when the dry prairie began to be settled, 160 acres was much too low for any viable land use (generally ranching and grazing.) As a result, very little western land came into private ownership for several decades. The resulting overuse of the land caused the destruction of western grass cover and much of the timberland.

With the importance of analysing the technological unit in mind, let us examine the ownership of airspace. Can there be private ownership of the air, and if so, to what extent?

The common law principle is that every landowner owns all the airspace above him upward indefinitely unto the heavens and downward into the centre of the earth. In Lord Coke's famous dictum, *Cujus est solum ejus est usque ad coelum*; this is, he who owns the soil owns upward unto heaven and, by analogy, downward to Hades. While this is a time-honoured rule, it was, of course, designed before planes were invented. A literal application of the rule would in effect outlaw all aviation, as well as rockets and satellites.[51]

But is the practical problem of aviation the only thing wrong with the *ad coelum* rule? Using the homesteading principle, the *ad coelum* rule never made any sense, and is therefore overdue in the dustbin of legal history. If one homesteads and uses the soil, in what sense is he also using all the sky above him up into heaven? Clearly, he isn't.

The *ad coelum* rule unfortunately lingered on in the *Restatement of Torts* (1939), adopted by the Uniform State Law for Aeronautics and enacted in 22 states during the 1930s and 1940s. This variant continued to recognize unlimited ownership of upward space, but added a superior public privilege to invade that right. Aviators and satellite owners would still bear the burden of proof that they possessed this rather vague privilege to invade private property in airspace. Fortunately, the Uniform Act was withdrawn by the Commissioners on Uniform State Laws in 1943, and is now on the way out.

A second solution, adopted by the Ninth Circuit federal court in 1936, scrapped private property in airspace altogether and even allowed planes to buzz land close to the surface. Only actual interference with present enjoyment of land would constitute a tort.[52] The most popular nuisance theory simply outlaws interference with land use, but is unsatisfactory because it scraps any discussion of ownership of airspace.

The best judicial theory is the "zone" theory, which asserts that only the lower part of the airspace above one's land is owned; this zone is the limit of the owner's "effective possession." As Prosser defines it, "effective possession" is "so much of the space above him as is essential to the complete use and enjoyment of the land."[53] The height of the owned airspace will vary according to the facts of the case and therefore according to the "technological unit." Thus, Prosser writes:

> This was the rule applied in the early case of *Smith* v. *New England Aircraft Co.*, where flights at the level of one hundred feet were held to be trespasses, since the land was used for the cultivation of trees which reached that height. A few other cases have adopted the same view. The height of the zone of ownership must vary according to the facts of each case.[54]

On the other hand, the nuisance theory should be added to the strict zone of ownership applied in cases such as excess aircraft noise injuring people or activities in an adjoining area, not directly beneath the plane. At first, the federal courts ruled that only low flights overhead could constitute a tort against private landowners, but the excessive noise case of *Thornburg* v. *Port of Portland* (1962) corrected that view. The court properly reasoned in *Thornburg*:

> If we accept...the validity of the propositions that a noise can be a nuisance; that a nuisance can give rise to an easement; and that a noise coming straight down from above one's land can ripen into a taking if it is persistent enough and aggravated enough, then logically the same kind and degree of interference with the use and enjoyment of one's land can

also be a taking even though the noise vector may come from some direction other than the perpendicular.[55]

While there is no reason why the concept of ownership of airspace cannot be used to combat air pollution torts, this has rarely been done. Even when *ad coelum* was riding high, it was used against airplane overflights but not against pollution of one's air, which was inconsistently considered to be a communal resource. The law of nuisance could traditionally be used against air pollution, but until recently it was crippled by "balancing of the equities," negligence rules against strict liability, and declaration that "reasonable" air pollution was not actionable. In the classic case of *Holman* v. *Athens Empire Laundry Co.* (1919), the Supreme Court of Georgia declared: "The pollution of the air, so far as reasonably necessary to the enjoyment of life and indispensable to the progress of society, is not actionable."[56] Fortunately, that attitude is now becoming obsolete.

Although air pollution should be a tort subject to strict liability, it should be emphasized that statements like "everyone has the right to clean air" are senseless. There are air pollutants constantly emerging from natural processes, and one's air is whatever one may happen to possess. The eruption of Mount St. Helens should have alerted everyone to the ever-present processes of natural pollution. It has been the traditional and proper rule of the common law courts that no landowner is responsible for the harm caused by natural forces originating on his property. As Prosser writes, a landowner

> is under no affirmative duty to remedy conditions of purely natural origin upon his land, although they may be highly dangerous or inconvenient to his neighbours... Thus it has been held that the landowner is not liable for the existence of a foul swamp, for falling rocks, for the spread of weeds or thistles growing on his land, for harm done by indigenous animals, or for the normal, natural flow of surface water (Prosser 1971, p. 354).

In sum, no one has a right to clean air, but one does have a right to not have his air invaded by pollutants generated by an aggressor.

Air Pollution: Law and Regulation

We have established that everyone may do as he wishes provided he does not initiate an overt act of aggression against the person or property of anyone else. Anyone who initiates such aggression must be strictly liable for damages against the victim, even if the action is "reasonable" or accidental. Finally, such aggression may take the form of pollution of someone else's air, including his owned airspace, injury against his person, or nuisance interfering with possession or use of his land.

This is the case provided that: (a) the polluter has not previously established a homestead easement; (b) the plaintiff proves actual harm in the case of invisible and insensible pollutants, while visible pollutants or noxious odors are per se aggression; (c) the burden of proof of such aggression rests upon the plaintiff; (d) the plaintiff proves strict causality from the defendant's actions to the plaintiff's victimization; (e) the plaintiff proves such causality and aggression beyond a reasonable doubt; and (f) there is no vicarious liability, but only liability for those who actually commit the deed.

With these principles in mind, let us consider the current state of air pollution law. Even the current shift from negligence and "reasonable" actions to strict liability has by no means satisfied the chronic special pleaders for environmental plaintiffs. As Paul Downing says, "Currently, a party who has been damaged by air pollution must prove in court that emitter A damaged him. He must establish that he was damaged and emitter A did it, and not emitter B. This is almost always an impossible task (Downing 1971, p. 13)." If true, then we must assent without complaint. After all, proof of causality is a basic principle of civilized law, let alone of libertarian legal theory.

Similarly, James Krier concedes that even if the requirement to prove intent or unreasonable conduct or negligence is replaced by strict liability, there is still the problem of proving the causal link between the wrongful conduct and the injury. Krier complains that "cause and effect must still be established" (Krier, pp. 107-108). He wants "systematic reallocation of the burden of proof," i.e., taking the burden off the plaintiff, where it clearly belongs. Are defendants now to be guilty until they can prove themselves innocent?

The prevalence of multiple sources of pollution is a problem. How are we to blame emitter A if there are other emitters, or if there are natural sources of emission? Whatever the answer, it must not come at the expense of throwing out proper standards of proof and conferring unjust special privileges on plaintiffs and special burdens on defendants.[57]

Similar problems of proof are faced by plaintiffs in nuclear radiation cases. As Jeffrey Bodie writes, "In general the courts seem to require a high degree of causation in radiation cases which frequently is impossible to satisfy given the limited extent of medical knowledge in this field" (Bodie 1976, p. 868). But as we have seen above, it is precisely this "limited extent of knowledge" that makes it imperative to safeguard defendants from lax canons of proof.

There are, of course, innumerable statutes and regulations that create illegality besides the torts dealt with in common-law courts.[58] We have not discussed laws such as the Clean Air Act of 1970 for a simple reason: None of them can be permissible under libertarian legal theory. In libertarian theory, it is only permissible to proceed coercively against someone if he is a proven aggressor, and that aggression must be proven in court (or in arbitration) beyond a reasonable doubt. Any statute or administrative regulation necessarily makes actions illegal that are not overt initiations of crimes or torts according to libertarian theory. Every statute or administrative rule is therefore illegitimate, and itself invasive and a criminal interference with the property rights of non-criminals.

Suppose, for example, that A builds a building, sells it to B, and it promptly collapses. A should be liable for injuring B's person and property and the liability should be proven in court, which can then enforce the proper measures of restitution and punishment. But if the legislature has imposed building codes and inspections in the name of "safety," innocent builders (i.e., those whose buildings have not collapsed) are subjected to unnecessary and often costly rules, with no necessity for government to prove crime or damage. They have committed no tort or crime, but they are subject in advance to rules often only distantly related to safety by tyrannical governmental bodies. Yet, a builder who meets administrative inspection and safety codes and then has a building of his collapse is often let off the hook by the courts. After all, he has obeyed all the safety rules of the government, and so has received the advance *imprimatur* of the authorities.[59]

The only civil or criminal system consonant with libertarian legal principles is having judges (and/or juries and arbitrators) pursue charges of torts made by plaintiffs against defendants.

It should be emphasized that in libertarian legal theory, only the victim (or his heirs and assigns) can legitimately press suit against alleged transgressors against his person or property. District attorneys or other government officials should not be allowed to press charges against the wishes of the victim in the name of "crimes" against such dubious or nonexistent entities as "society" or the "state." If, for example, the victim of an assault or theft is a pacifist and refuses to press charges against the criminal, no one else should have the right to do so against his wishes. For just as a creditor has the right to voluntarily forgive an unpaid debt, so a victim, whether on pacifist grounds or for any other reason, has the right to "forgive" the crime so that the crime is annulled.[60]

Critics of automobile emissions will be disturbed by the absence of government regulation in view of the difficulties in proving harm to victims from individual automobiles.[61] But, as we have stressed, utilitarian considerations must always be subordinate to the requirements of justice. Those worried about auto emissions are in even worse shape in the tort law courts, because libertarian principle also requires a return to the now much scorned 19th-century rule of privity.

The privity rule, which applies largely to the field of products liability, states that the buyer of a defective product can sue only the person with whom he had a contract.[62] If the consumer buys a watch from a retailer and the watch does not work, it should be only the retailer whom he can sue, since it was the retailer who transferred ownership of the watch in exchange for the consumer's money. The consumer, in contrast to modern rulings, should not be able to sue the manufacturer, with whom he had no dealings. It was the retailer who, by selling the product, gave an implied warranty that the product would not be defective. Similarly, the retailer should be able to sue only the wholesaler for the defective product, the wholesaler only the jobber, and finally the manufacturer.[63]

The privity rule should be applied in the same way to auto emissions. The guilty polluter should be each individual car owner and not the automobile manufacturer, who is not responsible for the actual tort and the actual emission. (For all the manufacturer knows, for example, the car might be used only in some unpopulated area or used mainly for aesthetic contemplation by the car owner.) As in the product liability cases, the only real justification for suing the manufacturer rather than the retailer is simply convenience and deep pockets, with the manufacturer presumably being wealthier than the retailer.

While the case against auto emissions for plaintiffs might seem hopeless under libertarian law, there is a partial way out. In a libertarian society, roads would be private owned. This means that the auto emissions would be emanating from the owner's road into the lungs or airspace of other citizens, so that the road owner would be liable for pollution damage to the surrounding inhabitants. Suing the road owner is more feasible than suing each individual car owner for the minute amount of pollutants he might be responsible for. In order to protect himself from these suits, or even from possible injunctions, the road owner would then have the economic incentive to issue anti-pollution regulations for all cars that will ride on his road. Once again, as in other cases of the "tragedy of the commons," private ownership of the resource can solve many "externality" problems.[64]

Collapsing Crime Into Tort

If there is no such entity as society or the state, or no one except the victim who should have any standing as a prosecutor or plaintiff, this means that the entire structure of criminal law must be dispensed with, leaving tort law, where the victim indeed presses charges against the aggressor.[65] However, there is no reason why parts of the law that are now the province of criminal law cannot be grafted onto an enlarged law of torts. For example, restitution to the victim is now considered the province of tort law, whereas punishment is the realm of criminal law.[66] Yet, punitive damages for international torts (as opposed to accidents) now generally are awarded in tort law. It is therefore conceivable that more severe punishments, such as imprisonment, forced labour to repay the victim, or transportation, could be grafted onto tort law as well.[67]

One cogent argument against any proposal to collapse criminal into tort law is that punitive damages are "fixed only by the caprice of the jury and imposed without the usual safeguards thrown about criminal procedure, such as proof of guilt beyond a reasonable doubt [and] the privilege against self-incrimination."[68] But, as argued above, standards such as proof beyond a reasonable doubt should be applied to tort law cases as well.[69]

Professor Epstein, in attempting to preserve a separate realm for criminal law versus a proposed collapse into tort law, rests much of his case on the law of attempts. In criminal law, an attempted crime that fails and causes no damage or invasion of the rights of the victim is still a crime and can be prosecuted. And yet, Epstein charges, such an attempted crime would not be an invasion of rights and therefore could not be a tort or be prosecuted under tort law (Epstein 1977, pp. 231-257).

Randy Barnett's rebuttal, however, is conclusive. Barnett points out, first, that most unsuccessful attempts at invasion result nevertheless in "successful," though lesser, invasions of person or property, and would therefore be prosecutable under tort law. He notes that "attempted murder is usually an aggravated assault and battery, attempted armed robbery is usually an assault, attempted car theft or burglary is usually a trespass" Barnett 1977, p. 376).[70] Secondly, even if the attempted crime created no invasion of property per se, if the attempted battery or murder became known to the victim, the resulting creation of fear in the victim would be prosecutable as an assault. The would-be criminal (or tortfeasor) could not get away unscathed.

Therefore, the only attempted invasion that could not be prosecuted under the law of torts would be one that no one ever knew anything about. But if no one knows about it, a crime cannot be prosecuted under any law.[71]

Furthermore, as Barnett concludes, potential victims would not be prevented under libertarian law from defending themselves against attempts at crime. As Barnett says, it is justifiable for a victim or his agents to repel an overt act that has been initiated against him, and that is, in fact, what an attempt at crime is all about.[72]

Joint Torts and Joint Victims

So far, in discussing invasions of person or property, we have confined ourselves to single aggressors and single victims, of the "A hit B" or "A damaged B" variety. But actual air pollution cases often have multiple alleged aggressors and multiple victims. On what principles may they be prosecuted or convicted?

When more than one aggressor has contributed to a tort, it is generally more convenient for the plaintiffs to join the defendants together in one suit ("joinder"). Convenience, however, should not be allowed to override principle or rights, and in our view the original common-law rule of joinder was correct: Defendants can be compulsorily joined only when all parties acted in concert in a joint tortious enterprise.

In the case of truly joint torts, it also makes sense to have each of the joint aggressors equally liable for the entire amount of the damages. If it were otherwise, each criminal could dilute his own liability in advance by simply adding more criminals to his enterprise. Hence, since the action of all the aggressors was in concert, the tort was truly joint, so that

> all coming to do an unlawful act, and of one party, the act of one is the act of the same party being present. Each was therefore liable for the entire damage done, although one might have battered the plaintiff, while another imprisoned him, and a third stole his silver buttons. All might be joined as defendants in the same action at law (Prosser 1971, p. 291).[73]

Unfortunately, for purposes of convenience the joinder rule has been weakened, and the courts in many cases have permitted plaintiffs to compel joinder of defendants even in cases where torts are committed separately and not in concert (Prosser 1971, pp. 317-318). The confusion in joinder for both joint and separate torts has caused many courts to apply the full or "entire" liability rule to each aggressor. In the case of separate torts encroaching upon a victim, this makes little sense. Here the rule should be what it traditionally has been in nuisance cases, that the courts apportion damage in accordance with the separate causal actions contributed by each defendant.

Air pollution cases generally are those of separate torts impinging upon victims; therefore, there should be no compulsory joinder, and damages should be apportioned in accordance with the separate causal factors involved. As Prosser writes:

> Nuisance cases, in particular, have tended to result in apportionment of the damages, largely because the interference with the plaintiff's use of his land has tended to be severable in terms of quantity, percentage, or degree. Thus defendants who independently pollute the same stream or who flood the plaintiff's land from separate sources, are liable only severally for the damages individually caused, and the same is true as to nuisance due to noise, or pollution of the air.[74]

But because the injuries are multiple and separate, it is then up to the plaintiffs to show a rational and provable basis for apportioning the damage among the various defendants and causative factors. If this rule is properly and strictly adhered to, and proof is beyond a reasonable doubt, the plaintiffs in air pollution cases generally will be able to accomplish very little. To counter this, environmental lawyers have proposed weakening the very basis of our legal system by shifting the burden of proof for detailed allocation of damages from the plaintiffs to the various defendants.[75]

Thus, compulsory joinder of defendants may proceed on the original common-law rule only when the defendants allegedly have committed a truly joint tort, in concerted action. Otherwise, defendants may insist on separate court actions.

What about joinder of several plaintiffs against one or more defendants? When may that take place? This problem is highly relevant to air pollution cases, where there are usually many plaintiffs proceeding against one or more defendants.

In the early common law, the rules were rigorous on limiting permissible joinder of plaintiffs to cases where all causes of action had to affect all the parties joined. This has now been liberalized to permit joint action by plaintiffs where the joint action arises out of the same transaction or series of transactions, and where there is at least one question of law or fact common to all plaintiffs. This appears to be a legitimate liberalization of allowing plaintiffs voluntary joinder.[76]

While permissive joinder of plaintiffs in this sense is perfectly legitimate, this is not the case for class action suits, where the outcome of the suit is binding even upon those members of the alleged class of victims who did not participate in the suit. It seems the height of presumption for plaintiffs to join in a common suit and to press a "class action" suit, in which even alleged victims who never heard of or consented to a suit are bound by the result. The only plaintiffs who should be affected by a suit are those who voluntarily join. Thus, it would not be permissible for 50 residents of Los Angeles to file a pollution suit on behalf of the class of "all citizens of Los Angeles" without their knowledge or express consent. On the principle that only the victim and his heirs and assigns may press a suit or use force on his behalf, class action suits binding on anyone except voluntary plaintiffs are impermissible.[77]

Unfortunately, while the 1938 Federal Rule of Civil Procedure 23 provided for at least one type of non-binding class action—the "spurious class action"—the revised 1966 rules make all class action suits binding upon the class as a whole or, rather, on all those members of the class who do not specifically request exclusion. In an unprecedented step, voluntary action is now being assumed if no action is taken. The residents of Los Angeles, who might not even know about the suit in question, are required to take steps to exclude themselves from the suit, otherwise the decision will be binding upon them.[78] Furthermore, most states have followed the new federal rules for class suits.

As in the case of voluntary joinder, the post-1966 class action must involve questions of law or fact common to their entire class. Fortunately, the courts have placed further limits on the use of class action. In most cases, all identifiable members of the class must be given individual notice of the suit, giving them an opportunity to opt out of the action; also, the class must be definitely identifiable, ascertainable, and manageable. Under this rule, the federal courts generally would not allow "all residents of the city of Los Angeles" to be party to a class action suit.[79] Thus, a suit allegedly on behalf of all residents of Los Angeles County (over seven million persons) to enjoin 293 companies from polluting the atmosphere was dismissed by the court "as unmanageable because of the number of parties (plaintiffs and defendants), the diversity of their interests, and the multiplicity of issues involved."[80]

Another sensible limitation placed on most class action suits is that common class interests in the suit must predominate over separate individual interests. Thus, a class suit will not be allowed where separate individual issues are "numerous and substantial," and therefore common issues do not predominate. In the case of *City of San Jose* v. *Superior Court* (1974), the court threw out a class action suit of landowners suing for damages to their land resulting from nearby airport noise, pollution, traffic, etcetera. Even though the airport affected each of the landowners, the court properly ruled that "the right of each landowner to recover for the harm to his land involved too many individual facts (e.g., proximity to flight paths, type of property, value, use, etc.)" to permit a class suit.[81]

Thus, class action suits should not be allowed except where every plaintiff actively and voluntarily joins and where common interests predominate over separate and individual ones.[82]

How, then, have the recent class action rules been applied to the question of air pollution? Krier says with dismay that while the 1966 Federal Rule 23 is indeed more liberal than its predecessor in allowing class action, the U.S. Supreme Court has virtually nullified its impact by ruling that class members may aggregate individual claims for federal courts only when they share a common and undivided interest.[83] According to Krier, this cogent limitation rules out most class action suits in air pollution cases. He adds that while this restriction does not apply to state suits, these are often even less viable than federal class suits before the new rules. Krier complains, in an unconsciously humorous note, that some class action suits don't attract any plaintiffs at all.[84D]

But the major problem of class action suits for the plaintiffs, Krier concedes, is manageable and ascertainable rules for suits with a large number of plaintiffs in the class, citing in particular the *Diamond* v. *General Motors* case. But whereas Krier attributes the problem solely to the lack of competence and facilities judges possess to balance the various interests, he fails to realize the still larger problem of lack of identifiability and of clear proof of guilt and causality between defendant and plaintiff.

Conclusion

We have attempted to set forth a set of libertarian principles by which to gauge and reconstruct the law. We have concluded that everyone should be able to do what he likes, except if he commits an overt act of aggression against the person and property of another. Only this act should be illegal, and it should be prosecutable only in the courts under the tort law, with the victim or his heirs and assigns pressing the case against the alleged aggressor. Therefore, no statute or administrative ruling creating illegal actions should be permitted. And since any prosecution on behalf of "society" or the "state" is impermissible, the criminal law should be collapsed into a reconstituted tort law, incorporating punishment and part of the law of attempts.

The tortfeasor or criminal is to be strictly liable for his aggression, with no evasion of liability permissible on the basis of "negligence" or "reasonability" theories. However, the liability must be proven on the basis of strict causality of the defendant's action against the plaintiff, and it must be proven by the plaintiff beyond a reasonable doubt.

The aggressor and only the aggressor should be liable, and not the employer of an aggressor, provided, of course, that the tort was not committed at the direction of the employer. The current system of vicarious employer liability is a hangover from pre-capitalist master/serf relations and is basically an unjust method of finding deep pockets to plunder.

These principles should apply to all torts, including air pollution. Air pollution is a private nuisance generated from one person's landed property onto another and is an invasion of the airspace appurtenant to land and, often, of the person of the landowner. Basic to libertarian theory of property rights is the concept of homesteading, in which the first occupier and user of a resource thereby makes it his property. Therefore, where a "polluter" has come first to the pollution and has preceded the landowner in emitting air pollution or excessive noise onto empty land, he has thereby homesteaded a pollution or excessive noise easement. Such an easement becomes his legitimate property right, rather than that of the later, adjacent landowner. Air pollution, then, is not a tort but only the ineluctable right of the polluter if he is simply acting on a homestead easement. But where there is no easement and air pollution is evident to the senses, pollution is a tort per se because it interferes with the possession and use of property by its owner. But the invisible and insensible crossing of another's air boundary—say by radio waves or low-level radiation—cannot be considered aggression because it does not interfere with the owner's use or enjoyment of his person or property. Only if such a boundary crossing commits provable harm, according to principles of strict causability and beyond a reasonable doubt, can it be considered a tort and subject to liability and injunction.

A joint tort, in which defendants are compelled to defend themselves jointly, should apply only if all acted in concert. Where their actions are separate, the suits must be separate as well, and the liability apportioned separately. Plaintiffs should be able to join their suits against a defendant only if their cases have a common element predominating over the separate and individual interests. Class action suits are impermissible beyond a voluntary joinder of plaintiffs because they presume to act for and bind class members who have not agreed to join in the suit.

Finally, we must renounce the common practice of environmental law writers of acting as special partners for air pollution plaintiffs, lamenting when plaintiffs are not allowed to ride roughshod over defendants. The overriding factor in air pollution law, as in other parts of the law, should be libertarian and property rights principles, rather than the convenience or special interests of one set of contestants.

Notes

1. Legal principles setting down certain prohibited actions as torts or crimes are to be distinguished from statutes or administrative edicts that lay down positive demands, such as "thou shalt pay X amount of taxes" or "thou shalt report for induction on such and such a date." In a sense, of course, all commands can be phrased in such a way as to appear negative, such as "thou shalt not refuse to pay X amount of taxes," or "thou shalt not disobey the order to appear for induction." Why such rephrasing would be inappropriate will be discussed below. See below also for a discussion of "torts" vis-à-vis "crimes."

2. Ronald Dworkin, however, has pointed out that even positive legal analysis necessarily involves moral questions and moral standards. Dworkin, *Taking Rights Seriously*, chapters 2, 3, 12, 13. Also see Charles Fried, "The Law of Change: The Cunning of Reason in Moral and Legal History, p. 340.

3. The Austinians, of course, are also smuggling a normative axiom into their positive theory: The law should be what the king says it is. The axiom is unanalysed and ungrounded in any set of ethical principles.

4. Again, these modern, democratic variants of positive legal theory smuggle in the unsupported normative axiom that statutes should mirror whatever legislators or voters wish to do.

5. See the article launching this analysis by Ronald H. Coase, "The Problem of Social Cost, p. 10. For a critique, see Walter Block, "Coase and Demsetz on Private Property Rights," pp. 111-115.

6. It is now illegal to bargain one's way out of an injunction by dealing with the injured party. In that case, of course, the Coase-Demsetz cost internalization totally breaks down. But even with bargaining allowed, it would probably break down. Moreover, there may well be farmers so attached to their orchards that no price would compensate them, in which case the injunction would be absolute and no Coase-Demsetz bargaining could remove it. On allowing bargaining to remove injunctions, see Barton H. Thompson Jr., "Injunction Negotiations: An Economic, Moral and Legal Analysis, pp. 1563-1595.

7. On the impermissibility of the social cost concept and its application here, see Mario J. Rizzo, "Uncertainty, Subjectivity, and the Economic Analysis of Law," and Murray N. Rothbard, "Comment: The Myth of Efficiency," pp. 71-95. Also see John B. Egger, "Comment: Efficiency is not a Substitute for Ethics," pp. 117-125.

8. Social efficiency is a meaningless concept because efficiency refers to how effectively one employs means to reach given ends. But with more than one individual, who determines the ends toward which the means are to be employed? The ends of different individuals are bound to

conflict, making any added or weighted concept of social efficiency absurd. For more on this, see Rothbard, "Myth of Efficiency," p. 90.

9.   Charles Fried has pointed out that efficiency is an attempted moral criterion, albeit unexamined, wrong, and incoherent. Fried, "The Law of Change," p. 341.

10.   The concept of social wealth suffers from the same disabilities as Coase-Demsetz, as well as other problems of its own. For devastating critiques of Posner, see Ronald M. Dworkin, "Is Wealth a Value?" and Richard A. Epstein, "The Static Conception of the Common Law," pp. 191-226, 253-276. Also see Anthony J. Kronman, "Wealth Maximization as a Normative Principle"; Mario J. Rizzo, "Law Amid Flux: The Economics of Negligence and Strict Liability in Tort"; Fried, "The Law of Change"; and Gerald P. O'Driscoll, Jr., "Justice, Efficiency, and the Economic Analysis of Law: A Comment on Fried," pp. 227-242, 291-318, 335-354, 355-366.

11.   The qualification of property being "just" must be made. Suppose, for example, that A steals B's watch and that several months later, B apprehends A and grabs the watch back. If A should prosecute B for theft of "his" watch, it would be an overriding defence on B's part that the watch was not really and justly A's because he had previously stolen it from B.

12.   For more on this libertarian, or "neo-Lockean," view, see Murray N. Rothbard, "Justice and Property Rights," pp. 101-122. In a sense, Percy B. Lehning is right when he comments that rather than being two independent axioms, the homesteading principle really follows from the single axiom of self-ownership. Lehning, "Property Rights, Justice and the Welfare State, pp. 323-352.

13.   Thus, John Stuart Mill calls for complete freedom of individual action "without impediment from our fellow-creatures, so long as what we do does not harm them." Mill, "On Liberty," p. 175. F.A. Hayek, after properly defining freedom as the absence of coercion, unfortunately fails to define coercion as physical invasion and thereby permits and justifies a wide range of government interference with property rights. See Murray N. Rothbard, "F. A. Hayek and the Concept of Coercion," pp. 43-50.

14.   Robert Nozick appears to justify outlawing all voluntary exchanges that he terms "nonproductive," which he essentially defines as a situation where A would be better off if B did not exist. But here, of course, Jim would be far better off if Bob had not existed. For a critique of Nozick on this point, see Rothbard, "Robert Nozick and the Immaculate Conception of the State," pp. 52ff.

15.   We may therefore hail the "absolutist" position of Mr. Justice Black in calling for the elimination of the law of defamation. The difference is

that Black advocated an absolutist stand on the First Amendment because it is a part of the Constitution, whereas we advocate it because the First Amendment embodies a basic part of the libertarian creed. On the significant weakening of the law of defamation in the last two decades, see Richard A. Epstein, Charles O. Gregory, and Harry Kalven Jr., *Cases and Materials on Torts*, 3rd ed. pp. 977-1129 (hereafter cited as Epstein, *Cases on Torts*).

16. There should be no assertion of a right to privacy that cannot be subsumed under protection of property rights to guard against breach of contract. On privacy, see Epstein, *Cases on Torts*, pp. 1131-1190.

17. "Apprehension" of an imminent battery is a more appropriate term then "fear," since it stresses the awareness of a coming battery and of the action causing that awareness by the aggressor, rather than the subjective psychological state of the victim. Thus, Prosser: "Apprehension is not the same thing as fear, and the plaintiff is not deprived of his action merely because he is too courageous to be frightened or intimidated." William L. Prosser, *Handbook of the Law of Torts*, 4th ed. p. 39.

18. It is unfortunate that, starting about 1930, the courts have succumbed to the creation of a brand new tort, "intentional infliction of mental disturbance of extreme and outrageous conduct." It is clear that freedom of speech and person should allow verbal insult, outrageous though it may be; furthermore, there is no cogent criterion to demarcate mere verbal abuse from the "outrageous" variety. Judge Magruder's statement is highly sensible: "Against a large part of the frictions and irritations and clashing of temperaments incident to participation in community life, a certain toughening of the mental hide is a better protection than the law could ever be." Magruder, "Mental and Emotional Disturbance in the Law of Torts, pp. 1033-1035; cited in Prosser, *Law of Torts*, p. 51. Also see pp. 49-62; Epstein, *Cases on Torts*, pp. 933-952.

   In general, we must look with great suspicion on any creation of new torts that are not merely applications of old tort principles to new technologies. There is nothing new or modern about verbal abuse.

   It seems that both the infliction-of-harm and the new invasion-of-privacy tort are part and parcel of the 20th-century tendency to dilute the rights of the defendant in favour of excessive cosseting of the plaintiff—a systemic discrimination that has taken place in tort rather than criminal proceedings. See Richard A. Epstein, "The Static Conception of the Common Law," pp. 253-275.

19. Prosser, *Law of Torts*, pp. 39-40.

20. Hence, the wisdom of the court's decision in *South Brilliant Coal Co.* v. *Williams*: "If Gibbs kicked plaintiff with his foot, it cannot be said as a matter of law that there was no physical injury to him. In a legal sense, it was a physical injury, though it may have caused no physical suffering,

and though the sensation resulting there-from may have lasted but for a moment." *South Brilliant Coal Co.* v. *Williams,* 206 Ala. 637, 638 (1921). In Prosser, *Law of Torts,* p. 36. Also see Epstein, *Cases on Torts,* pp. 903ff.

21. *Courvoisier* v. *Raymond,* 23 Colo. 113, 47 Pac. 284 (1896), and discussion by Epstein in *Cases on Torts,* pp. 21-23; and in Richard A. Epstein, "A Theory of Strict Liability, p. 173.

22. As Epstein puts it, "Under a theory of strict liability, the statement of the prima facie case is evident: the defendant shot the plaintiff. The only difficult question concerns the existence of a defense which takes the form, the plaintiff assaulted the defendant. That question is a question of fact, and the jury found in effect that the plaintiff did not frighten the defendant into shooting him." Ibid.

23. Barnett has since pointed out that his article was in error in mentioning "specific intent to commit a crime"; the important emphasis is on action constituting a crime or tort, rather than the intent involved.

24. See *Morris* v. *Platt,* 32 Conn 75 (1864), and the discussion by Epstein in *Cases on Torts,* pp. 22-23.

25. On the relationship between criminal and tort law, see section entitled "Collapsing Crime Into Tort."

26. While modern law discriminates against the defendant in economic cases, it discriminates heavily against the victim in his use of personal force in self-defence. In other words, the state is allowed to use excessive force through the courts in economic cases (where corporations or the wealthy are defendants), but individual victims are scarcely allowed to use force at all.

27. For the current state of legal doctrine, see Prosser, *Law of Torts,* pp. 108-125, 134ft. As Epstein indicates, basing the proper limits of self-defence on permissible punishment would imply that in jurisdictions that have abolished capital punishment, no one may use deadly force, even in self-defence against a deadly attack. So far the courts have not been willing to embrace this *reductio ad absurdum* of their own position. Epstein, *Cases on Torts,* p. 30.

28. This is the same concept under a different name as Williamson Evers' pioneering phrase, "the proper assumption of risk." The current phrase avoids confusion with the concept of "assumption of risk" in tort law, which refers to risk voluntarily assumed by a plaintiff that therefore negates his attempts at action against a defendant. The "proper burden of risk" is related to the legal concept but refers to the risk that should be assumed by each person in accordance with the nature of man and of a free society, rather than the risk that had been voluntarily incurred by a plaintiff. See Rothbard, "Nozick and the State," pp. 49-50.

29. Or, an overt act against someone else. If it is legitimate for a person to defend himself or his property, then it is equally legitimate for him to call upon other persons or agencies to aid him in that defence or to pay them for this defence service.

30. Thayer, in his classical treatise on evidence, wrote: "There is a principle...a presupposition involved in the very conception of a rational system of evidence...which forbids receiving anything irrelevant, not logically probative." James B. Thayer, *Preliminary Treatise on Evidence* (1898), pp. 264ff., cited in E.W. Cleary, ed., *McCormick's Handbook of the Law of Evidence*, 2d ed., p. 433.

31. Benjamin R. Tucker, the leading individualist-anarchist thinker of the late 19th century, wrote: "No use of force, except against the invader, and in those cases where it is difficult to tell whether the alleged offender is an invader or not, still no use of force except where the necessity of immediate solution is so imperative that we must use it to save ourselves." Benjamin R. Tucker, *Instead of a Book*, p. 98. Also see pp. 74-75.

32. E.W. Cleary puts the point well, although he unfortunately applies it only to criminal cases: "Society has judged that it is significantly worse for an innocent man to be found guilty of a crime than for a guilty man to go free... Therefore, as stated by the Supreme Court in recognizing the inevitability of error in criminal cases...'this margin of error is reduced as to him [the defendant] by the process of placing on the other party the burden...of persuading the factfinder at the conclusion of the trial of his guilt beyond a reasonable doubt.' In so doing, the courts have...the worthy goal of decreasing the number of one kind of mistake—conviction of the innocent." E.W. Cleary, *McCormick's Handbook of Evidence*, pp. 798-799.

33. The burden of proof is also on the plaintiff in contemporary law. Cleary writes: "The burdens of pleading and proof with regard to most facts have been and should be assigned to the plaintiff who generally seeks to change the present state of affairs and who therefore naturally should be expected to bear the risk of failure of proof or persuasion." Ibid., p. 786. Cleary also speaks of "the natural tendency to place the burdens on the party desiring change." Ibid., pp. 788-789.

34. See section entitled "Collapsing Crime Into Tort."

35. See *McCormick's Handbook of Evidence*, pp. 794ff.

36. Ibid., p. 796. Here we must hail the scorned trial judges in *Molyneux* v. *Twin Falls Canal Co.*, 54 Idaho 619, 35 p. 2d 651, 94 A.L.R. 1264 (1934), and *Williams* v. *Blue Ridge Building & Loan Assn.*, 207 N.C. 362, 177 S.E. 176 (1934).

37. C. Shiveley, ed., *The Collected Works of Lysander Spooner* (Weston, Mass.: M&S Press, 1971), II, pp. 208-209. It should be pointed out that

Spooner, too, made no distinction between civil and criminal cases in this regard. I am indebted to Williamson Evers for this reference.

38. *St. Louis Union Trust Co.* v. *Busch*, 36 Mo. 1237, 145 S.W. 2d 426, (1940); *Ward* v. *Lyman*, 108 Vt. 464, 188 A. 892, 893 (1937). *McCormick's Handbook of Evidence*, pp. 797-802.

39. According to Epstein: "Once it is decided that there is no hard content to the term causation, the courts are free to decide particular lawsuits in accordance with the principles of 'social policy' under the guise of proximate-cause doctrine." Epstein, "Strict Liability," p. 163. Such nebulous and unworkable concepts as "substantial factor" in a damage or "reasonably foreseeable" have been of little help in guiding decisions on proximate cause. For an excellent critique of "but for" tests for "cause in fact" in negligence theory, as well as the Chicago-Posnerite attempt to scrap the concept of cause altogether in tort law, see ibid., pp. 160-162, 163-166.

40. If a long-time smoker who develops lung cancer should sue a cigarette company, there are even more problems. Not the least is that the smoker had voluntarily assumed the risk, so that this situation could hardly be called an aggression or tort. As Epstein writes, "Suppose plaintiff smoked different brands of cigarettes during his life? Or always lived in a smog-filled city? And if plaintiff surmounts the causal hurdle, will he be able to overcome the defence of assumption of risk?" Epstein, *Cases on Torts*, p. 257. Also see Richard A. Wegman, "Cigarettes and Health: A Legal Analysis," pp. 696-724.

A particularly interesting cancer tort case that is instructive on the question of strict causality is *Kramer Service Inc.* v. *Wilkins* 184 Miss. 483, 186 So. 625 (1939), in Epstein, *Cases on Torts*, p. 256. The court summed up the proper status of medical causal evidence in *Daly* v. *Bergstedt* (1964), 267 Minn. 244, 126 N.W. 2d 242. In Epstein, *Cases on Torts*, p. 257. Also see Epstein's excellent discussion, ibid., of *DeVarre* v. *Parten* (1964), in which the plaintiff was properly slapped down in an absurd attempt to claim that the defendant was responsible for a disease she had contracted.

41. In his *Harvard Law Review* articles on "Agency," 1891. See Epstein, *Cases on Torts*, p. 705.

42. *Kerlin* v. *Southern Telephone & Telegraph Co.* (1941) (Ga.), 191 Ga. 663, 13 S.E. 2d 790; *Ballard* v. *Dyson* (1808) 1 Taunt. 279, 127 Eng. Rep. 841. In William E. Burby, *Handbook of the Law of Real Property*, 3rd ed., pp. 84-85.

43. Also see Burby, *Law of Real Property*, p. 78. *Sturges* v. *Bridgman* (1879), 11 Ch. Div. 852.

44. *Bove* v. *Donner-Hanna Coke Corp.*, (1932) 236 App. Div. 37, 258 N.Y.S. 229, quoted in Epstein, *Cases on Torts*, p. 535. Contrary to Epstein,

however, the coming-to-nuisance is not simply an assumption of risk on the part of the plaintiff. It is a stronger defence, for it rests on an actual assignment of property right in the "nuisance" creating activity, which is therefore absolute, overriding, and indefeasible. Cf. Richard A. Epstein, "Defences and Subsequent Pleas in a System of Strict Liability," pp. 197-201.

45. Also see Glen Edward Clover, "Torts: Trespass, Nuisance and E = mc2," p. 118ff.

46. A nuisance generally emanates from the land of A to the land of B; in short, stems from outside B's land itself. Prosser's attempt to rebut this point (defendant's dog howling under plaintiff's window or defendant's cattle roaming over plaintiff's fields) misses the point. The offending dog and cattle themselves wandered over from the land of A, and since they are domesticated, their deeds are the responsibility of their owners. On animals, see pp.496-503.

47. During the 1920s, the courts were working out precisely such a system of homesteaded private property rights in airwave frequencies. It is because such a private property structure was evolving that Secretary of Commerce Hoover pushed through the Radio Act of 1927, nationalizing ownership of the airwaves. See Ronald H. Coase, "The Federal Communications Commission," p. 1-40. For a modern study of how such frequencies could be allocated, see A. De Vany, et.al., *A Property System Approach to the Electromagnetic Spectrum.*

48. On prescriptive rights, tangibility, and the concept of "coming to the tort" in relation to air pollution, see William C. Porter, "The Role of Private Nuisance Law in the Control of Air Pollution," pp. 107-119; and Julian C. Juergensmeyer, "Control of Air Pollution Through the Assertion of Private Rights," pp. 1126-1155.

49. Terry James Yamada, "Urban Noise: Abatement, Not Adaptation," p. 64. Unfortunately, like most authors writing on environmental law, Yamada writes like a fervent special pleader for environmental plaintiffs rather than as a searcher for objective law.

50. Note, however, that in our view the requirement of "unreasonable" for actual injury or discomfort is correct for noise but not, say, for visible smoke or noxious odors, unless "discomfort" is interpreted broadly so as to include all interference with use.

51. See the discussion of various theories of land and air ownership in Prosser, *Law of Torts*, pp. 70-73.

52. In *Hinman* v. *Pacific Air Transport*, 9 Cir. (1936), 84 F. 2d 755, cert. denied 300 U.S. 654. In ibid., p. 7.

53. Ibid., p. 70.

54. Ibid., pp. 70-71. See *Smith* v. *New England Aircraft Co.*, (1930), 270 Mass. 511, 170 N.E. 385. Also see Prosser, *Law of Torts*, pp. 514-515.

55. *Thornburg* v. *Port of Portland* (1962), 233 Ore. 178, 376 P. 2d 103. Quoted in Clover, "Torts," p. 121. The previous view was based on *United States* v. *Causby* (1946). Also see Prosser, *Law of Torts*, pp. 72-73.

56. *Holman* v. *Athens Empire Laundry Co.*, 149 Ga. 345, 350,,100 S.E. 207, 210 (1919). Quoted in Jack L. Landau, "Who Owns the Air? The Emission Offset Concept and Its Implications," p. 589.

57. See section entitled "Joint Torts and Joint Victims" for a discussion of joint tort-feasors, multiple torts, and class action suits.

58. With respect to air pollution regulations, see Landau, "Who Owns the Air?", pp. 575-600.

59. For an excellent discussion of judicial as opposed to statutory or administrative remedies for adulteration of products, see Wordsworth Donisthorpe, *Law in a Free Society*, pp. 132-158.

60. Criminals should have the rights to buy off a suit or enforcement by the victim, just as they should have the right to buy an injunction from a victim after it has been issued. For an excellent article on the latter question, see Thompson, "Injunction Negotiations," pp. 1563-1595.

61. See section entitled "Joint Torts and Joint Victims."

62. For hostile accounts of privity and a discussion of implied warranty, see Richard A. Epstein, *Modern Products Liability Law*, pp. 9-34; and Prosser, *Law of Torts*, pp. 641ff.

63. Some of the practical difficulties involved in such suits could be overcome by joinder of the various plaintiffs. See section entitled "Joint Torts and Joint Victims."

64. On the "tragedy of the commons" and private ownership, see, for example, Garrett Hardin, "The Tragedy of the Commons,"pp. 1243-1248; Robert J. Smith, "Resolving the Tragedy of the Commons by Creating Private Property Rights in Wildlife," pp. 439-468.

65. Notes Prosser: "A crime is an offense against the public at large, for which the state, as the representative of the public, will bring proceedings in the form of a criminal prosecution. The purpose of such a proceeding is to protect and vindicate the interests of the public as a whole... A criminal prosecution is not concerned in any way with compensation of the injured individual against whom the crime is committed." Prosser, *Law of Torts*, p. 7.

66. . For an illuminating discussion of the roots of the modern split between criminal and tort law, with the former as pursuing crimes against the "king's peace," see Barnett, "Restitution," pp. 350-354.

67. On punitive damages in tort law, see Prosser, *Law of Torts*, pp. 9ff. This is not the place to set forth a theory of punishment. Theories of punishment among libertarian philosophers and legal theorists range from avoiding any coercive sanctions to restitution only, restitution plus

proportional punishment, and allowing unlimited punishment for any crime whatsoever.

For my own view on proportional punishment, See Murray N. Rothbard, "Punishment and Proportionality," pp. 259-270. On the concept of transporting criminals, see Leonard P. Liggio, "The Transportation of Criminals: A Brief Politico-Economic History," pp. 273-294.

68. Ibid., p. 11. Also see Epstein, *Cases on Torts*, p. 906.

69. As should the privilege against self-incrimination. In fact, the ban against compulsory testimony should not only be extended to tort cases, it should be widened to include all compulsory testimony, against others as well as against oneself.

70. Barnett adds: "In this way the law of attempt is actually a form of double counting whose principal function is to enable the police and prosecutor to overcharge a crime for purposes of a later plea negotiation. Furthermore, some categories of attempt, such as conspiracy laws and possessory laws—eg., possession of burglarious instruments—are short-cuts for prosecutors unable or unwilling to prove the actual crime and are a constant source of selective, repressive prosecutions." We might add that the latter laws would be illegitimate under libertarian law.

71. According to Barnett: "The only type of unsuccessful attempt that would escape liability [under tort law] would be the case of someone who unsuccessfully tried to commit a crime without otherwise violating anyone's rights and without anyone knowing about it... In any case, no system governed by any principle can prosecute acts that no one knows about." Ibid., pp. 376-377. Professor Ronald Hamowy of the University of Alberta should also be mentioned as contributing significantly to this solution to the problem.

72. One can agree with Barnett here without adopting his own pure-restitution-without-punishment variant of tort law. In our view, elements of criminal law, such as punishment, could readily be incorporated into a reconstructed tort law.

73. Also see, ibid., pp. 293ff. In this situation, joinder is compulsory upon the defendants, even though the plaintiffs may choose between joinder and separate actions.

74. Prosser, *Law of Torts*, pp. 317-318.

75. See Katz, "Function of Tort Liability," pp. 619-620.

76. However, a better course would be to require that common interest predominate over separate individual interests, as is now being required for class action suits. See the discussion of *City of San Jose* v. *Superior Court* below.

77. The type of class action suit once known as "spurious class action," in which a judgment binds only those members actually before the court,

was not actually a class action suit but a permissive joinder device. Fed. R. Civ. P. 23 (1938).

78. The 1938 Rules provided that, in some cases, any class action must be of the spurious kind mentioned in the previous note. The revised 1966 Rules made all class action suits binding by eliminating the spurious action category. See Fed. R. Civ. P. 23 (1966).

79. Fed. R. Civ. P. 23 (a) (1966). On the question of whether individual notice to class manners is mandatory, see Fed. R. Civ. 23(b)(1), Fed. R. Civ. P. 23(b)(2), Fed. R. Civ. P. 23(b)(3), Fed. R. Civ. P. 23(d)(2), Fed. R. Civ. P. 23(e), *Mattern* v. *Weinberger*, 519F.2d 150 (3d Cir. 1975), *Eisen* v. *Carlisle & Jacquelin*, 417 U.S. 156 (1974), *Cooper* v. *American Savings & Loan Association*, 55 Cal. App. 3d 274 (1976).

80. The case was *Diamond* v. *General Motors Corp.* 20 Cal. App. 2d 374 (1971).

On the other hand, some state court decisions, such as in California, have been highly favourable toward class action suits. The California court actually allowed a class action of one man against a defendant taxi company for alleged overcharges, on behalf of himself and several thousand unidentifiable customers of the company. *Dear* v. *Yellow Cab Co.*, 67 Cal. 2d 695 (1967).

81. *City of San Jose* v. *Superior Court*, 12 Cal. 3d 447 (1974).

82. Epstein provides an interesting note on ways in which plaintiffs, in a purely libertarian way, were able to overcome the fact that neither joinder nor class action suits were permitted because of the extent and diversity of individual interests involved. The drug MER/29 was taken off the market in 1962, after which about 1,500 lawsuits were initiated against the drug company for damage. While the defendant successfully objected to a voluntary joinder, most of the attorneys voluntarily coordinated their activities through a central clearinghouse committee with fees for services assessed upon all lawyers in the group. Epstein reports that the lawyers who participated in the group were usually more successful in their respective suits than those who did not. Epstein, *Cases on Torts*, p. 274.

83. In *Snyder* v. *Harris*, 394 U.S. 332 (1970). Krier, "Air Pollution."

84. In short, what if they filed a pollution class-action suit and nobody came? Krier cites the case of *Riter* v. *Keokuk Electro-Metals Co.* 248 Iowa 710, 82 N.W. 2d 151 (1957), Krier, "Air Pollution," p. 217. Also see John Esposito, "Air and Water Pollution: What to Do While Waiting for Washington," p. 36.

References

Barnett, Randy E., "Restitution: A New Paradigm of Criminal Justice," in *Assessing the Criminal: Restitution, Retribution, and the Legal Process*, R. Barnett and J. Hagel, eds. (Cambridge, Mass.: Ballinger Publishing Co., 1977).

Block, Walter, "Coase and Demsetz on Private Property Rights," *Journal of Libertarian Studies*, Spring 1977, pp. 111-115.

Bodie, Jeffrey C., "The Irradiated Plaintiff: Tort Recovery Outside Price-Anderson," *Environmental Law* 6 (Spring 1976).

Burby, William E., *Handbook of the Law and Real Property*, 3rd edition (St. Paul, Minn.: West Publishing Co., 1965).

Cleary, E.W., ed., *McCormick's Handbook of the Law and Evidence*, 2nd ed. (St. Paul, Minn.: West Publishing Co., 1972).

Clover, Glen Edward, "Torts: Trespass, Nuisance and E=mc^2," *Oklahoma Law Review* 11 (1966).

Coase, Ronald H., "The Federal Communications Commission," *Journal of Law and Economics* 2 (October 1959), pp. 1-40.

_____, "The Problem of Social Cost," *Journal of Law and Economics* 3 (October 1960).

De Vany, A., *et al.*, *A Property System Approach to the Electromagnetic Spectrum* (San Francisco: Cato Institute, 1980).

Donisthorpe, Wordsworth, *Law in a Free Society* (London: Macmillan, 1895), pp. 132-158.

Downing, Paul B., "An Introduction to the Problem of Air Quality," in *Air Pollution and the Social Sciences*, Downing, ed., (New York: Praeger Pubs., 1971).

Dworkin, Ronald, *Taking Rights Seriously* (Cambridge: Harvard University Press, 1977).

_____, "Is Wealth a Value?" *Journal of Legal Studies*, March 1980, pp. 191-226.

Egger, John B., "Comment: Efficiency Is Not a Substitute for Ethics," in *Time, Uncertainty, and Disequilibrium: Exploration of Austrian Themes*, M. Rizzo, ed. (Lexington, Mass.: Lexington Books, 1979).

Epstein, Richard A., "Note, Deposit of Gaseous and Invisible Solid Industrial Wastes Held to Constitute Trespass," *Columbia Law Review*, 60 (1960).

_____,"A Theory of Strict Liability," *Journal of Legal Studies* 2 (January 1973).

_____, "Defenses and Subsequent Pleas in a System of Strict Liability," *Journal of Legal Studies* 3 (1974), pp. 197-201.

_____, "Crime and Tort: Old Wine in Old Bottles," in *Assessing the Criminal: Restitution, Retribution, and the Legal Process*, R. Barnett and J. Hagel eds. (Cambridge, Mass.: Ballinger Publishing Co., 1977).

_____, *Modern Products Liability Law* (Westport Conn.: Quorum Books, 1980).

_____, "The Static Conception of the Common Law," *Journal of Legal Studies*, March 1980, pp. 253-276.

Epstein, Richard A., Charles O. Gregory, and Harry Kalven Jr., *Cases and Materials on Torts*, 3rd ed. (Boston: Little, Brown & Co., 1977).

Esposito, John, "Air and Water Pollution: What to Do While Waiting for Washington," *Harvard Civil Rights/Civil Liberties Law Review*, January 1970.

Fried, Charles, "The Law of Change: The Cunning of Reason in Moral and Legal History," *Journal of Legal Studies*, March 1980, pp. 335-354.

Hardin, Garrett, "The Tragedy of the Commons," *Science* 162 (1968), pp. 1243-1248.

Juergensmeyer, Julian C., "Control of Air Pollution through the Assertion of Private Rights," *Duke Law Journal*, 1967, pp. 1126-1155.

Katz, Milton, "The Function of Tort Liability in Technology Assessment," *Cincinnati Law Review* 38 (Fall 1969).

Krier, James E., "Air Pollution and Legal Institutions: An Overview," in *Air Pollution*, Downing, ed. (New York: Praeger Publishers, 1971)

Kronman, Anthony J., "Wealth Maximization as a Normative Principle," *Journal of Legal Studies*, March 1980, pp. 227-242.

Landau, Jack L., "Who Owns the Air? The Emission Offset Concept and Its Implications," *Environmental Law* 9 (1979).

Lehning, Percy B., "Property Rights, Justice and the Welfare State," *Acta Politica* 15 (Rotterdam, 1980), pp. 323-352.

Liggio, Leonard P., "The Transportation of Criminals: A Brief Politico-Economic History," in *Assessing the Criminal: Restitution, Retribution, and the Legal Process*, R. Barnett and J. Hagel, eds. (Cambridge, Mass.: Ballinger Publishing Co., 1977).

Magruder, Calvert, "Mental and Emotional Disturbance in the Law of Torts," *Harvard Law Review* 40 (1936), pp. 1033-1035.

Mill, John Stuart, "On Liberty," *Utilitarianism, Liberty, and Representative Government* (New York: E. P. Dutton, 1944).

O'Driscoll, Gerald P. Jr., "Justice, Efficiency, and the Economic Analysis of Law: A Comment on Fried," *Journal of Legal Studies*, March 1980, pp. 355-366.

Porter, William C., "The Role of Private Nuisance Law in the Control of Air Pollution," *Arizona Law Review* 10 (1968), pp. 107-119.

Prosser, William L., *Handbook of the Law of Torts*, 4th ed. (St. Paul, Minn.: West Publishing Co., 1971).

Rizzo, Mario J., "Uncertainty, Subjectivity, and the Economic Analysis of Law," in *Time, Uncertainty, and Disequilibrium: Exploration of Austrian Themes*, M. Rizzo, ed. (Lexington, Mass.: Lexington Books, 1979).

_____, "Law Amid Flux: The Economics of Negligence and Strict Liability in Tort," *Journal of Legal Studies*, March 1980, pp. 291-318.

Rothbard, Murray N., "Justice and Property Rights," in *Property in a Human Economy*, S. Blumenfeld, ed. (LaSalle, Ill.: Open Court, 1974).

_____, "Punishment and Proportionality," in *Assessing the Criminal: Restitution, Retribution, and the Legal Process*, R. Barnett and J. Hagel, eds. (Cambridge, Mass.: Ballinger Publishing Co., 1977).

_____, "Robert Nozick and the Immaculate Conception of the State," *Journal of Libertarian Studies*, Winter 1977.

_____, "Comment: The Myth of Efficiency," in *Time, Uncertainty, and Disequilibrium: Exploration of Austrian Themes*, M. Rizzo, ed. (Lexington, Mass.: Lexington Books, 1979).

_____, "F.A. Hayek and the Concept of Coercion," *Ordo* 31 (Stuttgart, 1980), pp. 43-50.

Shiveley, C., ed., *The Collected Works of Lysander Spooner* (Weston, Mass.: M & S Press, 1971).

Smith, Robert J., "Resolving the Tragedy of the Commons by Creating Private Property Rights in Wildlife." *Cato Journal* 1 (Fall 1981), pp. 439-468.

Thompson, Barton H. Jr., "Injunction Negotiations: An Economic, Moral and Legal Analysis," *Stanford Law Review* 27 (July 1975), pp. 1563-1595.

Tucker, Benjamin R., *Instead of a Book* (New York: B.R. Tucker, 1893).

Wegman, Richard A., "Cigarettes and Health: A Legal Analysis," *Cornell Law Quarterly* 51 (Summer 1966), pp. 696-724.

Yamada, Terry James, "Urban Noise: Abatement, Not Adaptation," *Environmental Law* 6 (1975).

Chapter 10

Environmental Problems, Private Property Rights Solutions

Walter Block[1]

A reconciliation between economics and the environment can be accomplished by using the institutions of the former as a means of attaining the goals of the latter. We can express this, alternatively, as a co-operative solution to the pollution problem. That is to say, we may be able to solve the problems of pollution by relying on the same behaviours and motivations that lead to economic growth and development. This is a solution that unleashes the tremendous power of self-interest.

There is a well-known expression to the effect that everybody's business is nobody's business. This applies with particular force to the issue of pollution. There is a problem because the air and the water and the forests that are polluted are in most cases everybody's property. For example, most of Canada's land area is owned by the Crown.[2] What that means is that it belongs to nobody in particular. Therefore, no particular person objects when his land is infringed by a polluter or when his trees are killed by airborne noxious chemicals.

Canadians who wonder what all the fuss is about when environmentalists raise alarms about the effects of acid rain on the forests react with outrage when the neighbour's dog performs *squatus smellibus* on their own front lawns. It may be said that this is different—after all, the front lawn is private property—but this is precisely the point.

If the same dog-owning neighbour happens to own an industrial plant that dumps a chemical effluent on some remote forest land, we have little reaction, even if we know about it. After all, the forest land isn't our private property. It's government land. The question is, how do we ensure that the protective reactions of private property ownership will leap to the aid of the forest in the same way that they protect front lawns? The answer is that as long as we persist in the myth of public ownership, it will be very difficult.

Blame

Unfortunately, instead of encouraging respect of property rights, governments all too often override them. This lies at the bottom of many of our pollution-related problems. Seldom, however, is this recognized. In fact, many commentators believe that private property ownership is part of the pollution problem.

Those who are most renowned for their interest in environmental protection—Greenpeace, unaffiliated environmentalists, the Sierra Club, "Green" parties around the world—frequently hold the *laissez-faire* capitalist system responsible for acid rain, the greenhouse effect, unclean air, and other such problems. A proponent of this view is Dr. David Suzuki, who uses his regular column in the *Vancouver Sun* as a vehicle for anti-growth and anti-capitalist sentiments.

A superficial response would be that there is pollution behind the Iron Curtain as well, and much of the mischievous interference with nature in the rest of the world is caused directly by government operations such as utilities, sanitation removal, and Crown corporations, or by subsidies to Third World nations that use the money to engage in wholesale destruction of rain forests.

A more basic answer is that private interests have indeed polluted the environment. However, in large measure their behaviour was encouraged and in some instances determined by the legislation and laws provided by the public sector.

Commercial transactions are only the most easily identifiable aspect of the marketplace. Of even greater importance are the laws that underlie the system, particularly the rules that define property rights. Unfortunately, in this crucial property rights area, legislatures and the courts have failed to perform their assigned tasks. The pollution problem is essentially a manifestation of this breakdown.

This chapter will first explain and elaborate upon the private property rights basis of a sound environmental policy, and then will illustrate this insight by applying it to several cases where ecological problems have emerged. It is important even for those who are antipathetic to the market system to understand the mechanisms that lead the market to malfunction, for only in this way will it be possible to devise solutions that will produce the desired result. The discussion will include the historical roots of the problem of air pollution, the case for recycling in general and baby diapers in particular, and environmental issues such as oil spills, forests, parkland, and species extinction. We begin with a brief historical account of how modern pollution problems have arisen as a result of the denigration of private property rights in western societies.

The Case History

In the 1830s and 1840s there were a spate of lawsuits in Canada, the U.S., and Great Britain that are pertinent to our modern experience. Typically, a woman would go to court under the common law provision of nuisance and complain that a factory belching smoke was dirtying the laundry she had hung out to dry, or a farmer would object to a railroad train passing by with sparks flying, which would burn his haystacks. The plaintiff, in other words, alleged that his or her private property rights were being violated and appealed to the judiciary for damages and an injunction to stop the affront. The courts, in a long series of decisions that established the precedents which rule us even now, admitted that private property rights were indeed being violated by the defendants. However, plaintiffs were commonly denied redress for their grievances on two grounds: the nuisance was either adjudged to be a common nuisance affecting everybody, and the plaintiff just happened to be the closest one to the smoking chimney, or the nuisance was determined to have been created by a project or service that was undertaken by a government authority or under public franchise of some kind.[3]

In the former case, the courts were, in effect, saying that if there was an element of general damage caused by activities there could be no particular determination of individual damage. The smoke from a factory affected all in its vicinity, and individual damages could not be ascertained by the courts. Public damage was not redressable by private damage claims and would have to be dealt with by the public authority—i.e., through legislation. In the latter case, the doctrine was that the public convenience was reflected in the actions of public authorities and provided that there was no negligence, anything that was done by the public authority must be deemed in the public interest—even if that meant that a farmer's fields were destroyed by sparks from a statutorily approved locomotive. "The onward spirit of the age" could not be restrained by considerations of a purely private kind.[4]

The historical developments surrounding the effective removal of private rights regarding nuisance or pollution have been traced back to their British roots by Professor Ronald Coase of the University of Chicago, one of the world's leading experts in economics and the law.[5] He points out that in the earliest days of rail transport the railways used steam engines under statutory authority, that is, with government permission. As such, they were not responsible at common law for any damage that may have been done by sparks. The law of England explicitly provided that if a cinder from an approved locomotive caused the destruction of a farmer's field, then the railway, except under extraordinary circumstances, would not be held responsible.

The reason, inherited by North American law, is the belief that since statutory permission was given to the railroad to operate the engine in the first instance, that permission must have reflected an attention to the public interest. And since the public interest must be served above private interests, no compensation would be paid to private farmers damaged by statutorily approved conveyance, even though privately owned. The implication of all this is that to a considerable extent the role of government, historically and up to the present time, has been to limit the natural private actions that would have tended to reduce the extent of pollution or the amount of nuisance caused by one party to another. Coase writes, "the effect of much of the legislation in this area is to protect businesses from the claims of those they have harmed by their actions. There is a long list of legalized nuisances."[6]

The defanging of nuisance laws, to which property owners historically could appeal if they were polluted or in other ways interfered with, explains why today governments are called upon to venture more boldly into the pollution sphere. Where the courts found common damage and therefore no possibility of private remedy, legislation has not been forthcoming or has been ineffectual in protecting property.

There was also a third ground for the denial of injunctive relief to plaintiffs in these early environmental cases. In a sense, this reason is even more important than the other two since it underlay them. It came to be commonly held that there was something even more important than private property rights, namely, "the public good."[7] And of what did the public good consist? It consisted of encouraging economic growth.[8] Since manufacturing plants of all kinds and varieties were deemed essential to this effort, they were protected, i.e., subsidized, by allowing them to engage in pollution activities that would otherwise have been denied them. With this doctrine in mind, the case of the plaintiff was often summarily dismissed. The needs of private property owners were denigrated on behalf of "progress"; and the manufacturer was allowed to use the water and atmosphere virtually as he saw fit.

Government Failure

There are several points that must be made with regard to this sorry tale. It should be clear that this is an example of governmental regulatory aspects of the system, not of the free market per se. In a true free enterprise system, the rights of the individual and his property are sacrosanct; they are not rendered inoperable by philosophically meaningless concepts such as the public good or public interest or the common good. These judicial findings were an instance of government failure, not market failure.

Secondly, it is clear that the concept of private property rights, although much reviled by self-styled defenders of the environment, is the key to its protection.[9] What we have here is a dramatic instance of the "tragedy of the commons." When people are allowed full title to property, they treat it as if they own it; that is, they tend to protect it. When property rights are unprotected, allowing others to violate them with impunity, they tend do so. Spoiling the environment is the result.

Thirdly, with this series of judicial decisions, even a public-spirited manufacturer would be forced to engage in pollution. If he alone invested in expensive smoke-prevention devices while his competitors invaded the property of their neighbours with dust particles, they would be able to undersell him and eventually drive him from business.

Unfortunate Precedents

The entire economy was thus encouraged to engage in pollution-intensive technologies. Had the judges found for the plaintiffs in these cases, the economy would have invested more in methods that had less pollution as a by-product. More research and development funds would have gone into creating better smoke-prevention devices and searching for cleaner burning fuels. Legal institutions that would have diminished the negative effects of environmental despoliation—such as restrictive covenants—might have sprung up faster and/or been strengthened. The sort of manufacturing process that produced smoke particles would have been forced to locate further away from population centres. In short, the environmental crisis could have been vastly reduced, or eliminated entirely, had the precepts of free enterprise been incorporated in our legal structure at the outset.

Let us now consider several current issues on the agenda of the environmental movement. We do so to illustrate how a greater reliance on the private property, free market system can serve as a means of attaining a more healthy environment.

Recycling

The packaging industry has come under fire because its bags, boxes, bins, and other wrappings, while serving the retail market adequately, are an environmental disaster when it comes to disposing of them. Styrofoam, for example, is cheap and convenient, but it is not easily biodegradable. And the same goes in spades for plastics of all varieties, sizes, dimensions, and manners of construction. Further, wrappings typically consist of not one but several materials. This makes recycling a nightmare. For instance, the "tin" in which frozen orange juice is sold to the public is composed of paper, cardboard, metal, and plastic. Each of these must first be separated if there is to be any hope of reusing the material.

How should the problems of solid waste disposal be dealt with? There are two schools of thought on the matter. According to the first, which might be called the liberal or interventionist view, the problem is caused by greedy capitalists who maximize their profits in sublime indifference to the well-being of society. They produce the Styrofoam, bottles, cans, and wrappers that subsequently litter our landscapes. Since the manufacturers are concerned only with producing the packaging—thereby drumming up more retail sales—and not with the ultimate destination of this material, they are blind to the ecological problems they leave in their wake.

In the view of the second school of thought on the issue of solid waste management, the reason for the problem has nothing at all to do with greedy capitalists. On the contrary, it is a result of the fact that garbage disposal has been organized through the public sector.

Why is this a problem? Simply put, government waste disposal is the very factor that accounts for the seeming irresponsibility of the packagers. In the jargon of economists, public sanitation is the cause of the negative externality. It is the phenomenon responsible for the fact that packagers now choose materials with no consideration for the difficulties of their ultimate disposal.

How would a fully private garbage collection industry function so as to solve the present impasse? While it is always a difficult task to anticipate the market, we now have enough experience with privatization to be able to predict, at least in broad outlines, how such an industry might conduct its business. To begin with, there would be a complete separation of solid waste sanitation and state. People would make arrangements for garbage removal with profit-seeking business firms on their own behalf. This task would be as completely private as any other paradigm case of market operation such as the provision of restaurant food, toys, or newspapers.

This does not mean that trash removal would cost more than at present. Many people think it is now done "for free," since the government does it for us. But the public sector, too, must be paid, so the money that formerly went to government would now be retained by the citizen for this purpose. (Legislation prohibiting the piling up of refuse in one's backyard would still remain in force, providing an incentive for the homeowner to make some arrangements for solid waste management). As it happens, it is almost certain that the costs would fall, probably by one-third to one-half or more, because of the greater efficiency of the private vis-à-vis the public sector.[10]

Privatization

How will privatization help the recycling effort? First of all, it will help determine whether recycling is justified at all. Reusing material is not an end in itself; it is merely a means of reducing waste. Only if the value of the resources saved is more valuable than the costs forgone is this process a worthwhile undertaking. If not, then recycling is part of the problem, not part of the solution.

Given that recycling is economically viable, it is likely that sanitation firms would set up a sliding scale: so much per hundred-weight of unsorted refuse, less if there is partial sorting, and still lower rates if there is full sorting. Some firms might be willing, for a price, to write any contract the client desires. Others might specialize in one or another level of sorting.

As well, there would be a sliding scale for refuse in terms of its "ecological friendliness." So much for easily recyclable material; more, proportionately, for plastics[11] or Styrofoam or orange juice tins containing several different types of material that are more expensive to separate.

The solid waste firms that deal on a retail level with homeowners would have to get rid of the refuse they collect. They would send it to a privately owned dump, which would charge or even pay them for the material, according to its usefulness and recyclability.[12] Retail firms would thus be led by Adam Smith's "invisible hand" to impose costs on homeowners according to the type of trash collected.

This would have a profound effect on the packaging industry. For consumers, knowing that they would later have to pay higher sanitation fees for harder-to-dispose-of materials, would tend to shun them. Or they would purchase them only if their prices are low enough to defray the additional removal costs.

No Imposition

For the first time, the system would be rationalized. Packagers would no longer be able to impose costs on the public sanitation service. Whenever a packager contemplated adding a new line of very attractive but non-biodegradable material to his offerings, he would be faced with customers who would look askance at it. They would say something like the following to themselves: "This looks good, but how much will it cost me to get rid of it?" For example, it might cost one penny to buy a paper or a plastic grocery bag. It might cost one penny to dispose of the paper product but $5.00 to get rid of its plastic counterpart. Then the options are these: a total of two cents for using and disposing of the paper bag versus $5.01 for the plastic variety. With a consumer in that mind-set, the ecological problem of solid waste management would evaporate.[13]

Under privatization, we would no longer face the difficulties of finding more space for garbage dumps. No longer would the spectre of unwanted garbage scows haunt our society. And the beauty of the plan is that it would not cost additional piles of money. All we need do is unleash the power of marketplace incentives; these can do our bidding.

However, it is almost a universally-held premise that better environmental protection necessarily costs more money. Consider the following statement, which is typical of this sentiment:

> The change in mood from the Reagan era's complacency about natural resources dates back to last summer's string of bad environmental news: medical waste washing up on beaches, the burning of Yellowstone Park, the mounting fears about global warming. In a national poll taken weeks *before* the Alaska (oil) spill, voters overwhelmingly said they wanted more, rather than less, money spent on environmental controls and cleanup (*Newsweek,* 17 April 1989).

Notice the *non sequitur* of the linkage between the two sentences quoted above. The first establishes that people are concerned with ecological problems. But the second fallaciously assumes that the only way to address this problem is by additional expenditures of funds. In contrast, it is our thesis that there is an alternative that need not call for any new out-of-pocket expenses—changing the legal system to conform more closely with a system of private property rights.[14]

Diapers

There are precious few people who have not had to decide which kind of diapers to use for their babies. In days of yore, the choice was simple: one used the cloth variety because there was no alternative. Now, however, the local convenience store features a bewildering plethora of choices: Huggies, Luvs, Pampers, and numerous others, each with their own particular features. Nor has modern technology bypassed the diaper industry; as a result, there are now disposables with "fit zones," "tucks," "moisture traps" and "two-point gather systems" from which to choose.

In purely economic terms, when the parent's alternative time forgone, the largest cost element in the decision, is taken into account, there is no contest. Throw-away diapers beat the washable type hands down. For in the latter case, there is disinfecting to do, washing, drying, and even, for the fastidious, ironing. It can take many hours per week to keep our youngest tax payers dry and comfortable. In the former case, one need only march down to the nearest store, plunk down a credit card, and walk off with a giant economy package containing five dozen easily disposable diapers.

But what of the ecological issue? Which baby care technique is more conducive to a sound environment? This is much harder to discern. Disposables are not easily recyclable. It is difficult to reuse the plastic derivatives and other synthetic material from which these diapers are constructed. Most problematic is the fact that human wastes, when mixed with ordinary garbage, cause diseases. As such, they constitute a "toxic waste" which might better be disposed of in sewers than in dumpsites. On the other hand, using cloth diapers implies using soap, which poses environmental threats of its own. Electricity is needed for washing, drying, and ironing, which necessitates the use of oil, gas, coal, or nuclear power, each of which is ecologically problematic. Further, there is the difficulty of disposing of the resultant dirty water.

Socialist Calculation

Which system is better? Under present institutional arrangements, where people may impose costs on others and on the ecosphere through trespass-invasions, it is not only difficult to answer this question, it is downright impossible to determine which mode is more conducive to a clean and healthy environment.

This problem has its analogue in the famous socialist calculation debate, which reached its heyday several decades ago. In that case, the question posed was: can rational economic planning take place under central control in the absence of a market? The result, based mainly on the writings of Ludwig von Mises and Friedrich A. Hayek, was that it cannot.[15]

In the present case, we maintain that just as economic planning is impossible without free markets that accurately reflect relative scarcities, neither can sound environmental decision-making occur without these conditions. We cannot calculate the economic cost to society of disposing of a non-biodegradable diaper because government has perverted market signals through its programme of ownership and management of waste disposal. Nor can we calculate the ecological cost of washing dirty cloth diapers or recycling plastic ones. Given the absence of the relevant markets, we certainly cannot compare these costs, whether financial or ecological, but no less is required to determine which of these items, cloth or disposable diapers, is the least harmful to the environment.

Opposite Sides of the Same Coin

Ecological and economic costs are inseparable. If, taking all costs into account, external and internal, it is determined that cloth diapers are the cheapest economically, this option will also be the best environmental solution. It is not only true that economic analysis is a means toward environmental goals but that ultimately there is no distinction worth making between the two endeavours. Ecology is really a branch of economics. Alternatively, for those who find this a bit much, we can say with equal accuracy that economics is a branch of ecology. The two are intellectually indistinguishable as far as our dealings with nature are concerned—but only if all costs are fully taken into account. The free enterprise system is devoted to doing just that—making sure that all costs are accounted for, so that no border crossings, trespasses, or violations of private property rights take place.

More than the choice between alternative types of diapers hangs in the balance since the same analysis can be applied to many other decisions. For example, is it better for the environment for people to use wood, plastic, or metal—all of which come in many kinds and varieties—to manufacture toys, boats, homes, home furnishings, musical instruments, and automobiles? Which fuels are most ecologically friendly? Without a free market that generates prices reflective of relative scarcities and a private property rights system that allows for the internalization of externalities, we cannot rationally decide which courses of action are most economically or ecologically sound.

Oil Spills

On 24 March 1989 the Exxon *Valdez* supertanker ran aground on Bligh Reef, over a quarter of a mile outside the regular shipping lanes on the approach to Valdez, Alaska. Over the next two weeks more than 10 million gallons of oil poured out into the sea, spreading out over 6,700 square kilometres, an area of the ocean exceeding the size of Prince Edward Island. The crude oil, emulsified with sea water into the consistency of mayonnaise, soiled 1,200 miles of coastline, killing all the fish, birds, mammals, and plant life that were unfortunate enough to come in its wake.

Even the strictly financial losses were gigantic. Early indications were that $75 million in the form of a commercial salmon harvest would be lost, along with millions more for herring and other fish resources, as well as the local tourist industry. But this estimate is only the tip of the iceberg. It doesn't even begin to account for costs to the areas not now affected which will become polluted as the oil spreads further and further.

But commercial losses are not the only consideration. The civilized world is now coming to realize that this earth is our only home. If we despoil it, we are fouling our own nest.

The Exxon *Valdez* tragedy, although the largest oil spill in North America, is only the third largest in world history. It is exceeded by the 1979 offshore oil well blowout in the Gulf of Mexico near the Yucatan peninsula, which released 155 million gallons of oil. The largest oil tanker spill was the sinking of the Amoco *Cadiz* off the French coast in 1978, which spewed forth 68 million gallons of oil. However, for every such stupendous violation of the ecological system there are hundreds more not brought to the attention of the public. Their cumulative effect presents a great danger to the continued functioning of our planet as we have known it.

Origins

This being the case, it behooves us to turn our attention to the cause of the Valdez spill. We must unearth the origins of this disaster, not so much to fix blame but to prevent repetitions. Strictly speaking, we can never hope to eliminate all such occurrences. Man is the "mistake-making" animal; thus it is quixotic to expect perfection in this regard. Rather, the obtainable ideal is to reduce the incidence of disasters of this sort to optimal levels. Upon first consideration, this may sound paradoxical, but there is a core of common sense behind it. It is not efficient to decrease oil spills to such a degree that this process actually costs more than it saves.[16]

In the present case, the antecedents are clear. Bligh is a charted reef, so culpability cannot be laid at the door of the geographers. Nor was the capital equipment in a state of disrepair. On the contrary, this vessel, which stretches the length of three football fields laid end to end and draws over 20 yards of water and contains almost 63 million gallons of oil, was only three years old and in splendid working order.

The reason for the mishap was human error. Allegations were widely made that the captain of the ship, one Joseph Hazelwood, was under the influence of alcohol while on duty. He was summarily fired by Exxon, but it is far too little too late to attain our goal of oil spill reduction—or better yet, optimization. This episode of alleged drunken "driving," however, was merely the proximate cause.[17] Exxon is responsible for hiring him in the first place, and for possibly failing to ensure that he was fit for duty.[18]

One remedy would be to hold the corporation legally liable for the damages. This solution faces serious obstacles. At present, admiralty law,[19] common law, and legislative enactments all seriously limit the company's liability to a fraction of the total damages due to oil spills. To the extent that fishermen and members of the tourist industry can collect damages, and this varies from country to country, they face many barriers in proving actual harm.[20] Further, oil firms are commonly held liable only for injury to shore-based interests, not for devastation of the ocean since no one owns bodies of water.[21] Private accountability is also vitiated by a welter of government "insurance" schemes and funds, which have the effect of socializing the risk. In Canada, for example, there is the Maritime Pollution Claims Fund.[22] The effect of these programmes is to shield oil companies from the responsibility for compensating the victims of spills.

Risk and Responsibility

Since these monies are raised through an import and export tax on oil, there is a sense in which industry is held accountable for environmental abuse. But these payments are not directly related to damage imposed on third parties, as they would be under a true private insurance plan. They cannot, therefore, repair the break in the link between risk and responsibility.

One private property rights-oriented solution to this problem would be to reaffirm the connection between damage and responsibility, to end all such governmental attempts to socialize risk[23] and shield oil companies from responsibility for the destruction they cause.[24] This would place accountability right where it belongs, in the hands of the perpetrators of environmental abuses. Under a regime of strict liability, the admiralty law, common law, and legislative enactments that now limit a company's liability for oil spillage would be repealed or reformed. By ending the policy of subsidy and protection, the externality can be internalized and the spill-over of harm to third parties (and to the environment) can be confined to the perpetrator. If such a policy were inaugurated, damage to the environment would be radically lessened. Firms in this industry would now be fully responsible for their acts. With these new incentives, they would either act more carefully or face severe economic losses and possible bankruptcy.

It might be claimed that ending limited liability for oil companies subjects them to an unfair attack. But why is it unfair to force those responsible for damages to pay for them? This is the procedure followed in every other line of endeavour. Oil companies, and everyone else for that matter, are "forced" to pay full market rents for the land and buildings they occupy, wages for the workers they employ, and interest for the loans they make. Likewise, they should be made to pay fully for damages they cause to the environment.

No Attack

Nor is it even true that such a policy amounts to an attack on the oil industry in any but the most temporary and superficial manner. With full responsibility, the price of oil would incorporate the true risks of this business. That is precisely as it should be, if we are to have an economic system where prices reflect the true and total costs of alternative activities. The market is now considered to be "imperfect" precisely because oil consumers are able to impose costs on the rest of society, through oil spills, for which they are not fully accountable.[25] Under a regime of full and strict liability for property rights violations, this external dis-economy is internalized—i.e., the oil industry is no longer allowed to impose costs on third parties.

As for the financial interest of firms in the oil industry, it will not be materially harmed. Profits in the oil industry cannot long diverge from profit levels prevalent elsewhere. Any differences will be met by movements of capital and labour that tend to reduce any incipient discrepancies to zero.[26]

We have seen that without a full and complete private property rights system, the tragedy of the commons prevails. Since those who destroy the environment do not suffer financial losses from their behaviour, they have insufficient incentive to curtail these acts. As well, while Exxon is a responsible corporation from which reimbursement may be obtained—at least in principle—many oil spills are the result of activities of "fly-by-night" ventures which are virtually unsueable. Under such conditions, there is little or no accountability for destruction to oceanic wildlife.

Private Oceans

These shortcomings may hint at another possible solution, a far more radical one than that now contemplated by even the most avid environmentalists. Why not carry the privatization trail blazed by Margaret Thatcher even further and privatize what now seems to be unprivatizable, that is, the oceans and seas and other large bodies of water into which oil can spill?[27] We know that private property rights bring in their wake a heightened sense of responsibility. We know that giving individuals a stake in resource ownership is the best, if not the only, way to overcome the tragedy of the commons where it is not in any one person's self-interest to act on behalf of the general welfare. There is no reason to think that this principle would not work for water as it does for land.

If people owned various patches of the ocean, they would have an economic incentive to protect their holdings. For example, they might well insist that any ship passing through their property with a cargo of oil be double-hulled.[28] Additionally, they would have more of a selfish interest not only in demanding that inebriated sailors be prohibited access to their property but in actually ensuring that this policy is enforced.

The idea that the oceans could be privately owned will appear to many as science-fictionish, idiosyncratic, lunatic, or just plain ludicrous. In the early 19th century, however, many people had similar opinions with regard to the question of fencing in (i.e., privatizing) the range in the western U.S.[29] Before the advent of barbed wire, that scenario, too, was technically dubious.

With regard to the oceans, we are now seemingly in even worse technical straights. There are lasers and electronic beams, but these have never been applied to setting up boundaries in bodies of water. It takes little imagination, however, to see that these and related techniques might conceivably be used for this purpose were it legal and economically advantageous to do so.

Evolution

We are now in the hunting and gathering stage in man's evolutionary pattern when it comes to the seas. If we are to move past that milestone to engage in aquaculture on a massive scale, as well as to protect the ocean environment against oil spills, we may be forced to embrace the institution of private property rights no matter how exotic the idea sounds. Solving the technical problems will be nothing compared to changing the political reality.

In order for ownership to be viable, in the ocean or anywhere else, two conditions must be met. First, ownership must be legal. If it is not, the entrepreneur will hardly make the requisite investment. Second, the costs of alienation or homesteading or caretaking or protecting one's stake in the property must be lower than the expected gains. This is why, even if it were legal to claim land on Mars and the moon, no one, under present technological conditions, would race off to these domains to assert ownership. This economic consideration presently also applies to peripheral lands near the Arctic, and certainly to many parts of the ocean.

What privatization of the seas amounts to is the proposal that at least this status be accorded legal protection. Then, as technology progresses, more and more of the Arctic land and ocean will come under private ownership. Even today it might be economically viable to bring some parts of the ocean into private property status. Initial candidates might include the Mediterranean Sea and the continental shelves of many coastal nations. But we will not be able to ascertain whether this is so until such activity is made legal.

Double Hulling and the Political Process

In *Chevron U.S.A. et al., Intercontinental Bulktank Corp et al. versus U.S.*, the court found against a regulation mandating double hulling for crude oil tankers.[30] The easy response to this shortsighted decision is to call for more stringent regulations, including the requirement that double hulls be fitted for all oil tankers.

But there is a serious difficulty with this as a public policy. If it is such a good idea, why was it politically impossible to implement it a long time ago? After all, oil spills are not a new phenomenon, and outfitting ships with additional hulls has long been within the realm of technological possibility. The reason that emerges from the decades-long work of Nobel Prize winning economists Milton Friedman, George Stigler, and James Buchanan is that people do not suddenly sprout angels' wings when they move from the private to the public sector.[31] On the contrary, they take with them all their human foibles of greed and avarice. This, coupled with the fact that producers are more highly concentrated than consumers—and in this case, the victims of oil spills—explains why economic regulation often works at the behest of the regulatees, not in the interest of the general public. Since large-scale business firms have long been able to "capture" their regulatory bodies, it is not sound public policy to rely unduly on this as a mode of amelioration.

An incident in British Columbia lends practical up-to-date support for the contention that the political process is imperfect at best and cannot in good conscience be relied upon to attain ecological ends. The oil spill of 23 December 1988 in Gray's Harbour, Washington, off the coast of Vancouver Island, focused a considerable amount of North American attention on the problem of pollution, and caused an increase in the clamour for more regulation and tougher involvement of government in the problem. Such well-meaning appeals largely emerge from the belief that pollution is a problem that only government can solve because the private sector, left to its own devices, cannot do so. The blobs of heavy bitumen that rolled up on the beautiful expanses of Long Beach, B.C., seem to provide mute testimony to the inability of private action to protect the natural environment.

Different Interpretation

Appearances apart, this recent mishap provides evidence for an entirely different interpretation of the pollution problem. Consider the revelation that the Department of the Environment in the state of Washington had actually ordered the leaking barge towed out onto the high seas rather than have its cargo seep onto the beaches of Washington state.[32] That decision implied the consequence that the oil would find its way onto British Columbia or other shores. It indicates that the government sector is not so much concerned with the protection of the environment as with its own selfish interests.

Even if its motive was the more attractive one of preserving the environment, it was a case of protecting the American environment even at the expense of the Canadian environment. The possibility that it may be this Washington property versus British Columbia property view that motivated the Washington Environment Department raises not a little disquiet about the reliability of public action in protecting the environment.

Meanwhile, environmentally conscious individuals have also been pressing the government to prohibit drilling for oil in the offshore areas of the continent. The general presumption of such well-intentioned folk is that the villains are the private firms operating either barge services or drilling rigs, and the government can be relied upon to protect the public interest in the form of legislation and other direct actions. The history of the matter is, however, somewhat different.

It is impossible to end this discussion of oil spills without at least briefly mentioning the moribund nuclear energy industry—moribund thanks in large part to the efforts of some of those environmentalists who are the most vociferous critics of the Exxon oil spill. In 1979, the year of the relatively harmless meltdown at Three Mile Island, 72 nuclear plants were in operation in the U.S. and, most important, 95 were under construction. As of 1989, 111 were in production, but only a minuscule 12 were being built.[33]

What is the relevance of this statement? Simply this. Because of environmental concerns, radical ecologists oppose offshore oil drilling and transportation (tankers, pipelines) and nuclear power. Coal is also dangerous (mining cave-ins, black lung disease, air pollution, acid rain). The only other options appear to be solar energy, windmill power, and other such technologies. But this would mean curtailing our living standards and consigning millions of poor and Third World peoples to an even more precarious existence. Such a move away from high-tech methodologies would render likely the death of many more people than the present course.

Forests

The wood products industry is a very important one. It directly employs some 4.95 percent of the total labour force in Canada.[34] In some regions and localities, it accounts for a far higher percentage of economic activity. As well, it is an important input into other sectors of the economy. It has been estimated that 14 percent of the cost of a new single-family home involves expenditures on the products of this industry.[35]

That being the case, it is of great importance that commercial activity concerning lumber and wood products be in private hands to the greatest possible degree. Without the incentives of profit and loss, the economic value of this resource can be dissipated. Marion Clawson, for example, estimates the commercial value of public lands in the United States to be at least $480 billion, and the cash flows generated by the bureaucrats now in charge of their management to be in excess of *minus* $1 billion.[36] In his review of the Clawson book, Steve Hanke comments on this state of affairs: "therefore, the case against current management practices is rather easy to make and generally not a point of contention among resource economists."[37]

However important it is for strict business purposes that timber resources be privatized, this is even more crucial when environmental considerations are contemplated. If government management of the woodlands has been a disaster for the bottom line, it has achieved even worse results on behalf of the ecological system. Government forestry policy in the U.S. and other nations has led to ruination of large swatches of timber lands, and consequently to mud slides, slumps, sloughs, earth flows, soil erosion, and river silting.[38] The massive removal of forests on the part of government is alleged to be a calamity in terms of the greenhouse effect, since trees reduce the carbon-dioxide level of the air, and excessive amounts of this gas play a pivotal role in whatever global warming of the earth's atmosphere already exists.[39]

The Yellowstone tragedy is only the tip of the iceberg.[40] Here, the bureaucrats in charge of these valuable lands were able to indulge their ideological views to the effect that forest fires are really healthy for the environment. It goes without saying that any private owners of a similar resource who sat on their hands in the early stages of a tragic forest fire—whether for this reason or any other—would have risked being consigned by the market to bankruptcy. In any event, there has been no automatic purge of those responsible for this dereliction of duty.

Clearing

John Baden describes one method of clearcutting commonly employed by the U.S. in the public sector:

> Chaining is a spectacularly ugly way to rid the landscape of trees and brush. Two hundred-thousand-pound D-8 crawler tractors are connected by a 600-foot anchor chain weighing 100 pounds to the link. As the tractors move forward, the chain uproots all trees and shrubs in its path, leaving gaping holes and unsightly tracks. The uprooted trees may then be burned, or simply left to the side of the clearing.
>
> Fortunately, chaining is such an expensive procedure that it is very rarely practiced on privately owned land. Unfortunately, the U.S. Bureau of Land Management (BLM), which maximizes its budget by providing subsidized

grazing rights to Western ranchers, faces a different set of incentives than entrepreneurs in the marketplace. The BLM has no incentive to keep costs down, or even to maximize revenues from grazing fees, which go into the overall U.S. Treasury, rather than its own coffers. Instead, the BLM builds its budget by winning political support from ranchers who then lobby for BLM expenditures.

It builds this support in part by charging less than market rate for grazing rights on public lands. The 20,000 ranchers with access to BLM lands pay from one-tenth to one-fifth the price paid for grazing rights on adjacent or nearby private land.[41]

When government is not itself laying waste to its own property, it pursues policies that subsidize the private sector to do the same. For example, it commonly encourages business firms to cut down trees on public lands by building logging roads at its own expense.[42] It is little wonder that under these conditions the profit-maximizing business concern will act in a counter-ecological manner. It pays no penalties for short-sighted clear-cutting behaviour since it is able to shift these costs onto the public as it does not own the land. In contrast, the firm that treats its own land in so cavalier a manner—clear-cutting without replanting—would soon enough have little or no land it could so mistreat.

Brazil

Consider the case of the wholesale depletion of the Brazilian rain forests, which have been called the last remaining healthy "lungs" of the earth. North American and European governments have been calling stridently for safeguarding this virgin preserve. These demands come with particular ill-grace from politicians who have presided over the destruction of their own natural woodland sanctuaries. If they are upset that there are fewer trees than might be desirable, let them first set their own houses in order. They can best do so by engaging in a policy of "separation of forests and state."

In any case, it is government yet again, not the free market, that is responsible for the cataclysm now taking place in Brazilian woodlands.[43] Says Jane Shaw in this regard:

> When property rights are insecure or incomplete, so that someone else bears the costs or reaps the rewards, accountability is missing. This is the case with the Amazon rain-forest.
>
> In Brazil, government policies encourage deforestation of the rain-forest through subsidies and tax credits. The biggest effect is that owners of land are reaping the rewards

of ownership without paying the costs, and thus are encouraged to act irresponsibly.

A study by the World Resources Institute (by no means a group committed to private property) concludes that cattle ranching and settlements by small farmers are the major factors behind deforestation. Both of those activities are heavily subsidized by the government. Author Robert Repetto says that the subsidies encourage the livestock industry to cut down trees to promote pastureland and encourage settlers to turn forests into farmland. In addition, the government subsidizes the forest products industry. "By supplying virtually free money, the federal government invited investors to acquire and clear large tracts of forested lands," says Repetto.[44]

While the foregoing analysis may be accepted amongst resource economists, the message has not yet filtered out into the popular press. One high-profile news magazine blamed the loss of timber stands not on public-sector mismanagement but on avaricious consumers:

Japan accounts for 40 percent of the imports of wood from the world's jungles. That harvest contributes to global warming by removing trees that breathe in gases that trap heat in the atmosphere, and also drives countless species into extinction. Every year an area almost the size of Connecticut is axed, largely in Indonesia, Thailand and Malaysia, mostly to feed the Japanese appetite for tropical hardwoods. Much of the wood goes to make forms for concrete and for furniture and construction. To ensure a constant supply, Japan supports logging with foreign aid which, says Saburo Okita, chairman of World Wildlife Fund-Japan and a former foreign minister, has resulted in massive destruction of virgin tropical rain forest. At today's pace, Asian forests will be stripped of usable wood within 15 years (*Newsweek,* 1 May 1989, p. 70).

But this attempt at Japan-bashing is as intellectually incoherent as it is morally repugnant. If mere demand for wood on the part of customers can deplete supplies, why confine the attack to the Japanese "appetite" for wood? Doesn't this nation of supposedly greedy, inconsiderate consumers purchase other items as well? The Japanese also buy massive amounts of wheat, vegetables, and meat, yet these products show no sign of catastrophic shortage. In the market, whenever increased orders for a good come in, the suppliers roll up their sleeves in glee, set to work, and expand their base of operations. This system works for every other item imported by Japan. It would function in the tropical hardwoods market as well, if the same economic incentives were operational. Under the conditions depicted, profits in this industry would skyrocket. Forestry entrepreneurs would fall all over themselves in their frantic efforts to plant crops of hardwoods favoured by the presumably insatiable Japanese, the better to exploit them. The reason for the disappearance of the jungle forest, whether in Brazil or in Asia, has little to do with consumers, and much to do with the absence of the institution of property rights.

If private ownership of forest lands is the public policy best suited to promoting the goals of the "Green" political perspective, the facts, unhappily, reveal that much work needs to be done to bring about this state of affairs.

Lion's Share

In the U.S., the government owns "only" 39.1 percent of the land, leaving a relatively hefty 58.7 percent to private enterprise.[45] But even this is far in excess of the land ownership required by government to pursue its legitimate and limited functions. Environmentalists of the private property school of thought complain of excessive governmental ownership in general, and in particular that 86.5 percent of Nevada, 92 percent of Alaska, 40 percent of California, and half of the mountain states come under the management and control of the public sector.[46]

In Canada, the situation is far worse. Table 1 depicts private and public land ownership in Canada. As can be seen from this table, the Canadian government, including federal and provincial levels, owns the lion's share of the land or 89.3 percent. This leaves only 10.7 percent under private ownership. True, when the Northwest Territories and the Yukon are excluded from consideration, the government's share falls to 82.4 percent, and that of the private sector rises to 17.6 percent. But this is still far too high and compares very unfavourably with our neighbour to the south.

Both nations currently suffer from large public debts and their fiscal balance sheets could improve by major land sales to the public. In addition, sales of land to private interest would help resolve perennial conflict over fair stumpage fees or timber rentals and would obviate the public sector bureaucracy presently needed to administer the overall system.[47] From the point of view of environmentalism, as well, such a policy of forest privatization is highly recommended. It may be politically impossible at present to implement this proposal because private interests have been subsidized into enthusiastic support for public land ownership, and the general public is not aware of the harm that is accomplished by this scheme. If we wish to safeguard the environment and promote better stewardship over forest resources, privatization is the only sound public policy.

Parkland

A recent debate about parkland in British Columbia has environmental implications for the entire country. When the relatively minor changes announced by

Table 1
Public and Private Land Ownership in Canada

	Newfoundland	P.E.I.	Nova Scotia	New Brunswick	Quebec	Ontario	Manitoba
Square Miles							
Private	6,830	2,050	15,670	15,350	43,500	45,160	55,870
Federal	980	20	620	620	1,010	3,680	2,220
Provincial	148,380	120	5,140	12,990	550,350	363,750	192,900
TOTAL	156,190	2,190	21,430	28,960	594,860	412,590	250,990
Percentage							
Private	4.3	93.6	73.1	53.0	47.3	10.9	22.2
Federal	0.6	0.9	2.8	2.1	0.1	0.8	0.8
Provincial	94.9	5.4	23.9	44.8	92.5	88.1	76.8
TOTAL	100	100	100	100	100	100	100

	Saskatchewan	Alberta	British Columbia	N.W.T. & Yukon	Canada	10 Provinces (excludes Territories)
Square Miles						
Private	106,140	99,840	20,780	90	411,280	411,190
Federal	3,800	23,600	3,460	1,513,220	1,553,230	40,010
Provincial	141,770	131,760	342,080	670	1,889,910	1,889,240
TOTAL	251,710	255,200	366,320	1,513,980	3,854,420	2,340,440
Percentage						
Private	42.1	39.1	5.6	0.0	10.7	17.6
Federal	1.5	9.2	0.9	99.9	40.2	1.7
Provincial	56.3	51.6	93.3	0.0	49.1	80.7
TOTAL	100	100	100	100	100	100

Source: Fraser Institute compilations based on data from *Quick Canadian Facts,* Canex Enterprises: Surrey, B.C., 37th edition, 1985, p. 17.

Indian reserves and settlements comprise only 9,740 square miles or .0025 percent of the total and are excluded from these calculations.

B.C. Parks Minister Terry Huberts were formalized through cabinet directive, some 4.5 percent of the territory of B.C. was covered by provincial parks (no mining or logging is allowed in such areas.)

"Striking the Balance," a parks policy statement released by the previous parks ministry, contended that the system was nearing completion and that about 6 percent of the province would ultimately be given over to such recreational areas.

But then the entire situation unravelled. A coalition of environmental groups, including the Western Canada Wilderness Committee, the Valhalla group, the Canadian Parks and Wilderness Society, Sierra Club of Western Canada, and Friends of Ecological Reserves, got into the act. They presented their wish list on a map, which showed a park system taking up about 13 percent of the land base of the province.

Who is right? Is the present 4.5 percent ideal? Should the percentage be moved up to former B.C. Parks Minister Bruce Strachan's 6 percent? Or perhaps the 13 percent proposed by the ecologically-minded constitutes the lucky number we are all searching for. Or maybe 4.5 percent is far too large and we should cut it down to 2 percent, 1 percent, or even less. On the other hand, might it be that the environmentalist groups are really too moderate, and that the ultimate goal should be 20 percent, 30 percent, 40 percent, or even a nice round 50 percent?

And what is the reaction to this puzzle from Parks Minister Huberts, in whose hands a large part of the decision will rest? Said Mr. Huberts, "Is 9, 10, 11, 12, or 13 percent the right number? I don't really know. I want to have input."[48]

Say what you will about Mr. Huberts, but at least credit him for intellectual modesty. Perhaps it indicates that he may be open, not to a definitive answer to this question, of which none can be provided, but at least to an efficient, time-tested and nonarbitrary method of resolving it.

Solution

In order to introduce the solution, let us first reflect upon the fact that the economic czar in the Soviet Union is continually presented with the same problem. Instead of having to answer it merely with regard to parkland, the central planner must decide how much of society's resources should be devoted to almost everything under the sun: to iron or steel, to wood or plastics, to computers or bicycles, to agriculture or chemicals, and to corn or barley.

The economic czar, like Mr. Huberts, may seek "input." The problem with this modest-sounding proposal is that it is no solution at all. All each of them will be given is yet another wish list from a special-interest group with an axe to grind. In any case, how would either a Canadian parks minister or a Soviet planning czar recognize any input as the correct answer to his conundrum? Both lack a criterion upon which to base a decision.

How does the Soviet central planner decide this issue? The short answer is that he doesn't, at least not very well. Otherwise, Soviets wouldn't be in the process of giving up their communist system and embracing the long-reviled principles of capitalism.

How does the free marketplace resolve these problems? Under capitalism, all property is privately owned. Each person is free to determine whether his land will be used as a wilderness park or for housing or commerce. Let us suppose that the ecologically-minded groups were on target with their estimate that 13 percent would most closely satisfy consumer demand. How would the market gravitate toward this level?

The invisible hand of Adam Smith rides to the rescue. If 13 percent were a correct assessment, and presently only 4.5 percent was being devoted to parkland, profits would be higher for this recreational purpose than for any other. This would lead entrepreneurs to convert land now in other uses (mining, forestry, agriculture) to parkland. Alternatively, if for example 2 percent of the land were sufficient for parks in the eyes of the consumer, then the marginal parkland in the present 4.5 percent holding would be less profitable for this purpose than for other uses. The owners would then have an economic incentive to switch, rather than fight.

The market may be anathema to many so-called environmentalists, but it is the only non-arbitrary solution to this problem.[49]

David Suzuki

In western culture, there is a long if not so honourable tradition of scientists who use the prestige garnered in their fields of specialization in order to publicize crack-pot views on economics and politics. Names such as Albert Einstein, Bertrand Russell, and Albert Schweitzer spring immediately to mind in this context.

Canada, too, has scientists who practice this legacy. Foremost among them is David Suzuki, a biologist and geneticist who is very active in the ecological movement in this country. He may not be as eminent a scientist as some of those who have blazed the path from the physical into the social sciences before him, but what he lacks in scientific accomplishments he more than makes up for in terms of innocence of even the most basic rudiments of economics. Coupled with a clear, clean writing style, a flair for the dramatic, and no little eloquence on behalf of the many issues and concerns he has articulated, this is a dangerous combination indeed.

Dr. Suzuki is a Canadian institution. His television science has delighted millions. He has recently begun writing on environmental concerns for the *Vancouver Sun,* having been a columnist at the *Globe and Mail* for several years. In his columns he frequently analyses subjects which take him out of his chosen profession and into the broader world of economics, politics, and ethics. Often, his purpose is to talk about the future implications of current institutions.

In a sense this entire chapter is dedicated to David Suzuki. The present discussion is devoted to providing an antidote to some of his more extreme attacks on profits, property rights, trade, consumption, growth, investment, land development, mining, finance, ownership, money, and commerce, which he undertakes in the false belief that these institutions are harmful to the environment. This, even in a backward manner, is ample testimony to the power and ability of Dr. Suzuki to influence a small but highly articulate sector of society. We now explore some issues that are of particular interest to this eminent Canadian.

Economic Growth

According to Suzuki, "so long as we live in a finite world of finite resources, we cannot keep expanding forever... Steady expansion over given increments of time is called exponential growth."[50] This is quite a scary phenomenon for Dr. Suzuki, who sees it as a fundamental threat to human survival.

He is concerned that most economic development tends to occur in those countries which are already the richest. If the nations of the Third World were ever to develop their economies to any great extent, let alone to this level, that would imply a gigantic increase in resource use, one which, in his view, is not possible.

In his column on the subject, Suzuki relates an experiment done by physicist Albert Bartlett involving a glass vial full of bacterial food. A bacterial cell is introduced into the vial and the cell divides every minute. At the end of one minute there are two cells, at the end of three minutes there are four, and so on until at the end of 60 minutes the vial is full of cells and the food is gone. According to Suzuki, this provides an analogy about the world in which we live—one from which human beings should learn.

Particularly, he notes that with exponential growth, at 58 minutes the vial is 25 percent full, at 59 minutes it is half full, and at 60 minutes it is completely full of bacteria. Suzuki says that mankind is at the 58th minute and wants to know when our global leaders will face up to reality and take firm action to stop the tragedy of the bacteria from overtaking us.

As unsettling as this scenario is, it would be fallacious to apply it to the real world. To begin with, the Suzuki tale of bacteria is no more than a scare story along the lines promulgated by Malthus. But the Malthusian doctrine has long since been confined to the dust bin of history by professional economists because too many historical occurrences are incompatible with this vision. Food, in relative terms, is becoming cheaper, not more expensive, as implied by this view. As well, the amount of the GNP accounted for by agriculture, and even the proportion of the labour force devoted to these pursuits, has been falling, not rising. Were food increasing at an arithmetic rate and population geometrically, with starvation consequently staring us in the face, these phenomena could hardly occur. Nor are real wages engaging in a free fall toward subsistence level—at least in the western industrialized and capitalistic nations—as they would be if population were about to outstrip our capacity to feed ourselves.

Faulty Analogy

People are not bacteria. The starvation scenario implied by the bacteria eating themselves out of house and home does not describe human reality. It may find some real world application in economically disintegrating places like Ethiopia, but this is due to their Marxist philosophy, with its concomitant centralized planning, collectivized farming, marketing boards, price controls, and other interventions. These are the policies which have kept agriculture in the doldrums for decades in even a technologically advanced nation such as the Soviet Union. The tragic Ethiopian experience simply does not apply to most other nations and has nothing to do with the Malthusian nightmare.

What Suzuki and his intellectual predecessor Malthus failed to realize is that if additional people must be fed, and must necessarily use up additional resources in this process, they can also create the wealth they need to maintain themselves and more, thanks to free markets and technological progress. All of this is completely understood even in the most elementary economic textbooks.[51] Indeed, it would be embarrassing to mention this but for the fact that an eminent scientist such as Dr. Suzuki so completely misunderstands the situation and is likely to successfully propagandize his views to the Canadian public.

Moreover, the earth is virtually empty, as anyone can attest who has taken an airplane ride and bothered to look out the window. States Thomas Sowell, "To get some idea of how crowded the planet is in actuality, imagine that every man, woman and child on earth were placed in the state of Texas... [Each person would have] approximately 1,700 square feet... A family of four would thus have 6,800 square feet—about the size of a typical middle-class American home with front and back yards. In short, every human being on the face of the earth could be housed in the state of Texas in one-story, single family homes."[52]

Overcrowding?

We speak of the "teeming masses" of places like India or China, and commonly suppose that their poverty is a result of overpopulation. Nothing could be further from the truth. What about the "teeming masses" of highly concentrated very wealthy areas such as Toronto, Los Angeles, Paris, London, or Tokyo? What about the dire poverty in extremely empty parts of the globe such as the Sahara?

In fact, there are rich nations (more than $5,000 in per capita income) with high population concentrations (500 or more people per square mile) such as West Germany, Belgium, Holland, Japan, and poor ones (less than $1,000 in per capita income) with low population densities (less than 100 people per square mile) such as Colombia, Afghanistan, Ethiopia, Kenya, Congo, and Bolivia.[53] No facile equation of poverty and population concentration can stand a scrutiny of the facts.

Far from economic growth and population expansion being a danger to the human race, the very opposite is true. Additional people can create more resources than they use up, thanks to technological improvements and a marketplace which allows specialization, division of labour, and world-wide economic co-ordination. This being the case, the lot of the average person will likely be improved, not worsened, by population growth.

The poor in advanced countries are economically better off than even the nobility in centuries gone by. Certainly, improvements in dentistry, medicine, public health measures, and access to clean water make the everyday life of a Canadian who lives below the "poverty line" preferable in many ways to that of a 16th century Duke in England or France. Unfortunately, there has been little or no improvement in the lives of those who live in some Third World countries. But this, as we have seen, is due to unnecessary government intervention, not to excessive population growth.[54]

Some of the poorest, most abused lands, ecologically speaking, have scant population and little economic activity. This applies in particular to some North African countries. In contrast, the most prosperous nations in the world have far better conservation records, even given all the ecological flaws in these societies. This, of course, is no accident. Conservation, and especially preservation, are the concern of the relatively wealthy. This is an argument for allowing market forces to promote whatever level of growth the voluntary savings and native intelligence of the population can achieve. It does not provide grounds for governmental attempts to try to enhance economic growth by denigrating rights. On the contrary, as we have seen, it is this attempt that is to a great degree responsible for present environmental difficulties. "That government is best which governs least" is no less true in the case of economic growth and sound environmental policy than it is for any other.[55]

Hunting Animals

Dr. Suzuki, in relating his own hunting experiences as a young boy, offers such a dramatic diatribe against the killing of animals that it is worth quoting at length:

> One year I saw an ad in a comic book for a metal slingshot.
> I ordered it, and when it arrived I practiced for weeks shoot-

ing marbles at a target. I got pretty good, and decided to go after something alive.

Off I went to the woods and soon spotted a squirrel. I gave chase and began peppering marbles at it until finally it jumped into a tree, ran to the top and found itself trapped. I blasted away, and grazed it a couple of times, so it was only a matter of time before I would knock it down.

Suddenly the squirrel began to cry—a piercing shriek of terror and anguish. That animal's wail shook me to the core, and I was overwhelmed with horror and shame at what I was doing—solely to prove my prowess with a slingshot, I was going to *kill* another being. I threw away the slingshot and my guns and never hunted again (*Globe and Mail,* 4 June 1988).

It is for reasons and emotions such as these that animal rights groups have held such strong sway. Groups such as Lynx, the Society for the Prevention of Cruelty to Animals, and the League Against Cruel Sports may have limited power, but they have been able to seize the moral high ground in opposition to the killing, especially of fur-bearing animals. It is time, then, to subject their case to careful analysis.

It is easy enough to oppose the brutal, sadistic, and vicious killing of creatures in ways such as leg-hold trapping, or Dr. Suzuki's amateurish attempts to kill a squirrel. But many of the protestors take a much more radical and comprehensive approach. In their view, any killing of fur-bearing mammals is wrong, even those that are farmed and killed humanely. This accounts for their antagonistic response to the wearing of all animal skins.

One response to this stance is the charge of hypocrisy. This argument can only be consistently maintained by vegetarians, since it would ill-behoove a meat-eater to cavil at other methods of using the cadaver of a once-living creature.

But mere vegetarianism is hardly sufficient. To be consistent, the animal rights advocate would also have to adopt the principles said to be employed by Mahatma Gandhi. He would have to refrain from killing any member of the animal kingdom, including such things as flies, rats, mosquitos, and germs. If every life is precious, whether human or not, we cannot make invidious comparisons between species. To do so would be to lower oneself to the status of "specie-ist." The logical implication of this, however, is that it would have been immoral for people to kill rats during the bubonic plague, or to eliminate the Anopheles mosquito in order to prevent yellow fever. Or even to exterminate a virus that causes AIDS, should this be found to be the case.

What, then, of the rights of animals? Do they have any? If they are to claim any rights of the sort human beings enjoy, they must do one of two things to establish some sort of cross-species linkage. One possibility is that they must petition for their rights in some manner or other. There are those who claim that chimpanzees and porpoises, among others, will be able in the future to do so, or to be taught to do so. On that day, humans will be honour-bound to consider their declarations.

Alternatively, if animals are to have rights, they must at least show that they respect the rights of human beings. That is, if the lion claims the right not to be hunted by us, then, we must both get up unharmed when the human and the lion lay down together. Why should we do more for the lion (or the bear, or others beloved by the animal "rights" organizations) than it is willing to do for us?

These protestors may be vociferous, they may be numerous, they may be cantankerous, but we must deny to them the moral high ground they so desperately, and unjustifiably, claim.

Species Extinction

Dr. David Suzuki waxes eloquent about the needless extinction of species. He states: "Today, 40 million years of evolution embodied in the rhinoceros is being snuffed out in decades for no other reason than profit and human vanity. Our inability to stop before the species is extinct is appalling. It is horrifying to reflect on the impoverished world that our children will inherit compared to the one we knew in our youth."[56]

In Dr. Suzuki's view, the villains of this piece are profit, development, and "a limitless demand for an increase in consumer goods." His solution? Cut down on excessive and frivolous consumption and end our reliance on the private property and profit systems.

We do owe a debt of gratitude to Dr. Suzuki, among others, for pointing out the perils to the rhinoceros. On the other hand, we cannot thank him for his insights on the cause of the problem or its likely solution. The fact that many species are brought to the edge of extinction and some, unfortunately, past this point, is usually for reasons opposite to those he suggests. The problem is not an excessive reliance on private property and the private sector, but a lack of private property rights and the natural actions of the private sector.

Consider the buffalo and the cow in this regard. Biologically, these are very similar animals, and yet it is only fortuitous that the buffalo—which for many years was allowed to run free, unowned by man—was saved from extinction. In sharp contrast, the cow has been domesticated for millennia; it has been owned and cared for by farmers and herdsmen from biblical times and even before.

What almost happened to the buffalo, and what is currently happening to the rhinoceros and elephant as well, is once again an instance of the tragedy of the commons. If no one is allowed private property rights over the buffalo, then it does not pay for anyone to protect it or see that it is not hunted to extinction. When a buffalo died in the non-private property days of "Home, Home on the

Range," no one lost any money. It can be expected that no one acted to prevent such occurrences. When a cow dies, in contrast, the owner suffers.[57]

Now consider the rhinoceros. The reason it is being driven almost to the vanishing point is not one of greed. The countries of the world in which the rhino can flourish have made it all but impossible for farmers to domesticate this animal and raise it in herds for purposes of profit. For many years there were no private interests aligned to support the rhino; there were only bureaucrats intoning platitudes about the importance of refraining from hunting the beasts. Like public servants the world over, these may be well-meaning people, but they have no real monetary incentive to perpetuate the species. What is needed is a private, profit-seeking supplier of rhinos responding to the evident demand.

The economics of the rhinoceros make this a highly likely scenario. At current prices, rhino horns sell for about $100 (US) per ounce, which translates into $160,000 for a full-grown beast with a horn of 25 pounds.

True, the rhino eats up a lot of fodder and cannot be kept for long penned up in a small cage, but market values of this sort can account for a lot of hay and relatively cheap pasture land.

Then, too, there is the argument that it is impossible, or too expensive, to fence in the rhino. But this is no great impediment to ranching this animal. Calvin Bentsen has installed a "six-bar iron fence" strong enough to withstand the best efforts of "a hard-charging 2,500-pound bull rhinoceros named Macho."[58] And this is an era when rhino farming is virtually nonexistent. If this enterprise were commercialized on a large scale, there would be more incentives to undertake the research necessary to develop better and cheaper fences, especially in an age of sophisticated barbed wire and electronic fences. Dr. Suzuki has it exactly backwards. If he really wishes to safeguard the rhinoceros population and see it prosper and grow, he should be a staunch advocate of private property.

But it is not true that the passing of every species is a clear loss for mankind. Some varieties of life constitute a positive harm to people and must be eliminated, or at least severely curtailed, if we are to prosper. Then there are the thousands, if not millions, of species that are neither clearly harmful nor beneficial at present. The snail darter is perhaps the most well-known example of this. Nevertheless, it pays to preserve such life forms, both for study and in case a need is discovered for them in the future.[59] The question that arises is who shall pay for these conservations? The best answer is for those who wish to preserve these species to pay. In practice, this would probably mean biology departments at major universities, chemical laboratories, and pharmaceutical companies. Not all, perhaps, will be saved in this manner, but we can take heart from the fact that if species unimportant to mankind have been vanishing for eons, new ones have also come into being.

Elephant Survival

Let us now consider the very emotionally charged issue of elephant survival. On July 18, 1989, Daniel arap Moi of Kenya burned more than 2,500 elephant tusks, worth an estimated $3.6 million dollars.[60] This set off a conflagration that transcended far more than just ivory. The action had implications for environmentalism in general, for free trade, and for the privatization movement that is now sweeping the globe as well as for that one resource.

Was Moi a pyromaniac? Not a bit of it. He set off the blaze in Nairobi National Park not for the sheer fun of it but to dramatize the plight of the African elephant. Poachers have been killing these gigantic beasts at such a furious clip that there is now fear in some quarters that the species may soon become extinct.

As a result, the price of ivory has been driven higher and higher. This resource has been called "white gold" and currently sells for about $150 per pound.[61] It is charged by Dr. Suzuki and his ilk that the lure of profits has only led, in a vicious cycle, to still more intensive poaching, to even higher prices, and to greater danger for the survival of the elephant.

The bonfire was set to underscore and gain adherents for a ban on the importation of ivory.[62] It was thought that this would reverse the cycle. With the trade ban, demand would decrease, as would ivory prices, and with softening markets there would be less incentive for poachers to operate. So powerful has this incident seized the public imagination that even some commentators otherwise receptive to the case for capitalism in general and to privatization and free trade in particular have gone along with the idea.

Whether or not Mr. Moi's dramatic gesture will turn out to be an efficient means toward his end, one thing is clear: the status quo can only be characterized as tragic. Gangs of poachers presently kill entire herds of elephants—bulls, cows, the old, the young, even those who are pregnant or still nursing. Then, they remove the tusks with a chain saw, leaving the carcasses to rot in the jungle. This spectre resembles nothing as much as the similar fate of the buffalo—tens of thousands of them slaughtered and decomposing on the plains so hunters could obtain their tongues.

Poaching, moreover, is extremely difficult to stop, at least under present conditions. For one thing, the elephant ranges far and wide; it is a formidable task to guard thousands of square miles of territory. For another, many of the governments who have taken on this responsibility, such as Tanzania, Kenya, and Zambia, "have been too inept or corrupt to prevent poaching."[63] The low salaries paid to the guards render them susceptible to bribes from the poaching gangs. In many cases, the guards are not even issued uniforms.

Their task is hopelessly complicated by the fact that the neighbouring villagers ofttimes actually support the poachers. This is because while the roving elephants destroy their crops, the locals are given no economic incentive which would offset this loss. Proceeds from the ivory and hides go not to them but to the central government.[64]

There are several issues worth exploring. Is privatization of the elephant a feasible alternative? How likely is this option to meet the goals of the environmentalists who are concerned with the present wasteful brutalization of the African elephant? Will a ban on the commercial use of ivory retard or enhance these goals? Let us consider these issues in the order mentioned.

Feasibility

Why is the case for privatization of the elephant often rejected out of hand? As has been demonstrated over and over again, privately-owned barnyard animals have been cared for and protected by their owners because of financial incentives. Never has extinction due to over-killing been even the remotest of threats for the cow, the sheep, the goat, or the horse. Why, then, not apply this lesson to the present case? Let us consider some of the criticisms that have been levelled against this proposal.

First, there is the argument that elephants are different from cows: they need much more space. At present, for example, what remains of the elephant herds range over hundreds of square miles, ofttimes refusing to recognize the sanctity of national boundaries. But this phenomenon is insufficient to destroy the case for privatization. Even if extremely broad horizons were a necessary condition for survival of the species Elephantidae, it is still possible to borrow a leaf from the wild wild West. In the epoch before barbed wire, cowboys would brand their charges and then let them run loose on the wide open prairie. A similar approach could easily be adopted in the present instance.

But this by no means exhausts the privatization option. Just because elephants at present under public ownership are allowed to range far and wide does not mean that this is necessary. Some say that the African elephant requires a truly gargantuan amount of terrain in order to prosper because more limited areas will not supply enough food. But this species is now at the brink of disaster in part because these large areas are too difficult for the public sector to safeguard against human predators. As to inadequate elephant food supplies, their private owners—be they ranchers, zoo-keepers, or private sector environmentalists—will find it in their interest to purposefully grow greater quantities of food if need be.

Then there is the argument that it is impossible, or too expensive, to fence in the elephant. But this, too, fails. Given that a fence is commercially viable in Texas for rhinos, the presumption is that private elephant entrepreneurs in Africa and elsewhere can, if need be, come up with something similar or otherwise suitable for their recalcitrant beasts, especially in an age of sophisticated barbed wire and electronic fences.[65] Nor have zoos been unable to keep their charges from wandering away from their assigned natural habitats.

All of these objections are really beside the point. Margaret Thatcher in England and the Labour Government of New Zealand have succeeded in privatizing numerous goods and services hitherto thought by many to be the intrinsic province of the state. There is nothing about elephants that renders them impossible to privatize. Nor need commercial elephant farms physically resemble cattle ranches. They need not be limited to small areas; they need no special technology. All that need be done is to privatize the herds and the publicly held lands on which they now roam.

Some critics contend that the absence of elephant farms shows that the idea is inconceivable or economically or technically impossible. But the facts are to the contrary. There are private wildlife game ranches all around the world. According to *Maclean's*, for example, "In Zimbabwe, where private ownership of game has been allowed since 1974, ranchers say that their herds are flourishing. Zimbabwean officials say that they view elephants as a renewable commercial resource, guarding them from poachers and then allowing big game hunters to kill them for a fee—a trophy licence costs $3,000 in Zimbabwe—or permitting them to be culled."[66]

True, elephant farming is hardly widespread. It is unknown in North America, for instance. But this is not due to any inherent impossibility; it is, rather, because of governmentally imposed barriers to entry.[67] Members of the world-wide American Association of Zoological Parks and Aquariums refuse to sell elephants to any would be farmer who intends to raise them on commercial principles.[68] Nor are they allowed to be imported into many countries because of sentiment now associated with the Convention on International Trade in Endangered Species (CITES). It is our contention, however, that this international pact against the commercial exploitation of endangered species has boomeranged and resulted in the exact state of affairs most feared by all concerned: danger to their continued survival.

Environmentalists' Goals

This book is predicated on the premise that most if not all the goals of the ecological movement can not only be met by the operation of the free enterprise system but can be better met by the market than by any other form of political-economic arrangement. Let us test this hypothesis by considering the specific goals of the environmentalists with regard to the elephant. As with any group composed of thousands of different individuals, their aspirations are not all the same. Beneath the different emphases, however, several broad patterns emerge. We consider them in decreasing order of specificity.

One common denominator on the part of all concerned with stewardship of the earth's resources is the desire that the elephant shall not be allowed to become extinct. It is for this reason that CITES is now in the process of attempting to place the African elephant on appendix I, its list of animals in the greatest need of protection.

But this goal is easily met, even under the present circumstances. The imminent or even eventual demise of the elephant is unlikely in the extreme, given that elephants can breed in captivity and that thousands of the beasts are spread around the world in zoos, circuses, ranches, and private sector wildlife preserves administered by non-profit environmental groups. This geographical spread is certainly an advantage to the survival of the species; no one forest fire, or any other such natural tragedy, could possibly reach them all.

A second goal of many environmentalistsis that elephants not be confined to small cages, barely large enough for them to pace around in. This goal, too, is already being met to a great degree. Numerous zoos already keep elephants and other large animals healthy in relatively large natural habitats varying from 100 to 700 acres.[69] To be sure, this is far less terrain than that commonly enjoyed in Africa; but it hardly amounts to small cages. Then there is the completely private Nature Conservancy, which has already acquired more than 1.5 million acres in more than a thousand preserves around the world. This is the largest private nature preserve system in the world, almost three times as large as the amount of land dedicated to that task now held by the U.S. Fish and Wildlife Service.[70]

Further, were the elephant to be raised commercially, private owners in North America and elsewhere might follow the pattern set by the rhinoceros farmer in Texas who has confined his small herd to a mere 80 acres out of a 2,200 acre spread. Although there can be no guarantees, to the extent that the elephant is exploited not only for his ivory and leather but also for safari and hunting purposes,[71] it is likely that it will be maintained on reasonably large tracts of land. Instead of picturing the commercialized, privatized elephant unhappily hemmed in and limited to a small stall or barn, one can envision a wide open "Disneyland" for elephants—run on profit and loss principles.

The Alligator

It is difficult for some people to see the elephant in the role of a barnyard animal because it does not give milk or lay eggs or provide wool. Nor is elephant meat a common dinner table delicacy in the west. But neither is alligator. It is perhaps possible to apply the valuable insights which emerge from the story of that previously endangered species to the now beleaguered elephant. If it is difficult to envision the elephant in the role of the placid barnyard cow, this goes in spades for that toothsome beast. But the alligator, too, was once decimated by poachers and on the verge of extinction as a species. Happily, however, 75,000 of these reptiles are being raised in 1989 on private farms, mainly in Louisiana.[72] This is triple the size of the herd as of 1987. As a result, the animal has been de-listed as an endangered species.

The economics of the alligator industry is similar to that which applies to the elephant. There are of course no tusks in this case, but a mature four-foot long farm fed alligator fetches $39 per linear foot for the hide (used mainly for women's handbags) and an additional $20 for the meat. They are fed nutria, a ground up swamp rat in abundant supply, croaker, an inexpensive fish, and vitamin fortified dry food.

But all is not well in the alligator business; there are still government regulations. The state requires alligator farm permits, and more than 200 people are on a waiting list to receive one. Another deviation from pure free enterprise principles is that the farmers are required to return a sizable proportion of their stock, 17 percent in 1989, to the wild. A further problem is that demand is less than it might otherwise be because, paradoxically, environmentally conscious consumers are avoiding alligator products in the mistaken belief that this is still an endangered species. But the moral of the story is clear: the private market has once again ridden to the rescue and ensured that a resource valued by human beings would not be dissipated through public ownership.

The Status Quo

For many environmentalists, achievement of this second goal is just not good enough. Not for them the rather modest amounts of land that private or commercial enterprise might easily be able to give over to the elephant. A third goal is that the vast terrains which are now home to the African wild elephants be preserved for them. Although less likely, it is at least conceivable that this goal, too, might be compatible with the operation of the market system.

To determine whether this is so or not, all the several African governments need do is turn over the elephants, and the vast lands they now occupy, to the private sector.[73] They could auction them off or disperse them over the entire citizenry à la BCRIC.[74] Alternatively, these governments could operate on Lockean homesteading principles,[75] and turn over these elephants and their lands to the villagers who have been dealing most directly with them in the past. One advantage of such a scheme is that it would reduce or even eliminate poaching. Instead of the villagers having a financial incentive to support these gangs, they would oppose them. If the villagers owned both the crops and the elephants, they would be in a position to maximize the value of both.[76] To the extent that the villagers and the poachers are one and the same, even the poachers would no longer engage in such activities, for private property rights puts an end to the tragedy of the commons, which creates the incentive for poaching in the first place. What farmer goes into his own lower 40 with a machine gun in the dead of the night? No; if you own the elephant, you care for it and protect it so you can rationalize the resource.

It is difficult to determine whether or not all the lands transferred to the elephant farmers in this privatization process would continue to be used for that purpose. The economist can only contribute to this discussion the general principle that if profits can be maximized in this manner, the overwhelming presumption is that this land usage will continue. At bottom, it is a contest between how much the elephant and these lands would be worth to human beings in that state versus how much they would be worth to us in alternative uses.

Assuming that the market price for ivory is $100 per pound and that the tusks of a mature elephant weigh 100 pounds each,[77] then the value of the elephant for this resource alone is an estimated $20,000. The value of the skin for leather is estimated as $2,000.[78] And elephant meat has additional value of perhaps several hundreds of dollars, although this depends on governmental restrictions and regulations of such sales. Of even greater financial importance is the value of these resources in order to satisfy human demands for safaris and tourism. But these are harder to estimate. The Zimbabwe trophy licence of $3,000 for hunting is only the tip of the iceberg. There are also bearers, drivers, cooks, jungle guides, and an entire support industry built around this activity. One research team has mentioned $25,000 as the value of the "average hunt in Zimbabwe."[79]

It is impossible to determine on the basis of these figures just how much of the present elephant lands, were they to be privatized, would continue to be dedicated to this purpose under a regime of free enterprise. Advocates of the marketplace are unable to provide guarantees in this regard. However, as can be seen, the estimated gains from such usage are far from insignificant. They are consistent with the scenario that many elephants would be preserved by the market, and much of those lands would continue to be used for this end.

Extremism

The fourth and most extreme goal of the environmentalists is that each and every African elephant, and all of this vast terrain, be forevermore preserved in its present usage. "Let not one hide nor hair of any elephant be disturbed," might be their rallying cry. This goal, it is safe to say, is highly incompatible with the operation of the free marketplace. As we have seen, most of the large adult males would be slaughtered under private ownership. And this is true, too, of females past reproductive age.[80] Just as very few bull cows are needed to maintain and expand the size of the herd, so it is for elephants.

It is highly probable that any government that would privatize land on such a large scale would also bring the benefits of free enterprise to other aspects of the economy. This, of course, would reverse population decline due to starvation, war, disease and outmigration into places such as South Africa. But with growing populations, human needs might well encroach onto the lands now reserved for elephants. Still another difficulty from the economic point of view is that if none of the elephants were killed by mankind, the elephant population would eventually swell to gigantic proportions given a lack of natural (non-human) predators.[81]

There is not much comfort at all to be drawn from the marketplace for the radical ecologists. Those who put elephant welfare above human welfare will always be disappointed by the operation of the free enterprise system. The market is the most efficient mechanism so far known for allocating resources and promoting wealth—on behalf of human beings—but it is no panacea. It cannot provide each and every item on the wish list of people in the radical ecology movement. This book is an attempt to reconcile the concerns of economists and environmentalists, but reconciliation can be carried only so far.

An Objection

What of the Indian or Asian elephant? It has been alleged that this animal is widely domesticated and therefore privately owned. Yet, it has been placed on appendix I by CITES as a highly endangered species in seeming contradiction of our thesis that privatization is the last best hope for the preservation of the elephant.

There are several difficulties with this allegation. First of all, the domesticated Indian elephant has not been completely privatized. There is a permit system, and a welter of regulations that restrict the scope and opportunities of the elephant owner. More important, the ownership rights over these beasts are tenuous, and at least theoretically liable to be revoked at any time. Under these conditions, it is no surprise that investment in this industry might be less intense than otherwise. While there are still wild elephants in the jungle and while it remains cheaper to capture one than to breed from domestic stock, there will be economic disincentives to do the latter. It is only when all elephants are under market control that this resource can be fully rationalized.

Secondly, it is the wild elephant, the one not subject to the control of an individual owner (however uncertain and attenuated that is) which is endangered. It is not the domesticated variety which is at risk. Yet the CITES finding does not distinguish between the two categories. Nor are CITES findings to be relied upon in any case. Take the wild cat as an example. According to Simmons and Kreuter:

> All wild cats were listed on CITES appendix I in 1976, and the fact that some leopard populations have been downlisted to allow sport hunting and some export for non-commercial personal use is claimed as an appendix I success. But, scientific data did not support listing these populations on appendix I in the first place, and the listing discouraged their preservation. The leopards in Zimbabwe, for example, were not endangered, and they posed a serious threat to local livestock. Consequently, until the CITES downlisting was

approved, leopards were killed in rural areas, not for skin sale
but for predator control.[82]

Third, Indian elephants are widely used to push, pull, or move large objects, especially in forestry. But mechanical bulldozers and other modern technological equipment has gradually been supplanting the elephant in these tasks.[83] This, too, would reduce the optimal size of the elephant herd, from the perspective of human beings. Any decrease in the elephant population due to these technological factors is thus rational from the economic point of view. But extinction is not in the cards as long as the elephant has some use for mankind.

The Economist states that "the African elephant's misfortune is its tusks."[84] We see that this is the exact opposite of the truth. In the market, it is only if the elephant has a value for us that it need not fear extinction. Under private enterprise, the tusk and any other valuable attributes, rather than a curse, become a blessing. Private owners would care for and protect the elephant in order to profit from the value it can provide. The tusks are a curse only in the present "common ownership" situation where economic incentives are perverted.

Ivory Import Ban?

There are two main arguments in favour of a ban on commercial trade in ivory. First is the claim that virtually all the ivory now traded is the result of theft. Just as it is quite proper to outlaw purchases of stolen property, so is it legitimate to prohibit ivory trade because poaching is equivalent to theft.

The difficulty with this otherwise valid argument is that it is impossible to reconcile its premises with the facts. First of all, not all traded ivory is stolen. True, some 80 percent of the current supply stems from poaching, according to the estimates of the conservationists,[85] but this means that roughly 20 percent of new ivory is sold in all innocence. Secondly, there are large amounts of ivory already stockpiled. The exact amount is unknown, but this includes unworked material as well as extant jewelry, sculptures, piano keys, billiard balls, chopsticks, and Asian signature stamps. Some of this wealth may have emanated from poaching, but most, especially that created long in the past,[86] likely has not. Third, not all African nations are likely to go along with the CITES ban to be proposed at the October 1989 meeting in Lausanne, Switzerland. *Maclean's* mentions South Africa and Zimbabwe as holdouts, and *The Economist* adds Zaire, the Central African Republic, Somalia, Sudan, and Burundi to the list. This means that still more legitimate ivory will be sold in the future.[87] One cannot therefore make the facile statement that if an object is made of ivory it must be the product of poaching/theft. As a trade ban would cover stolen as well as legitimate property, it cannot be justified on these moral grounds.[88]

There is as well the problem that commercial bans and importation restrictions simply don't work. According to *The Economist,* "a much more probable effect of a ban will be to drive up the price of ivory even faster... That will raise the profitability of poaching, and increase the risks poachers are willing to take... A ban will drive the ivory trade underground, making it as hard to police as cocaine smuggling from the forests of Latin America."[89]

But suppose that, contrary to all experience, the ban is successful. To the extent that it is, it will drive down the price of ivory. This, unfortunately, will harm the prospects for elephant survival, because those countries which have been most successful in preventing poaching will lose revenue. This is why several of the African countries oppose this plan. The ban, in effect, would be a reward for those countries which have not been able to stem the poachers, and a penalty for those which have.

Then there is the *reductio ad absurdum* argument. If trade bans can be justified in the ivory case on the grounds that commercial activity in partially stolen material is improper, this would put quite a spoke into the wheel of world trade. Not only would trade with South Africa be banned, but so would trade with China, the Soviet Union, and Eastern Europe. In all of these cases, the labour of some of the inhabitants is in effect stolen from them.[90] But this is only the tip of the iceberg. These are not the only governments in the world that engage in massive theft and exploitation of their citizenry. Many countries in South and Central America, in the Caribbean, and in Africa and elsewhere in Asia fit this bill as well. If we are to go along with a ban on ivory imports for this reason, and we are to be logically consistent, we must refuse to trade with very large parts of the world.

Short-run Considerations

Let us consider one last objection. It is claimed that the poaching problem is so serious that unless something is done immediately, there won't be any elephants left to be privatized. But the process of turning over the elephants and the land they inhabit to private enterprise in Africa will take months, if not years. Therefore, it is contended, while this idea might be a good one in theory, in would be a disaster in practice.

There are several flaws in this argument. It concedes, in effect, that privatization is desirable, but due to human ineptitude it cannot be carried out quickly enough. Therefore, the state must remain in control for the foreseeable future. As such, this perspective is vulnerable to yet another *reductio ad absurdum* argument. It applies to all cases of deregulation and privatization. One could object to the repeal of rent control,[91] or to the privatization of the Post Office, Air Canada, or the CBC[92] on these grounds. In each case, it was at one time seen as "politically impossible" that these alterations be made.

Therefore, it was thought, better to bring about more efficient government control than try to substitute the marketplace for the public sector.

But this does not apply to those cases, and it does not apply to the elephant either. The confusion consists of a failure to distinguish between the role of the economist and that of the politician. Economically, the case for elephant privatization is airtight. And thus the role of the economist is to make that case, and not to engage in self-censorship because public policy which emerges from economic analysis is not likely to be acted upon. Elephant privatization could be accomplished literally in weeks, were the political will but there. By all means let the government do what it can in the meantime to preserve the elephant, but the best long-run solution is privatization. In any case, a ban on ivory trade will also take months or years to inaugurate, if ever this is accomplished. The argument that it would take too long to privatize is thus only an excuse.

Further, when applied to this case, there is always the danger of profoundly racist implications. The assumption on the part of some commentators is that capitalism may be appropriate for whites, but when it comes to blacks, socialism is the preferred option. However the writings of Sowell, Williams, Bauer, and Leow/Kendall[93] should have long since consigned that myth to the dust bin of history. They have shown that contrary to popular conception, blacks are fully as able as whites to participate in marketplace institutions. That they have not historically done so is not due to lack of ability but rather to political interferences.

We have seen that none of the arguments against privatization and free trade can stand the scrutiny of analysis. In seeking a ban on imports, Daniel arap Moi is thus barking up the wrong tree. His tusk bonfire captured the imagination of the world and must be counted a public relations success, however, as a ban ignores the basic cause of the problem—public ownership—all Mr. Moi really succeeded in doing was wasting over $3 million of badly needed resources. It is simply not true that "the African elephant's misfortune is its tusks." On the contrary, the adversity now afflicting this stately animal is the fact that it is publicly owned. The goal adopted by CITES, preservation of this species, is exemplary. The means, a trade ban and continued public ownership, will not achieve this end. Indeed, it will likely worsen matters.

We have considered a number of ecological issues and in each case have put forth an analysis that relies on the utilization of the marketplace. We conclude that free enterprise is not the cause of environmental problems but rather the solution. At the outset this will not appeal to many people who are involved in environmental, ecological, and other "green" movements. But a careful consideration of this material will convince those who are open-minded that there is no intrinsic conflict between the market and the environment. A reconciliation between economics and ecology is not only possible but desirable as well.

Notes

1. The author wishes to thank the following for helpful comments and criticisms: John Baden, Steve Hanke, Karl Hess III, Morton J. Horwitz, John Howard, Michael M'Gonigle, Calvin Sanborn, Rick Stroup, Philip Bryden, Jeff Bush, James Dailley, John Heppes, Brian McClay, William Munro, Richard Parsons, Greg Terry, Raul Valdez, Barry Saunders, Randy Simmons and, especially, Mike Walker. The usual disclaimers apply.
2. See table 1.
3. I owe this point to Mike Walker.
4. See Morton J. Horwitz, *The Transformation of American Law: 1780-1860* (Cambridge: Harvard University Press, 1977) pp. 74-78.
5. See his seminal article, "The Problem of Social Cost," The Journal of Law and Economics, October 1960, Vol. III, pp. 1-44.
6. Ibid., p. 24.
7. See Morton J. Horwitz, *The Transformation of American Law: 1780-1860* (Cambridge: Harvard University Press, 1977) pp. 67-78.
8. Horowitz (1977) calls the chapter dealing with this subject "Subsidizing Economic Growth."
9. It must be acknowledged that there are technological problems in tracking invasions by polluters of the property and persons of others. When a manufacturer pollutes the air or water, and when this cannot be quantified or traced back to its originator, then any system seems likely to fail. This is a problem for the market, but it is a problem for any other system as well. However, when private property is firmly established, the owner has an incentive to do whatever is necessary to defend his rights in court. Whatever the efficacy of entrepreneurship, it is enhanced when rights are properly established. (I owe this point to Rick Stroup.)

   In addition, there is every reason to expect that under a legal regime that penalizes such pollution-invasions, the technology necessary to determine precisely who is responsible for what will be much enhanced.

   There will always be continuum problems. We can distinguish clear cases of pollution from clear cases of non-pollution, but there is a grey area in between. A jurist aided by experts in chemistry and biology—not a legal philosopher who can only set up general principles—can best make determinations in such cases.

   Similarly, there is a continuum in rape. On one hand there are consensual adult sexual relationships; on the other hand, there is the initiation of force by one of the partners. But in between, there are cases where the "victim" is neither willing nor unwilling, but rather ambivalent. In such cases, a jurist, aided perhaps by a psychologist, is best able to make a determination. The legal philosopher can argue only in terms of general principles, focusing on the importance of distinguishing between consent and non-consent.

10.   See *Privatization: Theory and Practice*, Michael Walker, ed. (Vancouver: The Fraser Institute, 1980); *Privatization: Tactics and Techniques*, Michael Walker, ed. (Vancouver: The Fraser Institute, 1988.)

11.   The claim that plastics pose a serious environmental threat has been authoritatively challenged by William J. Rathje, *Atlantic Monthly*, December 1989, pp. 99-109.

12.   In a free enterprise system, there need not be any Not-In-My-Backyard-You-Don't (NIMBY) problems of the sort that currently beset the field of solid waste management. Under economic freedom, dumps can be located anywhere at all—provided there are no boundary crossings of noxious fumes or trespass of air-borne pollutants. In actual practice, this means they will be located in the centre of very large tracts of privately held land, used as landfill, stored in abandoned mines, or placed in hermetically sealed containers to eliminate violations of the property rights of others. For a demonstration of the market incentives that will in effect force their location far away from population centres, see *Zoning: Its Costs and Relevance*, Walter Block, ed. (Vancouver: The Fraser Institute, 1980).

13.   These numbers, of course, are for illustration purposes only. If Rathje (op. cit.) is correct, the disposal costs for paper and plastic might be similar or even inverted. Economists, thus, hold no brief for either plastic or paper. As long as there is a free market in garbage disposal, the total costs of using paper or plastic will be taken into account. The externality will be internalized, in economic jargon, and resources will be rationally allocated.

14.   When newspapers and periodicals are required to use recycled newsprint, this can have chilling implications for free speech rights. The gravest danger to free speech is likely to emanate not from the political realm but rather from the economic realm. When governments explicitly regulate the content published by the print media, the populace is likely to object, and to do so vociferously. Our tradition of free speech is a strong one. But laws regulating or limiting paper, ink, and other such economic factors of production are just as important for the stoppage of a free press. Since they are far less likely to be seen as infringements on free speech, they are even more insidious. A case in point is the regulation recently enacted in Connecticut and Florida mandating the use of minimal percentages of recycled-content newsprint. (I owe this example to Brian McClay.) There is a danger here. If government can force our dailies to use a certain kind of paper on environmental grounds, will they one day dictate the number of pages which can be published? Is a newsprint

recycling statute only the entering wedge in a more general censorship programme inspired by ecological considerations?

15. For the theoretical proof of this contention, see the following:

Hayek, Friedrich A., "The New Confusion About Planning," *New Studies in Philosophy, Politics, Economics and the History of Ideas* (University of Chicago Press, 1978); Hayek, Friedrich A., "The Nature and History of the Problem," "The Present State of the Debate," *Collectivist Economic Planning*, F.A. Hayek ed. (Clifton, N.J.: Kelley Publishing Company, 1975); Hayek, Friedrich A., "Social Calculation: The Competitive 'Solution'," in *Individualism and Economic Order* Chicago: Regnery, 1972); Hoff, Trygve J.B., *Economic Calculation in a Socialist Society* (Indianapolis: Liberty Press, 1981); Hoppe, Hans, *A Theory of Socialism and Capitalism* (Boston: Kluwer, 1989); Lavoie, Don, "A Critique of the Standard Account of the Socialist Calculation Debate", Richman, Sheldon L., "War Communism to NEP: The Road to Serfdom", Steele, David Ramsey, "The Impossibility of Economic Calculation Under Socialism", *Journal of Libertarian Studies*, Vol. V, No. 1, Winter 1981; Kirzner, Israel, "The Economic Calculation Debate," *Review of Austrian Economics*, Vol. II, 1988; Mises, Ludwig von, *Socialism* (Indianapolis: Liberty Press/Liberty Classics, 1981); Mises, Ludwig von, *Human Action*, 3rd rev. ed. (Chicago: Contemporary Books, 1966); Mises, Ludwig von, "Economic Calculation in the Socialist Commonwealth," *Collectivist Economic Planning*, Friedrich A. Hayek, ed. (Clifton, N.J.: Kelley Publishing Company, 1975); Murrell, Peter, "Did the Theory of Market Socialism Answer the Challenge of Ludwig von Mises?" *History of Political Economy*, 15(1), Spring 1983; Rothbard, Murray N., "Ludwig von Mises and Economic Calculation Under Socialism," *The Economics of Ludwig von Mises*; Salerno, Joseph, "Ludwig von Mises as Social Rationalist," *Review of Austrian Economics*, Vol. IV, 1990, forthcoming.

For practical proof, one need do no more than consider the unravelling of the economies of the U.S.S.R., The People's Republic of China, and the eastern European nations, and their attempts to replace their central planning regimes with market institutions.

16. Similarly, we could conceivably reduce the crime rate to virtually zero—by spending the entire GNP on police, locksmiths, and guards. This would be unwise, since we would all die of starvation or lack of health care. Instead, sound public policy consists of spending so much on crime reduction but no more, so that an extra dollar spent on this task would just equal its value in accomplishing other ends.

17. Actually, Hazelwood was not at the helm of the ship when it plowed into Bligh Reef. The third mate, Gregory Cousins, was on the bridge at the time, but he was not licensed to operate in these waters.

18. This corporate culpability is greatly mitigated by the fact that the government has determined that alcoholism is a "handicap," and by its consequent requirement that firms try to rehabilitate, not fire, employees suffering from affliction. In fact, to the extent that this mishap resulted from alcoholism, the blame for it should be given to this well-intentioned government programme and not to the Exxon Corporation.

19. See 46 U.S. Code, section 183 (183) which states that the liability of a company in the position of Exxon is limited to the value of the ship and its cargo, an estimated $100 million.

20. See Michael M'Gonigle and Mark Zacher, *Pollution, Politics and International Law: Tankers at Sea*, University of California Press, 1979.

21. The Hickey case (*Hickey vs. Electricity Reduction* (1970) 21 D.L.R. (3d) 368), for example, made it more difficult for fishermen to collect damages, in that it determined they had no standing since they do not own the fish in the sea. See also Willard Estey, "Public Nuisance and Standing to Sue," 10 *Osgoode Hall Law Journal*, 1972, p. 563.

22. This was organized under part XX of the Canadian Shipping Act (R.S.C. 1970, c.S-9) and has a current endowment of some $140 million.

23. This socialization of risk is by no means limited to the oil industry. The Price-Anderson Act plays a similar role in the nuclear power industry.

24. Private insurance companies, before accepting industrial risks, normally conduct inspections and establish their own "regulations" regarding the behaviour of the insured. In this way, risks are spread but accountability is not destroyed. While the principal-agent problem remains, it is strongly mitigated. (I owe this point to Rick Stroup.)

25. Via their agents, the oil companies.

26. If profits in the oil industry are 5 percent, and 10 percent is obtainable elsewhere, investment will flow from the former to the latter. But as capital leaves oil, its rate of return will rise there. Similarly, as capital enters other industries, the level of profit there will tend to fall. Perfect equilibrium will, of course, never be reached, but this tendency will ensure that profits do not diverge significantly when due consideration is given to risk and psychic income factors.

27. See Terry Anderson's contribution to this book, "The Market Process and Environmental Amenities," chapter 4, where he makes the case for privatization of smaller bodies of water.

28. The failure of the political process to ensure double-hulling is discussed below.

29. Such views have long since filtered into our mass culture, where they still retain a powerful hold on the popular imagination. Consider the celebrated songs "Home, Home on the Range," and "Don't Fence Me In."

30. U.S. District Court, District of Alaska A77 195 Civil, November 1981.

31.   See Milton Friedman, *Capitalism and Freedom* (Chicago: University of Chicago Press, 1962); George Stigler, *The Organization of Industry* (Homewood, Il., Richard D. Irwin, 1968); James M. Buchanan, *The Demand and Supply of Public Goods* (Chicago: Rand McNally, 1968); James M. Buchanan and Gordon Tullock, *The Calculus of Consent: Local Foundations of Constitutional Democracy* (Ann Arbor: University of Michigan Press, 1971); *Theory of Public Choice: Political Applications of Economics*, James M. Buchanan and Robert D. Tollison, eds. (Ann Arbor: University of Michigan Press, 1972). See also Gabriel Kolko, *The Triumph of Conservatism* (Chicago: Quadrangle, 1967), as well as chapters 3 and 6 of the present volume.

32.   See *Summary of Events and News Coverage 1988/1989 Grays Harbor Oil Spill*, Washington State Department of Ecology, 1989.

33.   See *National Review*, April 21, 1989, p. 10.

34.   Forestry employs 62,700, wood industries 115,300, furniture and fixtures 65,000, paper and allied industries 125,800, and print and publishing 139,800. "Employment, Earnings and Hours," Ottawa: Statistics Canada, #72-002, November 1988.

35.   *Forest Service Timber Sales: Their Effect on Wood Product Prices*, Congressional Budget Office, Washington D.C., 1980.

36.   Marion Clawson, *Federal Lands Revisited* (Washington D.C.-Baltimore: Resources for the Future, Johns Hopkins University Press, 1983).

37.   Steve H. Hanke, "Federal Lands Revisited," *Land Economics*, Vol. 61, No. 2, May 1985, p. 222. In the view of Barney Dowdle and Steve H. Hanke, "Public Timber Policy and the Wood-Products Industry," in *Forestlands Public and Private*, Robert T. Deacon and Bruce M. Johnson, eds. (Cambridge: Ballinger, 1985) p. 101, "The most obvious reform for faulty public timber management policies would be to remove governments from the business of timber production. This could be achieved simply by selling commercial public timber holdings into private ownership. By privatizing these lands, and establishing an incentive system based on free enterprise, the unnecessary waste associated with government timber management could be eliminated."

38.   See John Baden, "Crimes Against Nature: Public Funding of Environmental Destruction," *Policy Review*, Winter 1987, p. 37.

39.   See chapter 5 in this volume for a discussion of this topic.

40.   States Fred Lee Smith, Jr., "Crisis: A Valuable Tool in Environmental Politics," *Competitive Enterprise Update*, September 1988, No. 5, p. 3, "The Yellowstone tragedy once again confirms the flawed vision of government as a benevolent, infallible steward... Even the 'Jewel in the Crown' of America's national park system in not safe from the whims of bureaucrats." See also, Lawrence Solomon, "Save the Forests—Sell

the Trees,170 *Wall Street Journal,* August 25, 1989. For the opposite perspective, see Peter Matthiessen, "Our National Parks: the Case for Burning," *New York Times Magazine,* Dec. 11, 1988.

Assuming no possibility of commercial exploitation of woodland resources, many more foresters might agree with a "free burn" policy. But the point to be underscored is that in a viable free market economic system, the possibility of commercial exploitation (on behalf of the consumer) would always be open.

41.   John Baden, op. cit., p. 38. There is nothing wrong with this method of clearing woodlands, per se. Wheat and other crops are harvested in this manner. When a private timber company engages in this activity on its own land, given that there are no third party trespass effects such as mud slides, it can take full responsibility for it. As such, if tree clearing of this sort is uneconomical, and/or if the firm fails to replant sufficiently to maintain the capital value of its asset, then it and it alone pays the penalty. The forces of profit and loss will thus discipline marketplace actors to act so as to preserve economic value. But when government engages in this sort of clearing on its own land (whether or not this task is subcontracted to private interests) or subsidizes firms to do so on theirs, then there is no automatic market reward and penalty system to guard against uneconomic and thus unsound environmental behaviour.

42.   Richard Stroup and John Baden, "Externality, Property Rights and the Management of our National Forests," *The Journal of Law and Economics,* October 1973, pp. 303-349. See also Randall O'Toole, *Reforming the Forest Service* (Covelo, Calif: Island Press, 1988).

43.   For the more popular and widely held alternative view, see *Newsweek* (May 1989, p. 50), which states: "If the profit motive has helped destroy the Amazonian rain forests, can it be used to save them? Estimates say that Brazil's ranchers, loggers and farmers have already eradicated as much as 12 percent of the world's largest rain forest."

44.   Jane Shaw, "Private Property and the Environment," *Freeman,* January 1989, p. 40.

45.   *Statistical Abstract of the United States,* Washington D.C.: U.S. Department of Commerce, Bureau of the Census, 1987, table #318, p. 182. Indian lands account for 2.2 percent of the territory of the U.S.

46.   Hanke, op. cit., *Land Economics,* 1985, p. 221; and Baden, *Policy Review,* op. cit., p 36.

47.   I owe this point to John Howard.

48.   *Vancouver Sun,* January 12, 1989, p. A20.

49.   See Terry L. Anderson and Donald R. Leal, "Inside Our Outdoor Policy," *Cato Institute Policy Analysis,* September 1988, No. 113. There are many reasons for privatizing parks in addition to thereby attaining a non-arbitrary allocation of land. Safety, consumer enjoyment,

efficiency—these are the hallmarks of free enterprise in every other industy, and the present one is no exception. Profit and loss incentives have made the owners of Disney World and the Edmonton Mall synonymous with excellence in amusement parks, and there is no reason to believe that entrepreneurs would not be able to play a similar role with regard to natural wilderness parks.

But not all authors and organizations ostensibly devoted to applying free market principles to the environment carry through rigorously and consistantly with the logic of their own analysis. For example, the Bozeman, Montana-based Foundation for Research on Economics and the Environment states in "Free Perspectives" (Vol. II, No. 3., p. 12): "Please note that this measure does *not* call for selling our national parks [to private owners]...title to the [park] properties [would] remain with the people as a whole."

Similarly, this analysis applies to the Agricultural Land Reserve Act, which forbids the conversion of fertile farms to housing development. As a result, the value of these lands, and thus the contribution they make to society, is only a small fraction of what it otherwise would be.

50. *Globe and Mail,* 25 June 1988.
51. For example, Nobel Prize winning economist Paul Samuelson, in his introductory textbook *Economics* (New York: McGraw-Hill, 1970, p. 714), states: "What did Malthus forget, or at least underestimate? He failed to realize how technical innovation could intervene—not to repeal the law of diminishing returns, but to more than offset it. He stood at the brink of a new century and failed to anticipate that the succeeding two centuries would show the greatest scientific gains in history." There is, of course, a good excuse for Malthus in adopting the Malthusian overpopulation doctrine: he could not foresee scientific progress. The same, alas, does not apply to Suzuki, with his advantages of hindsight.
52. Thomas Sowell, *The Economics and Politics of Race,* New York: William Morrow and Co., 1983, p. 209.
53. *The World Almanac Book of Facts.*
54. See Walter Block, "Population Growth: Is It a Problem?" in *Resolving Global Problems into the 21st Century: How Can Science Help?,* Peter S. Ross, Sheila Riordon, and Susan Macartney, eds., Ottawa: Canadian Student Pugwash Publications, 1989, pp. 2-61.
55. For an insightful account of the causes of economic development, and an explanation for the poverty that endures in the Third World, see Peter Bauer, *Dissent on Development* (Cambridge: Harvard University Press, 1972).
56. *Globe and Mail*, May 21, 1988. *Newsweek*, op. cit., takes a similar tack, criticizing Japan as "The World's Eco-Outlaw" for importing ivory tusks and thus threatening the African elephant with extinction.

57.   Ken Boulding, the well-known economist and poet, has produced a set of limericks to illustrate this point:

The buffalo, nobody's property
Went o'er the plains, Clippity, Cloppity
In thunderous herds where now only birds
Fly and rabbits go Hippity, Hoppity.

The cow, now, is kept on the farm
And flourished and came to no harm,
For its owners to thrive
Had to keep it alive
So property worked like a charm.

See *The Morality of the Market: Religious and Economic Perspectives*, Walter Block, Geoffrey Brennan and Kenneth Elzinga, eds. (Vancouver: The Fraser Institute, 1985) pp 263-264.

58.   "Raising Rhinos, Texas-Style," *Time*, 10 July 1989, p. 13.

59.   The movie *Star Trek IV* was predicated on the idea that whales become extinct several centuries in the future and yet are necessary for the preservation of human life on earth. To bring things back to the present day, Greenpeace is very concerned with the survival of the whale and the dolphin. In their analysis, however, the danger to these creatures emanates from "international corporate greed" and the attempt "to maximize tuna company profits" (undated fund raising letter, received August 1989, p. 2). Unfortunately, there is no appreciation of the role that private property in bodies of water could possibly play in the attainment of their goal. There is no understanding that the "tragedy of the commons" can apply to these sea creatures as well as to land animals.

60.   "Kenya Lights a Fire to Help African Elephants," *Maclean's*, 31 July 1989, p. 37.

61.   *Maclean's*, ibid., claims that the 12 tons of tusks burned were worth an estimated $3.6 million on the international market. This yields a value of $150 per pound. On the other hand, according to the *Globe and Mail*, 13 June 1989, p. A6, ivory sells for $200 per kilogram, which is equivalent to $90.90 per pound.

62.   Singapore, Hong Kong, Japan, Macao, and Belgium are the main importers of raw ivory. See *The Economist*, 1 July 1989, p. 16.

63.   Ibid., p. 16.

64.   See Randy T. Simmons and Urs P. Kreuter, "Herd Mentality: Banning Ivory Sales Is No Way to Save the Elephant," *Policy Review*, 1989, forthcoming, p. 2, galley format. See also the *Wall Street Journal*, 16 August 1989, p. A10.

65.   States C. Peter Small, "Big Game Ranching in South Africa," *Proceedings: First International Wildlife Ranching Symposium—May*

16-21, 1988, Raul Valdez, ed., Las Cruces, New Mexico: New Mexico State University, 1989, p. 145: "To discourage the straying of large, fence-breaking animals such as the elephant, rhino, and buffalo the use of electric fencing is becoming popular."

66. *Mclean's,* op. cit., p. 37; Simmons and Krueter, op. cit. See also C. Peter Small, "Overview of Wildlife Ranching in Africa," Bart W. O'Gara and Li Zhenying, "Overview of Wildlife Ranching in Asia," and C. Peter Small, "Big Game Ranching in South Africa," *Proceedings: First International Wildlife Ranching Symposium,* op. cit.

67. The New Mexico legislature, for example, has restricted entry into wildlife game ranching. See David Hopcroft, "An Ecological Approach to Natural Ranching," *Proceedings: First International Wildlife Ranching Symposium,* ibid., pp. 73 and 74, on the difficulties in obtaining the necessary governmental permissions. Also see Ronald J. White, *Big Game Ranching in the United States,* Mesilla, New Mexico: Wild Sheep and Goats International, 1987, pp. 139-157, who discusses a myriad of restrictions and regulations placed on game farming in general; and L.R. Shelton, "Constraints on Development for Wildlife on Private Lands," Trans., North American Wildlife Natural Resource Conference 47:464-469, 1982.

68. See "Code of Professional Ethics" of the American Association of Zoological Parks and Aquariums. Item K states: "As a member of the AAZPA, I pledge to make every effort to assure that exotic animals do not find their way into the hands of those not qualified to care for them properly." And according to the Addendum of 1981, "AAZPA members offering wildlife for sale at auctions attended by the general public are in violation of the AAZPA Code of Professional Ethics, especially item K." Based on discussions with several zoo officials, it is clear that a farmer wishing to raise endangered species for commercial purposes would be judged as a member of the general public who is per se not qualified to care for them properly.

69. One great benefit of this method is that animals are more likely to breed in captivity in these natural settings. See "Wilder Places for Wild Things," *Newsweek,* 17 July 1989, pp. 58-59. Strictly speaking, it is improper to list zoos as examples of free enterprise in action since virtually all of them are now, unfortunately, in the public sector. They are discussed here, however, because, apart from the political will to do so, they could easily be privatized (that is to say, there are no great technical impediments to auctioning them off), and they furnish an example of large wild animals thriving on rather limited amounts of land—compared to the amount now given over to elephants in the wilds of Africa.

70. *Wall Street Journal,* 24 May 1989, p. A18.

71.   The rational owner would tend to confine such activities to adults, to males (since one bull elephant can cover numerous cow elephants), and to females past the breeding age. In private hands, the harvesting of elephants would thus conform to the principles which apply to other domesticated species. In sharp contrast, under present public arrangements, the poachers kill elephants indiscriminatorily—pregnant cows and young females along with all the rest. It is for this reason that hunting privately-owned elephants would no more threaten them with extinction that does the present careful and discriminatory culling of cows endanger their existence. See Wayne Long, "Marketing Hunting Opportunities," Ross Shelton, "Fee-Hunting Systems," Edward L. Kozicky, "Hunting Preserves," and E. Lee Fitzhugh, "Pros and Cons of Fee Hunting," *Proceedings: First International Wildlife Ranching Symposium,* op. cit.

72.   *Wall Street Journal,* 2 August 1989, p. 1. See also S.R. Broad and R.A. Luxmoore, "Crocodile Ranching and the Potential Impacts of Commercial Wildlife Production on Conservation," *Proceedings: First International Wildlife Ranching Symposium,* op. cit., And R.W.G. Jenkins, "The World Conservation Strategy and CITES: Principles for the Management of Crocodilians," pp. 27-31; T. Joanen and L. McNease, "The Management of Alligators in Louisiana," pp. 33-42; and T.C. Hines and C.L Abercrombie, "The Management of Alligators in Florida," pp. 43-47; in *Wildlife Management: Crocodiles and Alligators,* G.J.W. Webb, S.C. Manolis and P.J. Whitehead, eds., New South Wales: Surrey Beatty, 1987.

73.   True, this is "politically impossible." These African states are amongst the most dirigiste in the world; the very idea would be anathema to politicians and tribal leaders dedicated to veneration of the public sector and to the denigration of the private. And this is to say nothing of the supposedly free enterprise Canadian government, which favours an ivory ban and opposes elephant privatization. Although it is a cliche, the task of the economist as scientist is to seek out and promote the truth whether politically palatable or not. If he engages in self-censorship because the truth will fall on deaf ears, there will never be the chance for it to win out. In like manner, it is the duty of the physician who discovers that smoking is injurious to health to make this point known, even if he lives in an era or in a country that is not receptive to that point of view. See in this regard, W.H. Hutt, *Politically Impossible...?,* Hobart Paperbacks, London: The Institute for Economic Affairs, 1971.

74.   Five free shares of the British Columbia Resource Investment Corporation (BCRIC), a former Crown corporation, were given to each citizen of that province in an early privatization effort. See *Privatization, Theory & Practice,* op. cit. It is claimed that this is an inept example

because the price of these shares dropped from a high of $9.00 after establishing an initial market value of $6.00 to a present low of less than $1.00. Contrary to this claim, however, the BCRIC giveaway was a success. It turned resources over to private enterprise, where they could for the first time be rationally valued and allocated.

75. See John Locke, "An Essay Concerning the True Original, Extent and End of Civil Government," in E. Barker, ed., *Social Contract,* New York: Oxford University Press, 1948, pp. 17-18. For a modern defence of this position, see Murray N. Rothbard, *For a New Liberty,* New York: Macmillan, 1973; and Rothbard, Murray N., *The Ethics of Liberty,* Atlantic Highlands, N.J.: Humanities Press, 1982.

76. For the general principle on the internalization of externalities, see Coase, op. cit. Also Walter Block, "Public Goods and Externalities: The Case of Roads," *The Journal of Libertarian Studies,* Vol. VII, No. 1, Spring 1983. On this specific case, Simmons and Kreuter, op. cit., p. 2, mention Zimbabwe, where "peasant communities [are given] the right to hunt a certain number of elephants. The communities can exercise this right themselves or sell the hunting permits to commercial operators. This has resulted in a much more positive attitude toward wildlife among Zimbabwean villagers."

It is preferable for the survival of the elephant that if government is to maintain overall control, it at least should set up rules which provide economic incentives for the villagers to preserve this species, as is done in South Africa and Zimbabwe. This is vastly superior to the systems which prevail in Kenya, Zambia, Tanganika, and other East and Central African countries where the herds have been decimated. However, even better than a system of relatively judicious government control would be one of full privatization.

77. More commonly, elephant tusks now reaching the market are vastly smaller than this, the upper or biological limit. Typically, the size is only 10 to 15 pounds. This appears to be because many of the mature elephants with long tusks have been killed by the poachers; the remaining elephants have less valuable tusks.

78. Randy T. Simmons, in personal conversation with the author.

79. Simmons and Kreuter, op. cit., p. 2. A similar situation prevails for other exotic animals. It costs $16,000 for a permit to kill the Mongolian wild sheep, $35,000 for the Soviet Marco Polo sheep, and $12,000 for the Mexican desert bighorn. (I owe these estimates to Raul Valdez.)

80. Radical ecologists would of course be free to contribute money to environmental groups dedicated to the preservation of all elephants. It is conceivable that they could amass enough money to outbid those who wish to consume elephants for other purposes such as ivory. In such a case, those who wanted ivory would have to wait until the elephant died

a natural death. But this scenario is extremely unlikely, given the demand for ivory compared to the amount of money which might reasonably be expected to be raised for this purpose. Of course, if tastes changed markedly, perhaps due to a successful public relations and advertising campaign on the part of the elephant lovers around the world, then market operation might even be compatible with this radical programme.

81. Despite their long gestation period, elephant populations could increase by an estimated 5 percent per year under such conditions.

82. Op. cit., p. 3. According to these authors, CITES has misapplied its listing in this manner in several other cases as well: the parrot, the black rhino, the white rhino, the alligator, and the crocodile. As well, this applies to the Siberian tiger and the spotted leopard.

83. Similarly, the horseless carriage supplanted the horse in an earlier day. This animal, however, was preserved by mankind because it still could yield other values.

84. Op. cit., p. 15. Pundits blame the problem of elephant overkilling on greed, not on the lack of private property rights. For example, according to the anti-Oriental and anti-consumerist *Newsweek* story, May 1, 1989, op. cit., "In 1988 Hong Kong passed Japan as the biggest importer of ivory, which threatens African elephants with extinction by the year 2005." But this is no more credible an explanation of extinction than were similar claims on the part of *Newsweek* in this story that Japanese demand for tropical hardwood lumber would lead to a depletion of that resource. Does anyone think that if the Japanese doubled, quadrupled, or even multiplied their present demand for cow products a hundredfold it would lead to the extinction of that animal? Increased demand would only raise the prices initially, which would encourage even more breeding and more care for the cow. Instead of being depleted, cow resources would rise. There is no difference, in this regard, between the cow, the buffalo, the rhino, and the elephant except for the fact that the former is subject to private property constraints and the latter three were, or are, not.

85. See *Maclean's,* op. cit., p. 37

86. It is possible to store raw ivory for up to 50 years without any significant attenuation of its value.

87. Legitimate, that is, on the highly questionable assumption that it is proper for government to be involved in this industry in the first place.

88. Suppose that a similar situation were to occur entirely within the borders of Canada. That is, assume that the government were to declare a ban on an entire commodity because a significant portion of it were stolen. The likelihood is that this would be declared unconstitutional under section 7 of the Canadian Charter of Rights and Freedoms. Any such ban would be a violation of the substantive due process rights of the legitimate owners of that part of the commodity which was not stolen. Further, our

entire common law, and the premises upon which western civilization is based, are predicated on the notion that the innocent should not be punished along with the guilty when it is impossible to distinguish between guilt and innocence. *Wilson v. Medical Services Commission of B.C.,* 30 B.C. Law Reports, 2nd series, 1988, page 1, is a case in point. (I owe this example and citation, but not the accompanying analysis, to Philip Bryden.) It was held that the substantive due process rights of recent medical school graduates were denied by not granting them doctors' billing numbers. The point was that whatever the merits of the plan to restrict billing numbers, or to make them conditional upon geographical location, the plaintiff (a new doctor) was innocent of any wrong doing and therefore suffered a denigration of his substantive due process rights due to this "ban."

There is, however, a caveat to the conclusion that a ban on ivory, were it a domestic industry, would not be upheld by the courts. There are also numerous precedents which cast doubt on this interpretation that substantive due process rights can readily apply to economic or commercial activity. But this caveat is of little relevance to the present discussion, all parties to which accept, with alacrity, the view that economic or commercial rights must and should be as fully protected as all other rights.

To reiterate, the present discussion under this heading is predicated upon the sanctity of property rights. Indeed, it is because of the very violation of property rights, ivory poaching, that the ban is being discussed in the first place.

89. 1 July 1989, p. 17. State Simmons and Kreuter, op. cit., p. 3: "One effect of the price rise [due to an unsuccessful ban on the international trade in ivory which leads to a black market] will be to encourage more people to be involved in poaching."

90. It might be claimed that any taxes above the level necessary to finance the legitimate and therefore limited functions of government would amount to theft. And since no country is "pure" under these stringent conditions, no one should be allowed to trade with anyone on the face of the earth. As against that it could be maintained that at least people in democracies have voted themselves into higher and higher tax brackets. Say what you will about this argument, at least realize that it cannot be offered in behalf of the non-democratic nations of the world. Therefore, dictatorships at least, cannot claim that they have a voluntary tax system. Their taxes, at least, are thus equivalent to theft. According to the logic of the moral argument in favour of the ban, imports of all their products should be prohibited.

91. See *Rent Control: Myths and Realities,* Walter Block and Edgar Olsen, eds., (Vancouver: The Fraser Institute, 1981).

92. See Steven Globerman, *Culture, Governments and Markets: Public Policy and the Culture Industries,* (Vancouver: The Fraser Institute, 1987); John Metcalf, *Freedom from Culture,* (Vancouver: The Fraser Institute); Douglas Adie, *The Mail Monopoly,* (Vancouver: The Fraser Institute) forthcoming; see also note 10.

93. Thomas Sowell, *The Economics and Politics of Race,* New York: William Morrow, 1983; Walter Williams, *The State Against Blacks,* New York, McGraw-Hill, 1982; Peter T. Bauer, *Reality and Rhetoric: Studies in the Economics of Development,* Cambridge, Mass: Harvard University Press, 1984; Leon Louw & Frances Kendall, *South Africa: The Solution,* Bisho, Ciskei: Amagi, 1986.